CW01617573
www.nissan.com.au

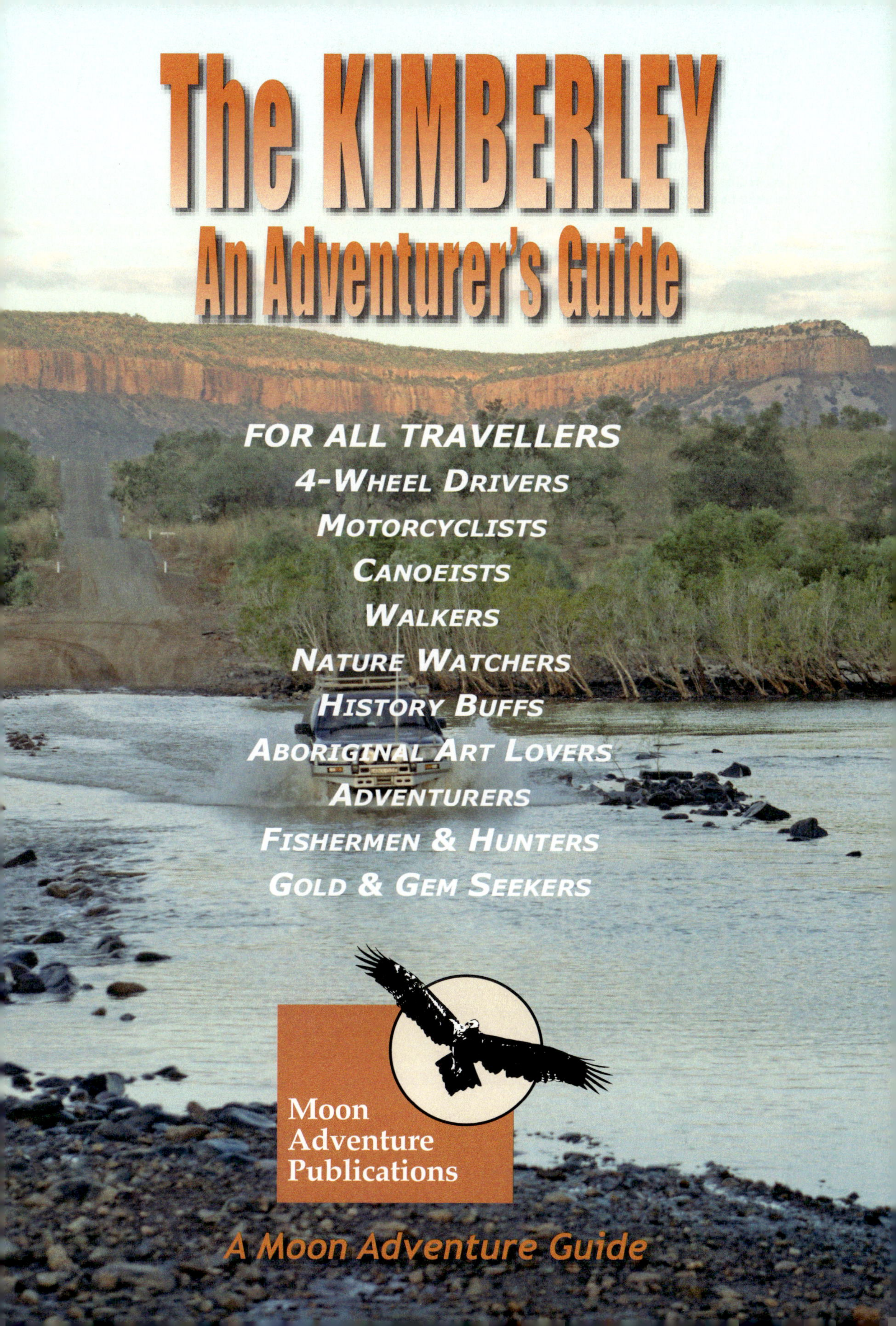
The KIMBERLEY
An Adventurer's Guide
FOR ALL TRAVELLERS
4-Wheel Drivers
Motorcyclists
Canoeists
Walkers
Nature Watchers
History Buffs
Aboriginal Art Lovers
Adventurers
Fishermen & Hunters
Gold & Gem Seekers
Moon
Adventure
Publications
A Moon Adventure Guide

Magnificent Bell Gorge is a popular spot to visit in the Kimberley.

ALL INFORMATION AND ADVICE IN THIS BOOK IS PROVIDED WITHOUT ANY RESPONSIBILITY OR LIABILITY ON ANY ACCOUNT WHATSOEVER ON THE PART OF THE AUTHORS OR PUBLISHERS, NOR DO THEY ACCEPT ANY RESPONSIBILITY FOR ANY ERRORS OR OMISSIONS, OR FOR ANY LOSS, INJURY OR INCONVENIENCE BY ANY PERSON USING THIS BOOK.

Disclaimer

The authors and publisher disclaim any responsibility to any person for loss or damage suffered from any use of this guide for any purpose. While considerable care has been taken by the authors and the publisher in researching and compiling the guide, the authors and the publisher accept no responsibility for errors or omissions. No person should rely upon this guide for the purpose of making any business, investment or real estate decision.

The representation on any maps of any road or track is not necessarily evidence of public right of way. Third parties who have provided information to the authors and publisher concerning the roads and other matters did not warrant to the author and publisher that the information was complete, accurate or current or that any of the proposals of any body will eventuate and, accordingly, the authors and publisher provide no such warranty.

The KIMBERLEY
An Adventurer's Guide

Published by: **Moon Adventure Publications,**
PO Box 1112,
PEARCEDALE, Victoria, 3912.
Australia.
Phone: (03) 5978 7066   Fax: (03) 5978 7093
Email: info@guidebooks.com.au
Web site: www.guidebooks.com.au

Typeset by: Moon Adventure Publications,
Pearcedale, Victoria.

Printed by: Brown Prior Anderson,
Burwood, Victoria.

Photographs by: Ron & Viv Moon (unless otherwise stated).
Maps by: Viv & Ron Moon (unless otherwise stated).

Computer/Technical Support: Just Macs, ph: (0412) 179 284

This Edition: 6th Edition, May 2006

National Library of Australia card number and ISBN 0 9578766 9 6

Front Cover: main pic On the remote track into Walcott Inlet.
inserts - (L) Drysdale River Camp.
(R) Great fishing on the Dampier Peninsula.

Pics from L to R: *Mustering cattle on Mt Elizabeth Station.*
Canoeing on Manning Gorge.
Aboriginal Art.
Crossing a small creek near Bedford Downs.
Background Pic: *Dimond Gorge, Mornington Wilderness Camp*

www.guidebooks.com.au
For updates on travelling the Kimberley, make regular visits to our site and keep up to date with what is happening.

A drive along 80 Mile Beach in the evening light is a great place to be.

CONTENTS

PEARL LUGGERS
THE SEA THE MEN THE LEGEND

TREK NOTES – PLEASE NOTE

Be aware that differences in tyres and speedos can result in significant variations to the figures given in our trek notes, ie most speedos are within +/- 5%, but that can mean 5 km every 100 km!

Abbreviations for Trek Notes –

PSA – Proceed Straight Ahead

T-junct – T-junction	Y-junct – Y-junction	Junct – junction
R/J – Road junction	T/J – Track junction	tk – track
TL – Turn left	TR – Turn right	LH – Left-hand
VL – Veer left	VR – Veer right	RH – Right-hand
SP – Signposted	LAF – Leave as Found	WP – Water Point

GPS Readings are detailed in **Datum WGS 84**, except when indicated. Most GPS units default to WGS 84, and with that you are approx 170 metres out in Latitude and 100 metres out in Longitude when compared to Datum AG 66.

MAPS SYMBOLS

- Major Towns
- Minor Town/Roadhouse
- Homestead (HS)
- Main Dirt Road (2WD)
- Minor Dirt Road (4WD)
- Bitumen - Major Road
- Bitumen - Minor Road
- Railway Line
- Walking Trail
- National Park (NP) Land (shading)
- NP Rangers Headquarters
- Reserve Land (shading)
- Aboriginal Land (shading)
- Rivers, Creeks, Sea, etc.
- Swamp
- Reef
- Mountain
- Crocodile Warning
- Boating
- Boat Ramp
- Diving/Snorkelling
- Fishing
- Lookout
- Bushwalking
- Mining Site/Area
- General store/supplies
- Hospital/Clinic
- Information Point
- Post Office
- Caravan/Camping Ground
- Camping/Bush Camping
- NO Camping/Bush Camping
- Accommodation
- Fuel
- Cemetery
- Airfield/Strip
- Toilets
- Fire Place
- Water

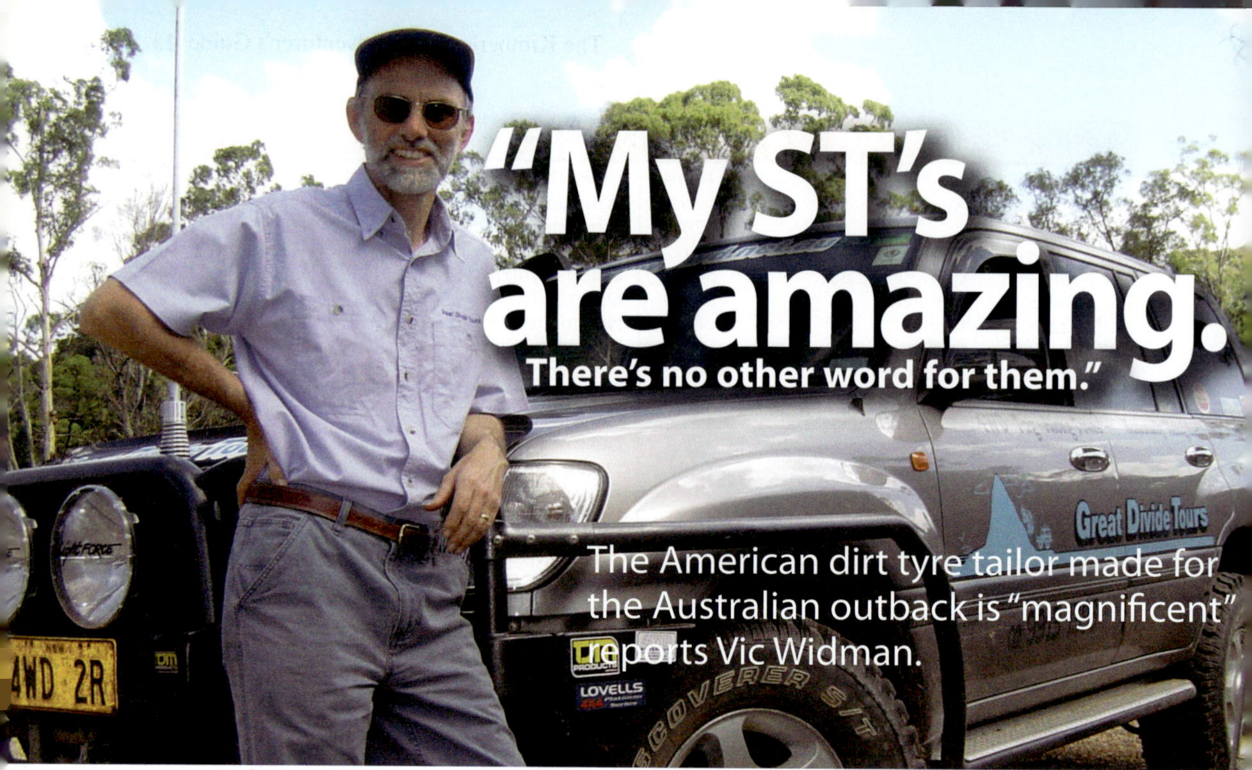

Professional 4WD tour operator and instructor for 25 years, Vic Widman reports that he's never had such magnificent performance from a tyre as Cooper Sure Trac.

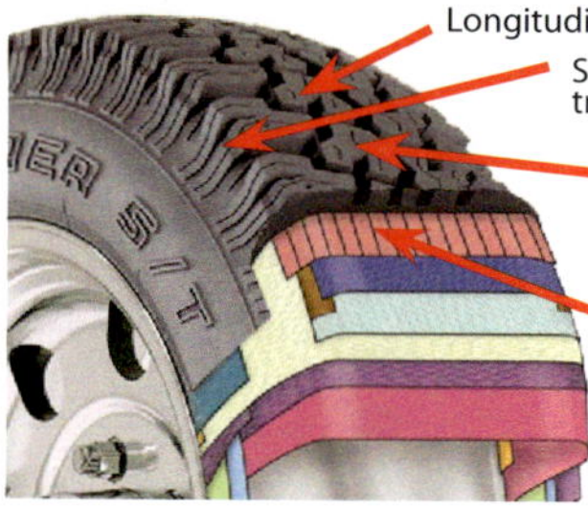

While America is recognised as the world leader in 4WD tyre design, many tyres are designed for American conditions only. That is, until Cooper's Sure Trac.

To show its commitment since 1920 to making tyres that last, Cooper Tires responded to an "Aussie Wish List" sent to them by Terry Smith of Exclusive Tyre Distributors Australia. Cooper identified that drivers in outback Australia, Argentina and South Africa share similar terrain and road conditions and experience the same damage to all terrain tyres.
After a year of intense research and development, Cooper produced the optimum outback tyre - the Sure Trac (ST).

Here Vic Widman shares his experience of the tailor made tyre.

"In the past year I have been using Cooper ST tyres on my Turbo Diesel Landcruiser and have clocked up 65,000 kms thus far. During that time I've crossed the Simpson Desert, driven the Oodnadatta Track and Birdsville Track, followed Len Beadell's famous Anne Beadell, Connie Sue and Gunbarrel highways, climbed the mountains in Victoria's High Country, explored the gnarly and shaly tracks of the magnificent Flinders Ranges and spent all the rest of my time driving the various four wheel drive tracks spread along the east coast of Australia.

The ST's have been amazing, there is no other word for them. In all that time they suffered just one pin-hole from a mulga stick which was easily repaired, dragged me through thick mud, over Sturt's Stony Desert, across the vast sand dunes of the Simpson, not to mention the ultra soft Stockton Beach dunes and through ice and snow in the mountains.

My Cooper ST's have tracked safely and surely on the black top, often with my fully loaded Landcruiser tipping the scales close to 3.5 ton."

For your closest authorised Cooper Tires dealer and free info pack call:

1300 COOPER

1300 266 737

Cooper TIRES

AMERICA'S MOST TRUSTED 4x4 TIRE

www.coopertires.com.au

ACKNOWLEDGMENTS

In the 17 years we have been producing this book numerous people and organisations have helped in keeping this book up to date and relevant to today's Kimberley traveller.

The Western Australian Department of Conservation and Land Management (CALM) have always been a great help, especially CALM's Kimberley Regional Managers and the staff based in Kununurra.

Other government departments including the WA Dept of Indigenous Affairs, the WA Water & Rivers Commission in Kununurra, DPI and their offices in the Kimberley were also of great assistance. Likewise the Shire Councils' of the region were extremely helpful.

For the early photographs and much of the early historic information that appears in this book, we'd like to acknowledge the WA Police Department, The Royal WA Historical Society, the J S Battye Library of West Australian History, the Derby Library, and the private collection of John Morgan, the Surveyor General of WA during the 1960s, 70s and early 80s. For the pics depicting the Kimberley in the early 1950s we'd like to sincerely thank our friends Alex and Jacky Sklenica who explored the area between Broome and Wyndham on push bikes! Now that was an adventure!

Thanks are also due to the tour operators and station owners who supplied us with help and information. We'd especially like to thank Peter & Pat Lacy from Mt Elizabeth, Cheryl Camp of Charnley River station and Anne Koeyers of Drysdale River station.

As well, there are the many others – station owners, jackeroos, publicans, miners, helicopter pilots, storekeepers, safari vehicle drivers, fellow travellers and office workers who, perhaps unknowingly at the time, contributed to this book. We know at times all we seemed to do was ask questions!

A special thanks must also go to Viv's sister, Linda Murray, for all her support and assistance in the office. Without her we wouldn't be able to get away as often as we do. There are also other friends along the way who have helped with information and collaboration.

Finally we'd also like to thank Nissan Australia for their support over the years.

Without everybody's help this book wouldn't have been possible. Thanks a lot.

Ron & Viv Moon

A WARNING and REQUEST from the Authors and Publisher

Everything changes.

Roads are improving, mining companies are opening up new areas and Government departments (National Parks, etc.) are continually upgrading their facilities. Aboriginal communities are opening their doors to travellers while asserting more control over their lands.

If you find things different to what we say, please don't blame us - well not too much anyway! We would really appreciate a letter or quick note on what you found, whether it is for the better or worse. If you have a comment drop a line to the publisher whose address you'll find elsewhere in this book.

INTRODUCTION

We first went to the Kimberley region in the early 1970s and our three month northern and central Australian trip didn't get much further. To say we fell in love with this wild land is an understatement. Its rugged ranges, wide sweeping plains and its jewel-like sources of water were, and still are, a magical inspiration to us. Most people who experience the Kimberley in one of her many moods will also be besotted with the region.

Most people travel to the Kimberley in the heart of the Dry season, but at that time of the year the area is putting on its cloak of brown. Access may be easier and the weather cooler during that period, but with an all bitumen road skirting its southern perimeter and air conditioned vehicles, travellers shouldn't solely restrict themselves to the Dry. You'll definitely see a different Kimberley in the Wet or just after the Wet finishes, than you'll see later in the middle or end of the Dry season.

The area covered by this book is huge – much bigger than the state of Victoria. In fact, the Kimberley region covers an area of 421,451 sq kms. Yet, the population is only around 35,000, with most of those clustered around the half a dozen major towns in the area. That, combined with the fact that the country is so rugged, means much of the region is completely untouched by modern man. You only have to consider that the Bungles were only 'discovered' in 1982, yet they were less than 100 km from Highway Number 1, to realise how pristine and unknown this area really is.

Along the Gibb River Road.

Our guide is an introduction to the area. Every person who visits the Kimberley and spends a bit of time there and gets out of their vehicle will discover some secret spots, known to just a few. That's one of the great attractions to the region.

This is a great region of Australia. Whether you are a four-wheel driver, a confirmed bushwalker, a lover of wildlife, a keen or casual fisherman, a canoeist or just a family man who loves camping with his wife and kids, then the Kimberley is the destination for you.

While this book is mainly meant for travellers who wish to experience the country on their own or in the company of a small select group, a large number of operators run trips throughout the Kimberley for those who wish to have tours organised for them. Remember though, that in this rugged country things can go wrong, even for the best equipped and organised operator. You may end up bogged, wet, bitten by insects (almost compulsory) and a number of other things, but it will be worth it – believe us!!

To truly appreciate the region visitors need to take the time to meet the people, learn the history and view the beauty of nature. You can drive from Kununurra to Broome or Derby in just over a day, but you'll miss seeing the walls of Windjana Gorge glow fire red in the evening light, or the sheer beauty of sunrise over the Mitchell Plateau, or feel a barra take a lure as it's trolled deep along some untouched waterway. You'll miss meeting the friendly people and won't even spy some of the incredible Aboriginal art or experience the cool blush of air as you enter Cathedral Gorge in the Bungles. Take your time!!

This is where individual travellers have a distinct advantage over those who choose package tours. With a lot of time and no set agenda they can slowly make their way through the country stopping where it pleases them and continually changing their next destination as they hear somebody mention some great place at a pub or camping spot. There are so many good places to stop and stay, to pitch a tent, to fish or to fossick for old relics that one Dry season is not enough!

With the popularity of the Kimberley to an ever growing number of people, rubbish and human waste are a problem in some parts. For the sake of everybody who comes to see a wild, unspoilt country (just like you did) do the right thing – carry out any rubbish you can't burn, and bury any human waste deeply away from any creek or river. Please don't make a tip of the place.

Above all, leave the area as you found it so others can enjoy the same pristine experience.

Our Favourite Attractions

Here's our list of favourites as they stand at present. Each trip we enlarge on it and we're sure you'll end up with just as good or even better after spending some time in the Kimberley.

1. Explore the wonders of the gorges of the Purnululu (Bungle Bungle) National Park and soak up the atmosphere of Cathedral Gorge.
2. Paddle the Ord River and enjoy the 'Everglades' during the quiet of the evening.
3. Marvel at the wonders of the Mitchell River Falls from the ground and a helicopter flight.
4. Drive the Gibb River Road and take a few days to enjoy it and the many gorges along the way.
5. Fossick for old relics among the ruins of the gold mines in the Halls Creek area.
6. View the magnificent Aboriginal art of the area and wonder at the power and majesty of the Wandjina figures.
7. Relax and swim on the beach at Broome, take a camel ride in the evening and take a drive along the length of Cable Beach.
8. Journey to Kalumburu and enjoy the friendship of the people, explore the coast and experience the fabulous fishing.
9. Catch a barra from any one of the rivers or, for the ultimate, take in a day or two of heli-fishing.
10. Camp beside a deserted pristine waterway surrounded by the rugged ranges that make up the Kimberley.

Cruising off Cable Beach at Sunset.
Camp ground at Kalumburu Mission .

The beautiful altar at the Beagle Bay church.
Wandjina heads near Edward River crossing.

PHYSICAL ASPECTS

GEOGRAPHY AND GEOLOGY

GENERAL

Located in the far north of Western Australia the Kimberley region is immediately recognisable on any geographic or topographic map of Australia. A deeply convoluted coastline borders the region on the north and west, while the sweeping arc of long, rugged mountain ranges cuts the Kimberley off from the sameness of the great deserts to the south.

Most people consider the Kimberley region as starting on the line of the 19° South of Latitude which crosses the coast some 170 km south of Broome in the west and some 20 km north of Wolfe Creek in the east. With its eastern boundary being the border of the Northern Territory/Western Australia, the total land mass is some 320,000 sq km, making it larger than the states of Victoria and Tasmania combined (total 296,000 sq km).

Situated as it is in the far north it is less than 500 km from Indonesia, with the port of Wyndham (the northern-most port in the State) nearer to Jakarta than Perth, and much closer to Singapore than Melbourne.

The population, including the quite large Aboriginal population, totals under 30,000 and most of these are located in the half-dozen major towns, Aboriginal settlements and homesteads scattered throughout the region.

Around 225,000 sq km of the total area is taken up with some sort of pastoral activity supporting 99 leases and carrying approx 350,000 to 400,000 head of cattle. Much of the remainder is designated Aboriginal land, while the rest is either unallocated Crown Land, or Reserved Crown Land such as water catchments, mining leases, national parks or nature reserves.

Near the mouth of Willie Creek, north of Broome, at high tide. A top fishing spot.

GEOLOGY

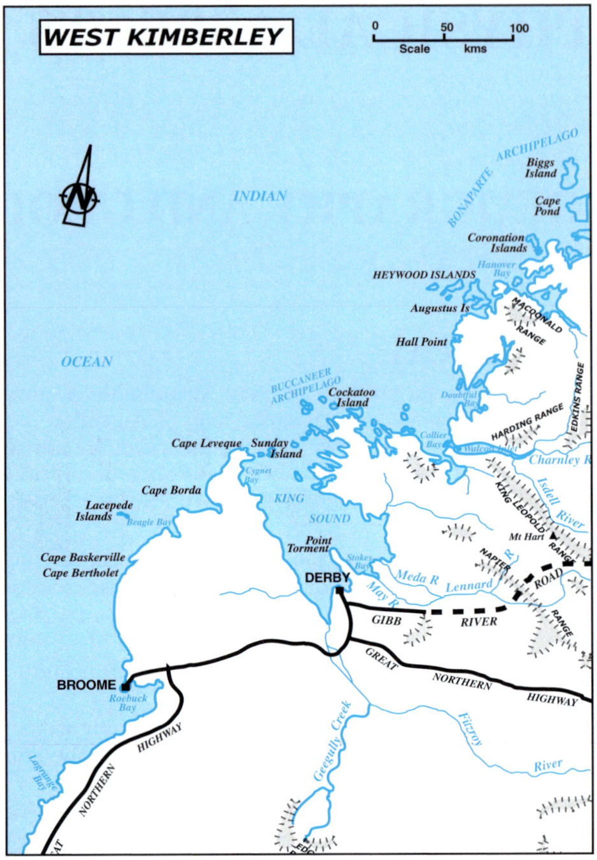

The geology of the Kimberley region is complex making it one of the most interesting regions in Australia, with rocks and geological formations ranging from the relatively recent to the most ancient times.

Basically, the most ancient formations dating back to the Pre-Cambrian times (greater than 600 million years) are represented by the beds of sandstone and shale of the Nullagine series and are located in and around the Hann Plateau or the Central Plateau region of the Kimberley and includes the King Leopold Ranges.

From the Archeozoic period (more than 2000 million years ago) schists, quartzites and metamorphosed sandstone occur in the flat topped ranges of the Carr Boyd Ranges, west of the Ord River, and on the fringes of the tableland country between Halls Creek and Fitzroy Crossing.

This extremely old land mass was very mountainous with peaks rising several thousand metres above sea level. Torrential rains generated erosion and silt loaded rivers flowed from these mountains, depositing sediment over a vast area. In places even huge boulders were transported and these later formed massive conglomerates such as that at Mt Behn, situated between Windjana Gorge and Tunnel Creek.

Upper Cambrian (550 to 600 million years ago) limestones and mudstones cover a considerable area in the headwaters of the Ord River, as do Lower Cambrian (500 million years old) basalts and these later basalts have eroded and given rise to large areas of grassland.

The red-brown sandy 'Pindan' country of the western Kimberley is underlaid by recent Jurassic (150 million years old) sediments, while in the east the large areas of sandy country called 'Cockatoo Sands', situated near Kununurra, are made up of Permian (250 million years old) sandstones and shales.

One of the most spectacular geological features of the region is the series of Devonian (380 to 400 million years ago) limestone reefs that stretch across the southern section of the Kimberley, and also outcrops just north of Kununurra. In the south this once great reef structure is now known as the Napier Range.

Salt flats border many of the streams and rivers close to the sea. These flood at extra high tide or during the Wet.

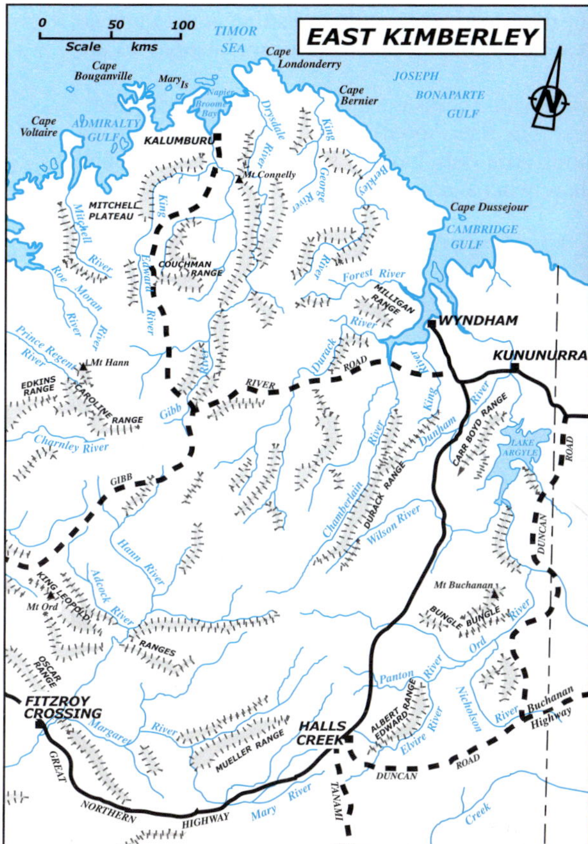

The spectacular, convoluted and twisted King Leopold Sandstone along the Gibb River Road

THE COAST AND OFFSHORE ISLANDS

Long, sandy beaches are all the go south of Broome and to a lesser degree to the north as well. From King Sound north the coastline changes and is indented with numerous bays, harbours, coves and large, sometimes cliff-lined river estuaries. It is often called the most outstandingly beautiful coastline in the world, but also one of the most dangerous. Dramatic tides that register a rise and fall of greater than 15 metres create swirling maelstroms and actual walls of water as they ebb and flow through the constricting channels of the many headlands, islands and bays along the mainland coast. The tide drops so quickly and so far that low, wide waterfalls sometimes occur on steep-sided reefs as the water cascades off the fast drying reef.

Offshore, numerous islands of varying shapes and sizes lay scattered along the coast. Some are no more than low mangrove covered mud islands, but many are virtually drowned hills, rough and rocky, like the nearby mainland. A few have small pleasant beaches and bays which are ideal for camping but, for the most part, you'd need local knowledge to find them.

A number of the islands have rich deposits of iron ore which have been, or still are, mined.

Permanent fresh water on many of the islands is a very rare commodity and animal life is very restricted. However, these islands are very important as biological reserves as they are isolated from the sometimes degrading influences of the mainland.

On the larger islands conditions are not so harsh, water may be found and a few trees and shrubs do survive, giving shelter to the occasional animal.

Coral reefs fringe many of the islands and further out to sea spectacular reefs, equal to the Great Barrier Reef in life and diversity, can also be found. The Rowley Shoals, Scott and Ashmore Reefs and Adele Island are just some that are dotted across this vast sweep of ocean.

Back on the mainland, as well as on some of the islands, where the coastline is not quite so rocky or steep, mangroves can be found in great profusion. At other places the mangroves are just a thin veneer along the water's edge.

Elsewhere, such as in King Sound, expansive salt encrusted mud flats stretch for miles. Inundated only a few times a year by the highest tide, these mudflats are prevented from being colonised by mangroves by the high temperatures (you only have to walk out on them around midday to know how hot it can get), a dry offshore wind and an unsuitable tidal pattern.

The Rowley Shoals

Three great circular coral reefs, Imperieuse, Clerke and Mermaid Reefs, stretched over 110 km of Indian Ocean, make up the Rowley Shoals. They are considered the best geological examples of atolls on the Australian continental shelf.

Discovered and named by Captain Phillip Parker King in 1818, who named Mermaid Reef after his ship, the three reefs and their surrounding waters are today protected. In the case of Clerke and Imperieuse reefs by a WA marine park, while Mermaid is a marine reserve under the management of the Australian Nature Conservation Agency.

For more information on these reefs see the chapter, 'National Parks and Nature Reserves'. Charter boats visit these reefs and the diving and fishing is superb. See our chapter 'Tour Operators' for a complete listing.

The spectacular reefs and marine life of the Rowley Shoals make for fantastic diving and fishing.

THE DESERTS

Approach the Kimberley region from anywhere down south and all you'll see for days is the vegetated ridges of the Great Sandy or **Tanami Deserts**. It is not that these deserts are uninteresting or dead, far from it, but compared to the Kimberley there is a lack of variety in landform, vegetation and animal life.

It's along the coast south of Broome that the only desert to reach the sea, officially, occurs in Australia. Here, along the stretch of 80 Mile Beach, the **Great Sandy Desert** meets the Indian Ocean.

This area of the Kimberley, south of the great sweep of the Fitzroy River, is much drier than the areas further north and the vegetation is typical of Australia's great deserts. Spinifex reigns supreme, with occasional stands of native pines and smaller grevilleas, hakeas, etc.

THE LOWLAND REGIONS OF THE SOUTH & EAST

Quite suddenly as one heads north from Port Hedland, the country changes.

As you approach Broome the **'Pindan' country** begins and extends north to close to the Fitzroy River. Found on the sandy plains that are the northern extension of the Great Sandy Desert, the Pindan country is dominated by tall dense stands of acacia.

Further to the west and south of **Halls Creek** is the better watered country around Lake Gregory and Sturt Creek and the tributaries of the mighty Ord River.

A vast sweep of grasslands parallels the mighty Fitzroy River, south of the ranges.

Centred along the sweep of the awesome **Fitzroy River** and its tributaries is the land of the great cattle properties of the Kimberley. Much has changed here since European man arrived with his sheep and cattle. Erosion and introduced weeds are a problem that are startlingly obvious as you cross the great floodplain of this mighty of mighty rivers.

It was through the Ord River and Fitzroy River basins that pastoral development started in the Kimberley and it is still where it is centred. It's also this area, due mainly to cattle grazing, where the land has suffered and it is relatively easy to see huge areas that are badly eroded. So bad was the erosion in the headwaters of the Ord that when the Ord dam was built much of the area was resumed by the Crown to protect the water catchment and to stop the dam silting up!

During the Wet season the monsoons bring heavy rains and the rivers run deep and fast. In their lower reaches (eg, where the main highway crosses the Fitzroy River south of Derby) the rivers flood out over vast areas, forming a mini inland sea.

During the height of the Dry most of the rivers contract to long chains of waterholes with only the occasional spring fed creek running. Such is the difference between the Wet and the Dry.

Rivers in Flood!

To give some indication of how much water the Fitzroy or the Ord Rivers carry, you only have to imagine the 1995 flood when the Fitzroy was running one metre deep over the Fitzroy Crossing bridge; or, the fact that when the Ord is running full bore it could fill all the water catchments that supply Perth from empty to full in just a couple of hours, or Sydney Harbour in four!!

While the Ord has been virtually tamed with two dams on it, the Fitzroy runs remarkably free with only a small weir and dam near Camballin, south-east of Derby. While great hopes have been held for the prospects of irrigation on the Ord and at Camballin, only the Ord has reached anywhere near its full potential and that has only been in the last few years!

Lake Argyle, the largest man-made lake in Australia, is the bigger of the two on the Ord. When full it covers an amazing 2000 sq km, is some 40 metres deep and holds – at normal full supply levels, some 10 Sydney Harbours – or so they say!

The Kununurra Diversion Dam, built across the Ord not far from the town of the same name, supplies the surrounding farms with gravity fed water. Now that the Ord flows continually and virtually at the same height all year round, below the dam the vegetation along the river has changed. The bird life has also increased dramatically – it's a real nature's paradise and in some areas open to all with a boat or canoe – see our chapter, 'Canoeing and Boating in the Kimberley', for more details.

While as yet the Fitzroy remains virtually undammed, that's not to say it hasn't been looked at. If dammed at Dimond Gorge, north of Fitzroy Crossing in the King Leopold Range, the resultant dam would be bigger than the Ord and one of the biggest in the world!

THE RANGES

North of the great plains of the Fitzroy is the first great arc of mountain ranges. And this is what the Kimberley is all about – its dominant feature and the image that stays in the mind.

The Napier Range

The first range is the jagged spires of the limestone Napier Range. Once a Devonian coral reef, around 400 million years ago, it swept north-west around the present coast of the Kimberley then east in a gigantic arc to around the NT/WA border.

The sheer, wall-sided edge of the Napier hindered access further north and for many years it formed the natural barrier to pastoral and hence European settlement of the country. In fact, in the 1920s and up to the 1940s there was only a handful of white people "over the range", as Ion L. Idriess so evocatively called it.

Today it is the site of many of the famous Kimberley attractions – Tunnel Creek, Geikie Gorge and Windjana Gorge, to name the most popular.

See our chapter, *Derby to Fitzroy Crossing*, for more information.

Gold is still found in the Kimberley.

The King Leopolds

North of the Napier Range begin the mainly granite foothills that build up to the highest range in the Kimberley, the King Leopold Ranges. **Mt Ord** in the Leopolds at 937 metres is the second highest peak in the Kimberley. (Mt Wells, situated in the southern end of the Durack Range, being the highest point at 983 metres.)

The King Leopold Range sweeps in from the west coast in a great arc, finishing north of Halls Creek where the Ord River rises and the equally spectacular Durack Range, with its **Elgee Cliffs**, strikes north along the Chamberlain River to the coast, south of Wyndham.

This great range of convoluted and twisted King Leopold Sandstone is a visual splendour with sheer cliffs rearing up at every quarter. Great gorges cut by the Lennard, Fitzroy and Margaret Rivers are other visual wonders of this range.

The great man-made lakes in the Eastern Kimberley have changed the landscape forever.

The Central Plateau

The Kimberley Plateau, the vast region of upland country that is centred around **Mt Elizabeth** and the cattle station of the same name, is a region of worn and torn rock covered in rolling waves of tropical woodland.

Mt Hann on the central tableland, or the Hann Plateau as it is often called, comes in as the third highest peak in the Kimberley, at just 854 metres.

From this central plateau, often called the **Gardner Plateau** on modern maps, many of the Kimberley's great rivers are spawned. To the south are the Isdell, Charnley and Hann Rivers, while to the north-west is the Prince Regent, Roe, Mitchell and King Edward Rivers, while to the east are the headwaters of the Drysdale and Durack Rivers.

Pics L to R: The impressive rock formations in the Purnululu National Park; sunset at beautiful Cape Leveque.

The Northern and Western Ramparts

Through these northern and western areas of the Kimberley, much of the geological formation is made up of very old beds of basalt rock overlaid with sandstone over 400 metres thick. Where this formation has been tilted by the tremendous pressures of the earth's crust, the creeks often follow the joining line, so that on one side of the creek will be basalt while on the other it will be sandstone.

These beds of sandstone have also formed many of the flat topped mesa-like mountains such as Mt Cockburn near Wyndham, **Mt Trafalgar** in the Saint George Basin, as well as the magnificent tabletop islands near Port Warrender.

Gorges, swamps, plateau and sheer escarpments are also all part of this magnificent country, while along the coast steep cliffs drop vertically into the sea. Much of the area is undisturbed and remains one of our greatest wilderness areas.

The **Prince Regent River,** in the very west of the Kimberley, has cut its course down a long straight fracture in the sandstone south of the Gardner Plateau, called the Prince Regent Lineament. Here the river runs near arrow straight between tall weathered cliffs for nearly 200 km while all its tributaries join the main stream through other fractures and at 90° to the main rock strewn channel.

On the **Mitchell Plateau**, further north, eons of time have leached the clay base soils to form a deep bed of rich bauxite. That area, such an attraction to mining companies, corresponds almost exactly to the area of richest palm growth and the very thing that makes the plateau different to every other region in the Kimberley. When and how much of it will be mined will most definitely depend on public pressure to conserve this unique place. See our chapter, *The Mitchell Plateau,* for more detail on this exciting place.

One of the most spectacular formations in the whole of the Kimberley and certainly one of the most distinctive is the **Carson Escarpment**. This tall line of cliffs stretches north along the Carson and Drysdale Rivers for over 200 km, from a break between the Central Plateau and the more easterly **Karunjie Plateau**, all the way to the coast near Cape Londonderry.

The wide expanse of the Victoria River .
Delightful Wrens Gorge.

The Ord River just below the Argyle dam wall.
The Walls of China, near Halls Creek.

THE EASTERN RAMPARTS

To the east of this central plateau, but separated by a stretch of lower country, is another vast area of upland country commonly called the **Karunjie Plateau**, whose northern extension is the **Bluff Faced Range**. Its southern and eastern boundary is the mighty Chamberlain River and for much of the distance the plateau ends abruptly at the edge of the river in a tall cliff, called the Elgee Cliffs. On the eastern side of the river the magnificent Durack Range rises, and further east, bordering the Ord River, the spectacular **Carr Boyd Range.**

Closer to the coast where the great rivers of the region – the Ord, Pentecost, Chamberlain, Durack and King to name just the major players, have deposited their eons of silt, vast areas of saltplain, mudflats, swamp and mangroves border the southern arms of Cambridge Gulf.

Between the King and the Pentecost Rivers is the escarpment ringed **Cockburn Range**, surely the most impressive sight along the eastern end of the Gibb River Road. Along the western circumference of the range tall sheer sandstone cliffs plunge downwards to large scree slopes that fall away to the flat plains below.

The bee-hive shaped domes of the Bungle Bungles.
Right: Echidna Chasm in the Purnululu National Park.

Further south, south of the **Osmond Range** and tucked into a sweep of the Ord River valley, is the **Bungle Bungle** massif, an area of dome shaped beehive sandstone structures which are cut by spectacularly sheer, and often narrow gorges. Similar structures are found near Kununurra and over the border in the NT in the Keep River region, however, it is the Bungles where this formation is at their grandest.

Formed during the Devonian era some 380 million years ago, the formations are of sandstone. Under the orange and black skin (layers of silica and lichen respectively) that give the beehive effect, is the soft white or yellowish sandstone.

CLIMATE AND WEATHER

The Kimberley has a monsoonal type climate, although it is much more arid than places in far north Queensland, or even in the Northern Territory. The climate is characterised by a warm, dry winter or Dry season, and a hot, wet summer or Wet season.

Ominous dark clouds form over the parched landscape towards the end of the Dry.

RAINFALL

Rainfall varies, but generally decreases as one heads inland away from the coast. In the northern Kimberley annual rainfall exceeds 1200 mm, while in the south, around the great arc of the Fitzroy River, yearly falls average around 350 mm.

January and February are the wettest months, but rain can occur anytime between October and March. Outside these times rain is definitely scarce.

However, the rainfall can vary greatly from season to season, especially inland. At Halls Creek for instance, rainy days have varied, for the wettest month, January, from two to 22 days of rainfall since records began nearly 100 years ago.

While the Mitchell Plateau records the highest rainfall for any site in Western Australia, you don't have to go that far inland, in fact just south of the mighty Fitzroy River, before you are in desert country.

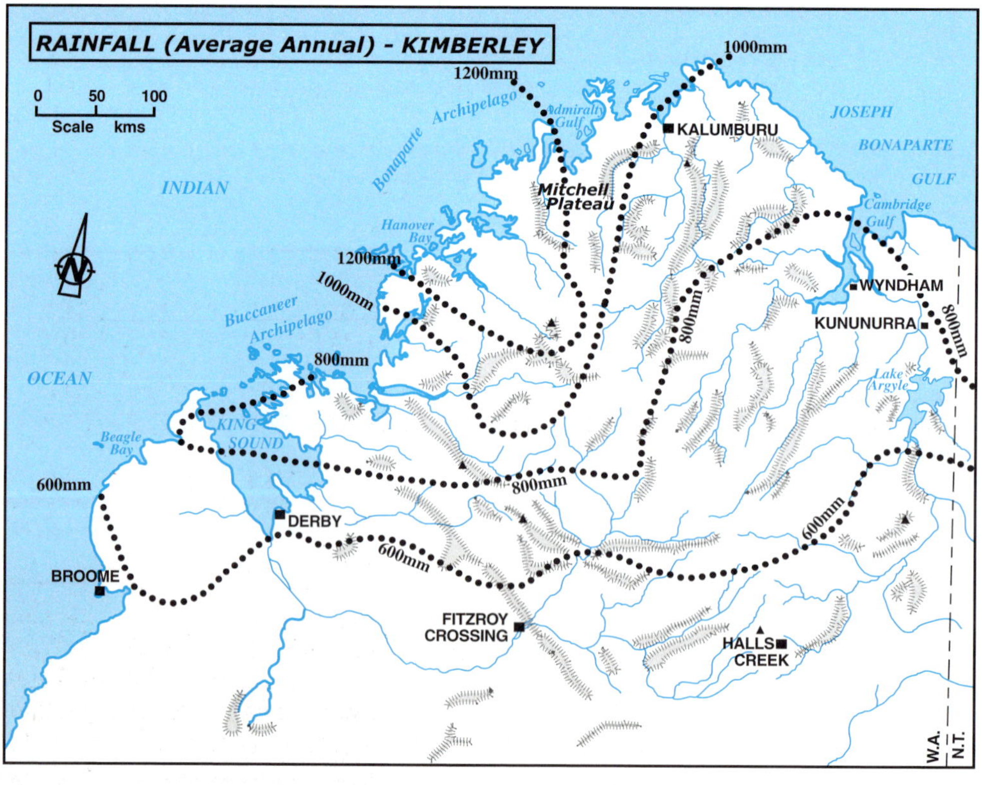

Evaporation is high and ranges between 1000 and 3000 mm per year, hence, the parched nature of the land at the end of the Dry season.

AVERAGE MONTHLY RAINFALL (MM)

	Jan	Feb	Mar	Apr	May	June	July	Aug	Sept	Oct	Nov	Dec	Year
Broome	178	162	94	26	31	20	5	2	2	2	9	42	573
Derby	177	184	98	26	21	9	8	1	2	3	10	45	584
Fitzroy Crossing	149	132	76	20	12	9	7	1	2	5	26	86	525
Halls Creek	144	127	56	21	17	5	7	3	4	17	30	67	498
Kununurra	195	201	115	44	12	3	6	1	3	26	62	128	796
Mitchell Plateau	337	372	323	40	43	5	13	2	13	52	130	202	1532
Wyndham	146	210	179	29	15	–	8	0	12	19	51	95	764

TEMPERATURE

Average annual maximum and minimum temperatures for selected areas within the Kimberley are given in the following table.

Temperatures vary from district to district, with the stations close to the coast receiving a modifying effect from the ocean. Inland it can get hot and in places like the Bungles, it can get very hot. In recent years daytime temperatures have been recorded in the high 40s, peaking in the low 50s – and that was in September!

The Southeast Trades (easterlies) are the prevailing winds in the winder months, (Dry season), while the Wet season rains are brought by the Northwest Monsoons.

AVERAGE DAILY MAXIMUM/MINIMUM TEMPERATURES (°C)

	Jan	Feb	Mar	Apr	May	June	July	Aug	Sept	Oct	Nov	Dec	Year
Broome													
Maximum	33.4	33.0	34.0	34.2	31.3	29.0	28.6	30.0	31.9	32.9	33.6	34.0	32.2
Minimum	26.2	25.9	25.4	22.6	18.3	15.1	13.6	15.1	18.4	22.1	24.9	26.4	21.2
Derby													
Maximum	35.1	34.4	35.2	35.3	32.4	30.2	30.4	32.3	34.7	36.9	38.0	37.8	34.4
Minimum	25.5	25.1	25.1	22.7	19.4	15.7	15.1	17.1	19.8	23.1	25.5	26.5	21.7
Fitzroy Crossing													
Maximum	37.7	36.8	37.0	36.4	32.3	30.0	29.7	32.5	36.2	39.4	40.8	39.9	35.7
Minimum	24.7	24.2	23.2	19.6	15.8	12.0	10.5	12.6	16.9	21.6	24.3	25.1	19.2
Halls Creek													
Maximum	36.7	35.9	35.5	33.9	29.5	27.2	27.0	29.8	33.7	37.1	38.4	38.1	33.6
Minimum	24.2	23.7	22.8	20.3	16.9	13.5	12.4	14.7	18.5	22.6	24.4	24.5	19.9
Kununurra													
Maximum	36.1	34.8	34.7	35.2	32.7	30.5	30.1	33.1	36.0	38.2	38.7	37.7	34.8
Minimum	24.8	24.5	23.7	20.6	18.5	15.5	14.3	16.3	19.7	23.1	24.6	24.9	20.9
Mitchell Plateau													
Maximum	32.4	32.0	32.6	33.1	31.5	29.6	30.2	32.5	34.5	36.0	36.1	34.1	32.9
Minimum	22.7	22.4	21.7	18.2	14.6	11.2	9.7	12.8	16.4	20.3	22.1	22.7	17.9
Wyndham													
Maximum	37.2	36.0	35.9	35.9	33.2	30.9	30.8	33.7	36.1	38.5	39.2	38.5	35.5
Minimum	26.1	25.7	25.1	23.4	20.8	17.6	16.9	19.4	22.7	25.6	26.7	26.7	23.1

How hot?

Daytime temperatures during the months of May to August are relatively cool ,with maximums in the low 30s and minimums around 15°C to 16°C. June and July are generally the coolest months and minimum temperatures can sometimes get down as low as zero at places such as Halls Creek and down to 5°C along the coast areas. October and November are the hottest months, when the temperature often exceeds 38°C.

Great waterways of the Fitzroy River are spawned by the annual Wet season and the cyclones it brings.

CYCLONES

A tropical cyclone is a circular rotating storm of tropical origin in which the average wind speed exceeds 63 km/h (gale force). Gale force is the threshold speed at which a cyclone is named, however it is normal for wind speeds to increase substantially as the storm develops. Wind speeds in excess of 100 km/h are common by the time a cyclone crosses the coast and higher wind speeds frequently occur. A speed of 248 km/h was recorded at Onslow as Cyclone Trixie crossed the coast in February 1975.

Tropical cyclones can blow up at any time of the year, but they are very rare outside the cyclone 'season' which occurs from the beginning of November to the end of April. Cyclones are most frequent however in February and March.

Traditionally cyclones are located with reference to the central 'eye', however it is important to remember that the damaging winds can sometimes extend over two hundred kilometres from the centre. When a cyclone directly approaches an area, the wind speed steadily increases and reaches a maximum just prior to the passage of the calm central eye. Once the eye passes the wind reverses direction, rapidly rises to peak strength again and then slowly weakens as the whole system moves away.

Once over land, cyclones tend to peter out within 24 to 48 hours and the strong central winds die away. Dangerous flooding can occur as heavy rain falls from the decaying system.

Category of Cyclones

Categories of cyclones range from '1' to '5'. A category '1' cyclone has the lowest risk with wind speeds up to 90 kph, while a category '5' cyclone is strong, very dangerous and has wind speeds over 200 kph!

Keeping Track of Cyclones

As cyclones often adopt an erratic course, or suddenly change speed, it is important that you be aware of any changes at the earliest possible time. In order to do this, keep your radio tuned to the ABC or the local commercial station and listen for the most up to date cyclone information, which is broadcast at regular intervals.

As a public service, radio stations in cyclone prone areas remain on air 24 hours a day when a cyclone is close to the coast.

The Bureau of Meteorology (BoM) issues current tropical cyclone advice from the **WA Tropical Cyclone Information Service, ph: 1300 659 210.**

The BoM also has offices which can be reached by phoning Port Hedland (airport) ph: (08) 9140 1440, as well as Broome, situated at the Broome airport, ph: (08) 9192 1211.

The safest place

The safest place during a cyclone is in a strong building on high, but not exposed ground. All glass should be removed or taped and on the side away from the wind and a door or window should be left open to reduce pressure inside the building.

The Bureau of Meteorology and Emergency Management Australia has a comprehensive guide about 'Surviving Cyclones in Australia' on their web page, check it out: **www.bom.gov.au/info/cyclone/**

If you are in a tent, find somewhere else to shelter! Even a van is not the best spot and if you are in one they will need to be tied down! Probably better to head for a motel!

Don't forget, the further inland you are the less effect a cyclone has.

WEB SITES

The following web sites can help you with current weather conditions in the Kimberley:

www.australiasevereweather.com/
Gives cyclone information and status of current activity, along with weather and climate information and links.

www.bom.gov.au/weather/wa/ - Bureau of Meteorology site with weather and flood information.

www.wunderground.com/global/AU_WE.html- Weather Underground Inc. site with up-to-the-minute information on towns and sites Australia wide, including the Kimberley region, covering temperature, wind conditions, moon rise and lots more, as well as astronomy.

Following a Pattern

From 1909 to 1975 there had been seven cyclones across the coast within 100 km either side of Derby. In comparison in the same period there have been seven cyclones across the coast within 50 km of Broome and a further 16 cyclones passing to the north and south of Broome outside the 50 km perimeter.

The significant difference in the two towns is that Derby is actually 115 km from the ocean, at the foot of King Sound and is therefore protected by land masses.

Our map shows just a few of the cyclones that have tracked across the Kimberley region.

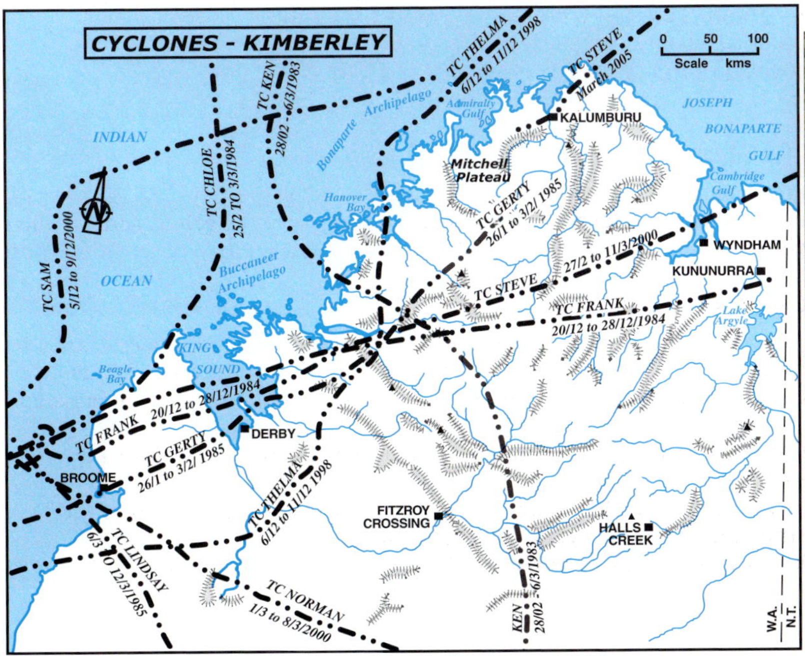

THE FLORA AND FAUNA

VEGETATION

GENERAL

The plants of the Kimberley are probably the least known in Australia and in recent years there have been numerous expeditions to the region to rectify this situation.

While the grasses, shrubs and trees of the plains and ranges are fairly well known, significant new discoveries are occurring amongst the smaller flower species and the pockets of rainforest that are scattered over the region. In recent years it is these micro habitats of jungle that have fired the imagination of scientists.

Amongst the great plains, and especially those bordering the Fitzroy and Ord Rivers, heavy grazing and the introduction of exotics have severely modified the plant communities. Heavy infestation of Noogoora Burr on the Fitzroy, below Fitzroy Crossing, through Camballin to Willare Bridge and beyond, has resulted in the whole area being placed in quarantine.

There is one plant specie of the Kimberley that, more than any other single feature, seems to be to many people the pure epitome of the region. That specie of plant is the Boab. Its huge bulk, topped with a mass of gnarled, twisted limbs, is an impression that stays in the minds of all who travel to and through the Kimberley.

As far as is presently known, the flora of the Kimberley contains over 2000 species, 1200 of them not occurring any further south in Western Australia. Indicating the Kimberley's closeness and likeness to the other great regions of the north, only 350 species are restricted to the Kimberley region.

As is the norm in Australia, it is the Eucalypts (gum trees and their cousins) and the Acacias (the wattles) that are the predominant trees in the region. More than 50 species of Eucalypts occur in the Kimberley (500 or more are known within Australia), while about 100 species of Acacia occur (of about 600 known in Australia).

Four Regions

A 1979 survey of the area divided the Kimberley into four broad natural botanical regions.

In the south-west, north to the King Leopold Ranges, the **Dampier Botanical District** is recognised, while to the east the **Hall Botanical District** takes in the dunes of the desert margin to the south, north across the ranges to the southern shores of Lake Argyle.

During the Wet, the Boab's usual characteristic bare-branched skeleton gets a covering of leaves.

The **Central Kimberley (or Fitzgerald) Botanical District** extends from Cambridge Gulf south-west across much of the plateau country to the King Leopold Ranges. The last and richest division is the **Gardner Botanical District** which extends across the well watered regions of the north-western and northern coasts from Walcott Inlet to beyond the NT/WA border in the east.

Soils and Vegetation

The variety of soils of the Kimberley have been derived from their respective geological formations and are the result of millions of years of weathering. This variety has in turn led to a wide range of vegetation associations, with many plants only being predominant in a particular soil structure. For example, the deep, reddish sandy soils of the west Kimberley, called Pindan, basically only support a mix of tree species that include a number of species, all called Pindan Wattle. Spinifex species occur on poor, sandy or skeletal soils, while the grasses, so valuable to cattle grazing, occur on the heavy clay and loam soils of the river systems.

THE GRASSES

Away from the great rock walls of the gorges, escarpments and mountain ranges, that is probably the lasting impression of the Kimberley, the grasses, vast seas of them, are often the first and still one of the most striking sensations of the region.

'Normal' Grasses

The grasses of the family Poaceae form the largest plant family in the Kimberley, and are found as ground cover throughout the region.

A number of species of Mitchell grass and Flinders grass are widespread through the region and provide good stock feed. Some of the grasses such as Bunch (or Black) speargrass, *Heteropogon contortus*, and Wind (Kerosene) grass, *Aristida contorta*, can be a real pain to walk through as the seeds penetrate and hang on to any clothing or skin.

Annual Sorghum or canegrass, *Sorghum stipoideum*, which grows up to four metres in height, often forms dense expanses on black soil in the better watered areas of the Kimberley and it can be a real pain to push a route through. This is especially so at the end of the Wet, in April and May, when the seed heads develop.

Other grasses include Kangaroo grass, *Themeda triandra*, usually found on granite derived soil and along creeks and well-watered creek margins, as well as Mauve sandgrass, *Whiteochloa biciliata*, that dominates the Cockatoo Sands area of the east Kimberley.

Tall grasses tower upwards after Wet season rains.

Spinifex

What is generally called spinifex covers a range of prickly grasses belonging to the *Triodia* and the *Plectrachne* genera. Plants belonging to the genus Spinifex only occur on coastal sand dunes.

Spinifex of the two aforementioned genera are the predominant plants over much of central and northern Australia. It is hard to identify them as the seed head is the only real way of telling them apart, and in the Kimberley they seed for only a very short time during the Wet. Common species include Hard spinifex, *Triodia basedowii,* (found in rocky ridges, gravel slopes and limestone country), Rock spinifex, *T. racemigera,* (occurring in sandstone areas and amongst rocks), Soft spinifex, *T. pungens,* (from basalt hills to clay pans) and Lobed, Gummy and Curly Spinifex, all of which are found over vast areas of the Kimberley.

Colourful images from the Kimberley including a yellow native hiibicius (top left); wild cotton or desert rose (top right); woolybut (above left); kurrajong (above right); one of the many Grevilleas (below left); the beautifuly marked Jabiru; flowering gum (bottom left) and native kapok tree (bottom right).

SMALL SHRUBS AND HERBS

There is a large range of herb type plants in the region with the most numerous being members of the Pea family, *Papilionaceae.*

Some of these plants are poisonous to animals such as the Crabs Eye Bean, *Abrus precatorious L.*, which has mauve flowers with the oblong shaped pods containing shiny black and red seeds. Just one of these seeds contains enough toxin to kill an adult, however the poison is contained within the seed and is not released until the outside coating of the seed is broken. Walkabout Poison (or Kimberley Horse Poison), *Crotalaria crispata,* is another short lived perennial which is commonly found on sandy plains, flowering from Feb to Nov. As its common name suggests, it often causes poisoning, especially in horses.

Other pea type flowers such as the Sesbania Pea, which is a common yellow flowered weed found growing along roadside verges, are not dangerous to animals.

The Cassia group (note: all *Cassia* L. species have been transferred to the genera *Chamaecrista* Moench. and *Senna* Miller) has a large representation in the Kimberley flora. All have symmetrical pinnate leaves with bright, yellow flowers with five petals and long, flattened sausage shaped seed pods, up to 10 cm long, which rattle when dry, bringing about the general name of 'Rattlepods' for this group. The Desert cassia, *Cassia nemophila,* is common in the more arid, sandy regions to the south, while the Cockroach Bush, *Senna notabilis,* occurs widely throughout the whole region. Randell, *Senna venusta,* is a shrub up to two metres high that grows along river courses and on rocky hills in the Kimberley, while the Ironwood (or Camel Poison), *Erythrophleum chlorostachys,* a toxic member of the Cassia family, grows well in loam soils over basalt. This deciduous tree, which in ideal conditions can grow to 15 metres, is extremely poisonous, especially to stock, with its dry, seemingly harmless leaves remaining toxic, as well as any sucker shoots also being very poisonous.

Mulla Mullas, *Gomphrena canescens,* sometimes called cottontails or batchelor's buttons, are the common names that cover a number of species of perennial herbs (*Gomphrena* and *Amaranthaceae* species). These species, with their purple or mauve flowers made up of short spikes in a ball or cluster, are papery in texture and often form quite a picturesque sight.

Mulla Mullas are a common sight.

SHRUBS AND TREES

THE WATTLES – *ACACIA* – FAMILY: LEGUMINOSAE

More members of the genus *Acacia* occur in the Kimberley than any other genus. Some of these small trees are predominant where the soil has been disturbed by heavy grazing or road building. Others tend to form thickets of dense, thorny plants to inhibit any form of progress by man or beast.

Species of Acacia that are common include the Sweet Mimosa Bush, *Acacia farnesiana*, an introduced specie which is found throughout the Kimberley, along with Prickly acacia (or Bardi bush), *Acacia victoriae*, an invader forming thickets on heavily trampled areas or along water courses. The Fitzroy Wattle, *Acacia ancistrocarpa,* is a slender, small tree often found in the western Kimberley, while the Broome Pindan Wattle, *Acacia eriopoda,* is especially common between Broome and Derby. The Corkybark Wattle, *Acacia suberosa,* is an erect, pine like tree common in the western Kimberley, while the Elephant-ear Wattle, *Acacia dunnii,* can be found scattered in the sandstone country towards the north coast.

THE GUMS – *EUCALYPTUS* – FAMILY: MYRTACEAE

The Eucalypts occur across the Kimberley in a whole range of habitats and include such well known and widespread trees as the River Red Gum, *Eucalyptus camaldulensis*, and the Northern Salmon Gum, *Eucalyptus bigalerita*, the latter common on poorly drained soils.

The Coolibah, the name of which, in fact, is given to two species – *E. coolabah* and *E. microtheca* (Flooded Box), is restricted to inland rivers and areas subject to flooding.

The Silver-Leaf Bloodwood, *E. collina*, occurs in almost pure stands in some sandstone, high rainfall areas and reaches an impressive 20 metres or more in height, while the Inland Bloodwood (or Plains Bloodwood), *E. terminali,* is often the dominant tree in the drier, open woodlands.

THE PAPERBARKS –*MELALEUCA* – FAMILY: MYRTACEAE

There are some 20 species of Paperbarks and Cadjebuts in the Kimberley and these trees usually occur in areas that are wet or at least damp for part of the year. Paperbarks often form almost pure stands along some water courses and their flowers, rich in nectar and pollen, attract birds, bees and flying foxes. The flower's heavy, sweet odour is a characteristic of many waterholes.

Coastal Paperbark, *Melaleuca acacioides,* is a small tree, up to 5 metres in height, with a dense crown and hanging branches which is commonly found on river banks and along the edges of mud flats, especially in the west Kimberley region.

The most common in the region are the Cadjeput, *M. cajuputi*, which grows to 30 metres, with narrow, bright green leaves, while the Silver Cadjeput, *M. argentea*, is a tree of between 5 and 12 metres high with narrow, silver leaves. A third species, Broadleaf Paperbark, *M. viridiflora*, is a similar tree with broad, dark green leaves, that can grown between 3 to 7 metres and up to 15 metres, depending on soil conditions and water availability.

All these provide pleasant places to rest under and spend the heat of the day.

GREVILLEAS – *GREVILLEA* – FAMILY: PROTEACEAE

About 20 species of Grevillea occur in the Kimberley and while most are tall shrubs, the spectacular Silky Grevillea, *Grevillea pteridifolia*, is a small tree to 8 metres found on well drained sandy areas. It is sometimes called the Kimberley Christmas Tree because that's what they were often used for. Flowering between May and July, the beautiful flowers, rich in nectar, are attractive to bees and kids.

One of the most common grevilleas in the Kimberley region and the sandy country to the south is Wickham's grevillea, *G.wickhamii.* A shrub up to 5 metres in height there are two sub species, both forms being very similar. One of the sub species is restricted to sandstone and quartzite ridges of the central and north-western Kimberley, while the smaller variety is found south from the central region of the Kimberley into the sandy desert country. Its blue-grey foliage and its bright orange-red coloured, honey-laden flowers make it stand out in any scene.

Other species of grevillea found in the region include the small Beefwood, *G. striata*, commonly found on alluvium areas; the Needleleaf grevillea, *G. erythroclada*, which prefers poorly drained sands, Rock grevillea, *G. heliosperma*, and a number of others. All have distinct colourful flowers.

HAKEA – FAMILY: PROTEACEAE

A number of species of Hakea occur across the Kimberley, with the Corkwood Hakea, *H. lorea*, of the sandy loam country, being the most spectacular, with yellowish flowers in cylindrical clusters. This small tree, with its cork-like bark, is common south of Halls Creek on the way into Carranya Station.

The Common Hakea, *H. arborescens*, a small tree up to 7 metres in height, with a rough, corky bark, is found throughout the Kimberley and has either small, white or pinkish-white, flowers.

The Figs – *Ficus* – Family: Moraceae

Figs are another common group of trees, especially along river and creek banks and amongst sandstone cliffs and the like.

The River Fig, *Ficus coronulata*, and the Stem-Fruit Fig, *F. racemosa*, are common along creek banks and amongst vine thickets, with the former reaching only 8 metres in height, while the latter grows to become a massive tree with solid branches.

While the Sandpaper Fig, *F. coronata*, is a small tree of the sandy, clay country, the Rock Fig can be either the smaller shrubby *F. platypoda*, or the Large-Leaf, *F. leucotricha*, which gets to tree size and has a silkier fig.

The Palm Community

There are a number of Screwpines (Pandanus Palm), genus *Pandanus*, to be found in the Kimberley, which come under the Family: Pandanaceae, of which a number of separate species are known from the Kimberley. The Common Screwpine, *Pandanus spiralis*, are widespread along river banks and swamps and grow to about 5 metres, often forming small, pleasant groves or thickets.

Tree Palms are represented by the genus *Livistona*, Family: Arecaceae, with five species being present in the Kimberley. *L. eastonii* is very common on the Mitchell Plateau where it forms a highlight of any visit and is in fact endemic to the Kimberley. In the Bungle Bungle Range a species of Livistona Palm is common, endemic and so new it is yet to be described. On both sides of the lower Drysdale River, amongst the low sandstone hills, the Fan-leaved Palm, *L. loriphylla,* is the only specie, again only occurring in the Kimberley region.

Cycads, *Cycas basaltica*, (Family: Cycadaceae), aren't really palms at all and are more closely related to Pines. However, they look like palms with their crown of large 1 to 2 metre long leaves spreading from a thick, erect trunk. The fruit, which is poisonous to stock and humans, is found in clusters at the base of the leaves. Five species are known from the region.

Mangroves

Along the coast many species of mangroves form dense forests along the water's edge. Some 17 species in 15 genera are known from this region, with the largest forests being around the estuaries of rivers such as the Glenelg, Prince Regent, Drysdale, Ord and Fitzroy.

The large forests of mangroves around Derby and Wyndham are probably the easiest to see and experience. Not particularly 'pleasant' habitats as far as humans are concerned, they are indeed rich, being the virtual nursery for untold species of fish and crabs.

Monarch of the Kimberley – The Boab

Adansonia gregorii – Family: Bombacaceae

The Boab tree, *Adansonia gregorii*, is a large, deciduous tree occurring on sandy plains, creek beds and stony ridges throughout the Kimberley, and in the nearby Victoria and Fitzmaurice River basins of the Northern Territory. In the Kimberley, they are especially common along the Fitzroy River valley, north along the Chamberlain and Pentecost Rivers to the coast around Kununurra and Wyndham.

The distinctive, immense trunk varies from bottle-shape to unusual, even grotesque shapes, sometimes with many stems. Mature trees can have a girth of 20 metres and canopies over 25 metres high.

Comprised of 5 to 9 leaflets up to 13 cm long, the Boab's leaves are green on the upper side, with white, silky matted hair underneath. During the Dry season the leaves fall off, revealing the characteristic bare-branched skeleton. Leaf fall enhances the tree's drought tolerance. The bark varies from dull grey-brown to bronze in colour, is smooth in texture and pock-marked or dimpled. The wood is soft and spongy.

Boabs have white waxy flowers about 10 cm long. The fruit, resembling pendulous gourds, is green and hairy at first, maturing to a brown, velvet textured surface on woody, but brittle shells. Mature fruit can be up to 25 cm long and 15 cm in diameter. Inside, dozens of hard, black, round, sometimes kidney shaped seeds, approximately 1 cm in diameter, are embedded in pulpy flesh.

During the Dry, Boabs shed their leaves, revealing their characteristic bare-branched skeleton, such as here at Marlgu Billagong, in the Parry Lagoon Nature Reserve..

Ancient Tree – Ancient Uses!

Australian Aborigines placed great importance on Boab trees. The explorer, George Grey, noted in 1838 that nearly all "gouty-stems" had evidence of an Aboriginal fire site beneath them.

The fruits were an important dietary supplement with the pulp containing malic, tartaric and ascorbic acids while the seeds have a high protein value. The pulp is eaten dry or mixed with water as a beverage.

The tree can also be a source of water when water becomes trapped in hollows inside the tree, or at the base of the branches. Moisture can also be extracted by chewing the stem or root fibre.

Strands of bark can be rolled to form twine, the gum used as glue and the fruit carved as ornaments, the latter being a handy source of income for artistic Aborigines who cater for the tourist.

Even the trees themselves have been known to be carved by Aborigines, with probably the best known one being located on Karunjie Station. This particular Boab shows a large crocodile carved into the soft layers of the tree.

Aboriginal names for the Boab are 'gadawon' (Kununurra), 'djungeri' (Kalumburu) and 'larrgid' (Bardi).

Seedlings are relatively quick growing (about 2 metres in the first three years in good conditions). Girth measurements of 2 metres in 30 year old trees have been recorded at a site on the Great Northern Highway, while the tree alongside the old Cable Station (courthouse) at Broome is believed to be less than one hundred years old, yet it has a girth of 7.01 metres.

Often the seeds accumulate under trees, and in ideal conditions the simultaneous germination of thousands of seeds takes place. Subsequently, the survivors beneath the canopy of the parent tree create the impression of a family gathering. In a couple of places along the Fitzroy River near forests of Boabs occur.

The longevity of Boabs is legendary, the oldest is perhaps aged over a thousand years. Mr. Aeneas Gunn of Elsey Station, N.T., (1895) wrote that *"...no one, through hundreds of miles where this tree grows, has ever seen a dead gouty-stem tree"*; which is how Boabs were known at the time. The name 'Boab' is probably a mispronunciation derived from the 'Baobab' of Africa.

The first Englishman to describe the Australian Boab was Lieutenant Phillip Parker-King, who in 1820 carved his cutter's name on a "gouty-stem tree" at Careening Cove, near the mouth of the Prince Regent River. This practice was remarked upon by Grey in his visit to the Kimberley coast in 1838, and he noted that Aborigines carved marks in Boabs, apparently to record the number of fruit taken.

Another historic blaze, signifying the encroachment of civilisation, was carved into a Boab on the banks of the Victoria River, in 1855, by celebrated explorer Augustus Gregory. He was leading an expedition into the Northern Territory and north-east Kimberley, and had with him the famous botanist Ferdinand von Mueller. Botanical specimens were collected and in 1857 the species was published as *Adansonia gregorii*, in honour of Gregory.

The Boab is extremely hardy. Examples can be seen of trees completely removed from the soil by wind, floodwater or earthworks, yet have continued growing and taken root in the new location. This has been exploited and large mature trees have been successfully transplanted, for example, along some of the streets in Derby and at the RAAF Airbase, near Yeeda.

Other Noticeable Species

The Wild Plum, *Terminalia platyphylla*, and the Wild Peach, *T. carpentariae*, both produce edible, but rather pithy fruit. The Wild Plum is found almost exclusively in and along creek banks where it grows to an attractive looking tree up to 20 metres in height. The Wild Peach on the other hand, is a small tree up to 12 metres in height that favours sandstone areas, stony, well drained soils or sandy plains.

On rocky hillsides the spectacular flowering Kurrajong, *Brachychiton populneus*, can often be seen in the better rainfall regions of the Kimberley. Having shed its leaves during winter, this small tree can put on a showy floral display of crimson coloured, large bell shaped flowers between May and August. In sandy soils and in medium to higher rainfall areas, the Northern Kurrajong, *Brachychiton diversifolius*, with its light green foliage, is found.

The Quinine bush, *Alstonia constricta*, is widely distributed, growing in a variety of habitats in higher rainfall areas of the Kimberley. The marble sized fruit starts off green, but turns bright orange and, as the name suggests, is very bitter in taste.

The Kapok bush (or Cotton Tree), *Cochlospermum fraseri*, is a small tree that loses its leaves in the winter and has large, showy yellow flowers and small fist size fruit. In the late Dry the fruit splits to release its seeds in white, silky parachutes. The Kapok bush is common on rocky hillsides throughout the region and is easily and readily seen by most Dry season travellers.

The Leichhardt tree, *Nauclea orientalis*, is a tall tree up to 20 metres in height with dark green foliage. Growing along river banks and in seepage areas in good rainfall regions, it provides deep shade, has cream coloured flowers and an edible, but dry fruit.

RAINFORESTS

A Recent Discovery

The rainforests or vine forests of the Kimberley are unique habitats that have been cut off from each other and from other similar large areas for hundreds of years by the dry country that's between them.

The Mitchell Plateau has a wide variety of flora, from palms, to open woodland forests, as well as patches of rainforest.

It is only relatively recently that researchers from the W.A. Department of CALM (Department of Conservation and Land Management) have actually begun to study them. While these areas and the plants and animals they contained were well known to Aborigines in the past, and that Allan Cunningham collected rainforest species in the Kimberley in 1819, S.A. Gardner noted, in 1923, *"...the total absence of rainforest in the Kimberley"*. Even in 1954 a CSIRO land systems survey failed to identify any rainforest. Finally, in 1975, a report released by the W.A. Herbarium reported rainforest patches in the Prince Regent Reserve.

Since then, research has shown that the rainforest patches of the Kimberley are sprinkled along the north-west coast, between Broome and the WA/NT border in a belt less than 150 km wide.

During the surveys it was found that the richest patches were in the coastal areas where they received a heavier rainfall. Such areas included the mouth of the Sale River, the Marigui Promontory and the Mitchell Plateau. Further inland the patches of rainforest were smaller and contained fewer species.

These rainforest patches never truly attain the size of a 'forest', with the biggest only covering one hundred hectares or so. Some are as small as just a few trees, and in total they number around 1200 separate patches.

Surveys of some of the most significant patches were carried out in 1987 and again in 1988, and despite their small size and total area, have been found to be much richer than previously known.

Three Types of Rainforest

Of over 20 types of rainforest in Australia, three are found in the Kimberley.

Complex mesophyll vine forests are found along water courses, with a variety of trees forming a dense canopy with little undergrowth.

Semi-evergreen mesophyll vine forest occurs on steep slopes. Where these occur, mainly deciduous trees, up to 15 m in height, are scattered and there is a dense understorey of vines and shrubs, but little else.

Deciduous vine thickets take up the drier areas and these contain scattered trees up to 9 m in height with a much more open understorey of scrubs.

A Treasure Trove of Species

More than 300 species of plants have been collected from these rainforest habitats, with 80% restricted to that environment.

Collected for the first time in W.A. are the trees of the genus *Ailanthus, Eugenia* and *Dimorphocalyx*. New species include *Alstonia* and *Buchanania*.

Over 80 species of birds have been recorded during surveys, with 20 species depending entirely on these remnant rainforests for their continued existence in the Kimberley. These include the Rose-crowned Fruit-Dove, Emerald Ground-Dove, Torresian Imperial-Pigeon, the Rainbow Pitta, Orange-footed Scrubfowl, Rufous Owl and the Great Bower Bird.

The python, *Melotis caronata*, the rarest of Australia's pythons having only been recorded once before, was also found during the 1987 surveys. As well, some 70 species of land snails were collected. One genus, containing 28 species, is endemic to the Kimberley, and has never been collected before.

Caring for Rainforest

These small patches of rainforest are extremely valuable and far outweigh their size in variety and importance. Surrounded by dry, open forests, they are vulnerable to damage by fire and wandering stock. Once the Aboriginal people who burnt the open forest regularly protected these rainforest clumps by back burning, etc. It's a pity we supposedly more civilised people couldn't be a little more careful with our use of fire and our animals.

When you visit these areas:

- Stay on the tracks or roads.
- Take your rubbish away with you.
- Don't light any fires. Use a portable gas stove, if required.

THE FAUNA

GENERAL

The fauna of the Kimberley region, while varied and in good numbers, is never conspicuous. The larger species, such as the kangaroos, remain well hidden in the rugged terrain, while other native mammals are shy or just plain secretive. Probably the most often seen animals are some of the introduced ones that have since gone feral.

For the most part the Kimberley shares its animals and birds with other areas of northern Australia, especially the Top End of the Northern Territory and Arnhem land. And, while the fauna of this region is exciting and relatively untouched, there are few endemic species.

MAMMALS

Introduction

Australia is home to some 230 species of mammals, nearly 70 of which exist in the Kimberley. Only three species – the Scaly-tailed Possum, *Wyulda squamicaudata*, the Yellow-lipped Bat, *Vespadelus douglasorum*, (a small insect eating bat) and the Monjon, *Petrogale burbidgei*, (a small wallaby – previously known as 'Warabi') are endemic, that is found nowhere else than in this region.

Testifying to its affinity with the Top End of the NT, the Kimberley shares with that area the Brush-tailed Tree-rat, *Conilurus penicillatus*, the spectacular Golden-backed Tree-rat, *Mesembriomys macrurus*, the Kimberley Rock-rat, *Zyzomys woodwardi*, and the locally common, Rock Ringtail Possum, *Petropseudes dahli*. These animals are not found outside these two areas.

Friendly Rats

The beautiful, large aquatic Water Rat, *Hydromys chrysogaster*, can sometimes be found in its watery abode of rivers and swamps, but it is never common. Forrest's Mouse, *Leggadina forresti*, and the Delicate Mouse, *Pseudomys delicatulus*, are both relatively scarce, small native rodents that are just two of the 12 species of native rats and mice which inhabit the region. These include the aforementioned species which the Kimberley share with the NT.

The House Mouse, *Mus musculus*, and the Black Rat, *Rattus rattus*, are also found around human habitation, but rarely elsewhere.

Bats

Twenty-three species of bats and flying foxes are known to occur in the region and as more research is done this is likely to increase.

Most of the animals in this group are small, insect eating bats which are often seen fluttering around the campfire at night or flashing through your vehicle's headlights on a narrow track.

The most obvious of these flying mammals are the fruit bats and flying foxes. These include the Little Red Flying-fox, *Pteropus scapulatus*, the Black Flying-fox, *Pteropus alecto*, and the Northern Blossom-bat, *Marcoglossus minimus*.

Most areas have their colony of fruit bats normally roosting during the day amongst the shady branches of tall paperbarks along the river's edge. In the evening they can be seen flying, in ever thickening clouds, to their latest feeding ground. The colonies can be quite large, with over thousands of animals in a single one. They are noisy, smelly affairs, good to look at from a short distance but definitely not a place to camp near.

Kangaroos and Wallabies

Common Wallaroo.

Of the kangaroos and wallabies, 9 occur within the area. Some, such as the Red Kangaroo, *Macropus rufus*, are found only rarely in the northern regions of the great deserts, south of the Fitzroy River.

The Agile Wallaby (or Kimberley Wallaby), *Macropus agilis*, and the Antilopine Kangaroo, *Macropus antilopinus*, are the most common kangaroos seen, with the occasional sighting of the Common Wallaroo (or Hill Kangaroo or Euro), *Macropus robustus*, in the southern sections of the Kimberley.

A couple of smaller rock wallabies and their close relatives, the rare Monjon, *Petrogale burbidgei*, and Nabarlek (Little Rock-wallaby), *Peradorcas concinna*, also call the Kimberley home. The northern Nailtail Wallaby, *Onychogalea unguifera*, and the smaller, reclusive, Spectacled Hare-wallaby, *Lagorchestes conspicillatus*, can also be found, with the former being common all over the region, while the latter is rare and only found in the southern areas.

Other Mammals

The desert country to the south of the Fitzroy River also has other animals rarely seen by anyone. These are the mouse sized, carnivorous, Stripe-faced Dunnart, *Sminthopsis macroura*, and the rare, burrowing, blind Marsupial Mole, *Notoryctes typhlops*, as well as the Bilby, *Macrotis lagotis*.

The Short-beaked Echidna (or Spiny Anteater), *Tachyglossus aculeatus*, is found all over the region, as is the beautifully marked Northern Quoll, *Dasyurus hallucatus*. The Quoll is surprisingly common in some areas, with the Mitchell Plateau taking the top spot in our book.

The Northern Brown Bandicoot, *Isoodon macrourus*, and the Golden Bandicoot, *Isoodon auratus*, are both found in the far north-west, with the former being common and the latter scarce. Once again the Mitchell Plateau is a good area for the Northern Brown specie.

Around the bays and inlets of the coast you may chance to see a Dugong, *Dugong dugon*, although they are not as common as they are further south, around Shark Bay or over around Torres Strait.

Introduced Animals

Dingoes, *Canis lupus dingo*, introduced by Aborigines or by Macassar fishermen in the last few thousand years, call the whole of the Australian continent home. In the Kimberley they are very common, but as they are killed by humans at every opportunity they keep themselves scarce and are rarely seen.

Introduced animals that have gone wild (feral) include the donkey, horse, cow, pig and goat. Rabbits and foxes sometimes occur in the desert country to the south of the Fitzroy River, but it is the donkey that causes the most problems. Most of the latter have been shot out in recent years.

BIRDS

Introduction

Birds are always one of the delights of our travels in the north and the Kimberley is no exception. While the region hasn't the large swamp areas of Kakadu or Cape York's Lakefield, and the waterbirds aren't as prolific, the birdlife still looks spectacular to tired, southern eyes.

Of Australia's 760 odd species of birds the 'Atlas of Australian Birds' (the results of a survey over 5 years) records no less than 300 species for this area of northern Australia.

Only one – the Black Grasswren, *Amytornis housei*, is endemic to the region, living amongst rough, sandstone boulders and spinifex between Mt Barnett Station and the mouth of the Mitchell River. With luck and an observant eye you may see them while walking to the Upper Manning Gorge or while going into the Mitchell Falls.

Some species, such as the Purple-crowned Fairy-wren, *Malurus coronatus*, while found elsewhere in Australia, has its own distinctive sub-specie in the Kimberley.

The White-quilled Rock-Pigeon, *Petrophassa albipennis*, has its stronghold in the Kimberley area, but is also found in similar habitats across the border in the Northern Territory. The gorge country of the southern Kimberley, especially around Windjana Gorge, is a top place to see this elusive little character, as is the Mitchell Plateau.

All in all the birds that inhabit the Kimberley are similar to those that hold sway across our northern region. And, while the Kimberley mightn't have the spectacular displays of waterbirds compared to some other areas, for many species the near pristine, rocky terrain, dotted with spinifex, is a stronghold.

The stately Brolga is a common sight, congregating in marshlands during the Dry season.

The Waterbirds

Around the rivers and swamps herons, egrets, grebes, night herons, ibis and bitterns can be seen. Both species of spoonbill – the black-billed Royal Spoonbill, *Platalea regia*, and the Yellow-billed Spoonbill, *Platalea flavipes*, are also found. The Magpie Goose, *Anseranas semipalmata*, Wandering Whistling-Duck, *Dendrocygna arcuata*, Plumed Whistling-Duck, *Dendrocygna eytoni*, and the Green Pygmy-Goose, *Nettapus pulchellus*, are also common waterbirds, along with the more widespread Pacific Black Duck, *Anas superciliosa*, and Grey Teal, *Anas gibberifrons*.

Black-necked Storks (or Jabirus), *Ephippiorhynchus asiaticus*, Brolgas, *Grus rubicundus*, and the similar looking Sarus Crane, *Grus antigone*, will also be seen, with the black and white Jabirus stealing the show. They are a magnificent bird and Australia's only stork.

Whistling Ducks are a common sight in wetlands, such as Marlgu Billabong.

In 1986 Birds Australia (formerly the Royal Australasian Ornithologists Union or RAOU) – birdwatchers in other words, conducted an extensive survey of the shallow southern and eastern sections of Lake Argyle. They surveyed approximately 40% of the available wetland, finding more than 180,000 waterbirds of 59 species. Groups of Hardheads (White-eyed Ducks), *Aythya australis*, and Eurasian Coots, *Fulica atra*, numbered in their tens of thousands, while some 17,000 Grey Teal and 11,000 Wandering Whistling Ducks and a like number of Magpie Geese were counted.

At the same time as this survey was carried out, Lake Gregory, south of Halls Creek, was also visited. Huge numbers of birds were on this transient lake that had been in existence at that time for an uncommonly long three years.

Bushbirds and Bigger

Along with a host of other birds countered around Lake Argyle by Birds Australia, probably one of the most surprising results was a count of 110 Yellow Chats, *Ephthianura crocea*. Generally if you see one or two of these birds you're going well!

Wrens, babblers, a wide range of honeyeaters and parrots, along with such well known birds as the Willie Wagtail, *Rhipidura leucophrys*, also inhabit the region.

The Rainbow Bee-eater, *Merops ornatus*, common in the region, is one bird that cries out to be looked at and its hunting antics on the wing are worth more than a cursory look.

The Great Bowerbird, *Chlamydera nuchalis*, the only bowerbird to be found in the region, is relatively common and often seen in the Windjana Gorge area.

Red-tailed Black-Cockatoos, *Calyptorhynchus banksii*, Little Corellas, *Cacatua pastinator*, and the ubiquitous Galah, *Cacatua roseicapilla*, can also be found in the Kimberley.

Peaceful Dove, *Geopelia placida*, and the Diamond Dove, *Geopelia cuneata*, are the small common birds of the pigeon family in the region, while the Crested Pigeon, *Geophaps lophotes*, is found in the central and southern sections of the Kimberley. The Spinifex Pigeon, *Geophaps plumifera*, a common inhabitant of rocky scrub and spinifex country, is a distinctive member of the pigeon family in the Kimberley area and to the desert country to the south-east and west.

Birds of Prey

Birds of prey, such as the Black Kite, *Milvus migrans*, and Whistling Kite, *Milvus sphenurus*, are often seen, along with a number of other hawks that are dispersed throughout the area.

In fact, every Australian bird of prey has been recorded in the Kimberley, including some of our rarest species.

Wader Heaven

One of the annual highlights of the bird world occurs around Broome each August/September. Between Broome and Port Hedland is the most important section of coast in Australia for waders – those annual migrants that fly in from Russia, Sibera, China and the Arctic. Literally millions of birds fly in to either spend their non-breeding months, or to rest while enroute to southern Australia. Red-necked Stints, *Calidris ruficollis,* Common Sandpiper, *Actitis hypoleucos*, Curlew Sandpiper, *Calidris ferruginea*, Great Knot, *Calidris tenuirostris*, Greenshank, *Tringa nebularia*, and Bar-tailed Godwit, *Limosa lapponica*, make up the majority of the birds that blot radar screens and cover remote beaches and mudflats. It's pretty impressive!

Rainforest Inhabitants

In the patches of rainforest scattered predominantly over the north-west Kimberley, birds that require this habitat are found. These include the Torresian Imperial-Pigeon, *Ducula bicolor*, the Orange-footed Scrubfowl, *Megapodius reinwardt*, Rainbow Pitta, *Pitta iris,* Yellow Oriole, *Oriolus flavocinctus*, Figbird, *Sphecotheres viridis,* Great Bowerbird, *Chlamydera nuchalis*, and the Green-backed Gerygone, *Gerygone chloronota*, to name just a few. While many of these rainforest species were considered rare in Western Australia, they are better classified as having a very restricted habitat, in which they can be locally common.

WHERE TO SEE BIRDS

Probably the best place to see waterbirds is on the Ord River, below the dam, and especially around Kununurra. The wetlands near the township of Kununurra and on the eastern side of **Lake Kununurra** is a real haven and a boat or a canoe is an ideal way to enjoy the scene.

Parry Lagoons, on the way to Wyndham and on the floodplain of the Ord River, is another top spot to watch waterbirds. As the Dry season progresses birds gather in their thousands at these verdant wetlands.

Lake Gregory, south of Halls Creek, if it has water in it, is another great area for watching waterbirds. As the latest surveys have discovered thousands of waterbirds flock to this transient lake. In the area surrounding the lake you have the birds that call the desert home.

In the central Kimberley, **Lake Gladstone** is the only spot that attracts good numbers of waterbirds and it is worth a stopover for birdwatchers.

One of the easiest spots to spy on some rainforest birds is the small patch of rainforest that is protected in the **Point Spring Nature Reserve**, north of Kununurra. Other small rainforest pockets good for the birdwatcher are those to be found around the **Mitchell Plateau** in the north- west of the Kimberley region.

Down the coast near Broome, along the shores of **Roebuck Bay** the waders, when they are in country are a sight to behold. There is much more than waders to see around the bay though as the mix of habitat from mangroves, to grass plain to bush and rich tidal mudflats make Broome a real Mecca.

Broome Bird Observatory

The Broome Bird Observatory, run by Birds Australia, is based at Crab Creek, 25 km east by road of Broome. While the immediate area has great birdwatching, the Observatory offers a range of accommodation, includng chalets, as well as camping (powered and unpowered sites), tours and courses.

For more information and bookings contact the Observatory by writing to PO Box 1313, Broome, WA, 6725, or ph: (08) 9193 5600, fax: (08) 9192 3364, web site:

http://www.broomebirdobservatory.com/

REPTILES

Frogs

Only about 30 of Australia's 190 odd species of frogs are found in the Kimberley. The most conspicuous of these are the tree frogs, with the Green Tree Frog, *Litoria caerulea*, being the most common.

Turtles and Tortoises

All six species of Australia's sea turtles occur around the Kimberley coast, with the Green Turtle, *Chelonia mydas*, being the most common.

Of the 15 species of freshwater turtles so far described in Australian waters only 4 occur in the region. The Northern Snake-Necked Turtle, *Chelodina rugosa*, is the most common, found in swamps, billabongs and slow moving rivers throughout the area.

Crocodiles

Both species of crocodiles occur in the Kimberley region.

The Freshwater Crocodile, *Crocodylus johnstoni*, is a shy animal, growing up to a maximum of around 3 metres, although anything over two is uncommon. These crocs feed on fish, crustaceans and occasionally other small animals and are considered *not dangerous* to man. The Freshwater Crocodile is found in freshwater rivers, billabongs and swamps and you'll see them at Geikie and Windjana Gorges.

The **Estuarine Crocodile (Salt-water Crocodile)**, *Crocodylus porosus*, is a much more dangerous animal that grows to 7 metres, although anything over 5 is uncommon. They inhabit coastal areas, saltwater estuaries and larger, freshwater rivers and billabongs and have been reported far inland up both the Fitzroy and Ord Rivers, as well as many Kimberley rivers upstream. They can be identified from the **Freshwater Crocodile**, *Crocodylus johnstoni*, by their heavier build, generally larger size and relatively short and blunter snout.

Lizards

The lizards of Australia consist of 4 major families, all of which have representatives in the Kimberley. In fact, it is amongst this group of animals that a number of endemic species occur.

Legless Lizards (Family: Pygopodidae)

Legless lizards are small, harmless snake-like animals of which about 30 occur in Australia. Seven of these are found in the Kimberley, with Burton's snake-lizard, *Lialis burtonia*, being the most common and widely distributed.

Geckos (Family: Gekkonidae)

Geckos are endearing animals that are found in a wide range of habitats across Australia. Out of Australia's 90 odd species some 19 occur in the Kimberley. These include the Northern Dtella, *Gehyra australis*, Spotted Dtella, *Gehyra punctata*, and the Desert Cave Gecko, *Heteronotia spelea*. Geckos endemic to the Kimberley include the *Oedura obscura, Oedura filicipoda, Oedura gracilis* and *Gehyra occidentalis*.

Skinks (Family: Scincidae)

The skinks are Australia's most numerous group of lizards with over 300 species. In the Kimberley some 40 species are recognised. These include well known skinks such as the Centralian Blue-Tongued Lizard, *Tiliqua multifasciata*, and the Eastern Blue-Tongued Lizard, *Tiliqua scincoides*, as well as unique animals such as the Broad-Banded Sand Swimmer, *Eremiascincus richardsonii*, while the *Cyclodomorphurs maxima*, *Egernia douglasi* and *Lerista Kalumburu* are found only in the Kimberley.

Goannas (Family: Varanidae)

Goannas or Monitors are Australia's most spectacular lizard. A group of about 30 species occur on the continent, with 9 occurring in this far northern area. These include the Ridge-Tailed Monitor, *Varanus acanthurus*, Long-Tailed Rock Monitor, *Varanus glebopalma*, Spotted Tree Monitor, *Varanus timorensis*, Mertens' Water Monitor, *Varanus mertensi*, (common around the Mitchell Falls/Merten Falls area), Mitchell's Water Monitor, *Varanus mitchelli,* and the beautiful, Gould's Goanna or Sand Monitor, *Varanus gouldii*.

Agamid (Dragon) Lizards (Family: Agamidae)

There are about 60 species of Agamid (or dragon) lizards found in Australia, of which around 28 are found in the Kimberley. These include the world acclaimed, once seen never forgotten, Frilled Lizard, *Chlamydosaurus kingii*. Other species include the Central Netted Dragon, *Ctenophorus nuchalis*, Ring-Tailed Dragon,*Ctenophorus caudicinctus*, Military Dragon, *Ctenophorus isolepis*, and Chameleon Dragon, *Chelosania brunnea*.

Snakes

The snakes of Australia are all contained in 5 separate families or groups. These include the Sea Snakes, File Snakes, Blind Snakes, Pythons, Colubrid Snakes, and the largest group of snakes, the Elapids.

Blind Snakes (Family: Typhlopidae)

Blind Snakes are all burrowing, harmless snakes, with about 30 species in Australia. Around eight are known from the Kimberley, with a couple found only in parts of the Kimberley such as the *Ramphotyphlops yampiensis* found only from Koolan Island, in Yampi Sound, and *Ramphotyphlops troglodytes*, at Tunnel Cave in the Napier Range.

File Snakes (Family: Acrochordidae)

Only 2 species of File Snake occur in Australia – the Arafura File Snake and the Little File Snake, both of which are non-venomous. The Little File Snake, *Acrochordus granulatus*, occurs in marine habitats along the north-eastern and northern coast of Australia, including the Kimberley coast.

Sea Snakes (Family: Hydrophiidae)

Australia is the world stronghold of sea snakes, with some 31 species occurring in offshore waters. About 18 of these inhabit in the waters around the Kimberley coast, which include the dangerous Yellow-bellied Sea Snake, *Pelamis platurus*, as well as the *Lapemis hardwickii* and *Astrotia stokesii.*

Pythons (Family: Boidae)

Pythons are non-venomous snakes, with some species attaining a very large size. Of Australia's 15 species, 6 occur within the region. These include the small, beautifully marked Children's Python, *Liasis childreni*, the Black-Headed Python, *Aspidites melanocephalus*, Water Python, *Liasis fuscus*, and the large, well marked Diamond Python, *Morelia spilota*, while the *Morelia carinata* is at present only known to be found around the Mitchell River Falls on the Mitchell Plateau.

Colubrid Snakes (Family: Colubridae)

Colubrid Snakes include Tree Snakes, Mangrove Snakes and the Keelback or Freshwater Snake, *Tropidonophis mairii*. Out of Australia's 10 species, six occur in the Kimberley, such as the Brown Tree Snake, *Boiga irregularis*, Common Tree Snake, *Dendrelaphis punctulata*, White-Bellied Mangrove Snake, *Fordonia leucobalia*, and the Keelback Snake. While some are venomous, none are considered dangerous to humans.

The Dangerous Elapids (Family: Elapidae)

The Elapids are the largest group of snakes in Australia and the most dangerous. While many are only mildly venomous and non-dangerous, this group also contains the most poisonous reptiles in the world.

Of Australia's 65 odd species, some 14 occur within the region. These include the Northern Death Adder, *Acanthophis praelongus*, Desert Death Adder, *Acanthophis pyrrhus*, Black Whip Snake, *Demansia atra*, Taipan, *Oxyuranus scutellatus*, King Brown or Mulga Snake, *Pseudechis australis*, and the Western Brown Snake or Gwardar, *Pseudonaja nuchalis*. All of these snakes are not only highly venomous, but they are DANGEROUS as well.

A Word of Warning

One last word on snakes, if you don't know what snake it is, treat it as deadly. The Kimberley is too remote a place for you to get bitten.

THE ABORIGINAL HERITAGE AND THE ART OF THE KIMBERLEY

INTRODUCTION

The Aboriginal heritage of the Kimberley dates back thousands of years and continues strongly today even though it's greatly changed.

About 11,500 Aboriginal people live in the Kimberley. Over 330 separate properties and six million hectares of the region is either declared Aboriginal Land, reserve, leasehold, pastoral lease, special lease, or freehold owned by the Aboriginal communities.

Probably the most outstanding feature, at least to visitors eyes, is the graphic art style that encompasses the whole region. Originally the Wandjina style of painting was used exclusively on rock faces, but today the art style has been transposed to wood and bark, much to the delight of the travellers.

HISTORY

THE BEGINNING

The Australian Aborigine almost definitely originated from South-East Asia – the when and where is a little harder to establish. Certainly the predecessors of today's people were inhabiting Australia at least 30,000 years ago. A number of sites in south-eastern Australia confirms that.

As the Kimberley is the closest piece of Australia to South-East Asia, it can be assumed that Aborigines first landed in this area and spread out around Australia from this region. A date of 50,000 to 55,000 years ago (B.P. – before present), has been given and is not hard to imagine. While places of such antiquity have never been found in the north, many reasons, and especially the climate, have been given for this.

The Miriwun Shelters

One site so far discovered that is a vivid example of how long Aboriginal people have been in the Kimberley is a site, known to archaeologists as the Miriwun Shelters.

These caves, or rock shelters, are situated on a steep rocky ridge above a stretch of the Ord River flood plain. Here, people camped and ate the food they found, or killed on the nearby, rich grasslands. Water lilies and shellfish, along with catfish, birds eggs, lizards and small mammals were the main food eaten.

Dating back to 18,000 B.P, the shelters were only used occasionally up to about 10,000 years B.P. Since then up to five shelters were in much more frequent use.

More recently, another site on Koolan Island, north-west of Derby, just above a protected bay, was found to be 27,000 years old. It is the oldest site so far discovered, but we have only just begun to look!

It should be remembered too, that the Kimberley coast has shifted greatly in the past 50,000 years. Nine thousand years ago the coastline was much further out, so that all the bays and gulfs that are part of the Kimberley scene today were kilometres inland. Twenty thousand years ago the land mass extended out hundreds of kilometres towards Timor and South-East Asia. Around that time the sea gap separating the two enlarged continents would have only been one hundred kilometres or so. As the Aborigines in the past, like we do today, preferred the coast, all their coastal sites would now be deep underwater.

These early Australians lived well, probably better than most people in Europe at the same time. Their diet, which basically remained unchanged for millennia, consisted of shellfish, fish, lizards, small mammals and wallabies, goose and even crocodile eggs.

Extensive trade routes crisscrossed the region and bought in goods from far away, while local products, such as pearl shell, were traded far and wide.

At least 15 of Australia's 29 distinct Aboriginal language groups were in the Kimberley, and while there was no written language, the languages had extensive vocabularies and complicated grammar.

THE LAST 500 YEARS

In recent times and before the coming of the Whiteman, Macassan Beche-de-Mer fishermen were plying the waters off the Kimberley coast and establishing fishing camps along the shore. Aborigines were seconded to work in these camps and almost certainly trade between these two people took place.

Initially there was little conflict between the Europeans and the Aborigines, but this changed with the opening up of the Kimberley by Alexander Forrest's expedition in 1879. Within a couple of years, pioneer pastoralists had moved in along the Fitzroy and Ord Rivers and confrontation often ensued.

When the Europeans arrived in the Kimberley it is estimated that there were about 10,000 Aborigines in the region. Within 50 years that population had crashed to less than 5,000. Diseases such as smallpox, measles and influenza almost definitely killed far more Aborigines than direct confrontation with Europeans!

ABORIGINAL

THE 'PIGEON' STORY

No history of the Kimberley, black or white, would be complete without mention of Pigeon, or as he was known amongst his own people, 'Jandamarra', sometimes also spelt, 'Sandamarra'.

Early Days – Early Trouble

Pigeon was only a young boy when Forrest passed through his people's country in 1879. By the mid 1880s he had sampled the Whiteman's way at William Lukin's recently established Lennard River Station, before returning to his people, the Bunaba, for the ceremonies that would make him a man.

An early Police Patrol with Aboriginal trackers and Aboriginal prisoners.

Pic courtesy of the W.A. Police Dept.

Influenced by the elders of the tribe, and especially one called 'Ellemarra the Cunning', Pigeon was in and out of trouble with the police because of sheep spearing. In 1894, after absconding from indentured labour, he was recaptured and put to work as a police tracker working with a police constable Richardson and another native called 'Captain'. It wasn't long before Pigeon had earned himself a fine reputation, backed up by good horsemanship, a skill with guns, and loyalty to his new boss. In fact, the team was so good that they were sent out to Pigeon's home territory (something not normally done) to deal with the growing Bunaba problem.

That first patrol by Richardson was remarkably successful, with 15 men all in chains heading for Derby. While the patrol rested at Lillimilura, Pigeon, in a magnificent coupe, captured his old hunting mate 'Ellemarra' and added him to the patrol's tally!

Later, while the young constable slept, Pigeon, in a dramatic about face, shot him from point blank range and released all the prisoners.

The Battle of Windjana Gorge

Soon afterwards Pigeon and his new found gang attacked a party of newcomers as they approached Windjana Gorge, one of the natural defiles in the sheer rampart of the Napier Range. A police patrol soon converged on Windjana Gorge and surprised the Aborigines on the morning of the 16th November, 1894. The 'Battle of Windjana Gorge' was to see a number of natives killed and both Ellemarra and Pigeon badly wounded.

Over the next couple of years ceaseless patrols scoured the country for Pigeon and his gang. While these patrols pushed north beyond the Leopold Ranges, Pigeon would suddenly turn up near Fitzroy Crossing, spear a few cattle or take the odd shot at a settler. His vanishing tricks became legendary!

In early 1896 both Ellemarra and Captain were betrayed and captured and a police patrol managed to follow Pigeon to his hideout at the entrance to the Cave of Bats, now known as Tunnel Creek. Camping at the cave mouth, the patrol was more than surprised when word was received that Pigeon had raided Lillimilura police post, a few kilometres away, while they had been absent.

ABORIGINAL

The Last Battles

In March 1897 Pigeon led a gang of 20 to 30 natives and attacked Oscar Range Station, killing Tom Jasper and continuing the siege all day before turning and vanishing back into the hills. The police patrols though were already in pursuit.

One patrol picked up Pigeon's tracks and, after following him for more than 50 km in a day, caught up with him. In the ensuing fight Pigeon and one of the patrol were wounded. Pigeon escaped, but next day attacked the patrol, killing one of the native trackers before slipping away into the bush once again. It was a brazen attack.

Now, a number of fast mounted patrols closed in on him and in the subsequent fight Pigeon was wounded twice more, this time seriously. Even so, he managed to escape into a small cave just a stone's throw from his hideout in Tunnel Creek.

Pigeon's stronghold, or the 'Bat Cave', now known as Tunnel Creek.
Pic courtesy of the W.A. Police Dept.

Next morning, the 1st April, 1897, the native police trackers picked up his blood trail and set off quickly in pursuit. Twenty minutes later they came across him and after a fight, which expended his last bullets and saw him wounded yet again, he fell to the ground where his life quickly ebbed away.

Time has changed our perception of these events. During his reign, he was considered by the white authorities as nothing more than an outlaw, murderer and a thief, albeit one that caused more trouble than most. Today we're inclined to see him more as a freedom fighter protecting his homeland from the white invaders. Whatever the reason and motives behind these events of so long ago, there is no doubt that his exploits have become the stuff of legends – black or white!

The Pigeon Heritage Trail

A Pigeon Heritage Trail has been established and while you can travel it from any direction it is better to start the Trail in Derby.

In Derby's historic cemetery you can view Richardson's grave, while just outside the town is the 'Prison Boab Tree', where police patrols once held their prisoners before the last day's march to Derby. The Trail then takes you on to Windjana Gorge National Park and Tunnel Creek National Park – Pigeon's 'Cave of Bats'. Nearby, at the base of the Napier Range, are the still standing ruins of Lillimilura Homestead where Richardson was killed.

THE MISSIONARIES COME

The church at Beagle Bay Mission is well worth a visit.

Continual problems occurred between the races, especially along the coast where contact between white and black was the most common. Pearling crews were especially troublesome as they plied the coast in search of rich shell beds. They needed divers, shellers and women and many of the crews were unscrupulous about when and how they got them.

It was during the late 1870s that the Catholic Priest, Father Gibney, started campaigning for a mission to be established in the Kimberley region.

In 1885, Father MacNab, a Catholic Priest from Scotland, founded a mission at Cunningham Point on the south-western shores of King Sound. Two years later the buildings were burnt to the ground and the Father decided he had had enough.

In 1890 Father Gibney founded a longer lasting enclave at Beagle Bay, followed by Lombadina in 1892. However, despite all Fr Gibney's efforts, the mission was taken over by the Pallotine Pious Society of Missions in 1901.

In 1897 a mission was also begun on the remote Forrest River in the north-east of the Kimberley, but was abandoned six months later due to native hostility. While it was later re-established, it gives some indication of the troubles the missionaries faced.

The Drysdale River Mission was founded in 1908 at a site called Pago, north of the mouth of the King Edward River. Much later the mission was transferred to its present site at Kalumburu.

Much of the area surrounding the missions were reserved in the late 1890s and early 1900s and placed under the control of the state government and the particular church group running the mission at the time. However, up until the early 1900s, the area reserved was normally less than 2000 acres, near useless, as even modern Kimberley pastoralists would agree.

In 1910 the Government established the 1.6 million hectare Marndoc Reserve, west of Cambridge Gulf, as a 'traditional hunting reserve' for the Aboriginal people. The surveyor Brockman sketched the boundaries in 1911.

By 1915 the WA Government had decided to buy and set up an Aboriginal run cattle station. Moola Bulla, just north of Halls Creek, was the first in Australia and was such a success that others were soon established. Violet Valley near Turkey Creek was set up in 1918 and Munja established north of Derby in 1926.

BATTLES AND THE FORREST RIVER MASSACRE

A police patrol brings in a group of Aboriginal prisoners. (Circa 1890s)

While the missions were areas of protection, the spearing of cattle and sheep still continued and Aborigines were still being hunted down and killed in 'battles' with police, stockmen and miners.

In 1901, Jerry Durack, one of the pioneer Durack family, was killed in his sleep and a police patrol soon captured the alleged culprits. It was just one of many reported in the police reports of the time. Justice was usually more than swift and more than one lawyer noted that the Kimberley pastoralists *'educated the natives with their rifles ...'*

In 1908 the East Kimberley was in the grip of fear that another Aboriginal uprising was likely. A number of Whitemen had been killed and 'Major' and 'Nipper', the leaders of the Aboriginal gang, were at large, threatening vengeance. In September 1908 a police force from Wyndham trapped the gang with the leaders being killed and many of the others being taken prisoner.

So tension continued to bring trouble to the boil. In 1921 a stockman was killed and the police patrol sent out to bring the killer or killers to justice raided over 20 camps along the Hann, Durack, and Chamberlain Rivers. The patrol captured, questioned and released hundreds of people and killed an unknown number.

In 1926 the infamous Forrest River Massacre took place. Yet another stockman had been killed by Aborigines and like previous pursuits, a party of 14 people under the command of two young policeman was sent out to find the killers. What really happened may never be known but at least dozens, possibly hundreds of natives were killed.

The alleged atrocities created a furore culminating in a Royal Commission, but no one was ever brought to trial.

ABORIGINAL

AFTER WORLD WAR 2

World War 2 saw many Aborigines shifted from their tribal land into the relative safety of the missions. However, even the missions weren't immune to attack, as the fledgling camp of Kalumburu discovered when the Japanese raided it in September 1943.

After the War, few of the people returned to their tribal land or way of life. Most stayed on at the missions or went and lived on cattle stations near their original homeland.

With 'equal pay' being granted in the late 1960s many cattle stations who had let local Aboriginal family members live on the property could no longer afford to employ them and the drift of Aboriginal people to towns in the region increased.

Relics from WW2 can still be seen at Pago, Kalumburu.

In 1972 the WA Government passed legislation to set up an Aboriginal Land Trust. Most of the communities in the Kimberley region are now incorporated under the Commonwealth Aboriginal Councils and Associations Act 1976, which sees them controlling access to their land and running their own communities. Most of the mission establishments and the various church groups that once ran the settlements now offer assistance to the local community and work in conjunction with them.

In 1980 the Kimberley Land Council was formed over the continual battle for mining rights on the Noonkanbah Station lease on the Fitzroy River. It was a battle fought on the pages of the national newspapers.

With Mabo and Land Rights being the latest battle lines in the 1990s, the Aboriginal people of the region are taking back and controlling more of the land in the area. Hopefully, access, communication and a mutual respect for each others' culture and aspirations will foster and improve relations over the next generations.

THE INCREDIBLE ART

INTRODUCTION

The first Whiteman to see and report on the dramatic art style of the Kimberley region, known as the Wandjina figures, was George Grey in 1838. His descriptions and drawings created a stir of interest throughout the scientific world, which continues to this day. No other body of art in Australia has generated as much interest or as much literature. While Kakadu may have its X-ray art, the Kimberley has as large a body of art, less well known to the general public, but just, or even more, spectacular.

FIVE ZONES OF STYLE

While the Wandjina figures may be the most well known of the Aboriginal art styles in the Kimberley, modern researchers have described five distinct regions of varying art styles throughout the area.

Zone 1 – The South-west

This art style is an extension of the art from further south along the coast and in the Kimberley pearl shell and wood were skillfully engraved with herringbone designs and interlocking parallel lines.

Zone 2 – Along the Fitzroy

In this region there is a mixing of the art styles from the desert country to the south and the eastern and central Kimberley art styles. The area is rich in rock art, with simple engravings depicting animal tracks often occurring.

Zone 3 – The Eastern Kimberley

This zone includes the Ord and Victoria River valleys, with the rock paintings in solid colours outlined, usually with fine white ochre painted dots. Fish, reptiles, birds and animals, as well as humans and vegetable food items, are the main objects depicted.

Zone 4 – Heart of the Kimberley

This is Wandjina country. Bradshaw figures are also often found. Other motifs include fish, reptiles, birds and animals, as well as humans.

Zone 5 – The Far North

Closely aligned with the central zone, this far northern region has few Wandjina figures but many Bradshaws.

WANDJINA ART

Wandjina Art, as the style is often called, is so named because of the giant, mysterious haloed figures that are symbolic of this style. Up to six meters in length and painted in vivid colours of black, red and yellow over a white background, they are sure to impress.

Some Wandjina art forms are depicted as complete figures, while others are of just head and shoulders, however all have the halo around the head, with eyes and a nose, but never a mouth. In some paintings though, the Wandjina has been stylised so much that the halo is more a number of concentric lines surrounding a pair of bold eyes.

The Wandjina Legend

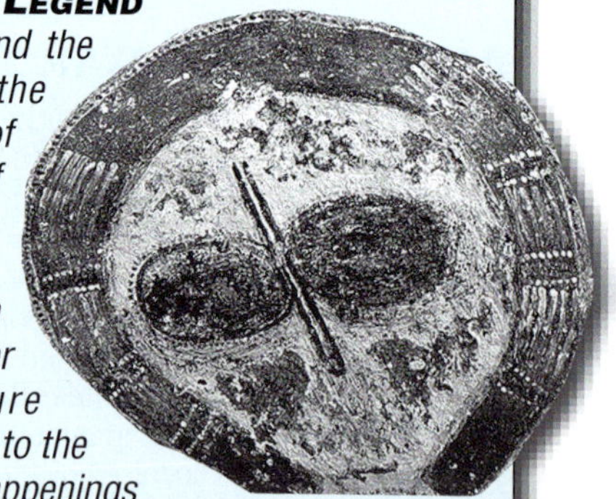

In Aboriginal legend the Wandjinas were the original creators of all the features of the land. Hence every gorge, rockhole, mountain range and any other prominent feature could be attributed to the wanderings and happenings of these Wandjinas.

It was said that the Wandjinas came in from the north-west and were associated with the annual monsoons. In fact, the Wandjinas are the 'spirit of the cloud' and can take both human and cloud form in their paintings. After their journeys through the land they went to a cave and died, leaving their body as a shadow on the wall. Other Wandjinas painted the figure that is now left for all to see.

Apart from their ability to create the landscape as we see it, the Wandjinas were also instrumental in the seasonal coming of the rains, and with the augmentation in plants, animals and babies.

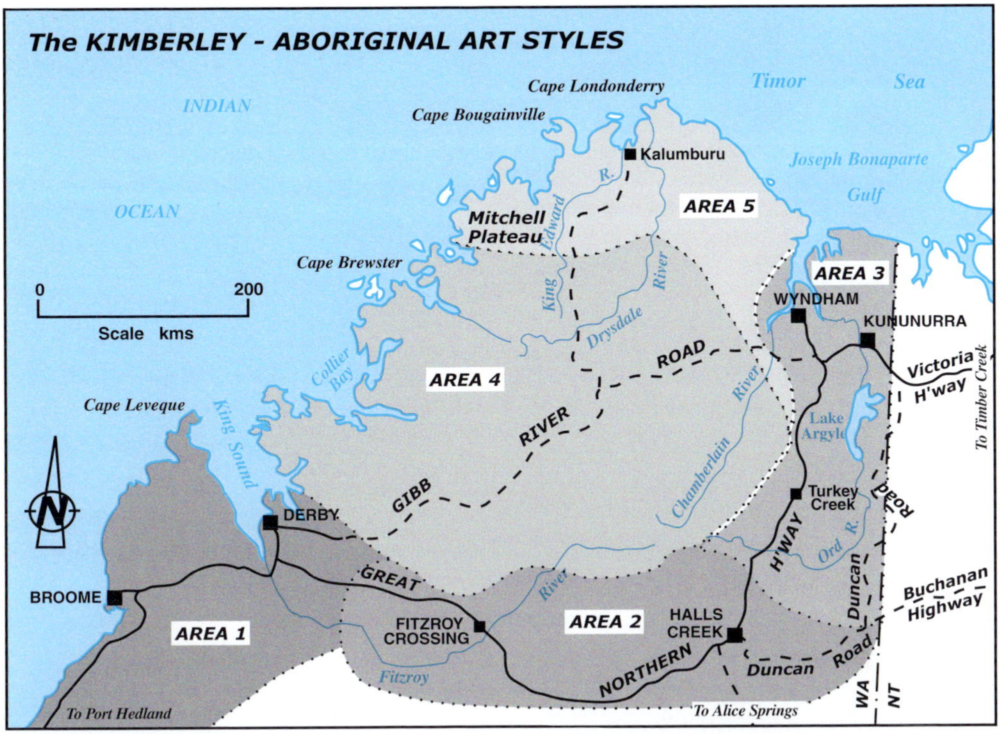

BRADSHAWS – THE OLDEST ART FORM ON EARTH?

As well as the many forms of Wandjinas, there are a number of other human-like figures that appear in the art of the Kimberley. Those known as Bradshaw Figures are some of the most artistic and elegant of these paintings.

These endemic figures are named after a Mr. Joseph Bradshaw, an early explorer and pastoralist who discovered and wrote about his findings while looking for pastoral land in the Kimberley. They closely resemble the Mimi Figures of the Northern Territory and like them have no real importance to Aborigines living today, or in the recent past. It seems they were once important but are considered 'rubbish' by the current Aboriginal custodians of the land.

Recent research though has almost definitely placed them at the forefront of human art. Not only that, the Bradshaws so eloquently painted all that time ago may predate the earliest art sites found in Europe which date back 27,000 B.P.

Whatever the background of these small, dynamic paintings, there is no doubt that the artists who painted them tried to capture the vitality and life of the scene they were painting.

OTHER MAGICAL FIGURES

While other human forms occasionally appear in the art of the Kimberley, with most of these depicting spiritual and ancestral figures, it is the paintings of snakes and pythons that are nearly as common as Wandjinas.

These large pythons, or 'Ungud' as they were most commonly known, played a similar role to the Wandjina. They too travelled the land, creating the important places, leaving their form on cave walls, and were once again associated with the rains and the fertility of the plants and animals.

The art in the Kimberley region is dramatic and takes many forms.

Viewing Wandjina art is an attraction of the Kimberley

Other animals appear in the paintings of the Kimberley. Crocodiles, kangaroos, fish, lizards, flying foxes and in fact all the animals that inhabit the area were painted. These people were close to the land and painted the animals that were around them.

All these paintings are dramatic and an integral part of the Aboriginal culture, being visible aspects of their religious beliefs, legends and stories that have been handed down over hundreds of generations. Probably more than any other single aspect, the art shows the deep spiritual heritage of the Aboriginal people.

VISITING THE SITES AND PRESERVATION

Some of the art sites throughout the Kimberley are well known and have been mentioned in this book. However, there are many hundreds, if not thousands of sites scattered through the region which are known to a select few. Many of these, especially the more important ones, have been recorded by the W.A. Museum, while others are yet to be described. In the more remote areas many of the sites have not been visited or seen by anyone, European or Aboriginal, for many years.

It may seem a little strange, but while we pay vast amounts of money for art galleries to protect art that is only a few hundred years old (at most), and we pay cold hard cash for Aboriginal artifacts decorated with traditional designs, we do nothing to protect the incredible outdoor galleries found throughout the Kimberley or anywhere in northern Australia, for that matter.

The most common cause of damage to these art sites is water and the general onslaught of weathering. Wasp nests, termite trails and birds nesting and roosting also add to the toll.

Human vandalism has so far caused little damage to most of the sites through the area, but some sites near the larger populated centres, have sadly been irreparably damaged.

PROTECTION OF SITES

All Aboriginal sites and objects in the Kimberley are protected under the Aboriginal Heritage Act 1972-1980 which is administered by the W.A. Museum. Sites found on National Park land are protected and managed under that Act as well.

Do the Right Thing

No matter which site you visit please remember the art is old and extremely fragile. It can never be replaced. Just a finger touch does damage – rubbing the ochre paint off and transmitting body oil to the surface.

So, when visiting a site :-

- Never touch any of the paintings or artifacts for any reason.
- Do not vandalise them or add any of your own handiwork.
- Pick up any rubbish and leave the site clean, so that other visitors can enjoy the site as you did.

VISITING ABORIGINAL COMMUNITIES & PERMITS

INTRODUCTION

There are about 198 Aboriginal communities in the region and many Aboriginal people also live in the towns. Aboriginal communities and their land take up vast areas of the Kimberley. To visit these communities requires a permit from the Community you wish to visit, and in most cases you must have the permit before you enter the Aboriginal land.

The **Aboriginal Lands Trust (ALT)**, established under the Aboriginal Affairs Planning Authority, has responsibility for the overall management of Aboriginal reserves, and travellers should apply to the ALT for any permit to enter Aboriginal reserves. You can contact them on the addresses given, or look at their web site detailed below for all the access details. You can also apply for a permit on line by filling out an application form.

www.dia.wa.gov.au/land/permits/

Dept. of Indigenous Affairs, Aboriginal Lands Trust, 197 St George's Tce, (PO Box 7770, Cloister's Square), Perth, WA, 6850, ph: (08) 9235 8000, fax: (08) 9235 8088.

Regional Office: Paspaley Plaza Centre, 25-37 Carnarvon St, (PO Box 1538), Broome, WA, 6825, ph: (08) 9192 2865, fax: (08) 9192 2850.

District Offices: Lot 2250 Coolibah Dve, (PO Box 672), Kununurra, WA, 6743, ph: (08) 9168 2550, fax: (08) 9168 2435; PO Box 88, Halls Creek, WA, 6770, ph: (08) 9168 5278, fax: (08) 9168 5287; and 273-274 Loch St, Derby, WA, 6728, ph: (08) 9191 2066, fax: (08) 9193 1466.

A More Practical Approach

Now all that is the official line but some of the communities are a little easier to visit than that. That's especially true of those communities that have opened their doors to travellers. However, don't abuse the privilege – you still need a permit, but that may just mean a phone call the day before you arrive, or to drop into the community office when you first enter the community. The best idea is to ring first but don't expect to get a permit out of normal office hours!

The Dampier Peninsula, north of Broome, is one such area and while access is restricted, some communities and outstations have embraced tourism and there are some wonderful and spectacular places to visit.

A contact list is given, but for more information on visiting each separate community see the section in this book, that covers that particular area.

The beach and some of the camping area available at Cape Leveque.

THE COMMUNITIES

DAMPIER PENINSULA

BARDI (ONE ARM POINT)

No accommodation or camping. For more information see our chapter on *Broome, The Dampier Peninsula.*

BEAGLE BAY

No accommodation or camping. For more information see our chapter on *Broome, The Dampier Peninsula.*

CHILE CREEK

For details on accommodation and **camping** see our chapter on *Broome, The Dampier Peninsula.*

DJARINDJIN

The Chairman, Djarindjin Aboriginal Community, via Broome, W.A., 6725, ph: (08) 9192 4940.

DJUGARARGYN

Walking tours.For details see our chapter on *Broome, The Dampier Peninsula.*

KALUMBURU

CAMPING - for more information see further on in this chapter.

KOOLJAMAN

For details on accommodation and **camping** see our chapter on *Broome, The Dampier Peninsula.*

LA DJARDARR BAY

Camping. See our chapter on *Broome, The Dampier Peninsula* for more details.

LOMBADINA

ACCOMMODATION (backpacker & self-contained units) - **no camping)** is available – see our chapter on *Broome, The Dampier Peninsula.*

MADDARR

Prearranged bookings for tours and camping only. See our chapter on *Broome, The Dampier Peninsula* for more details.

MIDDLE LAGOON

Accommodation and **camping** – see our chapter on *Broome, The Dampier Peninsula* for more details.

MUDNUNN

Camping. See our chapter on *Broome, The Dampier Peninsula* for more details.

WEB SITES

Western Australian Indigenous Tourism Operators Committee (WAITOC) raises the profile of Indigenous Tourism in the State. For info on tourism within Aboriginal Communities in the Kimberley, check out their comprehensive web site: **http://www.waitoc.com.**

All Aboriginal Tourism Operators in the Kimberley region – Kullarri Country, Wunan Region and Malarabah Country are listed with details of tours, are all covered, detailing tours, accommodation, camping, etc.

HALLS CREEK / TANAMI ROAD

BALGO

Accommodation is available - See chapter *Around Halls Creek,* page 91, for details.

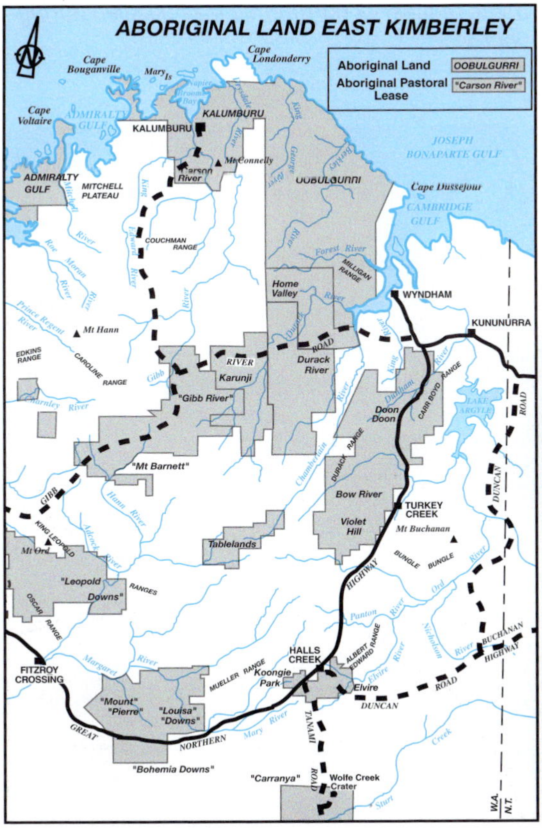

MINDIBUNGU (BILLILUNA) COMMUNITY

Basic **accommodation** and **camping.** (See chapter *Around Halls Creek,* page 92, for details.)

MULAN COMMUNITY

Camping. (See chapter *Around Halls Creek,* page 91, for details.)

Just part of the mural on the outside wall of the Art Centre in Balgo.

East Kimberley

Kalumburu

Camping and accommodation is available - See chapter, *The Mitchell Plateau & Northern Kimberley,* page 133, for details.

Warmun (Turkey Creek)

Day tours and tag alongs. See chapter, *'The Eastern Kimberley'*, page 122 for more details.

Oombulgurri

4WD access. See chapter, *'The Eastern Kimberley'*, page 106 for more details.

West Kimberley

Doon Doon (Woolah)

See chapter, *'The Eastern Kimberley'*, page 122 for more details.

Pantijan

No Access allowed. Permission from Pantijan community now based in Derby.

If you're lucky, a corroboree may be seen during your visit.

The art is dramatic and takes on many forms.

EUROPEAN HISTORY

EARLY CONTACT

Jutting northwards like some clenched fist, the Kimberley coast, or ancient variations of it, was almost definitely the first region of Australia to have been discovered by ancient people. As detailed in the last chapter, the forebears of the Aboriginal people only needed to sail their primitive craft across 70 to 80 km of open water to cross the Straits separating an ice-aged enlarged Australia from South-East Asia.

Legends of a Great South Land

In more recent times, Greek, Roman and Chinese legends mention a great south land.

During the reign of the Ming Dynasty, around 1405 AD, a great Chinese navigator sailed a fleet of junks southwards in search of wealth and fortune for his Emperor. He established Chinese rule over Malaysia and Indonesia and later the voyage extended around the coasts of Burma and India to the Persian Gulf, the Red Sea and finally Africa. Eastwards he almost definitely reached Timor and some conjecture suggests he reached as far as Darwin in the Northern Territory.

Certainly the **Macassans** sailed the straits of present day Indonesia fishing for Trepang or Beche-de-Mer, and long before the coming of the Europeans were visiting the northern coast of Australia on an annual basis. These were not just fleeting visits, but organised extended stays that saw fishing camps established and Aborigines seconded into the work force. Such fishing voyages not only travelled along the Kimberley coast, but penetrated far to the east, possibly even to the Barrier Reef waters of Queensland. Later navigators such as Matthew Flinders and Phillip King reported seeing them along the Carpentaria Gulf coast.

THE EUROPEANS ARRIVE

The Portuguese had colonised the island of Timor in the early 1500s and were the first Europeans into the fabled 'Spice Islands' of South-East Asia. A map produced around 1540 and known as the 'Dauphin Map' shows a vast south land called, Java La Grande. There's an uncanny resemblance to much of the Australian coastline and a vast bay, in the right place, that we know as King Sound.

While the Portuguese dominated Indonesia for a short time, the Spanish controlled the Philippines. When the Spanish Armada was defeated by Drake in 1588, the Dutch and English began to exert their control over the fabled Spice Islands.

The Dutch Arrive but Don't Stay

The Dutch, using the 'Roaring Forties' to blast their way across the Indian Ocean before turning north to Batavia (now Indonesia), sooner or later were going to plough straight into Australia.

In 1605 the Spanish navigator, **Luis Vaez de Torres**, sailed through the Straits that bear his name off the northern tip of Queensland, not suspecting the presence of a great continent to the south. Less than a year later **William Janzoon** charted nearly 400 km of coast around the Gulf and Arnhem Land.

Further south, on the Western Australian coast, on the islands off Shark Bay, **Dirk Hartog** left his famous pewter plate in 1610. In 1622 the *Tyral* became the first English wreck along the Australian coast, but little is known of her voyage. Further south, around the Abrolhos Islands, other Dutch wrecks occurred – *Batavia* (1629), *Gilt Dragon* (1656) and others much later. Survivors no doubt made landfall, but as was the case with the *Batavia* they tried to head back to Batavia itself.

In 1644 **Abel Tasman**, that famous Dutch navigator who discovered our island state, sailed along the Kimberley coast charting much of it as he went.

Dampier Arrives and Leaves Unimpressed

The English buccaneer, **William Dampier**, visited Australia's western coastline twice and became the first Englishman to set foot on Australian soil in the vicinity of the Buccaneer Archipelago in 1688. His first trip in the *Cygnet* was remarkably short, probably because he remained very unimpressed about the country and its inhabitants.

In 1699 the British Admiralty commissioned Dampier to chart the north-west coast of Australia. In the *HMS Roebuck* he sailed northwards from around Shark Bay (named by Dampier because of the number of sharks he saw there), through the Dampier Archipelago and north. Disgusted by the lack of fresh water, he left the coast just north of King Sound and headed for Timor.

Contrary to popular belief, he never landed at Roebuck Bay, buried treasure or careened his boat there. However, he did write two books of his adventures and they created considerable interest in the Great South Land.

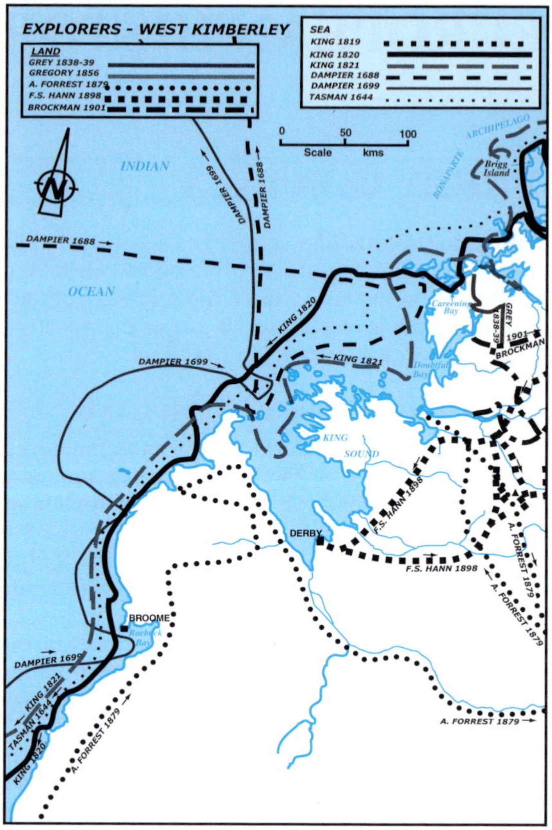

The French Take an Interest

The French navigator **Francois de St. Allouarn** landed in Shark Bay in 1772, hoisted the Tri-colour and claimed the land in the name of France. Pushing northwards he sailed past the Kimberley coast, but reported little about it. Reaching Timor he turned south-west and headed back home.

Nicolas Baudin's expedition of 1800 to 1804, in the ships *Le Geographe* and *Naturaliste*, scattered French names along the coast, even though they didn't approach too closely. La Grange Bay, Gantheaume Point, Cape Boileau, Bertholet and Leveque, along with Carnot Bay, the Lacepede Islands and the Bonaparte Archipelago are just some of the names bequeathed upon us by this French navigator.

For the next 100 years or so the Kimberley coast saw no European navigators, or at least none we know of.

Matthew Flinders completed his epic circumnavigation of Australia in 1801 to 1803 without ever spying the indented north-west coast.

Kings Voyage of Discovery

Dispatched in 1818 by the Admiralty to chart the virtually unknown coast, **Phillip Parker King** sailed in the *HMS Mermaid* around southern Australia and up the Western Australian coast past North West Cape to the rugged Kimberley region. On this first trip he virtually bypassed the Kimberley, concentrating on the North West Cape and later, Arnhem Land.

In 1819 he returned in the *Mermaid*, this time from the east, discovering and naming Cambridge Gulf. While there he sketched and named a mass of hills he called Mount Cockburn. From this point he sailed along the coast to Admiralty Gulf, naming Cape Londonderry, before heading to Timor and back to Sydney.

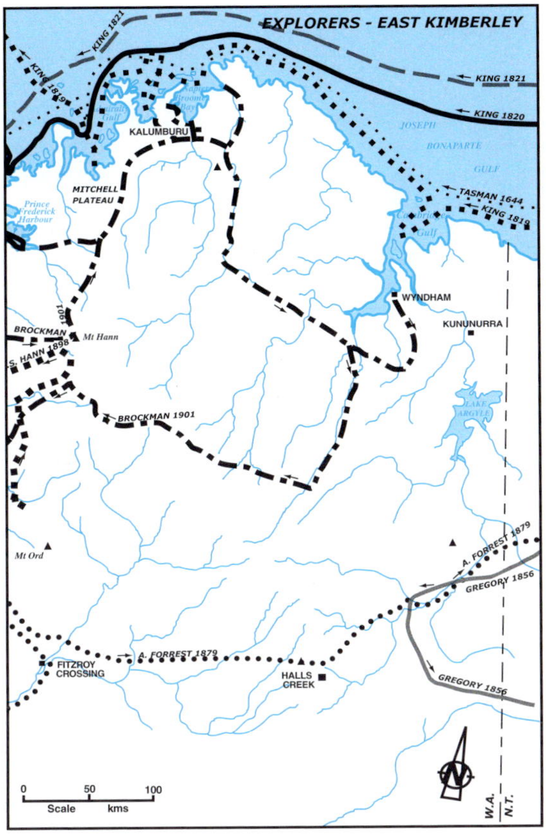

King's third voyage of discovery began in Sydney on the 13th June, 1820. Damaged in a storm, the *Mermaid* was beached at a small inlet, named by King 'Careening Bay'. The boat was found to be so rotten that there was nothing to do but head back to Sydney once again.

For his final voyage King used the brigantine *Bathurst* and by the 26th July, 1821, was back in the Prince Regent River. Using the ship's long boat, he pushed upriver to the magnificent falls that he sketched before having the boat carried around the cascade and pushed onwards for a few more kilometres. Sailing southwards he named the Buccaneer Archipelago just inside King Sound to commemorate Dampier's visit, before sailing to Roebuck Bay and then onwards to Mauritius for resupply and then back to Sydney.

Stokes and the Beagle

HMS Beagle, famed ship of Charles Darwin, returned to Australia in 1837 under the command of **Captain John Wickham** and **Lieutenant John Lort Stokes.** Naming Beagle Bay, they started their surveys at Disaster Bay in King Sound.

Later, while investigating a river mouth south of the present day Derby, disaster almost struck them. They named the river the Fitzroy and while Stokes knew there would be a large tidal surge, he wasn't quite expecting what actually happened. During the night he was awakened by a sound like thunder and then the boats were hit by a wall of water over a metre high. The small yawl they were using to explore and map this section of coast was turned over and almost lost. Luckily, nobody was drowned. Later Stokes sailed over 35 km up this great river.

For the month of April the Beagle's crew mapped Brecknock Harbour and were very impressed by the well watered country inland. On the 15th of that month they met up with the explorer George Grey, who was vainly trying to head south overland.

Stokes in the *Beagle* continued eastward and for the next few years concentrated on mapping the coast of Queensland and Northern Territory.

Grey's party under attack by a group of Aborigines. Pic courtesy of the S.A. Library Board

LAND EXPLORATION BEGINS

GREY'S FAILURE

Army **Lieutenant George Grey** (later Sir George, and Governor of South Australia), followed by Governor of New Zealand and then Cape Colony) was the first to lead a major expedition inland. It was hardly well thought out though. When they left England none of the expedition members had ever seen northern Australia before, let alone knew what to expect.

They landed at Hanover Bay on the 2nd December, 1837, with one water bottle each, no food and a few dogs. They immediately lost themselves in a deep ravine where they couldn't find water and two of their dogs died of thirst. Returning to the coast Grey was almost drowned in a tidal surge.

Finally, a camp was set up and the ship they had arrived in was dispatched for supplies. Meanwhile Grey and his men made several forays into the nearby region to familiarise themselves with the land.

In late January 1838 they set off southwards to Perth. Forced by Wet season rains into the high rocky country, they were attacked by Aborigines, with Grey being speared. After a month of tribulation, they finally came across the Glenelg River, which Grey enthused about. Climbing and naming Mt Lyell, the party struggled south and, near the head of the Glenelg River, became the first Whitemen to see and describe the spectacular art called 'Wandjinas'.

Forced to retreat, they returned to Hanover Bay and sailed to Mauritius.

While Grey had hardly discovered anything, his enthusiasm for this richly watered and grassed land (don't forget he saw it at the height of the Wet season) and his vivid descriptions, 'the best grazing land in Western Australia', set the scene for other grander attempts.

Grey was one of the first Whitemen to see the spectacular art called 'Wandjinas'.

Cave with Wandjina Heads found by George Grey near the Glenelg River.

Pic courtesy of the S.A. Library Board

EUROPEAN HISTORY

GREGORY EXPLORES THE VICTORIA RIVER AND STURT CREEK

In 1855 **Augustus Charles Gregory** led an expedition that planned to cross Northern Australia, from the north-west coast to Moreton Bay in the east.

Shipped to the Victoria River, they explored this mighty river, following it inland and discovering the creek they named Sturt Creek. They traced this ephemeral stream inland a distance of 500 km to near Lake Gregory itself. From that point they retraced their steps and then headed east across the continent.

One of the great things to come out of this expedition were the paintings and sketches by the artist, **Thomas Baines**.

THE FIRST SETTLEMENTS

By the 1860s pearl shell had been found along the W.A. coast from as far south as Shark Bay. As the waters north and south of Roebuck Bay yielded increasing amounts of shell, more boats appeared on the scene. By the 1870s many boats were using the Roebuck Bay and all along the coast Aborigines were being forced or conned into working for the skippers.

FIRST TO ROEBUCK BAY

A group of Western Australians, led by Kenneth Brown in the schooner *Flying Foam*, entered ***Doubtful Bay***, north of present day Derby, in June 1863. With a base established on the Glenelg River, the party explored the surrounding area then withdrew trying to land at Roebuck Bay before giving up altogether.

The following year saw another group head north in the *New Perseverance* to investigate a report of gold in or around ***Camden Harbour***. Failing to find anything, they entered Roebuck Bay and set up a depot there.

In November 1864 a party of men sailed from Perth in the *Hastings* and took up land around ***Roebuck Bay*** in an effort to start a sheep station. Three of the party were killed by natives soon after and a reprisal raid by the white settlers saw a number of Aborigines killed in what became known as the 'Battle of Roebuck Bay'. The sheep station was doomed to fail and in 1867 the settlement was abandoned.

EUROPEAN HISTORY

THE GLENELG RIVER PASTORAL COMPANY

Around the same time as the doomed Roebuck Bay experience, another venture was being mounted to colonise the Kimberley, this time from gold rich Victoria. The Glenelg River Pastoral Company, spurred on by the reports of George Grey, released a glowing prospectus on the pastoral bounty to be had by those willing to invest.

In December 1864 the hopeful immigrants landed on the rocky shore of ***Camden Harbour*** from their ships, the *Stag, Helvetia* and *Calliance*. In total there were over 110 settlers along with their families, 4700 sheep, 40 odd horses and 20 or so goats.

The settlement never went well from the start. The natives were hostile, the incredible tides swept away many of their provisions, the temperature was in the high 40s and fever and sunstroke raged. The Glenelg River for its part was salty where they planned to build their township and many of the settlers almost died before finding fresh water. One ship was wrecked and most of their sheep died from thirst or from eating poisonous weed. And, apart from all that, the country was near all rock and spinifex!

Within six months their hopes were shattered and they abandoned their settlement and headed back south. The site today at Camden Harbour is hardly noticeable, although a few headstones mark the graves of those that passed away in this remote spot. In 1978 a team from the WA Museum recovered a few meagre artefacts from the site, which are still held by the Museum.

The story of this failure is told in, ***'There Were Three Ships'*** by Christopher Richards.

ON THE FITZROY

The mouth of the Fitzroy River, where Stokes had been so rudely awakened, was first explored by **Alexander McRae** in 1866. He had headed overland from the station at Roebuck Bay, but it wasn't until 1879 that a further step inland was taken.

ALEXANDER FORREST OPENS UP THE KIMBERLEY

This large, old boab was carved by Alexander Forrest during his exploits in the Kimberley.

Leaving Beagle Bay on 22nd April, 1879, **Alexander Forrest** and seven other men travelled east through good pastoral country reaching the Fitzroy River on the 8th May. By the end of that month he had reached a point known as present day Fitzroy Crossing and headed north to discover the ***Oscar*** and **King *Leopold Ranges***.

Under government direction he pushed north-west across rugged country, along the southern flank of the mighty King Leopold's towards the coast. However, he only managed to sight the ocean near Collier Bay before being forced back by the sheer cliffs and gorge-riddled country he encountered.

Pushing eastwards from the Fitzroy, Forrest passed just to the north of Halls Creek, naming Mount Barrett and discovering and naming the mighty ***Ord River***. With supplies running low, the party made a dash for the Overland Telegraph Line in the Northern Territory. From there, they pushed north to Darwin and took a ship the long way around back to Perth.

On the party's return to Perth a land rush ensued and soon settlers were taking up land and stocking it with sheep and cattle.

PASTORAL PIONEERS AND GOLD

AT BEAGLE BAY

The Murray Squatting Company was the pioneer leaseholder, taking over more than 48,000 hectares near ***Beagle Bay*** in 1881 and shearing sheep on their Yeeda Station property the year after. The Kimberley Pastoral Company secured extensive river flat lands forming Liveringa and Meda stations. Within two years nearly three million hectares were under lease along the Fitzroy River.

For many years in the western Kimberley settlement was confined to the land along the Fitzroy. Slowly the pastoralists spread out. In 1887 ***Lillimilura Station*** was founded on the banks of the Lennard River, under the brow of the Napier Range, but progress further north through the King Leopold's thwarted many attempts.

SURVEYS AND GOLD

During the mid 1880s quite a few survey expeditions were sent to the Kimberley region.

John Forrest led a number along the Fitzroy River while Edward Hardmen, a geologist, followed the Fitzroy, crossed the ranges and then followed the Elvire and Ord Rivers downstream to the Negri River. Along the way he reported finding many minerals and set the scene for the gold rush that was to come.

In 1886 gold was reported near Mt Barrett and in 1887 the Halls Creek field was discovered by **Charley Hall** and **Jack Slattery**. A rush ensued with men and equipment walking from Derby in the west or from the new port of Wyndham to the north. Wyndham and Halls Creek boomed and both towns were rip roaring affairs.

Frank Hann and his companion on many trips, Talbot.

Alexander Forrest's party returning south along the King Leopold Range near camp F112.
Pic courtesy of the J.S. Battye Library of W.A. History.

FRANK HANN – BUSHMAN AND EXPLORER

Frank Hann was the younger brother of William Hann who did much to open up northern Queensland and Cape York.

After loosing his Lawn Hill Station because of drought, on the 1st April, 1896, at the age of 50, he headed west, his only possessions being 67 horses. He past through Halls Creek and looked for gold in the area to the south of Derby.

In 1898, he headed for Mt Broome where gold had been discovered and successfully crossed the King Leopold's, becoming the first Whiteman to do so.

On this expedition and a later one he discovered the fine cattle country around ***Mt House*** which he also named, along with the ***Adcock River*** and ***Bell Creek***, following the Adcock south-west past Mt Hamilton to the junction of the Adcock with the mighty Fitzroy River. He discovered the ***Hann River***, which he called the Phillips, discovered and named ***Lake Gladstone***, before pushing on and discovering and naming, amongst others, the Isdell River, Manning Creek and ***Barnett River***, as well as Mt Barnett.

He camped near the junction of the Manning and Barnett streams, blazing a Boab that is near the old Mt Barnett homestead, but now out of bounds to most travellers as it is on Aboriginal land. While camped at this spot his six Aboriginal companions, '... *caught a large quantity of fish*'. Most Kimberley travellers would know the place – the Manning Gorge near the camping ground at Mt Barnett Roadhouse.

A Boab with the distinct blaze of 'H' as marked by the explorer Frank Hann.

THE FAMOUS PIONEERS

Nat Buchanan

In the eastern Kimberley, along the Ord River, Nathaniel Buchanan, one of the greatest stockman, explorer and pioneer pastoralist to ever crack a whip, took up Ord River Station for his bosses, the Osmand's and Panton's of central Queensland in 1884, followed by Wave Hill over the WA/NT border soon afterwards.

In 1886 he opened up the Murranji Track in the NT and soon afterwards formed a new station on Sturt Creek with cattle from Wave Hill. Much of his route is now followed by the Buchanan Highway.

*Nat died on his farm near Tamworth, NSW, in 1901. His story is told in the book, '**Packhorse and Waterhole**', by G Buchanan.*

Patsy Durack's grave can be seen at the Argyle Homestead & museum, at Lake Argyle.

The Duracks

The Durack family was close behind Nat Buchanan, driving a huge mob of cattle from Queensland to establish Argyle Downs Station in 1885. They had left their family property, Thylungra station on the Cooper Creek, in the middle of 1883, taking just over two years to reach their destination.

The Durack family, responsible for opening up more of the eastern Kimberley than any other, soon had not only Argyle Downs Station, but also Ivanhoe, Dunham and Lissadell, plus other properties across the border in the NT.

During the gold rush days they also formed the 'Argyle Downs Gold Mining and Quartz Crushing Company', but they had better luck with cattle.

Their reign was to last over 100 years. The last station owned by a Durack in the area was Spirit Hill, just over the NT/WA border from Ivanhoe station. It was sold in 1989.

*Their story is eloquently told in the books by Dame Mary Durack – '**Kings in Grass Castles**' and '**Sons in the Saddle**'.*

The MacDonalds' of Fossil Downs

Leaving their property near Goulburn, NSW, the MacDonalds' took 670 head of cattle and 36 bullocks on what was to become the longest cattle drive in history. The 5600 km took just over three years and the dray that accompanied them was the first vehicle to cross northern Australia.

Still owned by the family, the property covers 430,000 ha (over a million acres) and is the largest property in Australia still owned by descendants of the founders.

*The story is told in the small book, '**Fossil Downs, a Saga of the Kimberleys**', by Gordon MacKenzie.*

MacDonald monument at Fossil Downs.

Further north Hann named and climbed ***Mt Elizabeth*** before heading west and following the Charnley River before striking south to find a way through the rugged range country that had turned Grey back 50 years previously, and Forrest 20 odd years earlier.

Later he was to head into the desert country around Lake Disappointment, which he also named, while also finding copper in the Warburton Ranges.

Yet it was his Kimberley trips that he is best known for and it seems from reading his reports that he, like many modern day travellers, was amazed by the country he discovered and traversed.

Hann died in the Perth suburb of Cottesloe on 22nd August, 1921. His prodigious notes and journals have been compiled into the book, ***'Do Not Yield to Despair'***, by M Donaldson & I Elliot. It is a fitting epitaph to a great explorer.

Brockman Opens Up the Northern Kimberley

Fred Brockman was the Western Australian Chief Inspecting Surveyor and leader of the 1901 Kimberley Exploring Expedition. The group left their Parry Creek camp, outside Wyndham, on the 9th May, 1901, with seven months of supplies. They headed south, then west, swinging along the southern ramparts of the Cockburn Range before arriving at the ***Pentecost River*** on the 17th of that month.

After a few days exploring around the junction of the rivers Brockman headed south along the Chamberlain River. The expedition left the ***Chamberlain River*** gorge about 110 km south of its junction with the Pentecost and struck north-west, meeting with the Hann River and following that to the vicinity of Mt Elizabeth. Heading west from their tracks at this point, they took in all points of the compass with the land dictating their travels.

Brockman's party and a distinctive boab on the upper reaches of the Chamberlain.
Brockman's party near Mt Hann

By the beginning of August they were on the southern rim of the Prince Regent and by the 16th September were further north when they discovered and named the ***King Edward River***. The beginning of October was spent exploring the coast around Napier Broome Bay and Vansittart Bay, further west.

By the 20th of that month Brockman was camped on the ***Drysdale River*** and after exploring the river to the coast headed south following the course of this rock shrouded river till the 6th November, to a point near where Banjo Creek joins it. From there he turned south-east, meeting with his starting point on the Pentecost on the 20th November and pushing on to Wyndham, which he reached on the 26th.

His report to the government of the day was full of hope for the six million acres of ' *good grass lands ...*' he discovered and considered, ' *eminently suitable for sheep, ...cattle or horses...*'.

THE 20s & 30s

Slowly, but surely, the Kimberley was being opened up. Other surveys followed in 1904 and 1922 but, while these were glowing reports, the number of white people remained low. In 1921 there were 945 males and 186 females in the Kimberley, with most being in Wyndham, Derby and Broome. Cattle stations and Aboriginal Missions were also dotted over the area but civilisation, you'd have to say, was pretty scattered.

While the gold at Halls Creek had long ago run out, between 1916 and 1927 cattle and sheep numbers also decreased, along with pearling. Sheep were later to leave the scene altogether and today the area is well and truly cattle country, while pearl shell is still searched for to supply the cultured pearl centres located around the coast.

The country languished during these years. Cotton growing was tried in Derby during 1922 and 1923, while the Freney Company began drilling for oil around that time, but met with little success.

In 1920 the Geraldton to Derby air service was extended to Wyndham, via Fitzroy Crossing and Halls Creek. In 1928 it was proudly reported that over 4500 passengers had been carried to these distant ports.

The Reverend John Flynn extended his mantle of safety over the Kimberley during this time. Since then the Royal Flying Doctor Service covering the region has been supported in cold hard cash by the state of Victoria.

By the late 20s there were some 2000 whites and about 7800 'others' (not including Aborigines) in the Kimberley region. Most were around the towns, including Broome that boasted a large population of Japanese and Malaysians engaged in the pearling industry. So the area slumbered on with the Federal Government offering to take control of all land north of the 26th parallel. That was rejected by everyone!

Transport throughout the area was severely handicapped by the rough terrain and the many large rivers. Camel and donkey teams were used extensively with more than 5000 camels in use in the late 20s. Police patrols were, up to the 1950s, still carried out on horseback.

The depression of the 30s didn't help the Kimberley at all.

A JEWISH STATE

In the turbulent 1930s the plight of Jewish refugees was becoming critical. After Britain had offered a number of other areas for a Zionist state, it was decided that the Kimberley offered the most suitable spot for a settlement.

On the 23rd May, 1938, Dr. Isaac Steinberg, Secretary to the Freeland League for Jewish Territorial Colonisation, arrived in Perth. A fine orator, he soon set about winning over people and politicians, the idea being to buy the 27,500 sq km of country owned by the Duracks and to offer it to 75,000 Jewish settlers.

Steinberg convinced a lot of people of the great advantages of a Jewish colony in the north. In late 1938 the WA government accepted the idea, but the Federal Government was harder to please. The concept was put on hold for many years and was finally rejected by the Curtin government in 1943. Still there was public support for the scheme and it wasn't until the foundation of modern Israel in 1948, that it died.

WORLD WAR 2

The war completely disrupted much of the Kimberley. The pearling fleet lost many of its boats, being conscripted for defence, and when Japan entered the war in late 1941 there were more serious problems.

During 1942-43 there were two big air raids on Broome, one on Derby and a number on the Aboriginal missions along the north coast. Many people were killed, although the death tolls were kept secret for many years.

Also in March 1942 a lone Royal Dutch East Indies Airlines DC-3 heading for Broome was shot down by Japanese fighters, and the pilot crash landed the plane on the sands of Carnot Bay, just south of Beagle Bay. On board was a fortune in diamonds. *See page 219 for the full details.*

Secret landfalls by Japanese reconnaissance units also occurred during the war years. In January 1944 a small Japanese army group made their way south from Timor to Cartier and Browse Islands and then to the mainland where they arrived on 17th January. They spent two days exploring and filming the area around the Admiralty Gulf before returning to Timor,

Flights and Fights for Survival

Two of the greatest aviation survival stories ever told came out of the Kimberley and both were centred on the wild and remote coast.

The Southern Cross is Down

By the time Charles Kingsford Smith and his friend Charles Ulm set off from Sydney in the Southern Cross to pioneer a route to England they were already national heroes and household names.

Heading north across the Tanami Desert the pilots missed Wyndham, hit the coast and, thinking they were east of Wyndham, turned west. They tracked along the coast until finally, out of fuel, they landed on a mud flat near the mouth of the Glenelg River.

Here they stayed, remaining with the aircraft and surviving on infrequent rain storms, and whatever they could scavenge from the mud flats.

Lighting smoky fires as a signal, it wasn't until 13 insect-ridden days later that they were found and rescued. The Southern Cross was refuelled and took off from its muddy airstrip that so nearly became its grave.

Blamed for the death of two others searching for them, Kingsford Smith and Ulm were rumoured to have set the whole events up as a publicity stunt. Cleared completely, the incident was named the 'Coffee Royal Affair', after the only drink the crew had on board.

A Flight into Hell

In May 1932 a German seaplane, named the Atlantis, a Junkers Ju W-33, piloted by Hans Bertram and mechanic Adolph Klausmann, left Timor for the final stages on their flight from Europe to Australia.

In atrocious conditions they lost their way and were forced to land on a stretch of coast, west of the Berkeley River.

For 33 days the two men fought against the odds in a desperate bid to survive. After trying to find their way south they used one of the planes floats and set sail, only to be swept out to sea and then swept back onto land just as remote at Cape Bernier. Once again they tried to walk out but to no avail. Nearly dead with thirst they were found by Aborigines from the Forrest River Mission and later rescued.

*The remains of their aircraft was found in 1979 and the story is graphically told in the Barbara Winter book, '**Atlantis: A Flight into Hell**'.*

WA 1954 police patrol visits a remote cattle station while on a four month patrol between Derby and Gibb River. Pic by A. Sklenica

The Last Explorer

In 1954 the last great horse-mounted expedition to be sent out to explore and chart unknown country in Australia left Wyndham in the middle of April of that year.

Stone arrangements found at Oogalanoongoo.

Led by John Morgan, later the Surveyor General of WA, the party consisted of 23 men and a small number of horses, mules and donkeys as well as four trucks, three 4x4 vehicles, a grader and a bulldozer. Split into reconnaissance, survey, transport and constructions sections their task was four fold. They were to not only explore and survey the area north of Gibb River and Karunjie stations (then the most northerly cattle stations in the Kimberley) to the coast at Kalumburu, they were to construct the first road access to the community, classify all the surrounding country for its suitability as pastoral land and to accurately fix key points observed from aerial photographs (flown by the RAAF in 1948) to allow for the accurate mapping of the region.

John Morgan and his small group in the recce section were mounted on horseback and were often well in front of the other sections blazing the way. The comprehensive report, still to be found in the Battye Library of WA, talks not only of the rugged country they passed through but spectacular Aboriginal art sites they found and of 'bush' Aboriginals who were still living their traditional nomadic life. As well there were the added dramas of food shortages, burning vehicles and sick men who had to be evacuated from isolated spots. It was exploration in the grand tradition of past Australian explorers.

The expedition didn't return to Wyndham until late October of that year. In their seven months of toil they constructed 670km of vehicle tracks and opened up 15,000sq mile of pastoral country, as well as carrying out the all-important survey work.

***John Morgan** has retired and lives in Perth.*

The survey work took many forms. (All pics by John Mogan)

AFTER THE WAR

By 1949 the population of Broome numbered less than 800 and where there were once six hotels, only three survived. Plastics had arrived and the mother-of-pearl market and the pearling industry had collapsed. It was to partly revive with the 'seeding' of pearls in the 1960s and today it is this cultured pearl market that keeps the dream alive.

During the 1950s the highway between Broome, Derby and Wyndham was improved. It couldn't have got any worse as it was only a goat track. It was not completely bitumenised until late in 1987.

Nomadic Aborigines still wandered through the central and northern Kimberley during the 1950s. The non-Aboriginal population of the region was only 4000 at this time.

The idea of damming the Ord River was first mentioned in 1941. By 1963 the dam holding back Lake Kununurra was finished and between 1969 and 1972 Lake Argyle, the biggest man-made waterhole in Australia, came into being.

While many minerals (including gold, bauxite, copper, nickel, iron and lead) were well known to the early geologists who explored this country in the late 1800s, early 1900s; diamonds, the glamour stone of today, weren't even talked about until the 1970s.

Oil was also sought earlier, but it wasn't until oil and gas were discovered at Blina, inland from Derby in 1979, that significant finds were reported. Even so, it is offshore that more important discoveries are being made and it is such finds as these, plus diamonds and bauxite, that are putting the Kimberley on the map.

Highway 1 was finally bitumised for its entire length in 1988, the last stretch being completed south of Halls Creek. Connected to the rest of Australia by good roads tourism began to boom in the following decades.

In was in 1988 to that the Ord River Project finally got into the black and since then there has been a gradual expansion of agricultural and horticultural production along the Ord.

In the mid 1990s plans were released for a large dam to be built on the Fitzroy River as well as on the Durack and Margaret Rivers, mainly for cotton irrigation on the lower Fitzroy and on country south and east of Broome. This isn't the first time such hopes have been promulgated, but it took until 2004 and a big public outcry before this plan was stopped. Other plans using the untapped waters of the great rivers of the Kimberley are sure to follow.

In 2005 a $50 million native title deal was finally settled between the WA government and the 1000 strong Miriuwong Gejerrong Aboriginal people in the eastern Kimberley region. This will soon see the second stage of the Ord River irrigation project come into being and the amount of irrigated land around Kununurra triple.

4WD truck on the track between Leopold Downs and Windjana Gorge in 1954. Pic by A. Sklenica

TRAVELLING AROUND THE KIMBERLEY

GENERAL

It is not our intention to write an instruction book on how to drive a 4WD, as there are a number of excellent ones available from bookstores around the country. If you are new to four wheel driving, join a club, read a book, check out a video and practise!

The following points are included to either reinforce the lessons from other publications or because we have found that the information is not widely known.

A NOTE ON THE DESCRIPTION OF ROADS AND TRACKS

Trying to describe how good or bad a dirt road is, is difficult and can be very misleading. Today, a section of dirt can be as smooth as a good bitumen highway and yet a couple of days later, with some rain and/or a few road trains, that same section can be a nightmare.

Your concept of what a dirt road is like also depends on what you have been subjected to. If you have never been off the bitumen, you may find the best dirt roads bone jarring and nerve-wracking experiences. Similarly, if you have just finished an east-west crossing of Australia you will find most of the tracks pretty good. It is all relative!! This guide is more aligned to the former traveller than the latter!

ROAD CONDITIONS

To check on road conditions throughout the Kimberley, contact the Main Roads Western Australia – road conditions (all hours) ph: 1800 013 314, or check out their web site:

www.mainroads.wa.gov.au/

You could also contact the Regional offices at Derby, Wodehouse Street, PMB 959, Derby, WA, 6701, ph: (08) 9158 4333, fax: (08) 9158 4334, or Kununurra, Messmate Way, PO Box 138, ph: (08) 9168 1755, fax: (08) 9168 1995.

Otherwise, check with the Police stations at Derby, Kununurra or Wyndham for the latest information. The Tourist Bureaus at Broome, Derby, Halls Creek and Kununurra should also be able to advise you on current road conditions, as can the local shires:

Shire of Broome	(08) 9191 3456	Shire of Derby/West Kimberley	(08) 9191 0999
Shire of Halls Creek	(08) 9168 6007	Shire of Wyndham/East Kimberley	(08) 9168 4100

BULLDUST, TRAFFIC & OTHER PROBLEMS

BULLDUST

In some parts of the Kimberley, especially around the riverine plains of the Fitzroy and the other major rivers, the bulldust is almost beyond belief. The track into the Purnululu National Park in parts is a classic! Needless to say, **slow down** on these tracks as some monstrous holes are hidden in the talc-like powder.

Bulldust can be a real problem on some tracks in the area.

Rough Tracks and Tyres

As a general rule most of the major dirt roads are pretty reasonable. Once off these and onto station tracks and the like, they can vary from reasonable to extremely rough and rocky. The rugged ranges that are part and parcel of the Kimberley experience ensure that.

The jagged rocks of the Kimberley are also a terror on tyres. The locals definitely favour 'rags' or conventional nylon tyres as the sidewalls are less prone to staking and damage. Radials can be expensive to replace and/or repair.

New 4WD vehicles are often shod with passenger type tyres ('P' or 'H/T' designated) and these are very prone to damage or staking on rocky or rough roads, and in scrub country. Better to have an LT (for Light Truck) or an A/T (for All Terrain) type tyres fitted. It can be expensive to replace and/or repair tyres when you are far from home!

On one of our trips to the Kimberley we had four vehicles in our group (three with radials and one with 'rags') and the toll was six radials and no rags! What really hurt was putting on a brand new widey only to find the sidewall slashed 300 km later!

We're not saying this will happen to everyone, but tyres definitely take more punishment here than they do on a normal Cape York or Central Australian trip.

Aircleaners

If you are driving in dusty conditions, especially in bulldust or if you are in a convoy of vehicles, you will need to check and clean your aircleaner daily. That simple precaution can save you a hefty repair bill as well as help keep your vehicle running efficiently.

A snorkel will help in dusty conditions as it will feed cleaner air to the aircleaner.

Don't let your air cleaner become this clogged with dust - daily maintenance of your vehicle is a very good idea.

Oncoming Traffic

When another vehicle approaches, move over to the left, slow down and, if need be, stop. Probably the most dangerous thing to do is travel in somebody's dust – oncoming traffic will never see you.

Don't forget, a **road train** will never get out of your way – appreciate that he has a huge load on behind him and keep out of his way.

When approaching bridges, watch for oncoming traffic and obey any give-way signs.

Trailers

On most of our trips to the Kimberley we've towed a well constructed camper trailer with good suspension and 16-inch wheels. We've had no trouble with it at all, but many people who take trailers end up with a load of scrap metal.

Choose your vehicle and trailer well – the Kimberley is no place for the family town runabout or a normal 6 x 4 trailer used to take rubbish to the dump. We learnt that really quickly when on our first trip through the region our boat trailer disintegrated on the Gibb River Road.

Roof-racks

For those people who choose not to tow a trailer, most have to carry their extra gear on a roof-rack. Don't forget, this raises the vehicle's centre of gravity and makes it easier to tip over.

Ideally only light gear should be carried on a roof-rack, but many people are forced to carry extra jerry cans of fuel there. If you do, (and we're not recommending it) then the best idea is to empty these drums ASAP. Don't let your main tank run dry before taking the fuel off the roof. Progressively empty the fuel cans at each major stop, eg, lunch and night-time camps. It might be a bit of a bother, but it's better than rolling!!

CARAVANS

It is best to keep your caravan on the bitumen roads, unless it is a dedicated 'off-road' van and you don't mind it getting knocked around a bit. The Gibb River Road has improved enormously over recent years and a good van will survive it with no trouble. For places further north many people choose to leave their van at Drysdale river station with only the dedicated few taking them further north.

RIVERS AND RIVER CROSSINGS

The Kimberley region has some of the greatest rivers in Australia and for the most part they run unchecked to the sea. One has only to take notice of the bridge and earthworks on the Fitzroy River, south of Derby, or to note that in 1984 and 1995 the Fitzroy went over the bridge, specifically built above flood level at Fitzroy Crossing, to gauge how much water flows down these rivers in a wet, Wet season!

However, during the Dry season these rivers quickly abate and generally there is no great problem in crossing the streams. Certainly the major highways and bitumen roads present no problem. While reasonable dirt roads, such as the Gibb River Road and the Kalumburu Road, are generally pretty good after they've had a grader down them, other tracks and routes may cause problems, even in the Dry season.

No matter where you travel, but especially in the Wet, a storm can cause rivers and creeks to flow strongly. 'Walls of water', up to 15 cm high (doesn't sound much, but it can have a dramatic effect on a vehicle) have been reported moving down rivers due to heavy rain in their upper catchments.

You should check each crossing before plunging in.

If you come across a flowing river, check to see how deep it is, that there are no deep holes or ledges and that the water isn't flowing strongly enough to sweep you away. Also check the bottom – if it's soft and deep it will be much more difficult to cross than if the bottom is firm.

Water depths up to 600mm shouldn't be too great a problem – deeper and you have to do a bit of preparation. Of course that all depends on the condition of the bottom, etc, etc. Let your experience be your judge. What's a cinch for some, isn't so easy for others.

If you can't cross it, then place a marker on the water's edge to see if the river is rising or falling. Sit down and wait. Have a brew and if the worse comes to worse set up camp and enjoy your riverside stay!

Crossing a fast flowing Kimberley stream can be hairy!

Snorkels

We are firm believers in fitting a snorkel to a vehicle, especially diesel-powered vehicles. Not only does it keep water away from the engine air intake it also helps feed the engine with dust-free air. They are the cheapest engine insurance you can buy!

Remember you are in pastoral country and be very careful with any camp fires.

RESPECTING THE PASTORALIST & THE RIGHT OF WAY

The majority of land over which public roads pass in the Kimberley is held under pastoral lease. This land should be regarded as private property, with the same laws of trespass as apply in farming areas. Additionally, not all roads marked on maps are public or gazetted roads. Many of them are private.

Permission is not required for travel on gazetted public roads provided you remain within the road reserve. However, anyone wishing to enter a pastoral lease beyond the road reserve, whether by using private roads or otherwise, should obtain permission from the occupier.

In pastoral areas main roads are not normally fenced, but station boundaries are usually indicated.

Unfenced roads mean that livestock and wildlife will often be found on the road or crossing it, so always watch for the unexpected, especially at night when speed should be reduced accordingly.

Don't forget, pastoral properties are a business operation with high operating and capital expenses. Any hindrance due to carelessness or vandalism can be extremely expensive to the owner.

Travellers in pastoral areas are requested to observe the following rules:-

- **Don't** impose on property owners along the way for help unless you are in <u>real</u> trouble. Property owners are not geared up to receive or resupply tourists. Before planning to enter their properties write to them for permission. At the very least, if you enter a property, proceed directly to the homestead and speak to the manager or owner.
- **Leave** all gates as you find them unless otherwise requested by the occupier. A gate may have been left open to allow stock to get to water.
- **Please refrain** from lighting fires unless approved by the occupiers. If you do have a fire, cover it completely with earth and ensure it is out before going to sleep or leaving camp. One small spark can start a devastating bushfire.
- **Littering** is an offence by law, the same as anywhere else and plastics and tin cans can be fatal when chewed or swallowed by livestock. Remove all litter and rubbish.
- **Chasing** or upsetting livestock can cause broken fences, injuries and even death, especially around calving time.
- **Livestock** need water too, so please do not bathe, swim or wash clothes in water tanks or troughs and **do not camp** near a watering place as stock will not come in to drink.
- **Fences** must not be cut, removed or driven over.
- **Travelling** on wet, unsealed roads can cause damage costing thousands of dollars and take months to repair. **You could be made to pay**, so always check with the local Shire, Department of Transport or the occupier before driving on unsealed roads after rain.
- **Dogs** should not be taken onto a pastoral property without the occupiers permission. Also your dog could die from eating a poison bait set to destroy wild dogs.

Already a number of owners have stopped people camping on their property. Careless acts by insensitive, non-thinking people have stuffed it up for others, as well as themselves, if they ever want to come back. Please take care and consider the rights of others.

CAMPING

Camping in a creek or river bed can be dangerous due to flash flooding, particularly during the summer months (the Wet season). There may not be any sign of rain where you are, but rain in another area can bring a wall of water and debris several metres high down a creek or river bed. Rain on a river catchment hundreds of kilometres away may take several days to reach where you are, with fatal results.

At all camp sites please don't leave your rubbish. Don't even bury it as wild animals, other people and flooding rivers can uncover the junk and spread it over the country. It's one of the greatest disappointments of a trip to travel through pristine wilderness and come across a delightful camping site marred – no, vandalised by rubbish!

For everybody's sake:-

- **Burn** all paper, plastics & scraps. Be aware however of local shire/council fire restrictions. In most cases all BBQs and cooking fires conducted outside townsite boundaries are banned during very high and extreme weather conditions.
- **Crush** tins and carry them out with you along with any glass containers. Rubbish drop-offs can be made at most towns and national park headquarters.
- **Use** a shovel to dig a deep hole for your toilet requirements. Keep it away from running water and other campers.
- **Don't** use soap in rivers. If you want to use soap, take a bucket or a bush shower well away from a river and wash and rinse yourself there. Nobody likes to drink water tainted by soap, not to mention its environmental effects!!
- **Take** care with fire – clean an area around the fire place before lighting.
- **Use** old fire places – don't erect new ones!

CONTACT PHONE NUMBERS

We've included over on the next page a fairly comprehensive list of phone numbers so that people wishing to traverse or visit privately owned land can contact the station in question. There is no guarantee that contacting them will get you the required permission, but at least you know you have done the right thing and now know where you can and can't go.

Roadhouse Contact Numbers

Included here is a list of phone numbers for the roadhouses along the Gibb River Road.

Imintji Store, ph/fax: (08) 9191 7471
Mt Barnett Roadhouse, ph: (08) 9191 7007
Drysdale River Station, ph: (08) 9161 4326
Home Valley station, ph: (08) 9161 4322.

Station Contact Numbers

Most of the stations now have STD phone facilities and it's a simple matter of telephoning them. And, while most have retained their HF radio for emergency communications, unless you have pre-arranged to talk to them on a given channel at a given time you would be hard pressed to raise anyone on the radio.

The Royal Flying Doctor Service (RFDS) no longer provides radio telephone calls in Western Australia, but can still be reached for medical and emergency services via the HF radio. See our chapter on *Safety and Medical Aspects* for more information on the RFDS network.

A pleasant camping area at Drysdale River homestead.

QUARANTINE REGULATIONS

STOP

Fruit and Vegetable Quarantine

Western Australia has strict quarantine regulations regarding the entry of a whole range of goods – including fruit, vegetables, plants, honey, fruit boxes, etc.

For travellers not aware of these requirements, they often find themselves at a quarantine station handing over all their produce. It is therefore important for travellers to be aware of the restrictions and the location of inspection stations so that they don't stock up on fruit, etc, before entering, or leaving Western Australia.

Probably the most important quarantine inspection point for travellers entering the Kimberley near Kununurra along the Victoria Highway, is the station situated on the Northern Territory/Western Australian border, and regulations apply whether you are crossing the border from either direction. The other station is situated at Eucla on the WA/SA Border on the Eyre Highway.

Don't forget that stiff penalties apply for breaking the rules!

To obtain any further information on quarantine measures and restrictions you can write to or contact WAQIS (WA Quarantine & Inspection Service):

Perth: 9 Fricker Rd, Perth Intl Airport, ph: (08) 9334 1555 or ph: (08) 9334 1800 or look up their web site: www.agric.wa.gov.au/quarantine.

Kununurra: in far north WA at the NT/WA border. For further information and current regulations contact the WA/NT Checkpoint, ph: (08) 9168 7354, fax: (08) 9168 7333.

You can also download a copy of their '***Travellers Guide***' off the web at:
www.agric.wa.gov.au/pls/portal30/docs/FOLDER/IKMP/PW/Q/Qflyer_2.pdf

Noogoora Burr Quarantine Area

Many parts of the Fitzroy River system and parts of the Ord River are heavily infested with Noogoora Burr. This introduced weed is poisonous when young and has vicious burrs that will reek havoc in Western Australia's sheep flock if it gets any further south. Hence the need for quarantine areas.

Basically all of the Fitzroy River below Fitzroy Crossing and much of the Ord River around Carlton Hill Station north of Kununurra are out of bounds to travellers.

Members of the public found in the quarantine area without permits may be fined up to $1000.

More information on these quarantine areas can be found in the relative chapter, ie, *The Eastern Kimberley* page 116 and *Derby to Fitzroy Crossing* page 189.

WEB SITES - For more Quarantine Information

Dept of Agriculture, ***Western Australian Quarantine & Inspection Service*** *(WAQIS):*

Derby*: Loch St, PO Box 278, WA, 6728, ph: (08) 9191 0333, fax: (08) 9191 0334*

Kununurra: *Durack Dve, PO Box 19, WA 6743, ph: (08) 9166 4000, fax: (08) 9166 4066*

Broome*: 27 Hunter St, PO Box 5502, WA 6725, ph: (08) 9192 2945, fax: (08) 9192 2946*

You an also find information on their web site: **www.agric.wa.gov.au/quarantine**

The Kimberley Development Commission *(KDC) also has a good web site with details on travelling and quarantine regulations, as well as info on travelling in the Noogoora Burr quarantine area along the Fitzroy River :*

www.kimberley.wa.gov.au/index.cfm?menu=357&page=vk_quarantinenog

FIREARMS

At the moment, WA does not recognise firearm licences issued in another State. You will require a Form 16 Temporary Permit, to bring a firearm into the State.

You must be 18 years of age or over to get a licence. If it is for use in hunting or shooting of a recreational nature, the owner of the land must give permission for that hunting or shooting.

For more information contact: WA Police Service (Firearms Branch), 210 Adelaide Terrace, Perth, WA 6004, ph: (08) 9223 7000, fax: (08) 9223 7029. Or check the web at:
www.police.wa.gov.au/services/FirearmsandWeapons.asp?FirearmsandWeapons
and also see the '*Frequently Asked Questions*' (FAQ's) in this section.

Access along the Lower Ord River is now allowed along the Parry Lagoon Road.

WHEN TO GO

A well defined Wet season normally extends from November to March, and isolates much of the Kimberley from vehicle access for weeks, possibly months. When routes become impassable, Kimberley people rely on air transport for supplies and travel.

However, with the bitumen **(Highway 1)** circumnavigating the eastern edges of the region from Kununurra to Fitzroy Crossing and onto Derby and Broome, travel in conventional vehicles is generally possible all year round. Only occasionally do the rivers flood and cut Highway 1.

The **Gibb River Road** however is a different matter and providing the Wet is not prolonged or early, it is normally safe to traverse the road in a 4WD or conventional vehicle between April and November. Sections, or all of the Gibb River Road, can be closed to traffic during or just after the Wet, and you may need to check on the current road conditions with the Main Roads Western Australia (see *Road Conditions* at the beginning of this chapter for full details).

It is also worth noting that the Kimberley region becomes extremely hot towards the end of the Dry season (October/November), especially in places such as the Purnululu National Park, making camping and exploration unpleasant, and tourists have had to be evacuated out of some areas due to heat exhaustion.

RUBBISH - DO THE RIGHT THING

There is no garbage collection service provided by Councils or Shires along the Gibb River Road, or any other route through the Kimberley.

Please deposit your rubbish in the designated rubbish pits along the way, or better still, and especially if none are provided, take it with you.

Many consider June to September the most opportune time to travel to the Kimberley. While this combines nicely with school holidays, etc, it is also the busiest and the driest time in the region. Earlier in the Dry season river crossings are deeper, but the country is greener, with less traffic and fewer people at camp sites. It is the time that we prefer to visit the Kimberley, however it is no place for the inexperienced traveller.

BANKING/PAYMENT FACILITIES

There are no banks to be found along the Gibb River Road, however travellers will find that at El Questro Station, Mt Barnett Roadhouse, Drysdale River Station and Imintji Community Roadhouse, **Eftpos** facilities are available and major credit cards are accepted as payment for goods and services.

There is a good range of **banks** and facilities at all the major town centres in the Kimberley and full details of banks and bank agencies are listed under *Facilities* in each town throughout the book.

While **credit cards** are widely accepted on in the Kimberley for services such as fuel and tours, they should not be relied upon completely.

Cheques are not generally taken as payment, unless you have made prior arrangement. However, Australian travellers cheques are accepted in quite a few places, but we suggest that you check beforehand before relying on this method of payment.

In many places **cash** is the only form of payment accepted, and many stations still only take cash as payment.

It is recommended that you have enough cash to cover fuel and food between major destinations – Eftpos is great, providing the machines are working. It is also advisable to have a **Commonwealth Bank** Keycard account, as all Post Offices are Commonwealth Bank Agents and you can withdraw cash from your keycard account.

Most water crossings are shallow by the middle of the Dry season.

HOSPITALS AND CHEMISTS

All of the communities and towns in the Kimberley will have either a health clinic or a hospital. While chemists may be few and far between, it is often possible to obtain medications, including prescription type items, through the hospital. Obviously this will depend on what supplies are available and if there is someone present who can dispense the medication needed.

Under each town or community we have listed the health facilities available and their contact number.

FUEL AVAILABILITY

All fuels (super, unleaded and diesel) are sold at numerous stations and roadhouses along the Gibb River Road, and throughout the Kimberley region.

LPG Autogas is only available in the major town centres.

Fuel can be much more expensive in remote areas, such as in the northern Kimberley and along the Tanami Track, so be prepared.

TOWING SERVICE

If you are far from home and you breakdown, there are a number of towing services available that basically cover the Kimberley. Breakdown services are offered by the following RAC branches:-

- *Broome Toyota,* Broome, ph: (08) 9192 1277
- *BP Colac Roadhouse & Service Station*, Derby, ph: (08) 9191 1256 / 9191 1429
- *Shell Roadhouse*, Fitzroy Crossing, ph: (08) 9191 5044
- *Elgee Toyota*, Kununurra, ph: (08) 9168 2236
- *Branko BP Motors*, Wyndham, ph: (08) 9161 1305

TREK NOTES – PLEASE NOTE

Be aware that differences in tyres and speedos can result in significant variations to the figures given in our trek notes, ie most speedos are within +/- 5%, but that can mean 5 km every 100 km!

See page 10 for full details of ***Abbreviations for Trek Notes.***

4WD VEHICLE PREPARATION & EQUIPMENT

It pays to have a well set up and reliable vehicle and to be well prepared when touring the remote places of Australia and it is no different when you are touring the Kimberley or the desert country further south.

Before you Go

- Check oil and coolant levels.
- Check tyre pressures.
- Check to make sure you have the following equipment and that it is in good working order.

Tools to Carry

You cannot make repairs to your vehicle if you haven't a reasonable set of tools. As a minimum you should carry:

- A set of ring spanners (either metric or what ever is suitable for your vehicle).
- A set of open end flat spanners.
- Adjustable spanner (200 mm or 250mm).
- Plug Spanner.
- Wheel brace, jack and jacking plate (30cm square x 2 1/2 cm thick board).
- Range of screwdrivers/Phillips head.
- Hammer.
- Chisel.
- Hacksaw & spare blades.
- Pliers and wire cutters.
- WD-40 or similar
- Battery jumper leads.
- Tyre levers.
- Tube/Tyre repair kit.
- Air compressor and pressure gauge for tyres.
- Maintenance Repair Manuals applicable to your vehicle.

Spares to Carry

The minimum spares you should carry include:

- Radiator hoses
- Length of heater hose
- Fan belt
- Electric wire - 3mm (5 to 10 metres)
- Fuses (assorted)
- Globes (assorted)
- Engine oil
- Fuel filter
- Insulation tape
- Silastic

Other Equipment

Other equipment you should carry includes:

- 10 litres of water
- First Aid Kit.
- Torch
- Fire extinguisher.
- Poly tarp
- UHF Radio
- Emergency food and stove
- Fire lighters
- Appropriate maps and navigation gear.

You may also want to have:

- Chainsaw (especially early in the touring season)
- GPS

Recovery Gear to Carry

Recovery equipment you should carry includes:

- Shovel
- Axe
- 9-metre snatch strap
- Two 'D' or Bow shackles
- Drag chain

If you have a winch (either manual or power operated) you require:

- Gloves
- Snatch block
- Two extra 'D' or bow shackles
- Winch extension strap

Vehicle Modifications for Touring

While any of the 'real' 4WD vehicles on the market will do a trip through the Kimberley, a well set-up vehicle will do it easier and with less damage being done to the vehicle and the environment.

Our 4.2 litre turbo diesel GU Patrol is well set-up with aftermarket product and while some of the gear is more important than others, a vehicle equipped like ours is set-up for any eventuality and for long distance touring and rugged operations.

Equipment Fitted

- ARB Bullbar
- Warn 9000i Electric winch
- IPF HIR Driving Lights (one driving and one spot beam)
- ARB 'Air Locker' front diff.
- ARB air compressor
- Piranha Dual battery system
- Piranha lighting loom and globes
- Safari snorkel
- ROH 'Monsoon' alloy wheel
- Cooper ST 285/75R16 tyres
- ARB steel roof-rack, or Thule roof-bars and roof basket (only when required)
- Codan HF NGT radio
- GME Electrophone UHF radio
- Garmin GPS II
- Suunto vehicle compass
- 4WD Interior Accessories 'Outback' roof console
- Milford cargo barrier
- Tanami 'Alumadrawer' roller drawer storage system
- 7-pin trailer plug plus 2-pin Anderson plug
- Kelsey electronic brake controller
- Piranha 12-volt power sockets
- Engel 40 litre fridge/freezer
- Kaymar rear step and towbar.
- Kaymar tyre carrier (dual tyre carrier when required)
- Kaymar extendible work light
- Kaymar HF antenna bracket.
- ARB 'Air Locker' rear diff

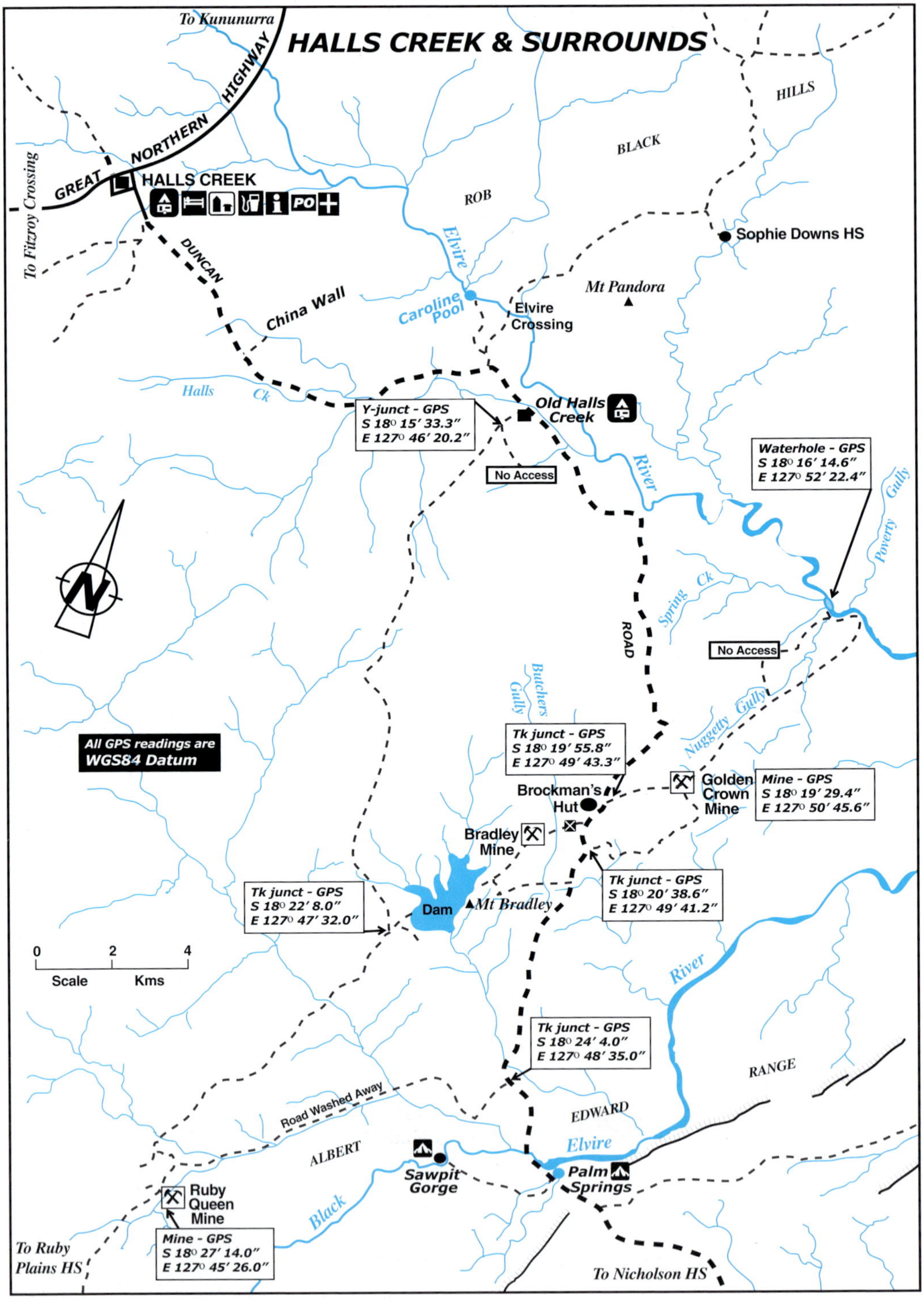

HALLS CREEK & SURROUNDS
To Kununurra
GREAT NORTHERN HIGHWAY
HALLS CREEK
PO
To Fitzroy Crossing
DUNCAN
ROAD
China Wall
Halls Ck
Elvire
Caroline Pool
Elvire Crossing
ROB
BLACK
HILLS
Sophie Downs HS
Mt Pandora
Old Halls Creek
Y-junct - GPS
S 18° 15' 33.3"
E 127° 46' 20.2"
No Access
River
Waterhole - GPS
S 18° 16' 14.6"
E 127° 52' 22.4"
Poverty Gully
Spring Ck
No Access
Butchers Gully
Nuggetty Gully
All GPS readings are
WGS84 Datum
Tk junct - GPS
S 18° 19' 55.8"
E 127° 49' 43.3"
Golden Crown Mine
Mine - GPS
S 18° 19' 29.4"
E 127° 50' 45.6"
Brockman's Hut
Bradley Mine
Tk junct - GPS
S 18° 20' 38.6"
E 127° 49' 41.2"
Tk junct - GPS
S 18° 22' 8.0"
E 127° 47' 32.0"
Dam
Mt Bradley
0 2 4
Scale Kms
River
Tk junct - GPS
S 18° 24' 4.0"
E 127° 48' 35.0"
RANGE
EDWARD
Road Washed Away
ALBERT
Elvire
Sawpit Gorge
Palm Springs
Ruby Queen Mine
Black
Mine - GPS
S 18° 27' 14.0"
E 127° 45' 26.0"
To Ruby Plains HS
To Nicholson HS

AROUND HALLS CREEK

INTRODUCTION

Halls Creek is located about 410 km south of Kununurra and Wyndham and over 500 km east of Derby in the very south-east portion of the Kimberley region, while the Halls Creek shire covers an area of 142,908 sq kms. The town site of Halls Creek was named after Charles Hall. Hall's name was first applied to the creek on which he found gold in 1885, before being used for the town site name.

The site of Western Australia's first gold rush, the town is not only headquarters for the vast Halls Creek Shire, but also acts as a major service centre for the surrounding pastoral area.

Tourism and mining are playing an ever increasing role in the town's development. For the traveller there is fuel and all supplies. Extensive repair facilities are available, as well as a large, camping/caravan park, postal and telecom facilities, a pub, stockmen's outfitter, etc.

HIGHWAY 1

ACCESS

Located on the Great Northern Highway and part of the Highway 1 complex, Halls Creek is now joined to major towns to the east and west by a good bitumen road.

To those travelling the bitumen from Derby, Broome, or Kununurra, Halls Creek seems little more than a wayside stop. Sadly few stop for more than an hour or so, or make an effort to see what's around.

THE TANAMI TRACK

For those travellers coming up from down south and driving the Tanami Road, Halls Creek can seem like a long way away. Still with nearly 1100 km of generally, well maintained dirt road it is pretty good. *See Trek Notes on following page.*

The Tanami Road is pretty good for most of the way.

Note:

- Ensure you have enough fuel. The distances between fuel stops is great.
- Carry drinking water and spares in case of mishap or breakdown. While easy, the country is extremely remote.
- Sections of the Tanami Track are used by cattle trains and they need a lot more road than you to manoeuvre. Take care when overtaking, or when one of these vehicles is approaching.
- When road conditions are dry, the trip is long, but easy. Allow at least 13 to 15 hours driving to go from Alice Springs to Halls Creek. When wet, the road can become impassable.

THE BUCHANAN HIGHWAY / BUNTINE HIGHWAY

The total distance along the Buchanan Highway / Buntine Highway is around 770 km and is either travelled on bitumen (160 km) or good dirt. It's not as scenic as the Victoria Highway, but it is pleasant and the remoteness and lack of traffic is a definite attraction.

The Buchanan Highway leaves the main north-south Stuart Highway, 862 km north of Alice Springs and some 35 km south of the Hi-Way Inn and Daly Waters in the NT. From the road junction to Top Springs it's a good dirt road, passing through well timbered, flat country.

TREK NOTES

TANAMI ROAD TREK

1052 km — 13 to 15 hours driving.

0.0 (0.0) Alice Springs*.*

Stuart Highway. Head north towards Darwin.

20.0 (20.0) Tanami Road Junction *— turn left (TL).*

125.0 (105.0) *Roadside stop on right.*

150.0 (25.0) *Gravel begins.*

188.5 (38.5) Tilmouth Roadhouse *(on right) & then Napperby Creek crossing. The roadhouse is open 7 days a week, from 7.00 am to 9.00 pm — supplying all fuels (no autogas) and limited supplies.*

Basic mechanical services, recovery, tyres and tyre repairs are also available.

Accommodation is available, along with a caravan park and ***camping*** *area with BBQs and all amenities, including laundry.*

All major credit cards are accepted.

Phone the roadhouse on (08) 8956 8777 or fax: (08) 8956 8787.

291.5 (103.0) T/J *- Proceed straight ahead (PSA). Right-hand (RH) track (tk) leads to* ***Yuendumu Community****. Fuel, limited supplies and take-away food are available at the Yuendumu Social Club-Store, Mon to Fri 8.00 am - 5.00 pm, Sat & Sun 9.00 am - 11.30 am and 3.00 pm - 4.00 pm, ph: (08) 8956 4006. (A permit is not required to enter this Community to obtain fuel).*

The Yuendumu Mining Company also dispenses fuel, along with limited spares, food supplies and has a telephone, ph: (08) 8956 4040.

545.0 (253.5) The Granites*. Old mining area on left. Take a break and check out the ruins - that is if you can as at times the area is closed off due to mining operations. Just up the road are the workings of a newer gold field. It closed down in the early 1990s but there is still no entry allowed.*

601.0 (56.0) T/J *- PSA. RH tk leads to* ***Rabbit Flat Roadhouse*** *- just under 2 km from junction, signposted (SP). All fuels (no autogas) are available, along with limited food supplies and camping facilities. Bar and Cafe. Cash and/or travellers cheques only. Open on Fri, Sat, Sun and Mon from 7.00 am to 10.00 pm. Closed Tues, Wed and Thurs. Ph: (08) 8956 8744, fax: (08) 8956 8750.*

644.0 (43.0) T/J *- PSA. RH tk (SP) leads to the* ***Tanami Mine*** *— no entry.*

724.0 (80.0) Northern Territory/ Western Australia Border*.*

810.0 (86.0) T/J *- PSA. Left-hand (LH) tk leads to the* ***Balgo Aboriginal Community****.*

Trek around Lake Gregory to Billiluna is possible from here.(For details see later in this chapter.)

877.0 (67.0) *Sturt Creek. Cement Causeway. Reasonable* ***camping*** *on right (upriver) on the west side. PSA for Halls Creek.*

880.7 (3.7) T/J *- PSA. LH tk leads to* ***Kururrungku (Billiluna) Store*** *and* ***Mindibungu Aboriginal community****. The general store, ph/fax: (08) 9168 8076, has fuel (unleaded and diesel), oils, tyres, tubes and a mechanic is available. Also food, drinks, ice and hardware items.*

There is also basic ***accommodation*** *in self-contained units with shared toilet facilities.*

Cash only for goods and services.

A medical sister, a public telephone and airstrip are located here.

Camping *is possible at Stretch Lagoon. See store for details.*

Trek around Lake Gregory to Balgo, via Mulan is possible from here.

This is also the turn -off for those heading onto the ***Canning Stock Route****.*

922.2 (41.5) T/J *- PSA on to Halls Creek. RH tk leads to* ***Wolfe Creek Crater*** *- (SP) 'Wolfe Creek National Park' (approx 23 km from the junction). A small* ***camping*** *ground can be found here.*

994.0 (71.8) T/J *- PSA. LH tk (SP) leads to* ***Ruby Plains HS.***

1034.2 (40.2) T-Junct *(bitumen road) - TR for* ***Halls Creek*** *onto the Great Northern Highway. Left for Fitzroy Crossing and Derby.*

1051.2 (17.0) Halls Creek.

Top Springs

At Top Springs, 190 km west, you'll hit the bitumen. Located at this point is a roadhouse, (open 7 days a week – major credit cards accepted), and the Wanda Inn Hotel Motel that will serve you a cold beer, limited take-away food and supplies, and dispense fuel, ph: (08) 8975 0767

Wave Hill (Kalkarindji)

Following the bitumen south takes you onto the Buntine Highway for 180 km leading west to Kalkarindji. The most obvious buildings are the Service Station and Store, ph: (08) 8975 0788. Here you can buy all fuels, groceries and take-away meals. The store has restricted trading hours on weekends. A small camping ground is also available. The Wave Hill Police Station, ph: (08) 8975 0790, is nearby.

A little further on you cross the *Victoria River*, a much smaller stream than at the Victoria Highway crossing. The bitumen runs out around here.

The WA/NT Border and the Flat Plains

The Northern Territory/Western Australia border is crossed 220 km further on and soon after you come to the junction with the Duncan Road that heads north 270 km to meet up with the Victoria Highway, approximately 20 km east of the NT/WA border (see below for more details).

Nicholson Homestead, just to the north of the road junction, gives its name to the surrounding flat plain and when we say flat, we mean flat. There aren't too many trees either! Mind you, it is magnificent cattle country and has been since the early pioneers began grazing their stock here in the 1880s.

Marella Gorge

Marella Gorge, located on the Nicholson River about 25 km west of Nicholson HS (ph: (08) 9168 7393), is on Nicholson Station property and **permission to visit this picturesque spot is essential.** There's ideal swimming and fishing, so the effort is worth it.

Around Lake Gregory

Lake Gregory is a near permanent inland sea south of the Tanami Road and one of the greatest water bird sanctuaries in inland Australia with over 600,000 waterbirds being recorded from here at different times. It is of immense cultural importance and is now managed as the ***Paruku (Lake Gregory) Indigenous Protected Area***.

Situated on Aboriginal land, this 260 km trek through the communities of Balgo, Mulan and Billiluna and back onto the Tanami Road takes you around this great lake. You need to allow at least two full days for this trip and a couple of camping areas are available for use. **Permission from the communities is required** and as it is through extremely remote desert country, including a short section of the Canning Stock Route, you need to be completely self-sufficient.

Lake Stretch, 15 km south of Billiluna, is a pleasant camp site.

Book through the store at Billiluna, ph: (08) 9168 8076.

Palm Springs and Sawpit Gorge

About 125 km from the Duncan Road/Buchanan Highway junction you come to Black Elvire River and Palm Springs (see later in this chapter for more detail) and you are just 50 km from Halls Creek.

Just before the Springs, which are on your right, there is a track on the left which leads to Sawpit Gorge. There is pleasant camping at Sawpit Gorge. (See this chapter for more detail).

Palm Springs is a popular swimming spot.

DUNCAN ROAD

The little used Duncan Road means travellers can cut from one east-west highway to the other before getting to Halls Creek or Kununurra.

Between Nicholson Station on the Buchanan Highway and the main Victoria Highway further north, it's a pleasant run over a mainly good dirt road, although the surface does change at times as it cuts in and out of the Northern Territory. The total distance between the Victoria Highway junction and the Nicholson Station intersection is around 270 km.

The Duncan Road passes through an area dotted with distinctive shaped hills.

The route traverses flat country in the south and more undulating country for most of the way. North of the Ord River Homestead views of the wide Ord River valley and the faint smudge of the Bungle Bungle massif can be seen.

The Negri River

Further north is the crossing of the *Negri River* which has an excellent **camp site** on its south-west bank. As the highway heads further north there are a few more pleasant creek and river crossings, including Hicks Creek, with some reasonable **camping** and overnight spots to stop.

Here, around Spring Creek Homestead there are some distinctive hills named by Alexander Forrest on his historic march east to the Overland Telegraph Line in 1879.

HISTORY

Reports of Gold

In 1879 Alexander Forrest first explored the Fitzroy River and then pushed on in a north-easterly direction to the Ord River. He reported that gold might be found in the East Kimberley and that the land was excellent for grazing cattle.

Looking for gold, Pat Ahern and a mate came from the NT, but neither were seen again. In 1882, well known prospectors and miners of the time Adam Jones and Phillip Saunders, led a small party through the area finding gold in the valley of the upper Ord River.

In 1883 the Government sent the second Forrest expedition to the Kimberley and on this occasion the party was led by John Forrest and included Edward Hardman, a geologist. On his return to Perth, Hardman marked on his map several places where he believed gold could be found, pinpointing the Ord again as one of the most likely sources.

Striking Gold!

Acting on this information, Charlie Hall and Jack Slattery set sail in a skiff from Roebourne to Derby in early 1885. They travelled along the Fitzroy River until they came across the tracks of the Forrest expedition and followed that to the Elvire River, and onward to around Mount Barrett, north of present day Halls Creek.

Hall's group of adventurers returned to Derby with 10 ozs of gold and reported their find. This was the first payable gold discovery in Western Australia, although the promised reward was never paid to the men.

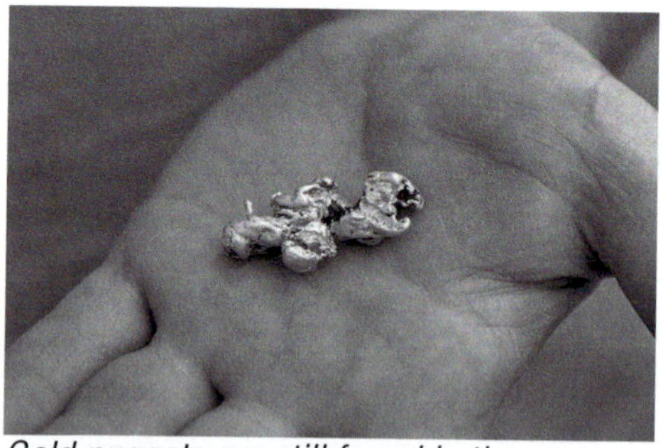

Gold nuggets are still found in the area.

A gold rush ensued and young and old men from all walks of life deserted their families, ships and civilisation for the trackless wilderness of the East Kimberley. Miners came from all over Australia and New Zealand by the shipload. They landed at the new ports of Derby and Wyndham and headed for the uncertain riches of Mt Pandora and the Black Elvire River. They searched in all directions, finding gold at Dead Finish Creek to the north, 12 Mile and Brockman to the west, and at Mt Dockrell 115 km to the south-west.

Between 1885 to 1887, reportedly some 10,000 men landed in the Kimberley with the hope of finding gold. The conditions in Halls Creek were extremely rough and only a few miners found gold of any quantity. When the 1886 Wet broke and the rivers came down, men were still arriving to try their luck.

Five thousand arrived at Wyndham and there was an endless procession from Queensland. Nobody knows how many died along the waterless stretches, from natives' spears, or at crocodile infested river crossings. They were just a few more marks to add to the tally of the new find.

Life on the Field

On a lighter note, even the gold had to wait when there was a sports day in the fields. It was reported that on the 27th December, 1886, over 100 people attended the sports day and the various events were fairly well contested. The price of gold in that year was about two pounds an ounce. A meal at the town was two shillings, which was made up of corned beef and vegetables. A large bottle of beer to wash it down was four shillings. Therefore, when you went to town you had to have an ounce of gold before you could even party!

The Legend of Russian Jack

From the hard days in the Kimberley gold fields came many tales of self sacrifice, such as the story of 'Russian Jack'. When he got to the fields he teamed up with another digger but in the bad conditions of the fields his new mate became seriously ill and was on the point of death. The nearest doctor was in Wyndham and Russian Jack loaded his mate into a wheel barrow and, with food and water for two, pushed him 300 km to the port.

Later Russian Jack was to join the other diggers when they left to take up new claims at Coolgardie, but his story lives on as part of Kimberley history. A monument to his endeavours can be seen in Halls Creek.

Monument to Russian Jack

The Town Struggles On

By the end of 1886 a few gold reefs were found but while these gave some hope for the field they were never rich finds and hardly paid for the machinery needed to open the mines up. When gold was discovered at Nullagine, many of the miners left Halls Creek and rushed south in search of their fortune.

Halls Creek was now a real shanty town of wood, stone, canvas, tin, bark and spinifex. Amongst the humpies were two hotels, a post office and a gold warden.

The population dropped to less than 500 by the middle of 1887 and within three years the European population was down to just 70 hardy souls.

The field produced, up to the late 1890s, an estimated 23,000 ounces of gold, although as tax was paid on any finds, the total amount of gold found could have been much more.

By April 1889 the telegraph link was opened to Perth and while it arrived too late for most of the gold seekers it helped establish the town as the main centre for the surrounding pastoral pioneers.

The 1900s

Another rush started again during the depression years of the 1930s. With no work and no money, men headed bush in the hope of finding a bit of colour to help them survive.

One of the mines, the Ruby Queen, started operation in the late 1800s and kept operating up until about 1954. Even today the battery is still standing. The mine is in a state of collapse, but there is still evidence in the creeks, around the shaft, of the work done. There is plenty to see and it makes an excellent day trip from the Halls Creek. Sadly, modern miners and their bulldozers have scarred the area surrounding the site, so it's not as good as it once was.

Where the old timers pushed wheelbarrows, and the well off rode horses (average price in 1887 for a horse was twenty pounds or 10 ounces of gold!), today's modern prospector drives a four wheel drive, searches with an electronic metal detector and rips up the land with bulldozers. Somehow I think the romance has gone out of it!

A New Town

By 1955 most of the Halls Creek town site was relocated 15 km away next to the airport and on less rugged terrain so that expansion could take place. The new buildings included a hospital, police station, school, hostel, post office, shire chambers, civic hall, churches and numerous privately owned businesses. These are far different from the mud and iron huts of the old town.

In 1956 the last camel train was brought into town by Sally Mohammed. Today road trains thunder into town bringing fresh produce from Perth and places further south.

The future of Halls Creek looks bright as mineral exploration is being carried out and platinum, rare earths, zinc and copper have been found. While the pastoral industry is being supported by steady beef prices, distances from markets remain a problem. Tourism is an ever increasing concern, especially as the fabulous Bungle Bungle massif is located in the Halls Creek Shire and access is easier, closer and cheaper from this town.

THINGS TO SEE AND DO

To the south and east of Halls Creek are the rugged ranges of the Bob Black Hills and the Albert Edward Range. Amongst the craggy bluffs and along the drying rivers and creeks are the remnants of the old gold rush days. If wild places and relics of our past are not enough to entice, there's always gold to get the blood pulsing!

PLACES OF INTEREST

OLD HALLS CREEK

Located 16 km south-east of the township of Halls Creek is Old Halls Creek that was abandoned in favour of the new site in 1955. The last resident left in 1959.

The ruins of the old post office are the most striking remnant of the old town, even though the shelter erected to preserve it does nothing for its looks. The town's cemetery, behind its stone slab fence, is very interesting. A grave yard of bottles from the old Kimberley Hotel could once be found just a little further away, but little remains of it today.

Located a short distance away is Halls Creek itself. A number of pleasant picnic spots are available between the old post office ruin and where the main road crosses the creek, less than a kilometre north. The water from the creek is not recommended for drinking.

Halls Creek Lodge

A caravan & camping ground was built on the small hill, near the cemetery, overlooking Old Halls Creek. The ***Halls Creek Lodge,*** ph: (08) 9168 8999, has powered and unpowered sites, along with air conditioned cabins. Meals are available, as well as takeaways, drinks, etc. It is also a good place to get some local information for fossicking and has metal detectors available for hire.

Tyre repairs are available here.

The graves at Old Halls Creek tell a little of the hardships endured by the early pioneers.

Ruins at the Ruby Queen mine site.

THE RUBY QUEEN MINE

Gold was discovered in this area in January 1888 and a rush soon set in. Little alluvial gold was found, but the reef gold was extensive and rich. The two most important mines were the Ruby Queen and the Saint Lawrence.

The battery that is the main attraction of the area is located some 2 km from the mine and once consisted of a 20-head stamper and four box crushers. Prior to 1897, 6000 tonnes of ore had been crushed with 4500 ounces of gold being recovered. The Saint Lawrence was the richer of the two mines producing nearly 1500 ounces of gold to just 1275 tonnes of ore.

The mine and stamper complex had its own small township, Ruby Vale, consisting of two hotels and two stores. Some of the stone ruins can be seen a short distance from the smelter site, but little else remains.

Getting There

From Old Halls Creek the best way to get to the Ruby Queen mine site is now out past the old cemetery. There's a few tracks for the first 1.5-2.0km from the lodge at Old Halls Creek. At the Y-junction (see map at start of this chapter) veer right and continue south on a rough slow track. Stick to the main track. At the track junction (marked on the map) veer left away from the dam. Right will lead to the back waters of the dam.

The tracks are four wheel drive and the Ruby Queen mine site (18° 27' 14"S 127° 45' 26"E) is 27 km from Old Halls Creek . Once you are close a number of tracks will confuse matters a little, but the GPS reading will get you to the main smelter and mine site fairly easy.

When exploring this area please use caution as there are a number of deep shafts still open.

The area is remote though, and if you are keen on prospecting or looking for old relics and bottles, there couldn't be a better place to camp, even if you have to bring your own water.

CHINA WALL

The turn -off to China Wall is located 5.7 km south of Halls Creek, on the Duncan Road, heading towards Old Halls Creek. The turn -off is indicated by a signpost and the left-hand track continues for 1.5 km to the parking area.

The China Wall is a sub-vertical quartz vein which projects above the surrounding rocks to form a natural white stone wall with an impressive blocky appearance.

China Wall, south of Halls Creek.

Originally the quartz was injected or precipitated into a fracture in the enclosing rocks which are sandstone and course grits. The quartz being harder and more resistant to weathering, has remained standing, whilst the softer surrounding rocks have been eroded away. The wall can be seen to wind its way over some tens of kilometres, appearing in its whiteness sporadically like the remnants of a miniature 'Great Wall of China', hence its name. Short stretches of the wall can be seen along the range running parallel to the road.

CAROLINE POOL

Approximately 13 km south of Halls Creek, along the Duncan Road, is the track to Caroline Pool.

Caroline Pool is a natural waterhole and was once the main social and sporting area for the Old Halls Creek town, boasting a cricket pitch and even competitive swimming events.

It is ideal for swimming during the Wet and into the beginning of the Dry. At the end of the Dry the pool becomes a series of smaller water holes. The walk along the banks of the water is very pleasant and the area is recommended as an ideal picnic spot where you can relax away from it all.

PALM SPRINGS

This idyllic spot is located 41 km south of Halls Creek on the Duncan Road, 28 km from Old Halls Creek. Palm Springs is a beautiful, natural spring located in a rocky, near sheer-sided gap in the Albert Edward Range, that the Duncan Road also passes through.

Used many years ago as a waterhole by cattle drovers, for themselves and their stock, today it's a popular swimming hole with kids from Halls Creek and passersby. Please, don't pollute the pool with soap or rubbish.

You can even set up a tent and enjoy the beautiful water of the springs, although it is a bit close to the main road.

Track to Golden Crown and beyond can be rough and slow.

Ruins at Golden Crown belie its richness

THE GOLDEN CROWN AND NUGGETTY GULLY

These two places south of Old Halls Creek are in a region known to gold prospectors as 'Brockman's'. Both sides of the Duncan Road in this area show signs of gold prospecting and the area still turns up good gold nuggets.

A reasonable dirt track leads off the main Duncan Road about 12 km south of Old Halls Creek and leads east to the Golden Crown mine site.

The ruins of **Brockman's Hut** are on the left of the Duncan Road, about 100 metres further on from the turn-off to the Golden Crown. Over the creek on the left and a little further on from Brockman's Hut is an old grave of a gold prospector.

Another track to the Golden Crown is found another 1.5 km further along the Duncan Road. It is rougher, passing through another well worked mining area before heading along a rough creek bed and up a ridgeline to the mine site. *See map at start of chapter for GPS points and detail.*

The **Golden Crown Mine** in its heyday produced nearly 1300 ounces of gold from the crushing of just over 1150 tonnes of ore. The ruins of the original workings, or what remains of them, are found just to the south of the old shack at the mine site.

Apart from the old shack, the scattered remains of modern mining equipment, sheet metal and assorted junk, along with a maze of tracks and benches hewn into the hillside from the open cut mining carried out up until 2004, litter the area.

For the prospector, nearly every gully in the area has produced gold, but as can be seen they have been extensively worked and some may again be under mining lease and entry prohibited.

The track to **Nuggetty Gully** heads north-east from near the shack and wanders through mined areas and meets the *Elvire River* about 6 km later. There's a couple of small **camp** sites around here and a waterhole which makes for a pleasant spot to stop. Up the hill to the west from here (on the south side of the river) are numerous signs of workings in and around Nuggetty Gully. Further on a leased mining area is closed to the public.

BLACK ELVIRE RIVER

Another spot you may choose to camp on is the nearby *Black Elvire River*, approx 1 km north of Palm Springs. Here is some nice **camping** close to the road crossing itself, but further away from the road than at Palm Springs.

SAWPIT GORGE

The track into Sawpit Gorge can be found just 100 metres south of Palm Springs. Turn right and follow the reasonable road for 2 km before reaching the gorge. The track continues into the gorge crossing the creek, which can be sandy.

Sawpit Gorge (alias Sawtooth Gorge) is the result of the *Black Elvire River* cutting through a ridge and leaving towering rock walls overhanging deep swimming and fishing pools.

There are a number of **camp sites** and many people find this an ideal overnight camping and picnic spot.

ABORIGINAL ART

The **Yarliyil Art Centre**, located adjacent to the Tourist information centre on the Great Northern Highway, specialises in Aboriginal art from the immediate area and the Warmun and Desert areas.

The art centre is a project of the Ngaringga Ngurra Aboriginal Corp., and is open to the public Monday to Friday 9am to 12pm and 1pm to 4pm and any other time by arrangement during these business hours on ph: (08) 9168 6466. You can also check out and even purchase the art works available on their web site at: www.yarliyilarts.com/index.html.

The famous **Warlayirti Artists** are located at Balgo Aboriginal Community. *See below for details.*

PROSPECTING FOR GOLD

There are a number of other areas around Halls Creek that are of interest to fossickers and prospectors. See the chapter on *Fossicking and Detecting for Fun and Fortune*, page 267, for more details.

PURNULULU (BUNGLE BUNGLE) NATIONAL PARK

It is from Halls Creek that the spectacular Bungle Bungle region is most accessible by air. It's also cheaper to fly from here than anywhere else.

See our chapter, *The Eastern Kimberley*, for more details.

ANNUAL EVENTS

The **Halls Creek Fishing competition** is held in April, while the **Halls Creek Agricultural Show** takes place in *July*. The **Campdrafting and Rodeo** is usually run during *July/August*, and the **Horse Races** are run in *October*. Dates vary from year to year, so contact the Tourist Information Centre, ph: (08) 9168 6262 or the Shire for exact timings.

WOLFE CREEK CRATER NATIONAL PARK

Wolfe Creek Crater is located approximately 150 km south of Halls Creek on the very edge of the Great Sandy Desert and is easily accessible from the main Tanami Road.

Formation and What we see Today

The Wolfe Creek Crater was formed when a large iron meteorite plummeted to earth about two million years ago. It is the second largest meteorite impact crater in the world, being exceeded only by the famous Arizona Diablo Crater. Fragments of the meteorite have actually been recovered from the crater.

The crater is almost circular in shape and between 870 and 950 metres in diameter. The outer slopes rise to form a ridge up to 35 metres above the surrounding plain. The inner walls are much steeper, in places forming cliffs, with the crater floor about 50 - 55 metres below the rim.

Even after hundreds of thousands of years the symmetry of the crater remains as it did after it was formed. Erosion has been slow due to the arid nature of the country. Originally the crater was much deeper, but the action of the wind and the weather, over a long period of time, has filled in much of the inner portion with sediment to an unknown depth. In fact, a large ridge of sand lies up against the eastern side of the crater.

The floor and walls of the crater support a mixed growth of mainly spinifex, a few shrubs and small trees. In the centre of the crater where water collects after rain, and a number of sink holes occur, along with a dense stand of larger shrubs and trees.

While most people simply walk up the defined path to the top of the rim (a short five minute walk), the more adventurous will descend into the crater and head for the centre. Take care when clambering down the steep walls of the crater – a number of people have been injured.

Legends and Discovery

To the local Aboriginal people the crater was formed when one of their Dreamtime rainbow serpents emerged from the ground after creating the nearby Sturt and Wolfe Creeks.

Wolfe Creek, which passes just to the west of the crater and gives it its name, honours the pioneer **Robert Tennant Stowe Wolfe** who arrived in the Kimberley in 1886. While the area was known to early European pioneers, it wasn't until 1947 that the crater was recognised as such. An F. Reeves and a D. Hart made extensive investigations of the formation and since then many other scientists have visited the area.

In 1969 the crater was designated a Class C Reserve and in 1976 a Class A Reserve. Today the National Park basically covers the crater itself and is just 1460 ha in area.

Access and Camping

To get to Wolfe Creek Crater follow the Tanami Road approximately 130 km south of Halls Creek, and take the turn-off (signposted) to the Crater. The ruins of Carranya Station are passed about 15 km from the main road. A few kilometres further on from the homestead is the parking/picnic and camping area for the crater.

An information board is located nearby. There is no water here. Accommodation, stores and fuel can be obtained from the Kururrungka Store at Billiluna, 45 km further south on the Tanami Road.

For Further Information

Contact CALM regional office: Messmate Way, PO Box 942. Kununurra, 6743
Ph: (08) 9168 4200, fax: (08) 9168 2179.
Web: **www.calm.wa.gov.au/national_parks/previous_parks_month/wolfe_creek.html**.

ABORIGINAL COMMUNITIES

BALGO (WIRRIMANU)

The Balgo Aboriginal Community is situated 250 km south-east of Halls Creek on the edge of the Great Sandy Desert. It has a population of around 500 people who are mainly desert people or 'lake people' from nearby Lake Gregory. They are from the Kukatja, Djaru, Walmadjeri, Wangkatjunga, Ngadi and Pintipi tribal groups. The main language is Kukatja. Balgo is called '*Wirrumanu*' in Kukatja.

The Community is incorporated as the Balgo Hills Community Aboriginal Corporation. The corporation's governing body consists of an elected ten member management committee and an appointed Council of Elders. The Corporation runs, on behalf of the Community, an airline, a store, a cattle station and a service station.

In 1986 an art show in Perth established the community as a leading indigenous art producer and the art centre was established the following year. The Warayirti Artists represents more than 300 artists from the surrounding area and many of these are world famous.

The Catholic church still run the school, church and missionary area.

VISITORS

While Balgo is not equipped to deal with large numbers of visitors, they are welcome, if the appropriate arrangements are made beforehand. Balgo is a closed community and entry requires approval. Motel style accommodation is available, but again you must telephone in advance.

Old historic church at Balgo.
Art at Balgo is rich and diverse, as depicted on the mural on the front of the Art Centre.

Intending visitors should write to the address below or contact the CEO, stating proposed dates, number of people, duration of stay, fuel and/or accommodation requirements, etc.

Access to the community to view the art at the art centre is a simple matter of contacting the art centre. A wide range of art is available for sale. The **Balgo Art & Cultural Centre** can be contacted on ph: (08) 9168 8960, fax; (08) 9168 8889, web: **www.balgoart.org.au**

Lake Gregory Trek: Access to the route around Lake Gregory is via Balgo. Permits are required from Billiluna, Mulan and Balgo. For a Balgo permit, ph: (08) 9168 8900.

The Wirrimanu Store at Balgo can be contacted on ph: (08) 9168 8894, fax: (09) 9168 9868.

For further information contact: The Chairman, Wirrimanu Aboriginal Corporation, Balgo Hills, 6770, ph: (08) 9168 8280.

MULAN COMMUNITY

The small community of Mulan, 45 km west of Balgo, was established by 'Lake people' from both Balgo and Billiluna. They wanted to move closer to their beloved lake and did so around 1980. The area around the lake was handed back to them in 2001 and today it is managed as Paruku (Lake Gregory) Indigenous Protected Area, of which they are immensely proud. Around 200 people live in this remote community.

The community runs a small store where limited supplies of food and fuel are available.

Lake Gregory Trek: The area around Lake Gregory is on land owned by the Mulan community. Permits are required from Billiluna, Mulan and Balgo. A fee is payable. Mulan is establishing a number of camping areas around Lake Gregory; one at Yuunpu on the south-west side of the lake; another at Kilang Kilang, close to the Canning Stock Route and another closer to the community. No facilities are provided in the bush camping areas at this stage.

For more info and permits contact the CEO/Chairman's office on ph: (08) 9168 8939.

MINDIBUNGU COMMUNITY (BILLILUNA)

This Aboriginal community, just south of the Tanami road and 170 km south of Halls Creek, was established in 1978 when the Billiluna cattle station was taken over by the Aboriginal Lands Trust, who still operate it for the local people. About 180 people call the community home.

The **Kururrungku (Billiluna) Store,** 2.5 km south of the main Tanami Road offers travellers diesel fuel, oils, tyres, tubes and a mechanic is available. There is also a well stocked store, where you can also get food, drinks, ice and hardware items. The store is open Mon-Fri 8.00am to 11.30am, 2.00pm to 4.30pm, Sat 9.00am to 11.00am, closed on Sundays and public holidays. The workshop is open Mon-Fri 7.00am to 3.00pm, Sat 9.00am to 11.00am. An afterhours call out fee applies. For more info contact the store, ph/fax: (08) 9168 8076.

There is also a **Telecentre** with internet and email access which is open Mon-Thur 8.00am to 12.00 noon, and Fri 8.00am to 12.00 noon, closed on weekends.

There is also basic **accommodation** in self-contained units with shared toilet facilities nearby.

The community also has a medical sister and an airstrip as well as a well set-up Telecentre for email, phone and web access. The main office is across the road from the store.

Lake Stretch, 13 km south of the Billiluna store, offers excellent camping beside a long wide billabong. This is just off the access route to the Canning Stock Route and the trek around Lake Gregory. See the store for a camping permit.

Lake Gregory Trek: To access the route around Lake Gregory demands a permit from Billiluna as well as Mulan and Balgo. A fee is payable. For more info and a permit contact the main office, ph: (08) 9168 8988.

For more info, permits, etc, contact the main office, Ph: (08) 9168 8988.

For more info on the Balgo, Mulan and Billiluna communities check out the web at:

www.users.bigpond.com/kutjungka/

Camping on the shores of Lake Gregory. Lake Stretch is a nice spot to camp.

MINDI MINDI ABORIGINAL CORPORATION

This community is located in Halls Creek. For more information, ph: (08) 9168 6470.

ACCOMMODATION, CAMPING & OTHER FACILITIES

ACCOMMODATION

Best Western Halls Creek Motel, Great Northern Highway, ph: (08) 9168 6001.
Kimberley Hotel/Motel & Halls Creek Backpackers, Roberta Ave, ph: (08) 9168 6101.
Halls Creek Lodge, Old Halls Creek, ph/fax: (08) 9168 8999.
Shell Roadhouse Halls Creek Cabins, McDonald St, ph: (08) 9168 6060.

CARAVAN PARKS/CAMPING

Halls Creek Caravan Park, Roberta Ave, ph: (08) 9168 6169, fax: (08) 9168 6277. Disabled facilities. Dogs on leash allowed. Accommodation available in air conditioned on-site caravans and cabins.

Halls Creek Lodge, Old Halls Creek, 16 km from Halls Creek, ph/fax: (08) 9168 8999 – Powered and unpowered sites. Limited accommodation in air-conditioned cabins. Facilities also include a restaurant along with take-away foods, cold drinks, etc. Pets allowed under control. In-house metal detector hire available.

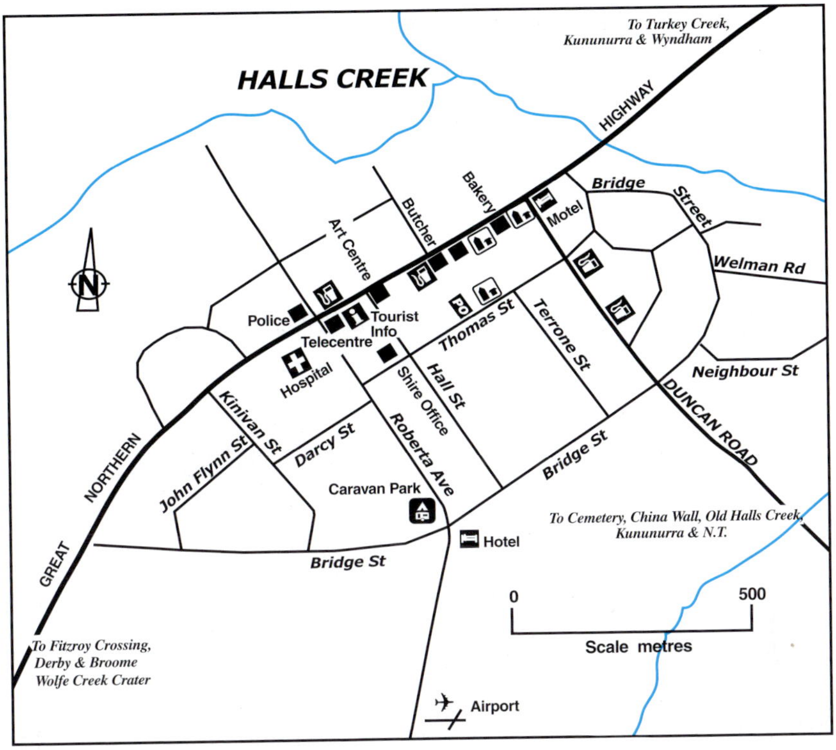

FACILITIES

ABC Regional Radio - Halls Creek

Halls Creek	**106.1 FM**
Radio National	**107.7 FM**

Hospital, Roberta Ave, ph: (08) 9168 6003
Police, ph: (08) 9168 6000
Fire, ph: (08) 9168 6007
Halls Creek Dental Clinic, Roberta Ave, ph: (08) 9168 9205
Banks – *BankWest Agency* (Halls Creek Trading Post – Card & Passbook facilities)
Commonwealth Bank (Agency Post Office – Keycard facilities)
Post Office, Thomas St, ph: (08) 9168 6111
Telecentre – internet & email access, cnr Great Northern H'way & Roberta Ave, ph: (08) 9168 5230.

Food and General Stores

Halls Creek Outback Fresh, Great Northern Hwy, ph: (08) 9168 5245.
Taylor's General Store, Duncan Road, ph: (08) 9168 6185.
Halls Creek Store, cnr Great Northern Hwy & Duncan Hwy, ph: (08) 9168 6125.
Thomas Supermart, 93 Thomas St, ph: (08) 9168 6090.

For a coffee and something to eat, drop into *Chok's Coffee House & Bistro*, beside the Tourist Information centre.

Bakery; Butcher; Liquor store; Newsagent.

TOURIST INFORMATION

HALLS CREEK VISITORS CENTRE

Great Northern Highway
(PO Box 242)
Halls Creek, WA, 6770
Ph: (08) 9168 6262
email: visitors@hcshire.wa.gov.au

Open March Mon-Fri 8.00 am to 4.00 pm, then April to December, 7 days, 8.00 am to 4.00 pm. If there is no one in attendance, the Shire Office should be able to help.

They will be happy to organise bookings for air charter, helicopter, road, camping tours and accommodation. It is also a good place for some historical information, souvenirs, maps, books and videos, etc.

SHIRE OF HALLS CREEK
Phone (08) 9168 6007 Fax (08) 9168 6235
Thomas St, Halls Creek.
Email hcshire@hcshire.wa.gov.au
Web: **www.hallscreektelecentre.org.au**

Service Stations, Fuel Supplies & Repairs:

Bailey's Auto Parts, Barry St, ph: (08) 9168 6508 – mechanical workshop, radiators, windscreens, tyres, range of vehicle parts and accessories.

Baz Industries, Duncan Rd, ph: (08) 9168 6150 – ***24 hour towing service.*** Also local Toyota dealer, as well as mechanical workshops/repairs, parts and accessories, tyres, oils, etc.

Poinciana Roadhouse (open 7 days a week – Eftpos/Credit Cards) – Great Northern Highway, ph: (08) 9168 6164.

Shell Roadhouse, Great Northern Highway, ph: (08) 9168 6018 – open 7 days a week, 24 hours per day – Eftpos facilities.

Aviation Fuel – Halls Creek Trading Post, ph: (08) 9168 6107

CRUISES & TOURS

The following **tour operators** specialise in offering tours around the Halls Creek area –

Air Tours

Discover the Kimberley Tours, Shop 4 'China Town' 25 Carnarvon St, PO Box 2615, Broome, WA, 6725, ph: (08) 9193 7267, web: www.bunglebungle.com.au/ – fly/drive tours of Bungle Bungle. Scheduled tours and specialised private charters

Oasis Air, Halls Creek, ph: (08) 9168 6462 or 1800 501 462 – air tours of Bungle Bungle massif, Wolfe Creek Meteorite Crater and Prince Regent River. Combination tours and others available.

4WD Safaris

Discover the Kimberley Tours, ph: (08) 91937267 – Departing from Halls Creek, they offer a 3 Day 4WD Safari Tour, Overnight Bungle Bungle self-drive, half day cattle station tour and half day goldfields tour.

See our chapter on *Tour Operators* for further listings.

TRANSPORT: To and From

Bookings for all domestic bus and air travel can be made at **Halls Creek Travel**, Great Northern Highway, ph: (08) 9168 6107. They can also arrange local scenic tours, air tours and camping safaris, as can the **Halls Creek Visitors Centre**.

Air Transport:

Halls Creek Airport, ph: 0439 092 726 – Air strip consists of a well gravelled runway and local air charter service **Oasis Air Charter** can be booked through Halls Creek Travel, ph: (08) 9168 6107, to provide a link to scheduled air services in Broome or Kununurra.

Golden Eagle Airlines currently operates regular scheduled services through the northwest Kimberley from Broome - Fitzroy Crossing - Halls Creek & return, Mon-Sat. The airline can be contacted at their offices in Derby, ph: (08) 9191 1132, or Kununurra, ph: (08) 9168 3103, web: www.goldeneagleairlines.com/regional.htm

Coach:

A coach service is operated by **Greyhound** stopping at Halls Creek. Bookings can be made through Halls Creek Travel, ph: (08) 9168 6107. You can also get current timetables and book a seat on their respective web sites: www.greyhound.com.au/

Hire 4WD

Poinciana Roadhouse Handyute and Car Hire, Great Northern Highway, Halls Creek, WA, 6770, ph: (08) 9168 6164, fax: (08) 9168 6227. Camping kits available.

Panning for gold is still a popular past time for visitors to Old Halls Creek.

THE EASTERN KIMBERLEY

INTRODUCTION

The eastern Kimberley region, centred around Wyndham, Kununurra and Lake Argyle, south to Turkey creek and the magnificent Bungle Bungles, is one of the most popular areas in the whole Kimberley. Kununurra itself is on the main, around Australia all bitumen highway, while the town of Wyndham, the tourist village of Lake Argyle and the dam itself are all connected by good bitumen roads. Such a network of tarred roads, almost insignificant by southern standards, makes it unique within the Kimberley.

On the main highway south towards Halls Creek is the small community of Turkey Creek and to the east along a 4WD track the hidden delights of the Bungles can be found.

ACCESS

FROM KATHERINE IN THE NT

Heading into Western Australia from the Northern Territory is via either the bituminised Victoria Highway or the mainly all-dirt Buchanan Highway. By far the most popular is the Victoria, but that doesn't mean you should write off the Buchanan. For more details on the Buchanan see the chapter, *Around Halls Creek*.

Katherine, approximately 350 km south of Darwin and 1200 km north of Alice Springs, is a major town that features everything a traveller requires.

VICTORIA HIGHWAY

Heading west along the Victoria Highway you'll pass a few wayside rest spots located at King River (30 km west) and Campbell Springs (170 km) before reaching the ***Victoria River Roadhouse.*** The roadhouse, open 7 days, is located near where the highway crosses the mighty **Victoria River,** 190 km west of Katherine. There's fuel and supplies available, meals and take-away food, and it's a good base to explore the nearby Gregory National Park. The roadhouse also has accommodation available in motel units or budget rooms, as well as a caravan park with all facilities, where you can have a dog. Phone (08) 8975 0744, fax: (08) 8975 0819, or write to PMB 59, Katherine, NT, 0852.

Just 90 km further on is **Timber Creek**, with its police station (ph: (08) 8975 0733) and various services. The ***Timber Creek Wayside Inn & Caravan Park*** offers motel accommodation and **camping** and has a general store, Eftpos, fuel, ANZ Banking agency and 24 hour service, ph: (08) 8975 0732. There is also a National Trust Museum and Victoria River Region Tourism.

Timber Creek Gunamu Tourist Park, Victoria Highway, offers fuel, 7 days, ph: (08) 8975 0631. Other facilities include Eftpos, phone, toilet, food, supermarket, licensed premises, motel accommodation, caravan and **camping** park (dogs accepted), swimming pool, Commonwealth Bank agency and post office Agency.

Max's Tours/Beverley's Booking Centre, Victoria Highway, ph/fax: (08) 8975 0850, has information and organises cruises, flights and 4WD tours in and around Timber Creek.

The **Timber Creek Garage** offers repairs and service, ph: (08) 8975 0835.

Gregory National Park covers an area of 13,000 sq km in two sections that straddle the Victoria Highway and take in much of the sheer escarpment country around the Victoria River. There is some fabulous **camping** and 4WD trails in this park, as well as great scenery, walking trails, Aboriginal art and fishing.

For more information contact the rangers at Timber Creek, ph: (08) 8975 0888, or at Bullita Station, ph: (08) 8975 0888, web: **www.nt.gov.au/ipe/pwcnt/**.

Big Horse Creek, 13 km west of Timber Creek, is a pleasant and free **camping** area beside the *Victoria River*. It's definitely worth a stop, especially if you have a boat and want to wet a line fishing for barra. There is a boat ramp nearby. Beware of Salt-Water Crocodiles.

The **Saddle Creek** rest area between Timber Creek and Keep River National Park is a reasonable overnight stop.

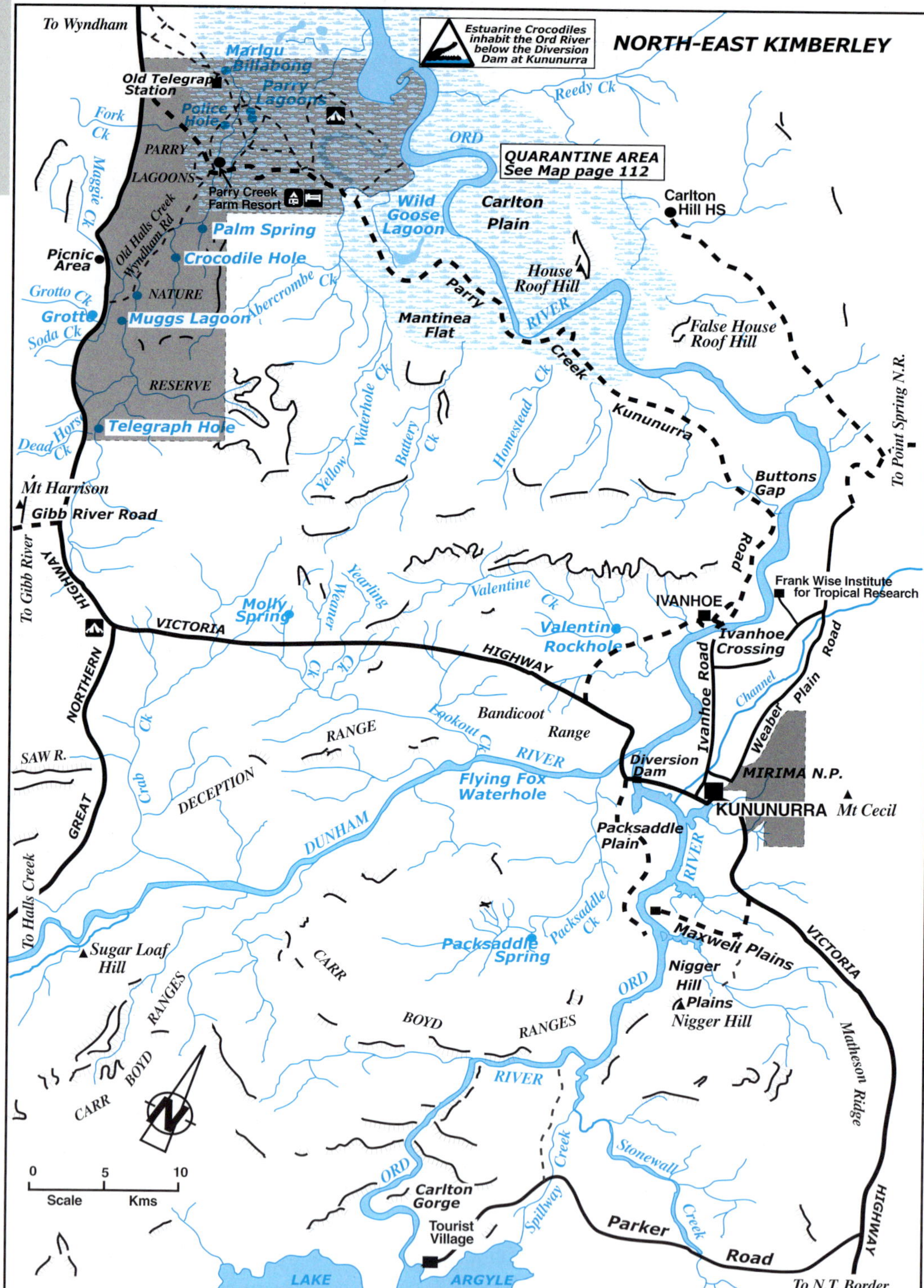

Keep River National Park, 460 km west of Katherine, takes in over 57,000 ha and is well worth exploring. Two **camping** areas are located in the park, one about 15 km north of the highway and the other just under 30 km north. There is some interesting Aboriginal art, spectacular rock formations and good bird and mammal life to keep you entertained.

For more details contact the Ranger, ph: (08) 9167 8827 and visit the park's web site at: **www.nt.gov.au/ipe/pwcnt/**

Heading into the Gregory National Park, which straddles the Victoria Highway, on the way to Kununurra.

As you cross the border don't forget your quarantine requirements – you certainly can't miss the check point!

Approximately 490 km west of Katherine you'll pass the turn-off to Lake Argyle and just 36 km further on enter Kununurra.

Quarantine Inspection Station

Kununurra is a major agricultural area and is the first town travellers encounter on their run across from the Northern Territory into Western Australia along the Victoria Highway. With its close proximity to the border, quarantine restrictions are most important.

A quarantine inspection station exists on the Northern Territory/Western Australia border and there are strict quarantine regulations regarding the entry of a whole range of goods – including fruits, vegetables, plants, honey, fruit boxes, etc. These conditions apply whether you are crossing the border from either direction.

Don't forget that stiff penalties apply for breaking the rules!

To obtain any further information on quarantine measures and restrictions you can write to or contact Agriculture Western Australia (WA Quarantine & Inspection Service):
Perth: 280 Bannister Rd, Canning Vale, WA, 6155, ph: (08) 9311 5333, fax: (08) 9455 3052, or look up their web site: **www.agric.wa.gov.au/**
Kununurra: WA/NT Checkpoint, ph: (08) 9168 7354, fax: (08) 9168 7333.

HISTORY

Early Days

On 19th September, 1819, Lieutenant Phillip Parker King, in his ship the *Mermaid*, sailed into the wide waters of an inlet he called Cambridge Gulf.

It wasn't until 1875 that the first land explorer arrived. In that year Alexander Forrest explored the valleys of the *Ord* and the *Fitzroy Rivers*, opening the way for European pastoral exploitation.

Patsy Durack of 'Kings in Grass Castles' fame arrived in 1885 on board the *Torinda Borstel*. His cattle and those of other outstanding overlanders such as the Buchanans' and the Costellos' were being driven across from Queensland and in the years soon after many great cattle properties were established. Among them were the Durack owned Lissadell, Argyle, Rosewood and Ivanhoe Stations.

Other pioneers of the time were the MacDonalds of Fossil Downs and the legendary bushman, Bob Dutton, who established the Ord River Station for the Buchanan family in 1884.

When gold was discovered at Halls Creek, Wyndham mushroomed and was well established by the end of 1896. By all accounts six hotels lined the streets, although only four of them were grand enough to have a name. By 1897 the town actually had a post office.

The decline in the Halls Creek field slowed the growth of Wyndham, but the construction of a T-shaped jetty at Anthon's Landing, that could handle live cattle, was a great boost to the cattle industry. In 1919 the meatworks was opened and gave new life to the town. In that same year an L-shaped jetty was built near the meatworks. In 1959 that was extended to connect to the shore at the southern end and in 1978 it was upgraded to its present standard.

In the late 1920s and early '30s Wyndham, being the most northerly port in Western Australia and the closest to South-East Asia, saw many great aviators pass through.

The Ord Irrigation Scheme

Little happened in the region until the WA Government, with some Federal assistance, began the Ord Irrigation Scheme. Stage 1 of the scheme was completed in 1963. It consisted of the construction of the Kununurra Diversion Dam and the development of the Kununurra township. Stage 2 consisted of the construction of a major storage reservoir called Lake Argyle. This was officially opened in June 1972.

While the dam provides as much water (and more) as required and the rich soil can grow virtually anything, the insects, birds, distances from markets and pure everyday economics initially slowed the Ord scheme from reaching its full capacity. However, in recent years the area has become a major producer of a wide variety of vegetables and fruit – a veritable market garden – and sugar. The latter is sure to transform the area and will no doubt spur on growth, hopefully bringing on the second stage of irrigation areas and possibly the power station.

After much negotiation the next stage of the irrigation scheme was finally allowed to proceed in 2006 when Aboriginal land claims were finalised. This will result in a doubling of the area under irrigation.

A Growing Area

In the late 1970s mineral, oil and gas discoveries began to revitalise the area. In 1988 the area was connected to the south and east via a bitumen highway. Kununurra, once a dying dream, suddenly became the service town not only to the surrounding area but to gas rigs in the Joseph Bonaparte Gulf, to diamond mine south of the great dam and to the ever increasing number of tourists who travel through here each year.

WYNDHAM

INTRODUCTION

Wyndham, the oldest town in the area, is the most northerly port in Western Australia. Terming itself the "Top Town of the West", it has its 'Top of the West' festival in August. Ten days of entertainment sees the town really jumping with a music festival, gymkhana and of course a race meeting. Certainly it's all good fun and worth seeing.

Governor Broome decided it would be named Wyndham, after Major Walter George Wyndham, and the townsite was gazetted in September 1886. The original town site can be explored at the Port area, situated on the Cambridge Gulf, while the main residential and shopping area has developed at Wyndham East, on the Great Northern Highway.

ACCESS

Wyndham can be reached by a good bitumen road just 101 km west from Kununurra, while Broome is 1100km away. The main part of town that includes the administration centre and most of the shops is located a few kilometres inland from the original port of Wyndham, now known as the Old Port.

Old Wyndham Town and Cambridge Gulf from Five Rivers Lookout.

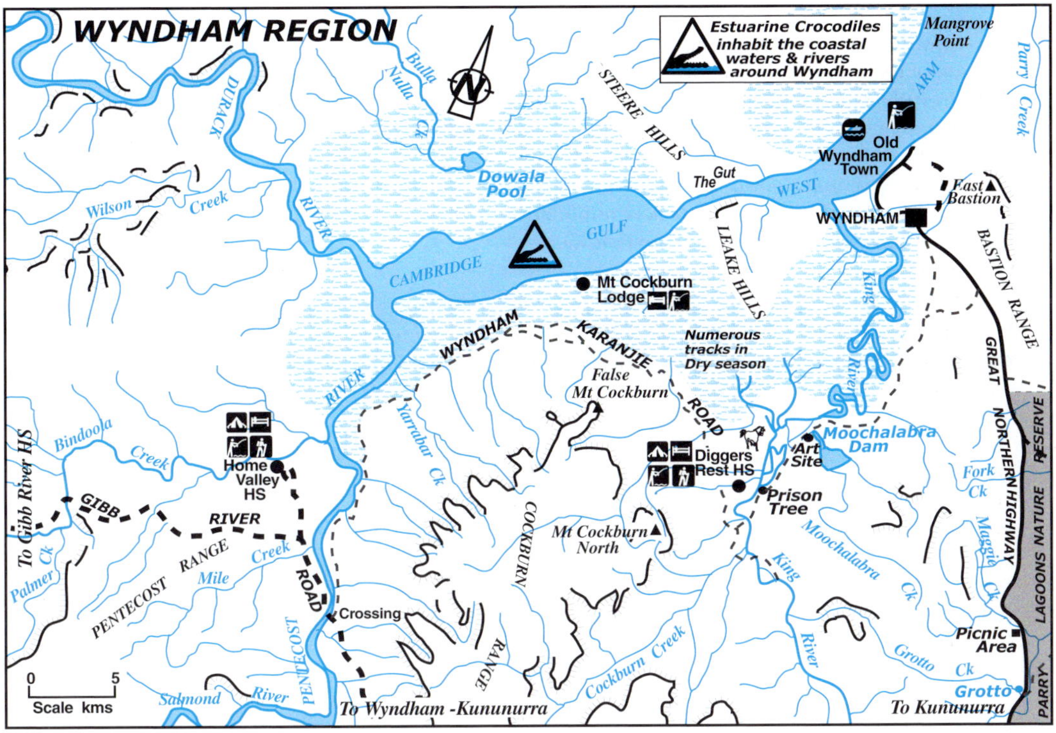

HISTORY

Wyndham was originally a tiny port, used mainly for exporting cattle to Perth and overseas. In 1886, with the State's first gold rush at Halls Creek, the town of Wyndham was officially established and a town site surveyed in the area where the old meatworks once stood. The first lots of land went on sale at a cost of 50 pounds per lot on the 30th August, 1886, in what is now known as the Port area and Gully.

During its early days Wyndham's hotels numbered six, however it never had a major industry until 1919, when the meatworks officially opened for its first season. The meatworks has long since closed down and Wyndham today survives mainly on tourism.

THINGS TO SEE AND DO

A great place to start any tour of Wyndham is to visit the **Old Port Post Office** in O'Donnell St. The Centre is not only extremely well set up with informative displays on Wyndham's history and sights, and you can also get some helpful tourist information as well.

MOOCHALABRA DAM – KING RIVER ROAD (4WD)

Moochalabra Dam, originally constructed in 1971, is Wyndham's major water supply and while fishing, camping and swimming are prohibited in the dam itself, there is plenty to see and do along the way. In the wet season, the reconstructed dam (1999) and spillway create a spectacular waterfall.

Heading out from Wyndham along the King River/Moochalabra Dam Road you skirt the edge of the *King River*, which gives reasonable access for fishing. Remember the river is tidal here and Salt-Water Crocodiles are common. Good catches of barra are not uncommon in the Wet along here, but they're more elusive in the Dry.

About 25 km from Wyndham you'll come to a track junction. Left will take you to the Moochalabra Dam, its picnic area and some **Aboriginal art**. On the right of the dam road, 600 metres before the dam itself and under the overhang in the cliff walls, can be found a number of faded Aboriginal paintings of spiritual figures and animals. As normal, the site is protected, so look, but don't touch.

By continuing straight ahead at the track junction to the dam, you'll drive beside a fast narrowing stream and 4.5 km later come to another junction where you keep right on the main track. Left leads to camp near what was the old pumping works. Shortly after, you'll cross the King River and then, on the right, is the old ***Wyndham Prison Tree***. This ancient Boab was used by the early police patrols as an overnight lockup.

Another track junction is reached 4 km further on. Veering right here leads to **Diggers Rest station** where camping and accommodation is available. Left at this junction takes you along the old Karunjie Road (see below).

PLACES OF INTEREST

THE OLD PORT AND SURROUNDS

The old port around **Anthon's Landing** is the historic centre of Wyndham and boasts many features retained from the early years. These include **Durack's Store** (now Wyndham Port Hardware), built in 1885 and still original in structure and design; the Port Post Office; the old Court House and Anthon's Landing itself. The main street is lined with Boabs as old as the town.

Down on the coast is a **boat ramp** from which spot you also get an excellent view of Cambridge Gulf. If you're launching a boat take care of the Salt-Water crocs though!

The **wreck** of the *M.V. Koolama*, a coastal trader attacked by Japanese bombers in World War II, has its last resting place 40 metres north of the present wharf, its existence given away by the swirling waters of the Gulf.

The **wharf** itself is used occasionally to service small tankers and fishing boats heading out into the Timor Sea or along the Kimberley coast. It's not a bad fishing spot!

Crocodile Lookout is only a short distance from the wharf. The creek which flows alongside was used as a blood drain by the meatworks and when the works was operating it wasn't uncommon to see up to 20 large Salt-Water Crocodiles resting on the mud. With the closure of the meatworks the numbers of visiting crocs have declined, but you can still often see one, two or more cruising about. The best time is three hours either side of low tide, and a pair of binos helps. Or to get a really close look at some crocodiles, pay a visit to the **Wyndham Zoological Gardens & Crocodile Farm** situated in Barytes Road, Wyndham Port. Set in scenic grounds, visitors have the chance to view Fresh and Salt-Water crocodiles as well as komodo dragons. There is a guided tour and crocodile feeding daily during the peak tourist season, ph: (08) 9161 1124.

For those with a fascination for history and headstones the **Pioneer Cemetery** (1886-1922), located on the highway towards the port, the **Gully Cemetery** (1922-1968 +,) in Gully Road, and the **Afghan Cemetery** (1890s), back on the outskirts of Wyndham, are reminders of how hard and unforgiving this land was when it was first settled and opened up. At the Afghan Cemetery you'll find the resting place of the Afghan camel drivers who provided the first freight service in the Kimberley, with all of the headstones facing Mecca.

The historic **Wyndham Museum**, located in the old court house between the original town jetty site and the hotel, not only has fascinating memorabilia, but houses the **Pioneer Photo Display** featuring pioneering activity and is open daily from 10.00am to 3.00pm during the tourist season, ph: (08) 9161 1713.

The Bastion – Five Rivers Lookout gives commanding views of Cambridge Gulf and the Forrest, Pentecost, King, Durack and Ord Rivers. The view is best in the early morning and from the lookout you gain an excellent feel for the country, its waterways and the almost insignificant signs of man around the meatworks and the old port. It is recommended that you leave your caravan in the parking area at the base or at the Tourist Information Centre.

At **Three Mile Valley**, situated just on the outskirts of Wyndham at the base of Mt. Bastion, you can see a rugged Kimberley range in miniature. It's also a scenic spot for a picnic or to do some bushwalking. Take the Five Rivers Lookout Road and the turn-off to the valley is just 1 km from the hospital.

At **Wariu Dreamtime Park** back in Wyndham, visitors can admire and ponder over tall bronze statues which represent an Aboriginal family and Dreamtime animals.

OLD WYNDHAM–KARUNJIE ROAD

This is an interesting run south around the bulk of the Cockburn Range and across or beside the flood plain of the region's great rivers. As such it can be flooded. However, many of the smaller creek crossings can be severely eroded at any time, but are generally dry.

Our trek begins at the Gibb River end of the old Karunjie Road and leads to Wyndham. If coming from the Wyndham end take care with the road junctions after the **Prison Tree**. They are easily missed.

El Questro Wilderness Park

The **Karunjie King River Road** passes through a private Pastoral Lease and camping and fires are not permitted. **You can get a good 4WD-Track Fact Sheet (mud map and info) on the Karunjie King River Road from El Questro Station** .

THE GUT

The Gut, a 150 metre wide constriction in the western arm of Cambridge Gulf, is formed by the Steere and Leake Hills. The tidal flow through the Gut is turbulent, spectacular and dangerous. It's not the place for anyone in a small boat.

THE GROTTO

Just south of where the old road joins the Great Northern Highway, 30 kms from Wyndham, the highway crosses *Grotto Creek*. The Grotto itself is a rock bound waterhole, said to be more than 122 metres (400') deep at its deepest point, complete with a staircase, 140 steps down, that takes you into the damp greenery that surrounds the cool waters. During the Wet water spills over the eleven metre sheer high rock face into the pool. It's a pleasant spot for a swim, but don't try it if the creek is raging.

Up the creek from the Grotto some Aboriginal art can be found, however the walk is difficult and the art site can be easily missed.

TREK NOTES *(Travel time 4 - 8 hrs)*

KARUNJIE KING RIVER ROAD
OLD WYNDHAM–KARUNJIE ROAD
Watch out for crocodiles! No Swimming.

0.0	***(0.0)***	***Gibb River Road*** *– track junction (TJ) on east side of Pentecost River – turn north on the Karunjie King River Road.* ***No camping.*** *GPS 15° 47′ 50″S 127° 52′ 57″E*
1.0	***(1.0)***	***Fence and gate beside boab tree*** *– proceed straight ahead (PSA). Please leave gate as you find it.* ***No camping or fires permitted.*** *There are numerous tracks in this area - stick to main track. Tracks on the left lead to the river.*
17.5	***(16.5)***	***Tk-junct -*** *VR to stay on main track. Left leads to El Questro River Lodge.*
19.5	***(2.0)***	***Yarrabar Cattle Yards. Please leave the gates as you find them.*** *Drive through slowly and do not disturb the cattle.*
24.5	***(5.0)***	***Tk-junct – VR.*** *The track is very rocky and slow.*
44.0	***(19.5)***	***Track junct – VL*** *to* ***Diggers Rest Station.*** *The RH track is the Old Karunjie Road. GPS 15° 37′ 46″S 128° 02′ 40″E.*
49.5	***(5.5)***	***Diggers Rest Station.*** *Accommodation, camping and tours available.*
52.8	***(3.3)***	***Y-junct - VL*** *onto* ***Karunjie Rd.***
56.5	***(3.7)***	***Y-junct - VL.***
56.8	***(0.3)***	***Prison Tree*** *on left.*
57.0	***(0.2)***	***King River*** *crossing.*
57.5	***(0.5)***	***Track on right - PSA.*** *RH tk leads to good* ***camp*** *site near where old pumping station once was. Road parallels river for next 4 km and tracks on left lead to possible* ***camp*** *sites.*
62.5	***(5.0)***	***Tk-junct – PSA.*** *RH track leads to Moochalabra Dam and* ***Aboriginal Art.***
80.5	***(18.0)***	***T-junct*** *with highway – TL onto the bitumen and towards Wyndham.*
86.5	***(6.0)***	***Wyndham.***

The Karunjie - King River Road is an excellent drive.

PARRY LAGOON NATURE RESERVE & MARLGU BILLABONG (4WD)

The 36,000ha Parry Lagoon NR and its wetlands are located about 15 km south-east of Wyndham and not only takes in Parry Lagoons, but also Marlgu Billabong, Police Hole and the extensive flood plains of the Ord River. The birdlife in the area is incredible.

A Changing Scene

Most of the area is inundated during the Wet season via a network of creeks and rivers. During these floods, overflow from the Ord River and Parry Creek introduce large numbers of juvenile barramundi, (and some larger adults to a lesser degree), mullet, riflefish and prawns. The abundant food supply and flooded savannah offer a major attraction to a multitude of water birds which flock to the area for breeding. Often at this time of year waterbirds can be counted in thousands and the spectacle of such concentrations is unmatched anywhere in the region.

As the Wet season subsides, the flood plain area divides into permanent pools, semi-permanent swamps and dry savannah grasslands. When this occurs, access into one of the permanent water courses, known as Marlgu Billabong (Aboriginal for wild bird), can be gained. A boardwalk and shaded bird hide allow visitors to enjoy some fabulous birdwatching.

An influx of ground nesting birds such as plovers, several species of quail, Kori Bustards (wild turkeys), bower birds and many others utilise the savannah for breeding.

Further into the year, as swamps dry out, many birds leave the area for other permanent swamps, lagoons and billabongs in the east Kimberley, only to make the return journey months later for breeding as the Wet season breaks. However, many birds remain permanently and are drawn to Marlgu Billabong by its constant water and food supply.

Transcontinental waders, often flying from as far afield as Siberia, land throughout the wetland system during the Dry. Some come to feed and regain energy to continue their annual migratory flights further south; others to nest and finally, later in the year, to return to their countries of origin with their offspring, having stored substantial amounts of body fat to be utilised as energy on the return flight.

The Parry Lagoons wetland system is recognised as an area of international significance and has been nominated as part of a migratory network of shorebird sites, aiming to establish and maintain appropriate managed sites along the East Asian-Australasian Flyway, which is a major pathway for migrating shorebirds.

Parry Lagoons is accessible to the public, but years of cattle encroachment and heavy vehicle traffic have taken their toll on vegetation. CALM have undertaken a development plan in recent years to manage access within the reserve, both to accommodate visitors and to provide the required protection of the fragile wetlands system to ensure that the area survives as a valuable ecosystem in the future. Vehicle access is restricted to certain planned roads and short walking trails will give easy access to points of interest.

Access and Facilities

Parry Lagoons Nature Reserve is easily accessible from the main highway just south of Wyndham. The main access road leads to **Telegraph Hill** and the ruins of the old wireless station, built in 1914 to assist ships entering Wyndham Port as well as being used for naval intelligence to intercept radio traffic during WWII. From this vantage point you can also get great views of the surrounding floodplain and distant hills. Dirt tracks give access to the centre of the reserve and such places as Marlgu Billabong, Parry Lagoons, Police Hole and the extensive flood plains of the Ord River. See the map, *Kununurra & Surrounding Areas*, in this chapter for access details.

A scenic lookout overlooks the Marlgu Billabong and the complete savannah system, with views to the Ord River and Bastion Ranges.

Bird hides have been erected as have information panels.

Camping is not permitted.

The spectacular wetlands of Marlgu Billabong.

TELEGRAPH HOLE

The Telegraph Hole is located 4.5 km south of *Naasra Creek* on the east side of the highway and is another waterhole that is a great swimming place.

MAGGIE CREEK

The *Maggie Creek* picnic and BBQ area is located on the Great Northern Highway, approximately 5 km north of 'The Grotto'.

OLD HALLS CREEK (WYNDHAM) ROAD (4WD)

This road, sometimes also called (Gold Rush road), was built around 1894 and is lined by stone kerbing laid down by prison convicts and makes up part of the old Halls Creek-Wyndham Road. These days the road, with its many stone creek crossings, gives access to some excellent fishing and picnic spots. *Palm Springs, Crocodile Hole* and *Muggs Lagoon* are three favourites. Accessible south of Parry Creek Farm, ending at the Great Northern Highway, 71 kms from Kununurra.

PARRY'S CREEK (KUNUNURRA) ROAD (4WD)

This road leads from Wyndham to Kununurra, following the Lower Ord River flats, passing through the Parry Lagoons Nature Reserve, past **Parrys Creek Farm & Tourist Resort** (accommodation/ **camping**) and pastoral country. There are five access points, freshwater fishing and picnic spots. The road continues on from the Reserve to Mambi Island (boat ramp), *Black Rock Falls/Pool, Middle Springs, Valentine Springs* and onto to Kununurra.

Middle Springs is a pleasant spot to stop.

MAMBI BOAT RAMP & PICNIC AREA (4WD)

Those wanting to launch a boat into the lower Ord River can access the river from this boat ramp on the Parry Creek Road and motor all the way down to the mouth of the Ord River, near Wyndham. You must have a permit however to access this area and the road may be closed during the 'Wet' season.

SPECIAL EVENTS & FESTIVALS

Barramundi Fishing Competitions are held April to October.

The months of July and August see a number of special events taking place in Wyndham. The **Wyndham Cup Horse Races** and **Race Ball** are held in August.

Contact the Wyndham Tourist Centre or the Wyndham-East Kimberley Shire for further details.

ACCOMMODATION, CAMPING & OTHER FACILITIES

ACCOMMODATION

Wyndham Town Hotel, O'Donnell St, Wyndham Port, ph: (08) 9161 1003.
Wyndham Community Club, 4 km East PO, Great Northern Highway, ph: (08) 9161 1130.
Gulf Breeze Guest House, 19 O'Donnell St, Wyndham Port, ph/fax: (08) 9161 1401.
Parry Creek Farm & Tourist Resort, Parry Creek Rd, Wyndham, ph/fax: (08) 9161 1139 or 0438 390 916. (Open from April to October.)

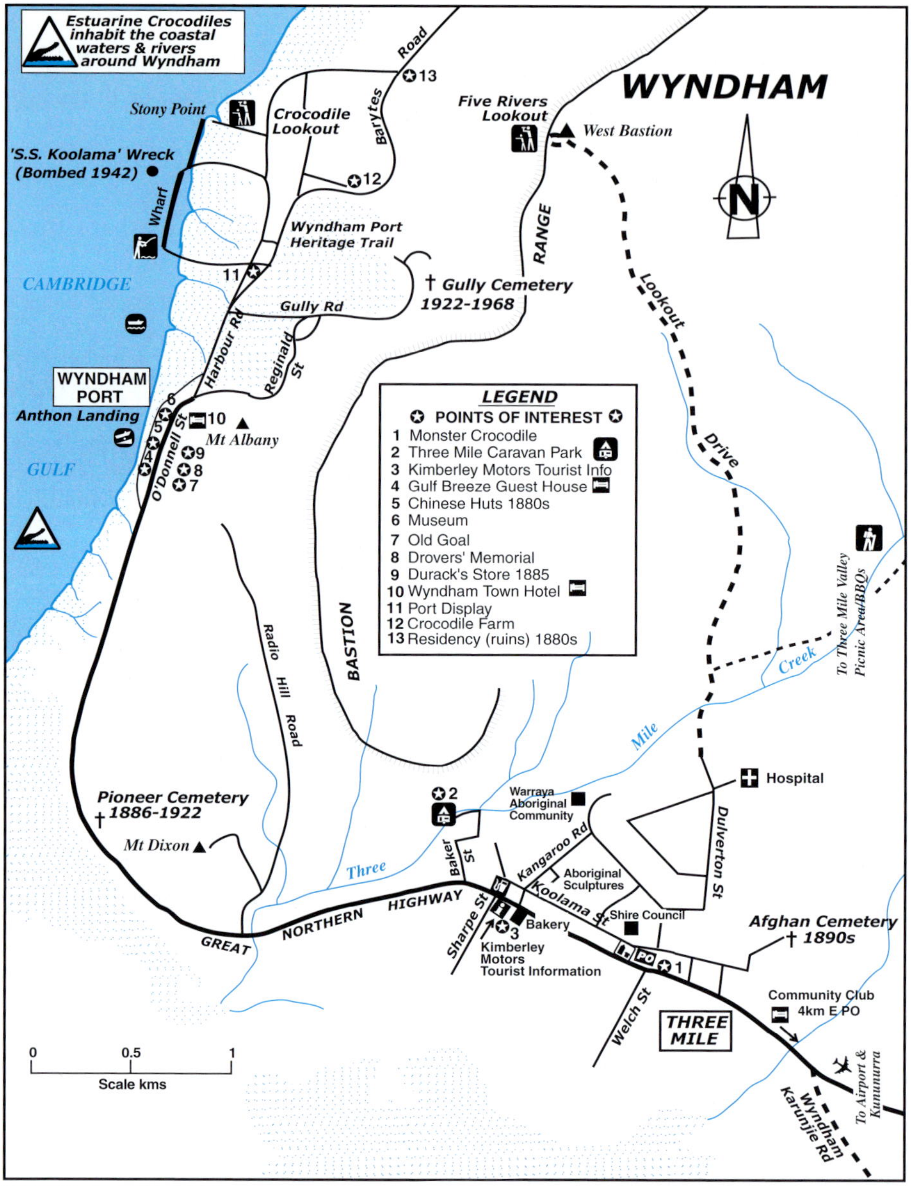

CARAVAN PARKS/CAMPING

Wyndham Caravan Park, Baker St, 3 Mile, ph: (08) 9161 1064. Disabled facilities, pool, BBQ, kiosk and pets allowed under supervision. Boat tours and scenic flights booked.

Parry Creek Farm & Tourist Resort, Parry Creek Rd, Wyndham, ph/fax: (08) 9161 1139 or 0438 390 916 – situated beside a lagoon, with shady camp sites or inhouse accommodation. Meals available during tourist season. Fishing and birdwatching. (Open from April to October.)

Diggers Rest Station, situated approx 37 km from Wyndham on the King River Road, PO Box 5, Wyndham, WA, 6740, ph/fax: (08) 9161 1029 – offers a range of accommodation and **camping** facilities. Hearty station meals available. While they have great horse trekking tours, there is also a wide range of activities the visitor can pursue such as fishing, bushwalking, birdwatching and photography. (See the following section on *Cruises & Tours*.) Web site: **www.diggers-rest.com**

Historic Pioneer Cemetery at Old Wyndham

FACILITIES

There is quite a wide range of facilities available, as detailed below. For anything else you may need you can always go back into Kununurra which is a very well serviced centre.

Hospital (and Dental Clinic), ph: (08) 9161 1104
Police, McPhee St, ph: (08) 9161 1055
Kununurra/Wyndham Dental Clinic, Kununurra, ph: (08) 9168 1529
Ambulance, ph: 000
Fire, ph: 000
Banks: *BankWest* (Agency in Shire Office)
GiroPost facilities in Post Office
Frontier News & **Post Office**, Koolinda Ave, ph: (08) 9161 1241.
Shire of Wyndham-East Kimberley, Koolama St, Wyndham, ph: (08) 9161 1002. Web: **www.thelastfrontier.com.au/**
Telecentre – 6 O'Donnell St, Wyndham Port, ph: (08) 9161 1166 - broadband internet access.
Supermarkets – open 7 days a week:
Tuckerbox, Great Northern H'way, ph: (08) 9161 1215
Wyndham Butcher & Supermarket, Koolinda Ave, ph: (08) 9161 1018 - 7 days.
Bakery Liquor Store
Fuel Suppliers/Service Stations:
Branko Motors, Great Northern Highway (turn-off to Caravan Park), ph: (08) 9161 1305 – **RACWA Agency** – *Emergency breakdown service* – Eftpos, fishing & camping equipment & tackle, boats & accessories, fuels, oils, mechanical repairs, tyres, etc, and licensed Firearms Dealer – open 7 days week.
Kimberley Motors, Great Northern Highway, ph: (08) 9161 1281, fax: (08) 9161 1435 – Mobil service station & Tourist Info Centre, repairs and service; tyres; batteries, parts & accessories; bait & tackle, etc.

WYNDHAM TOURIST INFORMATION

KIMBERLEY MOTORS

Great Northern Highway, 3 Mile,
Wyndham, WA, 6740.
Ph: (08) 9161 1281
Email: mail@thelastfrontier.com.au
Open 7 days.
Local free maps and tide charts as well as tour bookings. Tourist information and advice, plus current road details.

KIMBERLEY TOURIST ASSOCIATION
Web site:
www.kimberleytourism.com/wyndham.htm
This site can provide you with lots of information on Wyndham and the Kimberley.

ABC Regional Radio - Kununurra	
Kununurra	***819 AM***
Radio National	***107.7 FM***

CLUBS OF SPECIAL INTEREST

Wyndham Historical Society, PO Box 379, Wyndham, 6740, ph: (08) 9161 1002 or 9161 1351, fax: (08) 9161 1295.

CRUISES & TOURS

The following **local tour operators** are based at Wyndham –

AIR

Wyndham Aviation, Wyndham Airport Wyndham 6740, ph: (08) 9161 1335 – offers air charter and rental services out of Wyndham, as well as scenic flights from Wyndham and Kununurra.

FISHING

Diggers Rest Station, King River Road, Wyndham, 6740, ph/fax: (08) 9161 1029 - guided fishing with gear supplied. Web: **www.diggers-rest.com**

Look Sea Tours, Dulverton St, Wyndham, ph/fax: (08) 9161 1775 or 0408 646 264 – group trips exploring the Cambridge Gulf and surrounding Rivers. Fishing eco adventure local and coastal, as well as scenic, sunset, BBQs, crocs, crabs and more. Web: **www.lookseatours.com.au**

TOURS & 4WD SAFARIS

Ilpaya Tours, PO Box 413, Wyndham, WA 6740, ph/fax: (08) 9161 1990 or 0418 517 436, web: **www.waitoc.com/wunan/default.htm** – based at Diggers Rest Station, specialising in Aboriginal Heritage, cultural and scenic tours from Wyndham and Kununurra. Tours include Fiver Rivers Lookout; Sunset Tour; half day tours and 2 day scenic safari.

Diggers Rest Station, situated approx 37 km from Wyndham on the King River Road, PO Box 5, Wyndham, 6740, ph/fax: (08) 9161 1029 – offers 2 to 7 day horse trekking tours, as well as rides from the station, from one hour to three or four hours. Web site: **www.diggers-rest.com.**

(See our chapter, *Tour Operators, Lodges and the Like*, for details on other operators who cover the area for contact addresses, etc.)

Bullcatching on Diggers Rest Station is only for the hardy and the adventurous!

TRANSPORT: TO AND FROM

AIR *Wyndham Aviation*, Airport, ph: (08) 9161 1335 – aircraft charter & rental.

OOMBULGURRI (FORREST RIVER) ABORIGINAL COMMUNITY

HISTORY

Before European settlement, the traditional tribal groups in the area are believed to have been the Djeidji, Dulngari and Aruagga tribes.

In 1897, with the founding of Wyndham, there was an unsuccessfully attempt to establish a mission on the other side of the Cambridge Gulf at Forrest River. In 1910 the vast Marndoc Reserve was proclaimed by the WA government and an area set aside for a mission. The Reverend Ernest Gribble, acclaimed as the greatest missionary to work with the Aborigines, arrived in 1913 and by March 1914, over 200 people were living at the mission.

Fifty-five years later the mission was forced to close due to lack of funds, food and water and the Aborigines moved to the reserves just out of Wyndham.

In 1972 about thirty Aboriginal men, women and children returned to the mission site, renaming it *Oombulgurri* in reference to the nearby flooded plains.

VISITING THE AREA

Address all correspondence to:-

The Chairman, Oombulgurri Aboriginal Community, via Wyndham, WA 6740, ph: (08) 9161 4303, fax: (08) 9161 4314.

Only a rough track leads to Oombulgurri. *(See next section for more details.)* The more normal and faster way to reach the community is via boat from Wyndham.

OOMBULGURRI ROAD (4WD)

A permit is required from the Oombulgurri Aboriginal Community, ph: (08) 9161 4303, to travel to the Forest River Mission region. This trip is for experienced, adventurous, well equipped drivers. Two vehicles or more recommended. The road is very rough and crosses the Wilson, Durack and Forrest rivers.

KUNUNURRA

INTRODUCTION

Kununurra first came into existence to service the Ord Dam and its irrigation project and the townsite was gazetted in 1961. Originally the Aboriginal name of 'Cununurra', said to mean 'black soil' and to be the Aboriginal name for the Ord River was put forward, but later changed to Kununurra. Today it has a new lease of life with a new sugar mill, an imminent expansion of the irrigation area and the continuing wealth of diamonds from the Argyle Diamond Mine. Tourism, however, is making its mark in Kununurra which has become a popular stepping off place to explore the mysteries and wonders that can be found in this spectacular region.

ACCESS

Kununurra is linked by bitumen to Derby by the Great Northern Highway and to Darwin on Highway 1. Derby is 913 km to the south-west, while Darwin is 825 km to the north and Halls Creek 359 km south.

STOP

*The **Ord River Irrigation Area** is the only major fruit growing area in Western Australia which is free from damaging fruit flies.*

Travellers should note that from April 1 to November 30 it is illegal to bring citrus and stone fruit into the Area unless they have been sourced from an area free of Mediterranean fruit fly or carry appropriate treatment certification.

It is also preferred that no fruit (including capsicum, chillies, tomatoes, cucumber, zucchini, squash, pumpkins and melons) be brought into this area.

Travellers coming from the west are requested to please place fruit in the special quarantine bins provided. DO NOT place fruit in ordinary garbage bins as this will provide a perfect breeding place for fruit flies.

You can contact the Dept of Agriculture, Kununurra District Office, Durack Drive, ph: (08) 9166 4000, for more details.

THINGS TO SEE AND DO

You can easily enjoy a few days exploring around Kununurra and for your effort you'll find some excellent spots, some of which are detailed below. Other places to explore include the Lily Creek Lagoon, the walking trail developed by the Kununurra Historical Society and the Zebra rock deposits.

IVANHOE CROSSING (2WD)

A popular fishing spot 13 km from Kununurra along the Ivanhoe Road and part of the original road to Wyndham. Don't try swimming here though as the volume of water flowing over the crossing makes it extremely dangerous, along with the Salt-Water Crocodiles. The crossing itself is closed to vehicular traffic during the 'Wet' when the water level is high. It's a very popular fishing spot for barramundi and a good place for a picnic.

Ivanhoe Crossing is a popular fishing spot but be careful .

LAKE KUNUNURRA AND THE 'EVERGLADES'

Lake Kununurra is readily accessible

Lake Kununurra, 7 km from Kununurra, lies behind the Kununurra Diversion Dam, and has a swimming beach upstream from the dam wall. The maze of channels, waterways and large interconnecting ponds found behind the dam have created an everglades type environment which offer some fabulous exploring by boat or canoe. The area is a rich haven for a huge variety of birds. (See our chapter, *Canoeing and Boating* for more details.).

KELLY'S KNOB (2WD)

Located 2.4 km from town, along Speargrass Road, Kelly's Knob offers a scenic lookout over Kununurra and the Ord Valley.

FRANK WISE INSTITUTE

Initially established by the CSIRO in 1945 as the Kimberley Research Station, the site is now called the Frank Wise Institute, run by Agriculture WA, and continues its role with its involvement in experimentation with crops and pest control. Unfortunately, no conducted tours are available, however the Institute is open to visitors Mon to Fri (April to November). Contact: ph: (08) 9166 4000.

ORD RIVER IRRIGATION AREA (2WD)

The irrigation area lies to the north and south of Kununurra and the dominant crops are sugar cane, melons, mangoes, pumpkins and bananas. Do the 42 km round trip by road via Ivanhoe Road and Weaber Plain Road, or by taking the Packsaddle Road, left after the Diversion Dam. You can either do it yourself or go on one of the local tours organised through the Visitors Centre. Along the Weaber Plains Road you'll pass the City of Ruins, natural sandstone formations that resemble an ancient city.

LIONS PARK PICNIC AREA

Drive across the Diversion Dam and turn right after Packsaddle Road into the road behind the Information Bay. This is a good spot to take photos of the dam, have a picnic, or launch your boat. Swimming is not allowed as Salt-water crocodiles inhabit the river here.

EXPLORING THE ORD RIVER

Canoeing has to be the best way to explore the delights of the *Ord River* above the diversion dam. Apart from the everglades, you can try the nearby river, or for those more adventurous put in a canoe below the dam wall at Lake Argyle and paddle down river for a day or two.

If you haven't got your own canoe you can join *Go Wild Adventure Tours* on one of their Eco-noeing trips from 1 to 3 days. Phone 1300 66 33 69, or check out their web site: **www.gowild.com.au**.

Big Waters Kimberley Canoe Safaris, based in Kununurra, ph: (08) 9169 1998, also offers a 3 day self-guided canoeing safari on the Ord river with all the gear you need supplied. Check out their web site at: **www.adventure.kimberley.net.au**

(See *Canoeing* on page 117 for more details, and the chapter, *Canoeing and Boating* for more details.)

VALENTINE SPRINGS (2WD)

This series of rock pools, situated on Valentine Creek, is a delightful swimming spot and a popular picnic area. The pools are at their finest during the Wet, and can be found about 18 km from Kununurra along the Parry's Creek Road, just a short distance off the main road to your left.

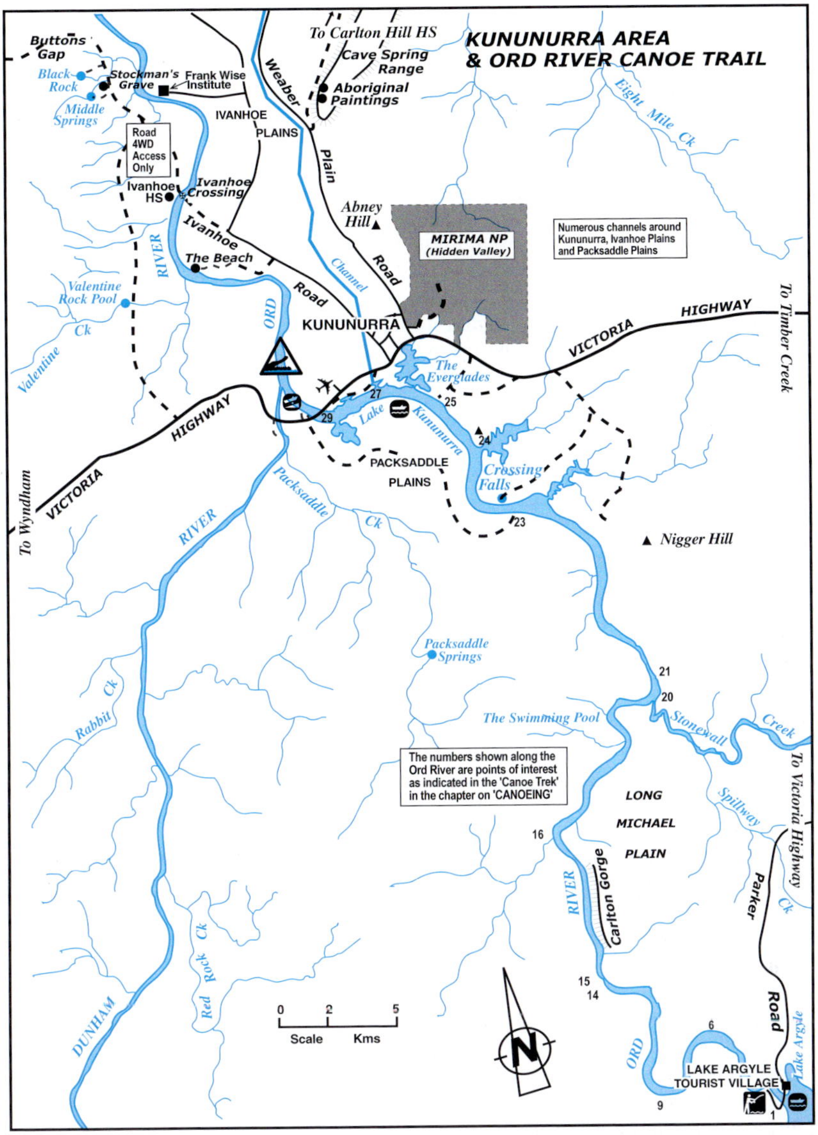

MIDDLE SPRINGS (4WD)

These springs are only reached by four wheel drive, 30 km from Kununurra on the Parry's Creek Road. During the Wet, a series of small pools are formed which offer some good swimming, however some climbing is required to reach them.

BLACK ROCK FALLS (4WD)

These falls are only accessible by four wheel drive and can be found on the Parry's Creek Road 32 km from Kununurra. During the Wet, water cascades over a 30 metre, semi-circular, rock cliff into a small pool area. The falls get their name from the colour of the rock cliffs which, over the years, have been stained black by the minerals in the water.

Black Rock Falls in the 'Dry' season still has a little water.

STOCKMAN'S GRAVE (4WD)

A tin plate cross marks the grave of pioneer stockman, David Suttie, who is featured in Jeannie Gunn's famous book, *We of the Never Never*. The grave is found on the Parry Creek Rd (the old Wyndham Road) (4WD access only), not far from Black Rock Falls.

ABORIGINAL CAVE PAINTINGS

Just 14 km north of town along Weaber Plain Road, (heading towards the Frank Wise Institute) and just past the Co-op on the opposite side of the road, you'll find some aboriginal cave paintings amongst the ancient rock formations. Remember that they protected and irreplaceable. Another site, at the south end of Carlton Ridge, can be visited by joining one of the boat tours along Lake Kununurra.

POINT SPRING NATURE RESERVE

This is a small reserve located 50 km north of Kununurra along the Weaber Plain (or Legune) Road. The Reserve surrounds a patch of rainforest at the base of the Weaber Range escarpment and contains a lagoon fed by natural springs.

It is one of the few areas that is relatively easily accessible where typical remnant Kimberley rainforest can be seen and enjoyed. Along with the plants and idyllic setting, you may see some birds that only live in these remnant forest areas.

There are no facilities and no camping allowed.

EAST KIMBERLEY ABORIGINAL COMMUNITY

There are about 2500 Aborigines in the East Kimberley Shire, with about 800 living in the Kununurra area, 1000 in the Wyndham region and the rest spread among small communities from Kalumburu in the north to Bow River in the south.

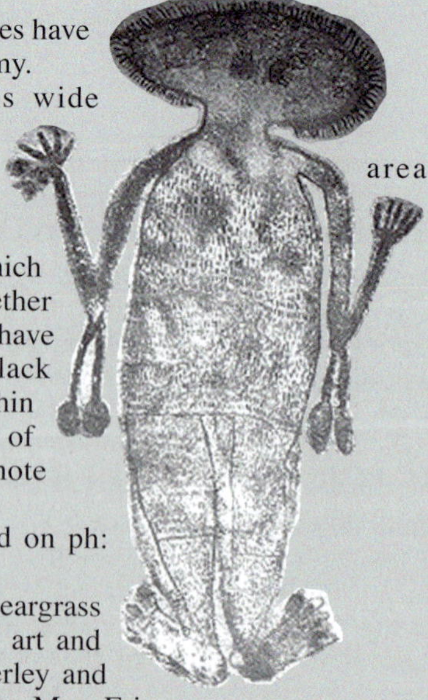

Although their numbers are relatively small, the Aborigines have contributed much to the region's history, culture and economy.

The cultural diversity within this small group is wide ranging and unique to the area. There are a number of different language groups within the East Kimberley area, including Mirriwung, Murin-patha, Malnigin, Gadjerong and Gidga.

Situated in Speargrass Road, Kununurra, Waringarri, which in the Mirriwung language means "Big mob coming together to resolve dispute", and its sister association, Balangarri, have done much to foster relations between the white and black communities, as well as encouraging self-determination within the Shire's Aboriginal population. It also provides a range of financial, technical and development services to the remote communities.

Waringarri Aboriginal Corporation can be contacted on ph: (08) 9168 1528, fax: (08) 9168 2081.

The ***Waringarri Aboriginal Arts Gallery***, situated in Speargrass Road (opposite Kelly's Knob) offers authentic, Aboriginal art and artifacts produced by Aboriginal artists of the East Kimberley and is well worth a visit. Gallery Hours are 8.30am - 4.00pm Mon-Fri, weekends by appointment, ph: (08) 9168 2212. You can also check out their web site at: **www.waringarriarts.com.au/**.

MIRIMA (HIDDEN VALLEY) NATIONAL PARK (2WD)

Just on the outskirts of Kununurra, approximately 3 km from the centre of town is Mirima National Park which covers an area of 2068 hectares.

Called by Europeans, Hidden Valley, Mirima is the name given by the Miriuwung people who inhabited the area for thousands of years. These people left an ancient heritage amongst the craggy cliffs and caves of this place. Rock paintings, engravings and other artifacts can be found. Remember these are all protected and please don't touch any of the paintings.

The Natural Wonders

Gradual erosion of the quartz sandstone cliffs by the waters of Lily Creek and its tributaries has created a large number of cul-de-sacs, amphitheatres and twisting valleys. The rock is some 300 million years old and its sedimentary nature can be seen in the layers or strata in which it has been laid down.

Much of the area is similar to the fabulous Purnululu National Park further south and the park is definitely worth at least a day visit.

Several species of eucalyptus dominate the area and these include the aptly named woollybutt which grows close to the cliff bases, and the long fruited bloodwood which grows in the moister areas of the main valleys within the park. Dotted over the area, often in seemingly inaccessible places, are the twisted shapes of Boab trees.

Frogs, tortoises, geckos, goannas, snakes and other reptiles can sometimes be seen, while the observant may encounter the Agile Wallaby or the Short-eared Rock-wallaby, fruit and insectivorous bats, dingoes or a Short-beaked Echidna.

Birds of many types abound in the area such as the Black Kite, the seed-eating finches, quails, pigeons, including the White-quilled Rock-Pigeon, and many more. A comprehensive bird list is available and further information on the fauna can be obtained from the ranger at Kununurra.

Walking Trails

Walking is the best way to see the attractions and there are three signposted walks, as detailed below, which show the best of the park.

Walk 1
Wuttuwutubin Trail (meaning short and narrow in the Miriuwung dialect) – a 500 metre return walk within a steep-sided gorge offering a view through to Kununurra.

Walk 2
Didbagirring Trail (lookout) – a more difficult walk of one kilometre up steep slopes with some loose rock, but the adventurous walker is rewarded with views of the area and the Purnululu (Bungle Bungle) like rock formations of Hidden Valley.

A rock formations found in Mirima National Park, an area similar to the well known Bungle Bungles.

CAUTION – much of the rock in Hidden Valley is brittle and crumbly. Do not stand on or walk close to cliff edges. Stay on marked tracks or, if venturing further, ensure that someone knows your proposed route and time of return.

If walking – go prepared. Wear a hat and sunscreen and wear sturdy shoes or boots. Take drinking water with you.

There is no camping permitted.

A **Day Pass** covers entry into the park, and is available from the Kununurra Ranger based at Mirima on ph: (08) 9168 4200, or the NP Ranger at Kununurra HQs, Messmate Way, PO Box 942, Kununurra, WA, 6743, ph: (08) 9168 4200, web site: **www.calm.wa.gov.au/**.

SPECIAL EVENTS & FESTIVALS

These are just some of the major events held during the year. For more details and timings, contact the Shire of Wyndham East Kimberley.

March: **Dam to Dam Dinghy Race**

May: **Argyle Diamonds Ord Valley Muster** – events exhibit the area's unique heritage, culture, industry and environment, including art, sport, youth, land and water. Contact the Kununurra Chamber of Commerce & Industry, ph: (08) 9168 2217, email: muster@ordvalleycommerce.com, web: **www.ordvalleycommerce.com**

May: **Kimberley Moon Experience**– set on the banks of the Ord River, this is the grand finale of the Ord Valley Muster, blending local talent and enthusiasm with first-class entertainment.
Rodeo

June: **Ord River Dragon Boat Marathon**.

July: **Agricultural Show** – sets Kununurra abuzz and is an interesting place for travellers to drop in and have a look around.

July/Aug: **Mardi Gra - Ord Festival**.

August: **Kununurra Rodeo**
Kununurra Races

September: **Kununurra Race Cup Day**
Kununurra Night Rodeo

NOOGOORA BURR QUARANTINE AREA

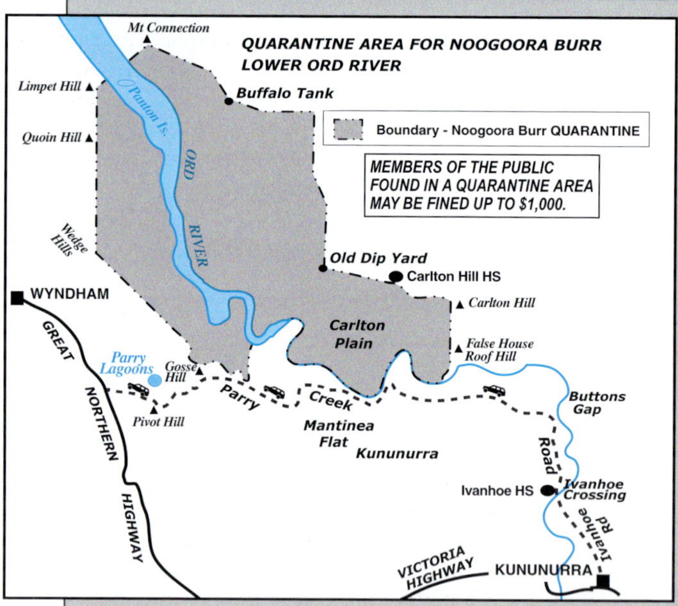

Part of the lower *Ord River* is infested with Noogoora Burr (Xanthium occidentale), which is one of the most destructive and widespread weeds in the world. To stop the spread of this weed in the Kimberley, all pastoral leases from Fitzroy Crossing to the River Mouth are quarantined.

To assist in controlling the spread of this weed please:

- Only go to public access areas. Signs showing where you can go are at main road parking bays and river access tracks.
- Pull out any Noogoora burr plants you find. Burn plants in your campfire if they have burrs on them.
- Check your clothes, camping equipment, pets and throw-nets for burrs before leaving the river. Remove and burn any burrs you find.

The accompanying map details the quarantine area where access requires a permit from the Dept of Agriculture. The Parry Creek Road however no longer requires a permit, and there are five access points along the Road . For any further information contact the:
Dept of Agriculture, Kununurra Office, Durack Dve, PO Box 19, ph: (08) 9166 4000, or check out their web site: **www.agric.wa.gov.au**

ACCOMMODATION, CAMPING & OTHER FACILITIES

ACCOMMODATION:

There is a wide variety of accommodation available in Kununurra, as listed below –

Big Boab Budget International, River Fig Ave, Kununurra WA 6743, ph: (08) 9168 1411.

Country Club Hotel, Coolibah Dve, ph: (08) 9168 1024, web: **www.countryclubhotel.com.au/**

Duncan House B&B, Coolibah Drive, ph: (08) 9168 2436.

Hotel Kununurra, Messmate Way, ph: (08) 9168 0400, web: **www.hotelkununurra.com.au/**

Kimberley Croc Backpackers YHA, Konkerberry Dve, ph: (08) 9168 2702 or 1300 136 702, web: **www.kimberleycroc.com.au/.**

Kununurra Backpackers, Nutwood Cres, ph: (08) 9169 1998 or 1800 641 998, web: **www.adventure.kimberley.net.au/**

Lakeside Resort, Casuarina Way, Lakeside, ph: (08) 9169 1092, web: **www.lakeside.com.au**/

Lakeview Apartments, Victoria Highway, Kununurra, ph: (08) 9168 000, web: **www.lakeviewapartments.net/**

All Seasons Kununurra, Cnr Messmate Way & Victoria Highway, ph: (08) 9168 1455.

ACCOMMODATION FURTHER AFIELD

Bush Camp Faraway Bay, is located 280 km NW of Kununurra on the Diamond Coast, on the edge of the Timor Sea. This resort is exclusive. Restricted air access makes this coastal bush hideaway the ideal getaway place for a relaxing wilderness experience. Accommodates 12 guests only in secluded cabins perched on a tiny headland. All meals, activities and use of facilities are included in the tariff. Activities include sportfishing, bushwalks, photography, exploring, freshwater plunge pool, flora & fauna watching. Contact: Faraway Bay, The Kimberley, PO Box 901, Kununurra, WA 6743, ph: (08) 9169 1214, email: farawaybay@bigpond.com, web site: **www.farawaybay.com.au/**

Bungle Bungle Wilderness Camp is located on Bellburn Creek within the Purnululu National Park. Permanent safari camp operated by *Kimberley Wilderness Adventures* offers travellers overnight tented cabin accommodation with all facilities and camp host. With a Safari Pass, travellers can utilise the camp on their self drive holiday for one or even two nights. Ph: 1800 675 222, (03) 9277 8444, web: **www.kimberleywilderness.com.au/**

CARAVAN PARKS - ACCOMMODATION & CAMPING

The following caravan parks not only offer the normal park facilities, but also a range of accommodation –

Hidden Valley Caravan Park, Weaber Plain Road, ph: (08) 9168 1790 (adjoining Mirima (Hidden Valley) National Park) – pool, BBQs – dogs allowed by arrangement for one week only. Partial access for wheelchairs. Accommodation: cabins. Web: **www.caravan-wa.com.au/hvtp.html**

Ivanhoe Village Caravan Resort, Ivanhoe Rd, ph: (08) 9169 1995 – BBQs, kiosk – no pets allowed. Accommodation: Cabins and on-site vans. Web: **http://ivanhoevillageresort.com**

Kimberleyland Holiday Park, Victoria Highway, ph: (08) 9168 1280 – shady grassed sites, BBQs, kitchen, pool, kiosk, launching ramp, canoeing, canoe hire – no pets allowed. Wheelchair access. Accommodation: cabins. Web: **www.kimberleyland.com.au**

Kona Lakeside Tourist Park, Lakeview Dve, ph: (08) 9168 1031 – BBQs, camp kitchen, kiosk, pool – no pets allowed. Canoe & bike hire. Wheelchair access. Accommodation: Bungalows, park homes, SC cabins and on-site vans. Web: **www.konalakeside.com.au**

Kununurra Lakeside Resort, Casuarina Way, Lakeside, ph: (08) 9169 1092 – shady trees catering for campers and campervans with limited caravan sites. Along with all the normal facilities there is also a private wharf to lake, canoe hire. Dogs allowed. Accommodation: motel rooms, cabins or self-catering studios. Web: **www.lakeside.com.au**

Town Caravan Park, Cnr Konkerberry & Bloodwood Dvs, ph: (08) 9168 1763 – BBQs, kitchen, shade, pool – no dogs allowed. Wheelchair access. Accommodation: SC villas & studio. Web: **www.townpark.com.au/**

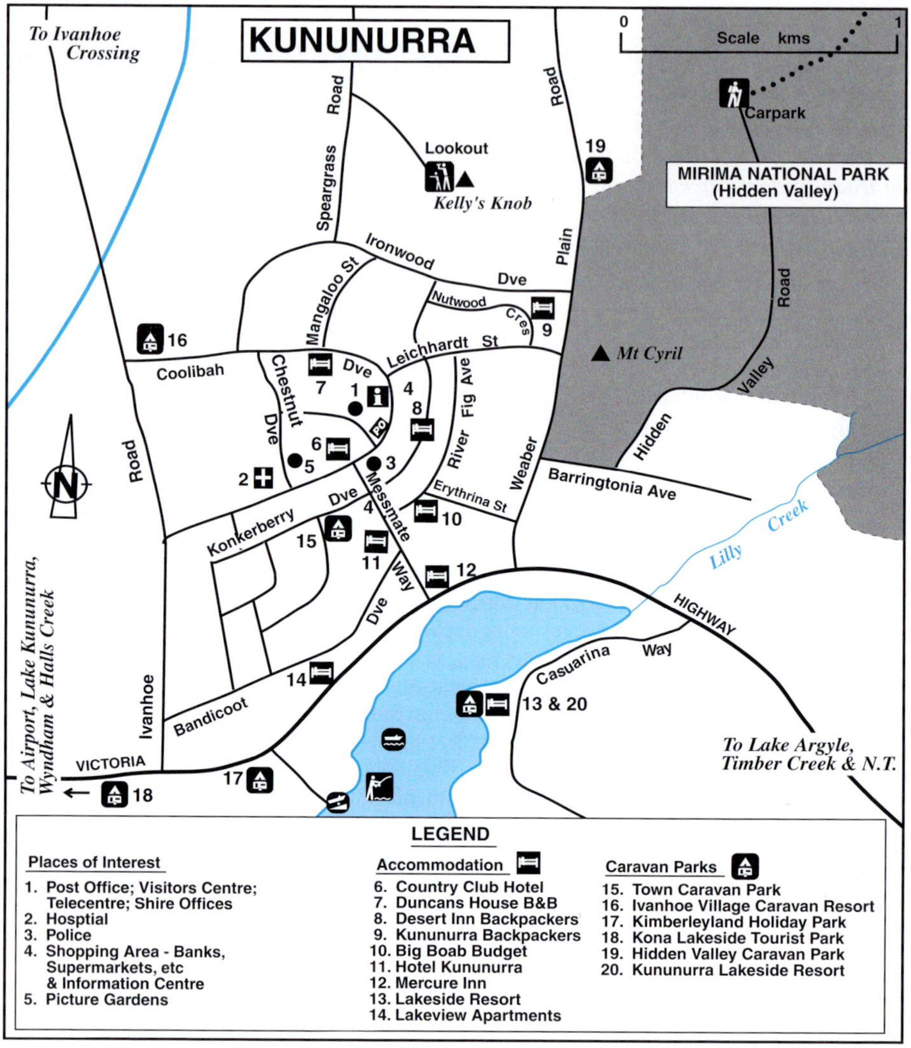

FACILITIES

Kununurra is a major town in the Kimberley and as such is well serviced. A brief outline of facilities available is detailed below –

Hospital, ph: (08) 9166 4222
Police, Coolibah Dve, ph: (08) 9166 4530
Ambulance, ph: 000 / (08) 9168 1522
Fire, ph: 000
Kununurra/Wyndham Dental Clinic, Lot 2429 Coolibah Drv, ph: (08) 9168 1529
Kimberley Vet Clinic, Cnr Leichhardt St & Riverfig Ave, ph: (08) 9169 1229
Post Office, Coolibah Dve, ph: (08) 9168 1072
Shire of Wyndham-East Kimberley, Coolibah Drive, Kununurra, ph: (08) 9168 1677, web site:
www.eastkimberley.com.au/
Banks –
BankWest - Coles Complex
Commonwealth Bank - cnr Cotton Tree Ave & Coolibah Drive

KUNUNURRA TOURIST INFORMATION

KUNUNURRA VISITORS CENTRE

Coolibah Drive, Kununurra
Ph: (08) 9168 1177
Fax: (08) 9168 2598
Email: kununurratb@bigpond.com
Web: **www.eastkimberley.com.au/**
Open 7 days. Booking and information agent for local operators and can organise scenic flights, cruises, 4WD safaris, accommodation and coach bookings. They can also design an itinerary to suit you and are up to date with the latest tourism activities available.

GiroPost facilities - Post Office
National Australia Bank - Ebony St
Westpac Bank - Kununurra Visitor Centre

Kununurra Telecentre, Coolibah Drive, ph: (08): 91691868 - internet access

ABC Regional Radio - Kununurra	
Kununurra	**819 AM**
Radio National	**107.7 FM**
Aboriginal Radio:	
Waringarri Radio	**693 AM**

Supermarkets –open 7 days a week:
Coles Supermarket, Kununurra Shopping Centre, Konkerberry Drive
Frontier Fresh, Gateway Shopping Centre, Messmate Way
Tuckerbox Stores, 191 White Gum St

Service Stations & Fuel Supplies:
D.D.K's BP Kununurra Service Centre, 1275 Bandicoot Drv, ph: (08) 9169 1799
Oliver & Co (Mobil), 518 Bandicoot Dve – mechanical repairs, parts, etc, ph: (08) 9169 1433
Ord River Roadhouse, 5 Messmate St, ph: (08) 9169 1188
Shell, 227 Messmate Way, ph: (08) 9168 1188
Shell Kununurra Road House (Coles Express), Lot 2259 Ivanhoe Rd, ph: (08) 9168 3177

4WD Repairers:
***RACWA** Kununurra ph: (08) 9169 1556*
Elgee Toyota, 231 Bloodwood Dve, ph: (08) 9168 2236
East Kimberley Towing, 1528 Poincettia Way, ph: (08) 9168 1816 - *24 hour breakdown service.*
Kununurra 4WD Spares, Lot 1492b Bloodwood Drv, ph: (08) 9169 1150
Kimberley Exhaust & Spring Centre, Mango St, ph: (08) 9169 1462 - 24 hour towing, RAC breakdown throughout the Kimberley region.
Kununurra Diesel Services, Lot 219 Bloodwood Drv, ph: (08) 9169 1054
Top End Motors & Marine, Bloodwood Dve, ph: (08) 9168 2207.

CLUBS OF SPECIAL INTEREST

Historical Society – Kununurra, Coolibah Dve, Kununurra, 6743, ph: (08) 9169 3337.

Historical Society Museum

The Historical Society Museum is situated in Coolibah Dve, and is a great place to learn more about the areas's beginnings and history, with accompanying displays of artefacts and photos. You can also pick up a booklet which describes the historical walking trail the Society has developed, as well as pointing out the best bird viewing locations in the area.

CRUISES & TOURS

There are a large number of operators running local tours from Kununurra and they offer a wide variety of tours to choose from. See our chapter, *Tour Operators Lodges and the Like,* for a complete listing of all operators.

Local Day Tours from Kununurra

Air Tours

Alligator Airways, Hangar No. 5 Kununurra Airport, PO Box 10, Kununurra, 6743, ph: (08) 9168 1333, 1800 632 533 – the oldest Kununurra based scenic and air charter service, offering a range of daily scenic tours from 2 to daily or extended tours, or try a float plane on a fishing safari or scenic flight. Web: **www.alligatorairways.com.au/index.asp.**

Golden Eagle Airways, Kununurra Airport, ph: (08) 9168 3103 – charter flights and twice a week flies the Mail Plane run north and south of Kununurra to cattle stations & Aboriginal communities. Web: **www.goldeneagleairlines.com/kimberley.html**

Northwest Regional Airlines, ph: 1300 136 629 – scenic flight tours include Bungle Bungle & Faraway Bay, as well as a 1 day tour Bungle Bungle / Emma Gorge. Web: **www.northwestregional.com.au/**

Slingair Heliwork WA, 319 Laine Jones Drive, Kununurra, ph: 1800 095 500 or ph: (08) 9169 1300 – offer a wide range of plane and heli flights to destinations such as Argyle Diamond Mine, Bungle Bungle, Kununurra and surrounds, Kununurra cruise combinations, indigenous art and cultural tours and extended safaris and Mitchell Plateau Heli flights. Web: **www.slingair.com.au/**.

4WD/2WD Coach Tours from Kununurra

2K Tours Kununurra Kimberley, ph: (08) 9168 1314, 0427 633 455 - 3 to 8 hour bus tour of Kununurra and surrounds. Web: **www.2ktours.com.au/**

East Kimberley Tours (see 4WD Safaris)

Kimberley Wilderness Adventures (see 4WD Safaris)

Triangle Tours & Charters, PO Box 1337, ph: (08) 9168 1272 – Choose from a selection of 10 tours from 2 hours to 2 days. Tours utilise a combination of Coach, Boat, Helicopter and fixed wing Aircraft. Special interest tour for farming groups - Tropical Irrigated Farming Technology.

River Cruises from Kununurra

Jabiru-Ord River Cruises, Packsaddle Plains Rd, Kununurra, ph: (08) 9168 3993 – boat charter service.

Kimberley Eco Houseboats, PO Box 812, ph: 0408 681 279 – cruise the upper Ord River in luxury on a houseboat. Daily or extended overnight hire.

Kununurra Cruises 'The BBQ Boat', 22 Dryandra Rd, ph: (08) 9168 1718, 0409 681 718 – sunset BBQ dinner cruise. Also available for private charter. Web: **www.thebbqboat.com.au/**

Lake Argyle Cruises, PO Box 710, ph: (08) 9168 7687 – morning, sunset or half day cruises on Lake Argyle incorporating bird and wildlife watching. Specialised tours and charters available. Web: **http://lakeargylecruises.com/**

Lower Ord Cruises, PO Box 407, ph: (08) 9168 2144 – boat, flight & bus combination tours. Riverside camp on the Lower Ord River.

Triple J Tours, ph: (08) 9168 2682 – cruises on the Ord River between Kununurra and the Ord River Dam. Combinations of boat and coach available. Web: **www.triplejtours.net.au/**

Fishing Trips from Kununurra

Alligator Airways (see Air Tours).

Kimberley Fishing, PO Box 2024, Broome, 6725, ph: (08) 9193 5689 – One Tree Beach fishing camp on the eastern side of Admiralty Gulf, accessible only by boat, float plane or helicopter. Web: **www.kimberleyfishing.com.**

Kimberley Sportfishing, PO Box 471, ph: (08) 9169 2752 – fishing charters, boats & guides.

Mackas Barra Camp, PO Box 1385, ph: (08) 9169 1759 – day or overnight boat fishing tours on the lower Ord River. Bungalow style accommodation. Overnight & extended tours to remote locations for coastal fishing.Web: **www.mackasbarra.com.au/**

Ultimate Adventures – Barra Fishing & Sportfishing Safaris, Parrys Creek Rd, ph: (08) 9168 2310 – day or overnight small boat barramundi fishing on the lower Ord River with croc spotting. Stay overnight in permanent bush style camp. Also offers remote location coastal sport fishing. Web: **http://members.westnet.com.au/web/ultimateadvent/welcome.htm**

Float planes can take you to out-of-the-way fishing spots.

The fishing on the Ord River can be good.
Canoeing around the 'Everglades' on Lake Kununurra is a great experience.

Canoeing, Rock Climbing & Abseil Tours from Kununurra

Big Waters Kimberley Canoe Safaris, based in Kununurra, ph: (08) 9169 1998 – Three day self-guided canoeing safari on the Ord river with permanent camp sites for overnight stops. Camping kits, barrels, maps and transfers supplied. BYO food. Web site: **www.adventure.kimberley.net.au**

Go Wild Adventure Tours, PO Box 487, Kununurra, ph: 1300 66 33 69 – offer a great range of outdoor activities and real adventure tours, challenging and inspiring. Try one of their Eco-noeing trips from 1 to 3 days on the Ord river with permanent camp sites for overnight stops. A boat pick up is available and a guide can take you bushwalking to explore more of the area. You can also hire canoes from them.

If caving or abseiling is more to your liking, there is a range of adventures to choose from. Check out their web site for all the details on all their activities: **www.gowild.com.au**.

Aboriginal Art and Eco Tours

The Kimberley Specialists runs a range of eco tours and Aboriginal art discovery tours from Kununurra. These include trips to Kachana Station south-west of Kununurra (see, *South Towards Halls Creek,* later in this chapter) and to places further afield where Wandjina and Bradshaw art are at their finest.

For more details on the tours available and Kachana Station contact, The Kimberley Specialists, ph: (08) 9168 2576 or check the web at: **www.kimberleyspecialists.com.au**.

Extended Tours from Kununurra

See our chapter, *Tour Operators Lodges and the Like,* for a complete listing of operators.

Air Safaris

Alligator Airways (see Air Tours)
*Golden Eagle Airways (s*ee Air Tours)
Norwest Regional Airlines (see Air Tours)
Slingair Heliwork WA, (see Air Tours)

4WD Safaris

Bungle Bungle Adventures, (Kununurra Backpackers Adventure Centre), Nutwood Cres, ph: 1800 641 998 – 4WD camping tours to the Bungle Bungles (2 & 3 days). Web: **www.adventure.kimberley.net.au**.

East Kimberley Tours, PO Box 537, ph: (08) 9168 2213 – Fly/drive & 4WD tours to the Bungle Bungles & Mitchell Plateau from Kununurra and Turkey Creek. One day or extended. Permanent camps with cabins in the Bungle Bungles. Charters on the Gibb River Road. Web: **www.eastkimberleytours.com.**

Halls Creek & Bungle Bungle Tours, PO Box 2615, Broome, 6725, ph: (08) 9193 7267 – variety of 4WD tours accommodated, camping, fly/drive. 7 day Kimberley Connection Tour ex Kununurra. Web: **www.bunglebungle.com.au.**

Kimberley Adventure Tours, PO Box 629, Derby 6728, ph: (08) 9191 2655 – 4WD & charter tours into the Kimberley. Darwin to Broome 9 day adventure. Web: **www.kimberleyadventures.com.au/**

Kimberley Wilderness Adventures, 475 Hampton St, Hampton, Vic 3188, ph: (03) 9277 8444 – permanent safari camps & accommodated safaris departing Kununurra, Broome & Darwin. 4WD and/or fly to the Bungle Bungles, Gibb River Road & the Mitchell Plateau (one day and extended tours). They also have a unique 6 day Bush University tour, ex Kununurra. Web: **www.kimberleywilderness.com.au/.**

Wilderness 4WD Adventures, PO Box 2071, Palmerston NT, 0831, ph: (08) 8941 2161 – 9 day Kimberley Challenge tour Darwin/Broome. Web: **www.wildernessadventures.com.au.**

Boat, & Fishing Safaris (see *Fishing Trips from Kununurra*)

Alligator Airways
Kimberley Fishing
Ultimate Adventures

TRANSPORT: To and From

For more information on tour operators, contact the Kununurra Visitors Centre.

Air

Airnorth, ph: 1800 627 474 (reservations) or (08) 9820 4000 – has regular scheduled services throughout the North-West and flies Darwin – Kununurra – Broome and return. Web site: **www.airnorth.com.au/**

Freight:

There are a number of general freight companies that operate from Kununurra, such as **Centurion Transport,** 97 Poinciana St, Kununurra, ph: 0408 097 230

Coach:

Greyhound sets down in Kununurra, connecting from Darwin and Broome. Bookings can be made through the Kununurra Visitors Centre, ph: (08) 9168 1177, or you can contact Greyhound direct on ph: 13 14 99. Bookings can also be made on their web site, where you can also check current timetables: **www.greyhound.com.au**.

Hire Boats

Top End Marine, Konkerberry Dve, Kununurra, ph: (08) 9168 2777.

Hire 4WD

There are a number of car hire companies based in Kununurra who have a range of 4WDs available for hire, and you may even be able to hire camping gear as well –

Avis Kimberley, Terminal Building Kununurra Airport, ph: (08) 9169 1258, web: **www.avis.com.**

Budget Rent A Car, Terminal Building Kununurra Airport, ph: (08) 9168 2033, web: **www.budget.com.au**

Europcar, 30 Poincettia Way, Kununurra WA 6743, ph/fax: (08) 9168 3385, web: **www.deltaeuropcar.com.au**

Hertz, 6 Coolibah Drv, ph: (08) 9169 1424, web: **www.hertz.com.au**.

LAKE ARGYLE

INTRODUCTION

Lake Argyle was formed by the damming of the Ord River which was completed in 1972 and covers an area of approximately 2000 sq km – the largest man-made lake in Australia. It offers great swimming, fishing, boating and exploring of the many inlets, bays and islands that form this huge expanse of waterway.

Spillway Lookout and the view of Lake Argyle that covers a vast amount of area - more an inland sea than a lake!

ACCESS

Lake Argyle is reached by travelling east 36 km from Kununurra on the Duncan Road (towards Darwin) and then turning right onto the Parker Road for another 34 km. The road passes the Lake Argyle Tourist Village just before crossing the Ord Dam. At this point the road continues for a very short distance down to a picnic area adjacent to the dam wall.

THINGS TO SEE AND DO

Some of the main places of interest to be found include the following:

Argyle Homestead (Museum)

Built in 1894 by the great pioneer Patsy Durack, the home was moved in its entirety to its present position to save it from the rising waters of Lake Argyle. The homestead is now a museum and gives you an insight into those early pioneer days. Nearby is a short bushwalk, one the whole family will enjoy. The museum is open daily, on Parker Rd, via the Lake Argyle Road, ph: (08) 9167 8088.

Argyle Homestead is an excellent museum that details the life of the Durack family

Spillway Lookout

From this vantage point you get a good look at the spillway which was cut through solid rock.

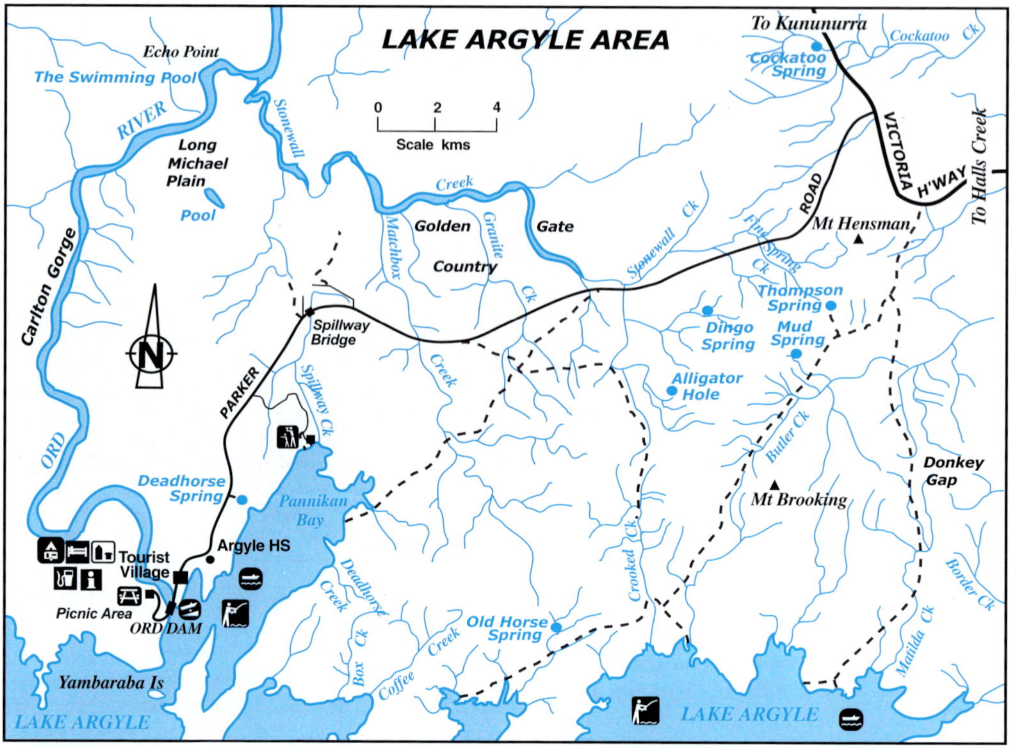

Ord Dam

This relatively tiny wall, measuring 615 metres in length and constructed of rock fill over an impervious core, with no concrete used in the construction, is said to hold back approximately 54 times the amount of water to be found in the Sydney Harbour..

Aboriginal Rock Paintings

A sample of the many Aboriginal rock paintings in the region can be viewed along the drive to Lake Argyle, on the edge of Parker Road.

Crocodile Ridge

A ridge on the skyline of the main body of water at Lake Argyle that takes on the appearance of a crocodile basking in the sun.

Thompson Spring

A pleasant picnic/swimming spot by a small pool surrounded by tropical vegetation. (See map, for track details.)

Fishing, Diving, Boating and Canoeing

The favourite pastime of many visitors to the vast lake is fishing. There's even a commercial fishery based here but amateur fishing folk will enjoy catches of forktail catfish and others.

Late in the Dry season Scuba diving on the ruins of the old Argyle Homestead is worth the trouble, for those who are qualified.

See our chapter, *Canoeing & Boating,* for info on these activities.

Lake Argyle with its many inlets, bays and islands is a great place to explore.

ACCOMMODATION, CAMPING & OTHER FACILITIES

ACCOMMODATION/CARAVAN PARKS:

Lake Argyle Tourist Village & Caravan Park is situated 72 km from Kununurra on Parker Road, near the main Ord River dam site, and has a number of facilities available.

The **Lake Argyle Inn** provides Tourist information and souvenirs as well as great meals and Motel rooms. Open 7.30am until at least 7.30 pm every day from April 1st until the end of October each year. During the wet season the village operates on limited hours, please call first (Oct - Apr).

A ***caravan and camping area***, with all facilities, is located at the Village, along with BBQs, pool and a kiosk, and pets are allowed on application.

You can contact the Tourist Village at PO Box 616, Kununurra, ph: (08) 9168 7360, or check out their web site for more info: **www.lakeargyle.com/english/intro.htm**

FACILITIES

The general store stocks a reasonable range of general supplies as well as souvenirs. Gas, ice and fuel are also available. The store can also help you out with information on the area and the booking office can arrange tours, cruises and scenic flights.

Fuel (Diesel, Super, Unleaded) is available, as well as outboard fuel for your boat.

A number of short tours, are operated in and around Lake Argyle and tickets/information can be obtained from the tourist village.

CRUISES AND TOURS

The following operators run tours in and around the lake and also run tours from Kununurra (see full listings under *River Cruises from Kununurra*):

Argyle Expeditions, PO Box 1310, Kununurra, ph/fax: (08) 9168 7040 – range of cruises on Lake Argyle including fishing charters, dive trips, bushwalking and birdwatching. Web: **www.ozhorizons.com.au/wa/kimberly/argyle/home.html.**

Lake Argyle Cruises, PO Box 117, Kununurra, ph: (08) 9168 7361 – variety of lake cruises (tour & cruise), as well as Kununurra Combo - Bungle Bungles / Lake Argyle / Ord River in a float plane. Web: **www.lakeargyle.com/english/tours.htm.**

SOUTH TOWARDS HALLS CREEK

ACCESS

Highway 1, or the Great Northern Highway, heads south some 45 km west of Kununurra. Spectacular views of the surrounding ranges makes the drive along this section of highway between Kununurra and Warmun on the way to Halls Creek well worth while, especially during the first 100 km or so.

There are also some nice **camping** spots passed on the *Durham River* and at the *Bow River* Rest Area.

Two small communities are passed on the way south and both offer tourists basic facilities and more.

Rugged range country south of Kununurra makes the drive to Halls Creek a scenic one.

DOON DOON

Situated 110 km south of Kununurra on Highway 1 is Doon Doon Roadhouse, which is operated by the local Aboriginal community

Facilities and **accommodation** are limited. The roadhouse has fuel, food, a small general store, grassy sites for camping, powered sites for vans and air-conditioned accommodation. For more details, ph: (08) 9167 8004.

WOOLAH ABORIGINAL TAG-ALONG TOURS

The nearby Doon Doon station in the Kimberley now features tag-along trips to a number of delightful gorges on the property. Led by local Aboriginal guides these day trips take you to fine swimming and fishing holes. For more info about Woolah Aboriginal tag-along tours contact the Doon Doon Roadhouse.

WARMUN (TURKEY CREEK)

Situated 200 km south of Wyndham and 161 km north of Halls Creek, Warmun, or Turkey Creek, is a small hamlet on Highway 1 south of Wyndham. For most travellers the roadhouse is the only reason to stop, but the small Aboriginal community of Warmun does have an art centre to attract people and from near the roadhouse you can also get a helicopter flight over the Bungle Bungles.

Helicopters take tourists out over the local ranges to the fantastic Bungle Bungles.

The **Warmun Art Centre** located in the Community has a gallery and art is available for sale. Visitors are welcome. A verbal permit is required to enter the community, and you can phone the Art Centre on (08) 9168 7496 for permission. For more info write to Locked Bag 24, Turkey Creek, via Kununurra, WA, 6743, ph: (08) 9168 7496. You can also check out their online gallery and learn more about the artists on their web site:
www.warmunart.com/centre.htm

TURKEY CREEK

Facilities and **accommodation** are limited. Powered caravan sites and **camping** facilities, including a BBQ area, are available, as well as motel accommodation at the ***Turkey Creek Roadhouse/Motel & Caravan Park***, ph: (08) 9168 7882 – pets are allowed. The following facilities can also be found at the roadhouse –

- Petrol, diesel, oils and autogas
- Garden picnic area
- Take-away food, cold drinks
- Limited groceries
- 4WD charter & safari tours
- Souvenirs
- Telephone

Heliwork WA, PO Box 165, Kununurra, 6743, ph: (08) 9168 1811, direct bookings ph: (08) 9168 7337, web site: **www.slingair.com.au** – operates a scenic helicopter flight from Warmun from April to November, that takes you over cattle station country and Purnululu National Park .

KACHANA STATION

Situated close to the banks of the remote Chamberlain River, south-west of Doon Doon Roadhouse, is Kachana Station. This small 77,500ha property was once a part of El Questro station but was considered an uneconomical section of the property for running cattle. Today it is run as an eco-tourism resort and is only accessible by air from Kununurra.

Tours are led by an Aboriginal guide and an archaeologists and include some fabulous art sites.

For more details on Kachana Station contact, *The Kimberley Specialists*, ph: (08) 9168 2576, or check the web at: **www.kimberleyspecialists.com.au**

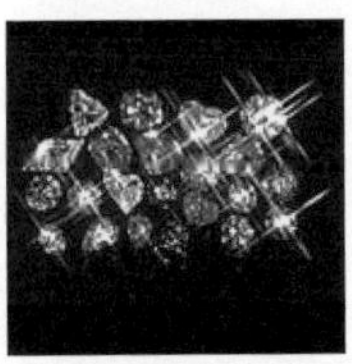

ARGYLE DIAMOND MINE

Situated 20 km east of the main highway amongst rugged hill country south-west of the southern shores of Lake Argyle is the world famous Argyle Diamond Mine. The world's largest diamond mine, it produces more than 25% of the world's diamonds. Amongst the bulk of the stones are truly rare and beautiful pink diamonds - the mine's signature stone.

Owned by Rio Tinto, diamonds were first discovered in the region in 1979 and an alluvial mining operation began four years later. The first ore was extracted from the open cut pit in 1985 and since then nearly 650 million carats of diamonds have been produced at an annual average of 34 million carats. The mine employs some 700 people which makes it the biggest single contributor to the Kimberley economy, with 25% of its workforce indigenous and 50% living locally.

In late 2005 Rio Tinto announced that it would develop an underground project at the mine site to extend the life of the mine from 2007 to 2018. Average annual production of the underground mine will be some 60% of its current open cut production.

What to learn more about the mine, its operation and the diamonds, then check out their web site at:
www.argylediamonds.com.au/homepage.asp

TOURS

Slingair Heliwork WA, Kununurra, ph: 1800 095 500 or ph: (08) 9169 1300 – offers a couple of tours incorporating a ground tour of the Argyle Diamond Mine. Tours generally orbit the Argyle Diamond Mine in the plane before landing to take an informative ground tour of the process plant and diamond display room. The tour includes lunch at the staff village. You can check out their web site for all the details: **www.slingair.com.au/**.

PURNULULU (BUNGLE BUNGLE) NATIONAL PARK (320,000 ha)

The Purnululu (Bungle Bungle) National Park is known best for its tiger-striped, beehive-shaped domes and has won accolades as one of the greatest wonders in Western Australia. It's certainly worth a visit and a scenic flight. The park is open only between April and December.

A NATURAL WONDER

The striped black and orange rock of the Bungle Bungle Range, so indicative of the area, owes its existence to a tough, thin, outer skin. The orange bands are formed of silica, while the black bands are of lichen. Once the rough outer layer is removed the soft white sandstone is exposed and for this reason **it is illegal for people to climb on the domes**. Once you see them you'll realise that climbing a dome is almost impossible anyway, and just a little dangerous.

Vegetation on the plain surrounding the massif consists mainly of hardy spinifex, dotted by spindly acacias and the occasional eucalypt. The rocks of the massif are bare of any soil, but where plants manage to anchor their roots in the cracks of the surface a number of species survive. These include silver-leaf bloodwoods, Wickhams grevillea, heath myrtle and some tough, wiry eucalyptus. In the cool of the valleys and tucked away in well protected spots, many ferns and the Bungle Bungle Fan Palm (a form of Livistona palm) can be seen.

The park is home to many newly discovered plants, and to wildlife such as the Agile Wallaby and the Green Tree Frog. Several species of rare animals also occur in the park.

From the air Bungles are impressive.

The beehive shaped domes of the Bungles have made them world famous.

HISTORY

Hidden from prying European eyes until 1982, the region was known to the local Aborigine people, a few cattle people and the occasional helicopter crew searching for minerals or oil in the huge untrodden expanse of north-west Western Australia.

The Aboriginal people knew the area as 'Purnululu' and in times past it was a favoured Wet season area that was rich in animal and plant food. Do not touch any art or take any artifacts you may find as these are still important to the local Aboriginal people who help manage this magnificent park.

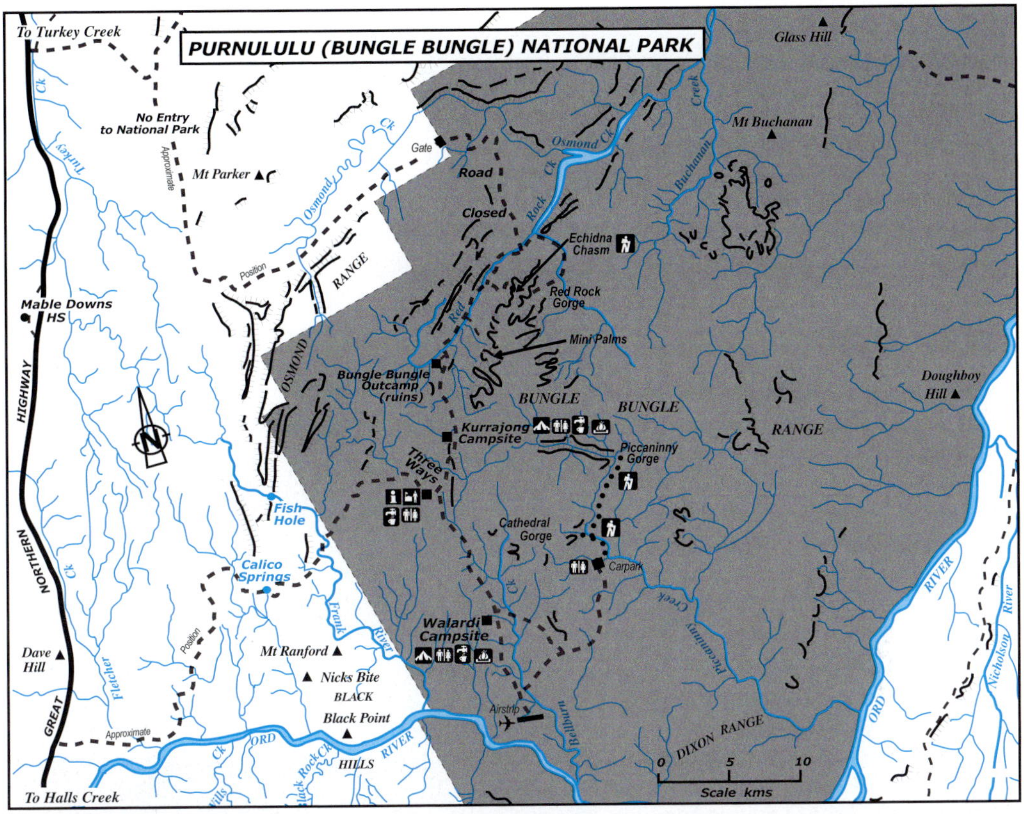

The origin of the name Bungle Bungle probably either came from a corruption of the Aborigine name for the area, or from misspelling one of the common Kimberley grasses – Bundle Bundle grass.

The first European to see the Bungles was the explorer Alexander Forrest in 1879. He camped on the Ord River about 10 km south of the ranges and while he was impressed with the surrounding grassland he was less than enthusiastic about the ‘rough and rangy’ mountains to the north.

Next was Edward Hardman, a geologist who was sent to join a party being led by Harry F Johnston who traversed from the West Kimberley to the East Kimberley in 1884. While he noted the existence of likely gold bearing quartz in the headwaters of the Ord and Panton Rivers, he was also enthused about the Bungle Bungle ranges, saying how they assumed ‘strange and fantastic form’ because of their geology and the weathering they endured.

Initially the ranges were part of the large Ord River Station which was taken up by J Panton and W H Osmand in 1884, the cattle being driven to the region by the famous Nat Buchanan. While the area in and around the Bungles was considered ‘rubbish country’ by the early pioneers, the cattle thrived on the property and it was estimated that numbers were doubling every four years or so, so that by 1902 the property ran 47,000 head!

The area around the range was officially taken up in a separate lease in the early 1900s by pastoralists’ named Wilson and William Madden who named the property, Stonehenge Station. Madden kept the lease until his death in 1927. The named changed to Red Rock Station when Arthur Muggleton from the adjoining Tickalara Station took over the lease in 1930 and he is supposedly the first to have used the name ‘Bungle Bungle’ for the rugged ranges that took up much of the lease. Then, by some accounts, later in 1941 the lease was taken over by William Skuthmore, who called it Bungle Bungle Station and had an outstation located close to the massif.

With continual over grazing, the area was resumed by the Crown in 1967 to help protect the Ord River catchment area from further erosion. Even so, few realised how spectacular this one particular area was; those that did, preferred to keep it quiet. In 1982 a Channel 9 camera crew heard about it, which resulted in the Bungle Bungle being blasted across the nation’s airwaves.

GETTING THERE

The Purnululu (Bungle Bungle) National Park, in the north-west corner of the Ord River Catchment Reserve, was declared in March, 1987. It covers an area of almost 320,000 ha – 110,000 ha is conservation reserve and 210,000 ha is national park.

Driving into the Bungles you can expect the track to vary quite a bit - but it is only suitable for 4WD vehicles!

By Road (4WD)

Spring Creek Track, off the Great Northern Highway (approximately 109 km north of Halls Creek), leads to the Three Ways intersection in the National Park. The first 40 km or so, runs through Mabel Downs Station.

Along this route very few sites are available for camping and permission from the property owner is required. However, **Calico Springs** (permission from the land owner is required), some 31 km from the main road, is probably the best camping spot in the whole region. It is not only shady and cool, but you can usually find a pool to splash in. Even to the casual observer the bird life around here is a delight, and if you look you may find many nesting – we did. The place is a real haven from the scorched surrounding country.

The distance from the highway to the Three Ways intersection is approximately 53 km, however, the trip will take two to three hours to reach this point and the track is suitable only for 4WDs with good clearance. 2WD vehicles are not permitted, and caravans will not survive the trip in.

Driving Distances and Times

From Visitors Centre – Three Ways intersection	
To Walardi Camping Area:	*16 km – 30 to 40 min*
To Echidna Chasm Car Park:	*20 km – 45 min*
To Kurrajong Camping Area:	*5 km – 15 min*
From Walardi Camping Area	
To Piccaninny Car Park:	*20 km – 30 to 40 min*

It is not advisable to attempt to tow standard trailers into the Park. Specially constructed, robust off-road trailers are more suitable and will survive driven appropriately.

The track into the Purnululu National Park and camping areas is well signposted.

Please stay on approved tracks and observe the 50 kph speed limit within the park.

Flights & Air Tours

One of the best ways to see the Bungle Bungle massif is to take a scenic flight over it or, if you want, you can fly into the park and be picked up by a tour operator and shown around.

Scenic flights regularly fly from either Kununurra, Wyndham, Turkey Creek or Halls Creek.

Kununurra and Wyndham, being further away, are generally more expensive and you spend less time over the Bungles. However, you do get a chance to view the great expanse of Lake Argyle and to take in the diamond mine.

For details on flights from Kununurra contact:

Alligator Airways, ph: (08) 9168 1333, web: **www.alligatorairways.com.au/**

Slingair Heliwork WA, ph: (08) 9169 1300, web: **www.slingair.com.au/**

For details on flights from Halls Creek contact:
Discover the Kimberley Tours, ph: (08) 9193 7267, **www.bunglebungle.com.au/**
Oasis Air, ph: (08) 9168 6462.

From Turkey Creek, or Warmun, *Heliwork WA*, ph: (08) 9168 1811, operates scenic helicopter flights over the Bungle Bungles and Mabel Downs Station.

During the peak of the tourist season helicopter flights are available from Bellburn airstrip within the park, operated by *Heliworks*, ph: (08) 9168 1811. The booking office is at the airstrip, 16 km south of the ranger base and not far from the Walardi camping area.

CAMPING

Camping is available at ***Bellburn Creek***, ***Kurrajong*** or ***Walardi Camps***, with the Bellburn site being for licensed tour operators bringing fly/drive tourists to the park.

APT Kimberley Wilderness Adventures operate Wilderness Camps throughout the Kimberley, including the ***Bungle Bungle Wilderness Camp,*** located on Bellburn Creek. This camp offers tented accommodation with shared facilities and cabins with private facilities.

Independent self-drive travellers can book to stay at any of the Wilderness Camps by obtaining a **Safari Pass** which allows access to the fully-hosted camps that feature hot showers, beds and dinners. All camps are exclusively sited on Aboriginal land and are open between April - October.

For more details ph: (03) 9277 8444, web: **www.kimberleywilderness.com.au/**

TOUR OPERATORS

The following tour operators have tours to, and incorporating, Purnululu. For more information see the section on *4WD Safaris* under *Extended Tours from Kununurra*, or the *Tour Operators listing* at the back of the book:

Bungle Bungle Adventures, ph: 1800 641 998, web: **www.adventure.kimberley.net.au**
East Kimberley Tours, ph: (08) 9168 2213, web: **www.eastkimberleytours.com**
Halls Creek & Bungle Bungle Tours, ph: (08) 9193 7267, web: **www.bunglebungle.com.au**
Kimberley Adventure Tours, ph: (08) 9191 2655, web: **www.kimberleyadventures.com.au/**
Wilderness 4WD Adventures, ph: (08) 8941 2161, web: **www.wildernessadventures.com.au**

FACILITIES

Both the **Kurrajong** and **Walardi camps** have toilets, water, individual camp sites, separate group sites, as well as generator and non-generator areas. There is also a phone available.

Fires are only allowed in the fireplaces provided and only with the firewood provided. Have a gas or fuel stove just in case!

There are no rubbish disposal facilities; please follow the example of past visitors and take out whatever you take in.

The many creeks, and even the Ord River (if you were allowed to get to it), are dry for most of the year. There is little running water for swimming, but you may find pools where the ground is rocky enough to trap water.

Ranger

The park is open only between April and September.

During the Dry season there is a ***Visitors Centre*** and ***Ranger Station*** located close to the Three Ways intersection. They will be happy to help make your visit more enjoyable and can tell you what to see, where to go, track conditions and other information. They can be contacted on ph: (08) 9168 7300 during the season. Also, consult the information shelters on the Spring Creek Track – one near the highway and the other at the Three Ways intersection.

At times, the rangers also have slide nights which are well worth attending to learn more about this magnificent area.

Entry/Camping Fees

A **Day Pass** covers entry into the park on any one day and currently costs $9/vehicle. Park passes do not include camping fees.

The **Annual All Parks Pass**, costing $51/vehicle, allows you to visit any park throughout WA as many times as you wish for a period of 12 months.

A **Holiday Park Pass** is available if you are on holiday and want to visit a number of national parks, this pass entitles you to as many visits to as many parks as you wish for any four-week period. Fee: $22.50/vehicle (up to 8 people)

There is a self registration/information bay near the ranger base at Three Ways.

See the *National Parks* chapter for full pass cost details.

For more information contact the NP Ranger at Kununurra HQs, Messmate Way, PO Box 942, Kununurra, WA, 6743, ph: (08) 9168 4200, web site: **www.calm.wa.gov.au/**.

WALKING AND EXPLORING

Best Season

From May to September. **The park is open from April to December 31st, weather permitting**. It often closes early, because of the heat and the onset of the Wet.

The Gorges

Walk Distances and Times (return trip)

From Piccaninny Creek Car Park			
To Cathedral Gorge:	*2.5 km*	*– 1 to 2 hour*	*Easy*
To Piccaninny Gorge:	*30 km*	*– 8 to 12 hours*	*Difficult (overnight)*
From Echidna Chasm Car Park			
To Echidna Chasm:	*2 km*	*– 1 to 1.5 hours*	*Easy*
From Froghole Car Park			
To Froghole:	*1.5 km*	*– 1.5 hours*	*Moderate to Hard*
To Mini Palms:	*3 km*	*– 2.0 to 2.5 hours*	*Easy to Hard*

Cathedral Gorge is the most visited spot and once you walk along it, to its cathedral-like source, you'll understand why. It's an easy to moderate 2 km return walk, well signposted from the car park, which is about 25 km from the ranger base. It is a fantastic place; stay a while, have lunch, or whatever in the cool and let the magic of the place soak into your soul.

Piccaninny Gorge is a much longer, harder walk, covering about 30 km return, but is well worth the effort. To penetrate up into the depths of the gorge requires at least an overnight walk, so be prepared. Please register with the ranger before setting out.

Echidna Chasm on the north-west side of the Bungle Bungle Range, 21 km from the ranger base, is stupendous. An easy to moderate 2 km return walk. As you penetrate deeper into the gorge the walls become sheerer and closer together. Finally they are an arm's width apart and tower upwards so they almost completely block out the light.

Located just to the south of Echidna Chasm both **Froghole** and **Mini Palms Gorges** are accessible from the Froghole Gorge car park. Froghole is a moderate to hard walk of 1.5 km return and it's best to keep to the left hand side of the gorge, while Mini Palms is a 3 km return walk that can be hard.

Once you get to the Bungle Bungle escarpment take your time and explore the area and its gorges. Access to the gorges is only by foot, along creek beds. Carry water on all your walking excursions! **Remember, climbing the rock domes is prohibited!**

For Further Information

The nearest CALM office to contact for information on the park is the Kimberley Regional Office, Cnr Konkerberry & Messmate Way, PO Box 942, Kununurra, WA, 6743, ph: (08) 9168 4200, or check the web at: **www.calm.wa.gov.au/**.

Walking into Cathedral Gorge.

Spectacular Cathedral Gorge.

THE MITCHELL PLATEAU AND NORTHERN KIMBERLEY

INTRODUCTION

The far north of the Kimberley region is one of the best areas for the adventurous traveller and for those that love good fishing.

The Aboriginal community of Kalumburu, on the far north coast, is one of the friendliest around and with a permit there is a choice of camping areas and fishing spots to enjoy.

Then there is the Mitchell Plateau, which has long been a favourite and today, with a helicopter based at the Mitchell Falls camping area during the tourist season, it is even better.

Finally there is the remote attractions of the Drysdale River National Park and if you can gain permission for access then this remote region offers many attractions.

HISTORY

This northern region of the Kimberley has been inhabited for thousands of years by Aboriginal people and being relatively close to Asia could well have been one of the first landfalls ancient seafarers came to in Australia. Certainly Macassan fishermen from Indonesia were sailing this coast and setting up their beche de mer (sea cucumber) processing bases well before Europeans arrived. In 1865 a fleet of boats and 300 Macassan fishermen were reported at Camben Harbour, and at Anjo Cove, at the furtherest tip of the Anjo Peninsula northwest of Kalumburu, the substantial remains of one of their bases can still be seen.

The early sea voyages of discovery by Tasman (1644), Baudin (1801-03) and King (1819-21), and then the land explorations of Grey in 1837, were followed up by the failed Camden Harbour venture by the Glenelg River Pastoral Company in 1864. (See the *European History* chapter.)

In January 1882 the Victorian Squatting Company took up a lease over much of the northern Kimberley, including the area around present day Drysdale River station. In 1886, Charles Burrows, who worked for the company, explored the region, naming the Drysdale River.

The lease, which included much of the area along the Prince Regent River, was next taken up by Captain Joseph Bradshaw. It was during one of his trips to his leases in April 1891 that he first discovered the ancient art that is now known as 'Bradshaw art'. He sent his own steamer, the *Red Gaunlet*, with his cousin, Mr Aeneas Gunn, (who's wife was to write the book, *We of the Never Never*), to set up and build stock yards for his cattle which he was to overland from Queensland. He never got to the northern Kimberley with cattle, but instead set up Bradshaws Station in the NT.

In 1901 Fred Brockman led a party that explored much of this region (see *European History*). Just seven years later the Drysdale River Mission at Pago was established (see *History of Kalumburu* in next few pages).

In 1916 the Presbyterian Church also established a mission at Kunmunya, just to the north of Camben Harbour and operated it until the Second World War. The mission is in ruins today, but the land is administered by the Mowanjum Aboriginal Community in Derby.

John Morgan led another major survey party through this country in 1954 (See *European History*) which heralded the roads we see today. Mineral exploration followed and the northern cattle properties of Theda, Doongan, Carson River and Barton Plains were established. The Drysdale River station lease was taken up by Dick Condon in 1967 and by the current owners, John and Anne Koeyers, in 1985.

Early in the Dry some of the creeks and rivers crossed on the road to Kalumburu can still have quite a bit of water in them.

ACCESS

Access to this region is via the Kalumburu road, which turns off the Gibb River road, 415 km north of Derby or 290 km west of Kununurra.

This road does not remain open during the Wet season and rarely opens before April. Early in the Dry season it can be badly chopped up and water crossings can be frequent and deep. By the end of the Dry, corrugations and bulldust are common. The route deteriorates north of Theda station, and improves again north of the Carson river crossing.

This route gives access to Kalumburu itself and the beaches further north as well as to the main access tracks to the Mitchell Plateau and the Drysdale River National Park.

DRYSDALE RIVER HOMESTEAD

Drysdale is a family owned and operated million acre working cattle station, running approx 7000 head. The homestead is reached around 52 km from the Gibb River Road junction. ***Homestead accommodation****, meals, a bar, beer garden and a licenced restaurant are available from this large well run cattle station which straddles the upper reaches of the Drysdale River.*

All rooms (twin, double & family) have bedding, soap and towels provided, while some rooms have own private lounge. The accommodation building also includes full cooking facilities for those wishing to self-cater meals, as well as a BBQ and outdoor dining area, along with the use of an automatic washing machine. All meals are also available from the Homestead Restaurant. There is a picnic lunch area and toilet facilities for all travellers. Travellers staying in the accommodation have use of canoes on the river.

Camping is available at the ***Homestead Camp*** *and at* ***Miners Pool*** *(camping fees applicable). The Homestead Camp area has hot showers and toilets and laundry available. Miners Pool, 5 km from the homestead and situated on the banks of the Drysdale River, is a pleasant open area with shady trees and basic pit toilets, overlooking the pool. No bookings are taken for either camp as there is plenty of space.*

A small general store can supply a range of basic tin and food supplies, and there is a public phone available as is fuel (diesel and unleaded). The workshop offers mechanical, welding and tyres repairs, along with tyres, batteries, springs and shocks. Rubbish can be disposed of here. There are Eftpos facilities, and the station also accepts travellers cheques, Visa, Bankcard and Mastercard. The store is open 7 days a week from 8.00 am to 5.00 pm.

The station also offers a free caretaking service for trailers and vans which can be left at the homestead for those travelling further north.

Alligator Air*, ph: 1800 632 533 or (08) 9168 1333, operates daily scenic flights from the homestead from May to September for the Mitchell Falls (which includes a helicopter flight) and to the Prince Regent River and spectacular Kimberley coastline. Individually tailored flights also available. It is advisable to book ahead. Web site:* **www.alligatorairways.com.au.**

Those fly-in visitors with their own plane or air transport can use the airstrip, by pre-arrangement, and the station is able to service all your refuelling requirements. Fly-in morning teas and lunches are available.

For more information contact the station on ph/fax: (08) 9161 4326, or write to PMB 9, via Wyndham, WA, 6740, or check out their web site:
www.drysdaleriver.com.au/

The camping area at the Homestead.

Crossing the Drysdale River.

TREK NOTES (WGS 84 DATUM)

KALUMBURU ROAD

Total Distance 256 km – allow 4 to 5 hours travelling time for the whole trip.

0.0	*(0.0)*	***Track junction (T/J) Gibb River Rd/Kalumburu Rd.*** *GPS 16° 7' 8"S 126° 31'12"E* *Head north to Kalumburu.*
2.5	*(2.5)*	*T/J – PSA. LH track leads to* ***Aboriginal art site****.* *GPS 16° 5' 59"S 126° 30' 53"E*
3.1	*(0.6)*	*Gibb River – some good* ***camps*** *with shade, river access and sand – a lovely spot. Firewood is scare.*
15.9	*(12.8)*	*Plain Creek - water, possible* ***camp*** *on LH side before crossing.*
58.2	*(42.3)*	*T/J – PSA. LH track leads 1.3 km to* ***Drysdale River HS****. Accommodation, camping, store and fuel. See this chapter for further details.*
60.4	*(2.2)*	*T/J – PSA. RH tk leads to* ***Miners Pool*** *(4.5 km from main road) where you can camp. Fee payable at Drysdale River Station.*
60.8	*(0.4)*	*Drysdale River – water.* ***No camping.***
93.5	*(32.7)*	*Begin to travel through an area of Livingstonia Palms. The first of many.*
94.9	*(1.4)*	*T/J – PSA. RH tk, to Doongan Station.*
103.7	*(8.8)*	*T/J – PSA. LH tk leads 12 km to* ***Marunbabidi Safari Camp****.*
156.0	*(52.3)*	*T/J – PSA to Kalumburu.* *GPS 14° 55' 44"S 126° 14' 9"E* *LH tk leads to* ***Mitchell Plateau****. See Trek Notes later in this chapter.*
159.0	*(3.0)*	*McDonald Creek – water can be fairly deep, especially early in Dry.*
164.0	*(5.0)*	*Ngoollalah Creek – nice* ***camp*** *spots on right and left before crossing.*
168.2	*(4.2)*	*Mud Springs Creek.*
179.0	*(10.8)*	*Creek crossing.*
188.2	*(9.2)*	*T/J – PSA. LH tk leads to Theda homestead.*
189.4	*(1.6)*	*T/J – PSA. LH tk leads to Theda homestead. Track worsens from here.*
191.9	*(2.5)*	*Station Creek.*
214.1	*(22.2)*	*Creek crossing. Road follows creek (water), with a* ***camping*** *spot on the left beside the creek.*
217.8	*(3.7)*	*Coondillam Creek – water.*
235.6	*(17.8)*	*Carson River* *GPS 14° 27' 10"S 126° 39' 47"E* ***Camping*** *possible on rocky creek bed. Beware of crocs!*
236.0	*(1.1)*	*T/J – PSA veering left. Track improves. RH track leads to* ***Carson River Station*** *and* ***Drysdale NP****. See Trek Notes later in this chapter.*
256.0	*(20.0)*	*Enter* ***Kalumburu*** *Community - Mission on left; store and Community office on right.* *GPS 14° 17' 46"S 126° 38' 34"E*

MARUNBABIDI SAFARI CAMP – *KIMBERLEY WILDERNESS ADVENTURES*

This safari camp is in a bush setting near the upper King Edward River and offers travellers overnight accommodation. All facilities, meals and a camp host are provided. Self-drive travellers can use the camps as part of their Safari Pass, but the accommodation must be pre-booked. For details freecall: 1800 335 003, or check the web at:

www.kimberleywilderness.com.au

Good bird watching in a pristine wilderness along with a range of Wandjina and Bradshaw art sites can be seen near here.

Access: Head along the Kalumburu Road north of Drysdale River Station to Doongan Station access track, and 8.8 km from this junction you will come to a fenceline marked with white steel posts. Turn left here, immediately after fenceline, and follow fence for 8 km and cross Edward River. Two (2) km later at KWR sign, veer left and 2 km later veer left into the camp.

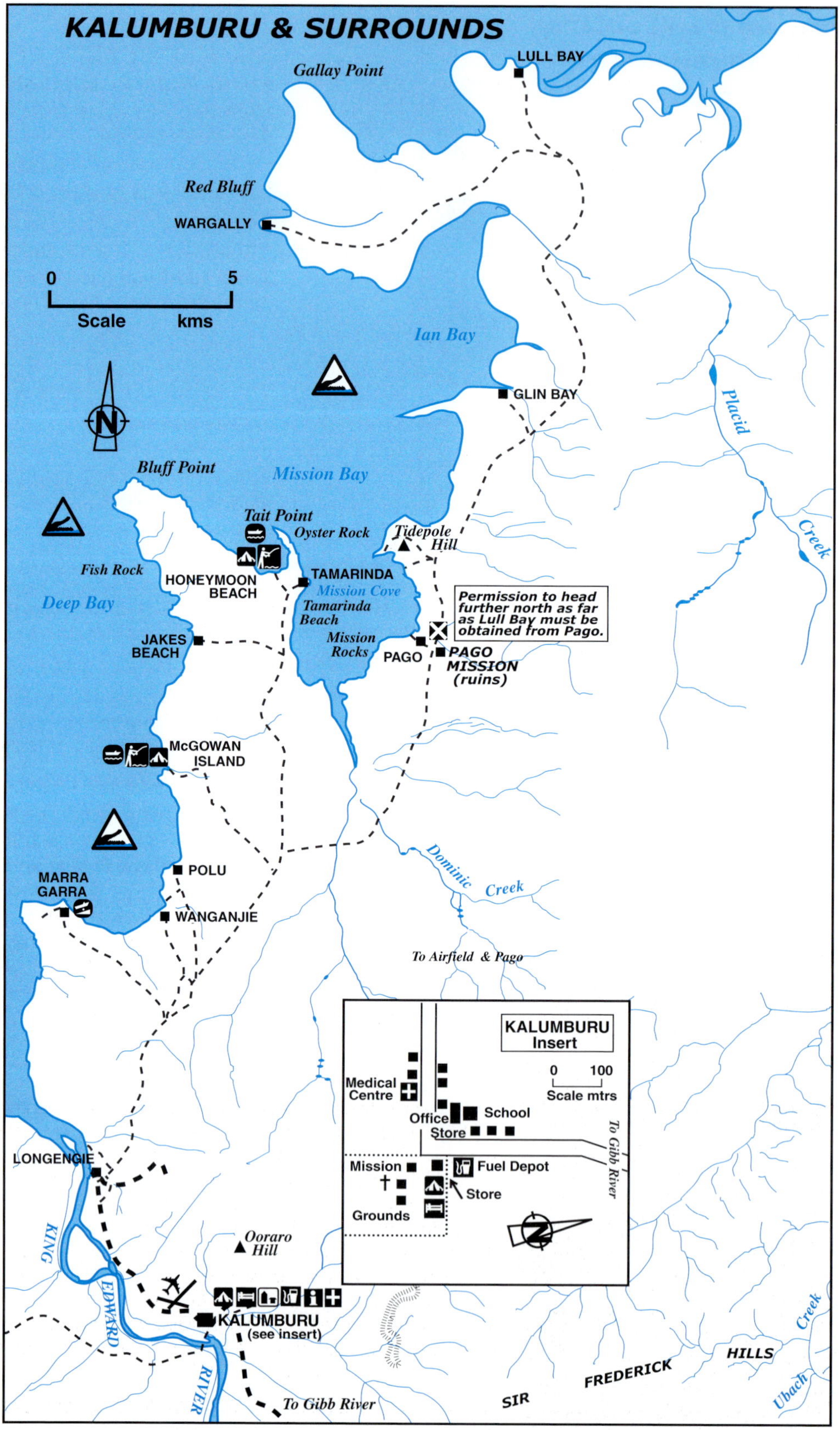
KALUMBURU & SURROUNDS
Gallay Point
LULL BAY
Red Bluff
WARGALLY
0 5
Scale kms
Ian Bay
GLIN BAY
Placid
Bluff Point
Mission Bay
Tait Point
Oyster Rock
Tidepole Hill
Creek
Fish Rock
HONEYMOON BEACH
TAMARINDA
Mission Cove
Tamarinda Beach
Deep Bay
Permission to head further north as far as Lull Bay must be obtained from Pago.
JAKES BEACH
Mission Rocks
PAGO
PAGO MISSION (ruins)
McGOWAN ISLAND
POLU
MARRA GARRA
WANGANJIE
Dominic Creek
To Airfield & Pago
KALUMBURU Insert
Medical Centre
0 100
Scale mtrs
Office
School
Store
To Gibb River
Mission
Fuel Depot
Store
Grounds
LONGENGIE
KING
EDWARD
RIVER
Ooraro Hill
KALUMBURU (see insert)
To Gibb River
SIR FREDERICK HILLS
Creek
Ubach

THEDA STATION

Theda Station, 130 km north of Drysdale River homestead and 70 km south of Kalumburu, is a 303,100 ha (750,000 acres) cattle station established in 1959, and with the adjoining Doongan Station, takes in a vast stretch of country stretching from the western edge of the Drysdale River National Park to the Mitchell Falls area and north to the Aboriginal lands.

The station is no longer open to tourists.

KALUMBURU

Kalumburu, situated on the northern coast of the Kimberley is situated 5 km from the mouth of the *King Edward River* and close to the King Edward River Gorge. It provides a picturesque setting with giant mango trees and coconut palms surrounding the historic Kalumburu Catholic Mission. The area has a rich history and offers the traveller a wide choice of experiences.

KALUMBURU'S HUMBLE BEGINNINGS

The Beginnings at Pago

In 1908 the New Norcia Benedictine Monastery founded the Drysdale River Mission at Pago. This was after some early exploratory work by Rev. Torres who, in 1906, almost single handedly inspected the coast between Broome and Wyndham looking for a suitable site for the mission.

There were a number of Aboriginal groups in the area, which included the Kwinis, Kularis, Walmbis and Arrawaris.

On Sunday 19th July, 1908, the first mass was said at Djemei in Deep Bight. The Missionaries first encounter with the local Aborigines though was not all that friendly, with the Aborigines attacking! Unfortunately, some of the Aborigines were hit by gun fire, whereupon all the warriors disappeared.

After some further exploration of the area, a site at Mission Cove, about 1 km from the coast at a place called 'Pago' by the Aborigines, was chosen for a temporary settlement. On the 15th August, 1908, the *Mission to the Aborigines of North Kimberley* was officially opened.

Exploration to find a passage to the Barton Plain was soon undertaken, and today the resultant road, and another one opened years later, are still the only roads through this long, rugged range.

During 1910 minor attacks by the Aborigines still occurred and in September, 1913, 103 Aborigines, both men and women, attacked the mission spearing the Fathers, and life on the mission became a state of siege. Slowly though a change was taking place, and the Aborigines had begun to show a more peaceful attitude.

Early in 1922 an expedition by the Fathers was undertaken by dinghy up Monger Creek. After inspecting the land on both sides of the creek, they walked towards the King Edward River and camped near a splendid pool – 'Kalumburu'.

In August 1927 Fr. Thomas went to Kalumburu to prepare two small blocks for cultivation, opening the way for the transfer of the mission from Pago to Kalumburu.

In the early development of the mission there was concern by the Fathers about the constant fighting amongst the Aborigines, and the fact that very few births were occurring. *"...the race seemed intent on its own destruction"*, was one comment made by the missionaries of the time.

The Mission, considering its isolation, had a number of interesting visitors – adventurous travellers and prospective settlers amongst them. There is a record of an Englishman walking around Australia who came one day from out of nowhere. The mission was also involved in the search for the missing German aviators, Bertram & Klausmann and the *Atlantis* in 1932.

Father Anscar has been at Kalumburu for over 22 years. His tours are delightful and insightful!

The German pilots were in fact found by 4 'mission' boys. Capt. Bertram, in gratitude, opened a subscription to obtain transmitting and receiving sets for both Drysdale and Forrest River Missions and sent a harmonium to the mission in Pago. Searches were also carried out from the mission for the plane the *Southern Cross* in 1929.

Kalumburu became a mission station in 1932 and by the end of 1936 most of the people at Pago had moved owing to the failure of the wells at Pago. The Drysdale River Mission was formally transferred to Kalumburu on 13th November, 1936, but it was not until 1951 that the name 'Kalumburu' received official recognition and replaced the original name, 'Drysdale River Mission'.

World War 2

Kalumburu played a major role during World War 2 with a large contingent of air force personnel utilising the air field. This activity caused Kalumburu to be a target for the Japanese, and on 27th September, 1943, Kalumburu was bombed. There was no serious damage to the aerodrome, but the mission was almost completely destroyed, with one of the Fathers being killed along with a native woman and four children. During this period the native community was reduced to 40 and they and the monks retired from the bombed mission to a place, about 3 km away, called Tingun. There they pitched tents until May 1945, when they returned to Kalumburu, which they reconstructed.

The remains of abandoned fuel drums are reminders of the role Kalumburu played.

Truscott Airfield

On 10th June, 1945, the military abandoned the buildings at Kalumburu and Pago and moved to the Sir Graham Moore Islands where they established a communication base and to Truscott which had already been established as an airstrip.

Truscott was named after a well known Australian RAAF pilot, Keith 'Bluey' Truscott, and was used extensively during the final stages of the war and afterwards. On the 20th May 1945, a bomber crashed at the end of the Truscott strip, killing all 11 crew. Today a monument and the scattered remains of the aircraft can still be seen along with the dumped remains of old trucks, buildings and fuel drums.

In recent years the Truscott strip and basic facilities are used and maintained by mining companies working the Timor Sea. As well, commercial adventure travel companies, mainly fishing charters, use the strip as a base for transferring people and equipment from plane to boat and vice versa.

After the War

The land around Kalumburu started being taken up and an Irishman, in the company of another countryman, arrived in March 1950 to establish himself in Carson (Carson City) and run a sheep station. There were many different crops cultivated at Kalumburu and a host of animals introduced by the missionaries. Cattle though, were to prove the most successful. However, the bullocks and donkeys which were released after their useful service had expired, can still be found wild in the Kimberley today.

In 1954, John Morgan and a small party of men surveyed a route from Gibb River Station to the Kalumburu Aboriginal Mission and graded a track through the wilderness. This survey along with the graded route provided the basis for the modern road link to the mission and subsequently to the Mitchell Plateau.

The Barton Plain Pastoral was obtained by the mission in 1958, giving new scope for their cattle breeding, and in August 1965 the mission also brought the lease of the Carson Station.

The Kalumburu Mission was developing and by innumerable visits, the Health Department was working on eradicating hookworm, whooping cough, Hansen's disease, trachoma and venereal diseases. New houses were being built and in April 1962 the first qualified school teacher took over the school from the mission Sisters.

Today the Community is run by the people themselves who also operate a cattle operation, while in recent years they have been catering for a growing number of travellers. In 2004 a large upgrade of the local school was undertaken while in 2005 the community received its first police station.

The Catholic church still owns and runs its small church grounds and school as well as a camp ground and store.

CAMPING AND VISITING

Visiting Requirements –

Travellers wishing to experience the delights of Kalumburu are most welcome by the Community, but it is a privilege, and not a right, to enter the Reserve.

Please follow the rules and guidelines below and note that a dual permit system is in place. Camping fees are in addition to these two permits.

- An **Entry Permit** is required from the **Aboriginal Land Trust**. These are issued free and generally take only a day or so over the net. Contact Estelle Donovan, ph: (08) 9235 8000, or email: estelle.donovan@dia.wa.gov.au, or check the web at: **www.dia.wa.gov.au.**
- A **Kalumburu Recreation Entry Permit** is also required to enter and stay on the Community's land. These costs $35 per vehicle and are valid for one week. Longer stays require a permit extension. Permits are available from the **Kununurra** and **Derby Visitor Centres**, or from the **Corporation's office,** the nearby **Uroro Store** or the **Mission** on your arrival in Kalumburu. If you arrive after hours you must check in when the office is next open.
- Permits can also be obtained in advance from the Community Office. Payment is only by money order or direct deposit. Allow 3 to 4 weeks to receive the permit by mail.
- The Community Office hours are: Mon - Fri 8.30am to 12 noon & 1.30pm to 4.30pm, ph: (08) 9161 4300, fax: (08) 9161 4331, email: kacadmin@bigpond.com, or write to Kalumburu Aboriginal Corporation, PMB 10, Wyndham, 6740.
- There are also camping fees applicable at McGowan Island, Honeymoon Bay and Pago. These are the only areas where visitors may camp.
- You must display your permit on your windscreen or dash.

  Severe penalties apply for any person apprehended on the Reserve without an Entry Permit, or camping in other than the allowed areas.
- **NO ALCOHOL or Non-Presciption Drugs OF ANY KIND** are allowed to be brought onto the Reserve and no firearms are to be discharged within its boundaries.
- You must not leave the roads and only use the tracks provided.
- **You are not allowed** to take bulk fish or oysters from the Community. You may only catch what you can eat while you are there.
- You must comply with any instructions issued by a uniformed Community Warden.
- **Prohibited Areas:** West of King Edward River; Winanghie Beach; and north of Pago.
- Don't cut down or deface any trees or vegetation.
- Please do not take photos or video within the Community environs without prior approval.

FACILITIES, FOOD AND FUEL

Uroro Store and Takeaway

A range of fresh, frozen and packaged foods, takeaway food, clothing, fishing equipment, and basic hardware items are available from the Community Store. Aboriginal artefacts can also be purchased at times. Store hours are: Mon 8.30am to 11.00am (closed pm); Tues to Fri: 8.30am to 11.00am and 1.30pm to 3.50pm; Sat 8.30 am to 11.00 am. The store has Eftpos facilities and can be contacted on ph: (08) 9161 4336. Eftpos banking facilities (BankWest Agency) also operate from a manned booth at the back of the store.

Takeaway food is available from Mon 8.30am to 1.00pm; Tues to Fri 8.30am to 3.50pm and 5.30pm to 7.00pm; Sundays from 6.00pm to 7.00pm. (Sat & public holidays closed.)

Mission Garage and Store

Fuel (unleaded and diesel) is generally available from June to November from the **Mission Garage**, just across the road from the Community store. Garage hours are Mon to Fri 7.15am to 11am and 1.30pm to 4pm. Credit Card payments accepted (Bankcard, Mastercard, Visa).

The **Kalumburu Mission Takeaway** ph: (08) 9161 4117, has basic food supplies (no fresh produce or meat), general fishing supplies, ice and takeaway food available, or you can dine-in. Open Mon to Fri 7.15am to 11am and 1.30pm to 4pm, plus Fri 6.00pm to 7.00pm, weekends 12.00 noon to 4.00pm. Eftpos and credit cards accepted.

You can contact the Mission office on ph: (08) 9161 4333, fax: (08) 9161 4349.

NOTE: There are **no vehicle repair facilities available at Kalumburu** and no spare parts. Carry all the spares you may need. Spare parts may be arranged to be delivered on the next supply boat!

Other Facilities

Other facilities available at the community include **police**, ph: (08) 9161 4580, airstrip & public phone. The **Community Health Clinic**, ph: (08) 9161 4335, is open 7.30-11.30am and 1.30-4pm. Emergency attention is available at all other times.

For those boat owners who don't want to launch off the beach, you can use the **boat ramp at Marra Garra Beach**. If the barge is in however, you won't be able to use the ramp.

CAMPING

You are only allowed to camp in the areas of **McGowan Island, Honeymoon Bay** and **Pago**. The usual camping fee is $10/person/day. For these three areas, bookings are necessary at the Kalumburu office, ph: (08) 9161 4300, but you should also contact the families involved as well. Facilities are pretty basic, especially at Pago. See below for more details. Camping at the **Mission** is also allowed.

Remember, this is a unique area, with a magical coastline and the fishing can be great – but don't forget that salt-water crocodiles inhabit these waters.

Mission – Camping & Accommodation

The historic grounds of the mission are now a pleasant camping area.

The **Mission** has a very pleasant grassy, shady **camping** area, with powered and unpowered sites and water, normal campground facilities, as well as BBQs and shaded picnic tables/seats.

Alternately, you can stay in their motel **units**, in either twin share or single rooms, all of which are air-conditioned and have a self-contained kitchen. Motel residents can also have use of television, undercover recreation, meals area and laundry facilities.

Contact the Mission on ph: (08) 9161 4333, for more details.

McGowan Island

A scenic spot on the coast of Deep Bay, this **camping** area is operated by the Maraltadj family, ph: (08) 9161 4386. In recent years the previously good facilities here had fallen into disrepair, but they have been rejuvenated somewhat. The camping area is flat and opens onto the beach, however there's little shade, the choice spot being under a small group of pandanus palms.

Fishing charters can be arranged from here for fishing the open water, nearby coast or the river. For those fishermen limited to the shoreline there's some fishing action from the nearby rocks where they stand a good chance of landing queenfish, trevally and mackerel.

TREK NOTES (WGS 84)

NORTH OF KALUMBURU

0.0 (0.0) **Mission** – *Kalumburu.*
GPS 14° 17' 46"S 126° 38' 34"E
Head west, keeping store on right. Exit community in 400 metres.

1.0 (1.0) *Veer left (VL) at end of airstrip.*

3.3 (2.3) *Track junction - PSA. Left leads 100 metres to* **Malindjar Gorge**.

3.5 (0.2) *Y-junction (Y-junct) – veer right (VR). Lefthand (LH) signposted (SP) 'Longengie' and* **King Edward River Gorge**.

4.8 (1.3) *Track Junction (T/J) – PSA. LH track (tk) leads to river.*

11.5 (6.7) *T/J – PSA. LH tk SP 'Marra Garra Beach'.*

13.6 (2.1) *T/J – PSA. LH tk SP 'Winaghie Beach'. No Entry.*

15.1 (1.5) *Y-junct – veer right (VR) for northern beaches and Pago.*
Left leads to McGowan Island – camp, fishing, 6.2 km from this junction; follow main track to fishing camp on beach.

17.3 (2.2) *Y-junct – VR for Pago and beaches further north.*
GPS 14° 10' 34"S 126° 40' 37"E
Left leads to Honeymoon Beach Fishing Camp, Jakes Beach and Tamarinda.

To Honeymoon Beach/Tamarinda

0.0 (0.0) *Above track junction*

6.0 (6.0) *T/J – PSA. LH tk to Jakes Beach.*

7.7 (1.7) *T/J – VL to Honeymoon Bay, VR to Tamarinda, 1 km from here.*

8.6 (1.7) *Honeymoon Bay.*
GPS 14° 6' 16"S 126° 40' 50"E

19.0 (1.7) *Creek crossing*

20.7 (1.7) *Creek crossing*

22.5 (1.6) *Creek crossing.*

26.4 (3.9) *T/J – PSA. LH tk leads to Pago Beach. Beach is good for launching a small boat.*

26.5 (0.1) *T/J – PSA. RH tk leads to ruins of Pago Mission.*

26.6 (0.1) *T/J – PSA. RH tk leads to beaches further north and Lull Bay.*

26.5 (0.1) *- Pago. House on right.*
GPS 14° 7 29"S 126° 43' 07"E
Beach and bay is 300 metres from here.

Access north of Pago, is currently not allowed.

The scenic coastline around Kalumburu offers some great boating and fishing.

The fishing off Honeymoon Bay can be awesome.

Honeymoon Bay

Located a little further around the coast from McGowan Island, on Mission Bay, is the pleasant **camping** ground of Honeymoon Bay, owned and run by the French family, ph: (08) 9161 4378.

It will take you about a 1/2 hour or so from Kalumburu to reach as the road is narrow, sandy and slow in places.

Facilities include toilets, showers and power. Camp sites are on the top of the hill less than 100 metres from the beach and there's a bit of shade to enjoy. There are a couple of smaller camps a little further down on the beach proper. If you want to use the power we'd suggest that you carry at least a 30m power lead.

Again various tours can be organised from the camp ground. Remember to take your own fishing gear though, it's not supplied. And take some heavy gear – the locals use 200lb line!

As with any spot on the coastline the sandflies can be horrendous. Come prepared!

MITCHELL PLATEAU

Pago

Located some 27 km from Kalumburu is Pago, which is not that far from the old Pago Mission. This small camping area is operated by the Wain family, ph: (08) 9161 4394. This camping area has few facilities but from near here you can launch a boat across the beach to get into the fish.

Fishing

There's some great fishing around Kalumburu, however, strict catch limits apply. **You are only allowed to catch what you can eat while you are there.**

Out to sea you can catch Spanish mackerel, queenfish, threadfin salmon, coral trout and cod, while in the river there are big barra, bream and more.

A good spot for barra is the 'Washing Machine', not far out of Kalumburu. A track leads to a rocky plateau and the *King Edward River*, just a short walk away. (The track is marked by an old washing machine dumped at the track junction.) Check with the locals for details.

See our chapter, *Fishing in the Kimberley*, for bag limits and other details.

Truscott Airfield

The World War 2 airstrip and base known as Truscott Airfield is not readily accessible to travellers. However the Uunguu traditional owner have established a tour of the Anjo Peninsula on which Truscott was established. This half-day tour takes in the once secret base, a crashed Liberator aircraft site, and a monument to 11 aircrew that were killed here in 1945. The scattered remains of other aircraft can still be seen along with the dumped remains of old trucks, buildings and fuel drums. The tour also includes traditional culture and the local rock art which includes Wandjina and Bradshaw figures.

You can organise a boat trip across independently or scenic flights can be arranged from Kununurra. For more info on the Mungalalu Tours contact the Kalumburu office, ph: (08) 9161 4300.

Mission Tours

The Mission runs a **museum tour** a number of days each week and can organise a tour to some **Bradshaw Art** nearby. Contact the Mission during your stay, or ph: (08) 9161 4333.

Mission buildings as they are today.

THE REMOTE DRYSDALE RIVER NATIONAL PARK

This is the largest national park in the Kimberley region, taking in 448,264 ha of rugged escarpment country. It's also extremely remote and for the most part completely inaccessible.

Situated in the northern area of the Kimberley, 150 km west of Wyndham and 100 km south of Kalumburu, the park is centred around the Drysdale River and the spectacular Carson Escarpment that parallels the Carson River for much of its length. This sheer rock face is one of the most significant features in the Kimberley running for over 200 km from the very heart of the Kimberley to near the northern coast at Cape Londonderry.

The area is rich in Aboriginal art and artifacts and its many rivers, waterholes and remnant patches of rainforests are important bird and mammal habitats. Over 600 species of plants have been recorded, along with 129 varieties of birds, 26 species of mammals, 13 frog species and 26 species of fish.

Included in the park are a number of gorges such as the scenic *Worriga Gorge* and a number of waterfalls including the two largest, *Morgan Falls* on the *Palmoondoora Creek* and *Solea Falls* on the *Drysdale River* itself. Access to both is difficult and you need to take to foot, or a combination of foot and canoe if you are early in the Dry season. The walk, or walk and paddle, upstream from the camping area takes a couple of days return. You really do need to be experienced before setting out on such a jaunt though.

For most people a visit to the remote **camping** area and a few leisurely strolls up and down the river will satisfy their wilderness experience because that is what this park is – a real wilderness experience!

ACCESS AND CAMPING 4WD ONLY

All visitors must register with the Kununurra office of the Dept of CALM before heading to the park. You can do that in person by phone or fax, or by writing. Include the number of people in your party, proposed dates and itinerary.

As there is now only one possible way to access the park, and that is through Carson River Station you must have permission from Kalumburu Aboriginal Community and Carson River. See below for details.

The official camping area in the park, is located at the north-east extremity of the park close to the Drysdale River. The spot is surrounded by taller trees with the high red cliffs of the escarpment just a short distance away over the river. There is plenty of water running past and heaps of shade and sandy camping spots.

Fires are allowed for cooking only!

Our trek notes give you full details of the route to the national park camping ground and the area around Drysdale Crossing.

Main access track into the Park (top); Drysdale Crossing; Carson Escarpment dominates the surrounding flat plain (below)

Access Via Carson River Homestead

The only accessible route into the park is via the Carson River homestead, the turn-off to which is located some 20 km south of Kalumburu. You need to contact the Kalumburu Aboriginal Corporation, ph: (08) 9161 4300, beforehand providing details of your intended visit. You will also need to call in at the office in Kalumburu to obtain and pay for your permit before entering Carson River Station.

In April 2006 access to the park was closed and entry and camping on Carson River station was not allowed. This may change at any time.

When **camping** is allowed on the property, the best spot is the **Drysdale Crossing** (GPS 14° 26' 53"S 126° 51' 29"E – AGD66 Datum) south of the old Barton Plains Outstation. Here, where a track crosses the *Drysdale River*, there is a rockbar with shallow running water, rock pools and shady trees scattered along the low sandy bank. It's a pleasant spot.

Warning:
Salt-water crocodiles inhabit the waters of the Drysdale River below Solea Falls. Do not swim and be wary near river banks. Camp well away from the river.

Access via Theda HS, Old Theda HS & King Edward River (Doongan) HS is no longer allowed.

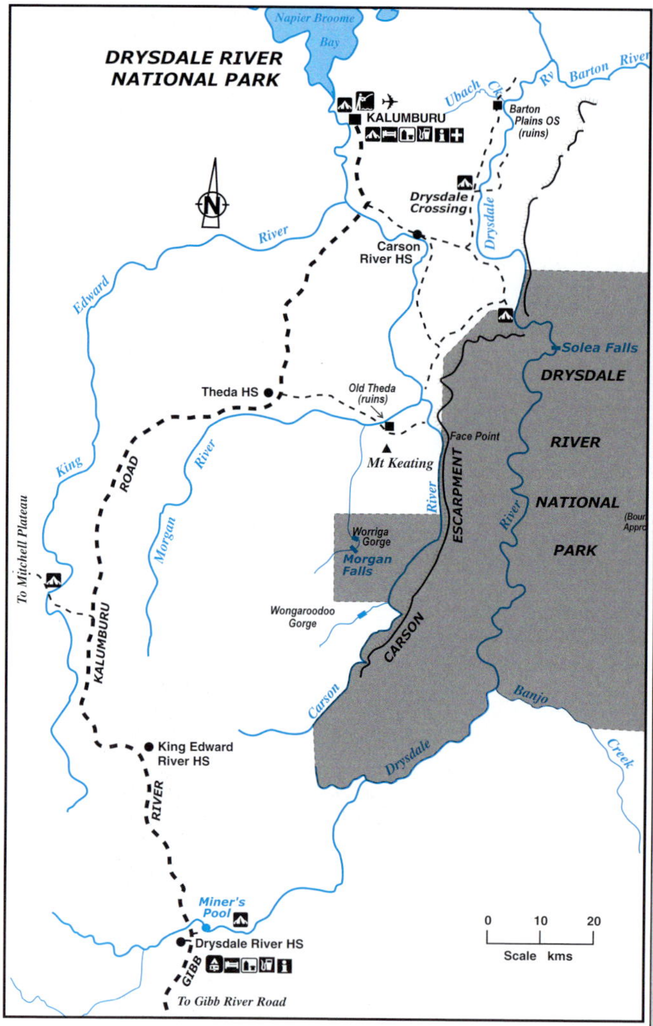

TREK NOTES (AGD 66 DATUM)

KALUMBURU TO DRYSDALE RIVER NATIONAL PARK CAMPING AREA

Travelling Time: from Kalumburu Road to campsite, approx 1 to 1hr 30 mins.

0.0 (0.0) **Track Junction** (T/J) 0.4 km north of the Carson River crossing, or 20 km south of Kalumburu itself – junction marked by a fuel drum. Veer east to Carson River Station.

16.3 (16.3) **Carson River Station** homestead. Stop and check in with homestead. **Permit required from Kalumburu Aboriginal Community.** Drive on past the homestead and sheds on right.

16.8 (0.5) Gate, then pass sign on left 'Drysdale River National Park 19 km'.

18.9 (2.1) Gate.

20.6 (1.7) Gate – Y-junct straight after gate – veer left (VL).

27.9 (7.3) Y-junct – veer right (VR). Righthand (RH) fork signposted (SP) by arrow, indicating direction to national park.

Left leads on to Drysdale Crossing which is 8.6 km north of this junction.

31.0 (3.1) Creek crossing – dry.

35.1 (4.1) T/J – PSA. Faint LH track (tk) leads to a crossing across the river. Escarpment can be seen on left.

37.3 (2.2) Main track veers left. Faint track continues straight on.

41.0 (3.7) T/J and yards on left – VL, SP 'Camping'.

44.0 (3.0) **Bulldust Yards Camping** Area – very pleasant spot on the river with shady trees within the Drysdale River NP.

GPS 14° 36' 50"S 126° 56' 40"E (approx)

FACILITIES:

There are no facilities. Visitors must be self-sufficient as this park is remote, isolated and extremely rugged. Visitors planning extended walks must be experienced bushwalkers and aware of potential hazards that could be encountered.

FOR FURTHER INFORMATION

Contact the CALM's Kununurra HQs, Messmate Way, PO Box 942, Kununurra, WA, 6743, ph: (08) 9168 4200, fax: (08) 9168 2179, web site: **www.calm.wa.gov.au/**.

TO THE MITCHELL PLATEAU & CRYSTAL CREEK

ACCESS

Access to the Mitchell Plateau area is via an often rough road that leaves the main Kalumburu road and crosses the King Edward River and then climbs up onto the Mitchell Plateau, before descending once more to the coast.

MUNURRU – KING EDWARD RIVER

CAMPING

The King Edward River is the first major watercourse encountered on the Mitchell Plateau track and is therefore used extensively by visitors for overnight camping.

A couple of designated camping areas are located near the King Edward River crossing, where you'll also find basic toilet facilities.

The river provides a good supply of permanent water and is a great place to swim. The large pools and small waterfalls are idyllic. After a late Wet, the falls and river will flow almost through to the next Wet.

Firewood is only to be collected from designated collection zones. Signs indicate where firewood can be collected on the way in.

ABORIGINAL ART SITES

There are a number of Aboriginal art sites to be seen in this area and these would include some of the best you'll see in the Kimberley. Please treat them with respect.

A track that veers off to the left just after the *King Edward River* crossing takes you a short distance and stops amongst some tall outcrops of rock. A short walk will take you to a boardwalk that allows good viewing of the Wandjina art.

About 5 km from the King Edward River crossing a track on the right leads into a series of low rock outcrops. A good keen eye and a short walk will result in a number of small but good sites being found. Both Wandjina and Bradshaw figures can be found in different areas of the rocks.

WALK TO THE FALLS

A three hour return walk downstream will take you to a second set of *falls*, falling approximately 15 metres vertically over a horizontal distance of 10 metres.

The walk takes you through varied and diverse ecosystems of pandanus, dry ridges, bubbling rapids, Cadjeput forests, ti-tree thickets and open rocky country.

OLD MINING CAMP/CAMP CREEK AREA

This area is now inhabited by the Kandiwal Aboriginal Community and out of bounds to travellers and access to Camp Creek is closed off, except to those areas around the Ungolan Safari Camp.

UNGOLAN SAFARI CAMP – *KIMBERLEY WILDERNESS ADVENTURES*

This Safari Camp is located on the banks of Camp Creek, amongst a forest of Livestonia palms, close to the Mitchell Plateau airstrip, and is an exclusive permanent safari camp operated by *Kimberley Wilderness Adventures*. All facilities, meals and a camp host are provided. Self-drive travellers can use the camps as part of their Safari Pass, but the accommodation must be pre-booked. For details freecall: 1800 335 003, or check the web at:
www.kimberleywilderness.com.au

TREK NOTES (WGS 84 DATUM)

MITCHELL PLATEAU

***Travelling Time**: From Kalumburu Rd to Mitchell Falls camping area allow 2 hrs 30 mins to 3 hrs.*

***Travelling Time**: From Kalumburu Rd to coast allow 4 hrs 30 mins to 5 hrs.*

0.0 (0.0) *Tk-junct (T/J) on **Kalumburu Road**, 156 km north of Gibb River Road and about 100 km south of Kalumburu. Turn westward to King Edward River and the Mitchell Plateau.*

GPS 14° 55' 44'S 126° 14' 9"E

3.3 (5.1) *Track parallels King Edward River and there are a number of **camp** spots on the left with a little shade.*

6.1 (2.8) ***Camp** site on right, under some large shady trees.*

6.3 (0.2) *King Edward River crossing – small camp site on right just after crossing.*

6.4 (0.1) *T/J – PSA. Lefthand (LH) track (tk) leads to some spectacular **Aboriginal art** sites.*

GPS 14° 54' 7"S 126° 11' 46"E

7.9 (1.5) *T/J – PSA. RH tk leads 300m to river and **No 2 Camping Area**. Good camp with shade. Beautiful rockholes ideal for swimming.*

8.2 (0.3) *T/J – PSA. RH tk leads to river and **No 1 Camping Area**. Good camp.*

11.5 (3.3) *T/J – PSA. RH tk leads to **Aboriginal art** sites*

GPS 14° 52' 50"S 126° 10' 16"E

19.9 (8.6) *Steep descent into valley. Thick forest of Livingstonia Palms begin and continue almost to coast.*

42.1 (22.2) *Lawley Lookout on the right on the edge of the escarpment. Great views.*

65.5 (23.4) *T/J – veer right (VR) for Mitchell Falls and coast.*

68.7 (3.2) *Cross Camp Creek.*

69.3 (0.6) *T/J – PSA. Left leads to 'Plateau Camp' or **Ungolan Safari Camp** on Camp Creek.*

71.0 (1.7) *Cross Roads – PSA. Left leads to Safari camp, Right leads to airstrip.*

71.6 (0.6) *Y-junct – VL.*

GPS 14° 47' 59"S 125° 49' 5"E

RH track leads to Surveyors Pool, Port Warrender & Coastal Access.

***TO MITCHELL FALLS** - Zero Trip Metre*

0.0 (0.0) *Above track junction*

6.9 (1.9) *Top of range with good views across valley.*

16.0 (9.1) ***Mitchell Falls Camping** area – large area with water along the creek and shade.*

TO WALSH POINT/CRYSTAL CREEK

Zero Trip Metre at Y-junct 71.6

0.0 (0.0) *Above track junction*

20.3 (20.3) *T/J – PSA to coast and **Port Warrender.***

GPS 14° 38' 21"S 125° 48' 8"E

LH track SP 'Surveyors Pool – Drive 6.5 km, walk 4 km'.

23.4 (3.1) *Lookout –Good views.*

29.8 (6.4) *Y-junct – RH track leads to **Port Warrender** and **Walsh Point**, SP 'Warning Port Warrender road badly washed out.'*

37.8 (8.0) ***Walsh Point Camping** area*

GPS 14° 34' 6"S 125° 50' 54"E

Travelling time: Allow 1 hour travelling for last 8 km!

Crocodiles and Sandflies abound here.

TO CRYSTAL CREEK

Zero Trip Metre at above Y-junct

0.0 (0.0) *Above track junction. VL*

RH Tk leads to Walsh Point.

8.0 (8.0) *Tk approaches closely to Crystal Creek which is lined by paperbark trees.*

11.0 (3.0) *Y-junct – take RH track to continue further on towards the mangroves. LH track leads 300 metres to a camp near an old Boab tree. Crystal Creek is another 100 metres walk away.*

12.0 (1.0) ***Camp** sites on left.*

12.2 (0.2) *Track ends just before the mangroves.*

Crocodiles and Sandflies abound.

Travelling time: Last 12 km to mouth of Crystal Creek, approx. 1 to 1 hr 30 mins.

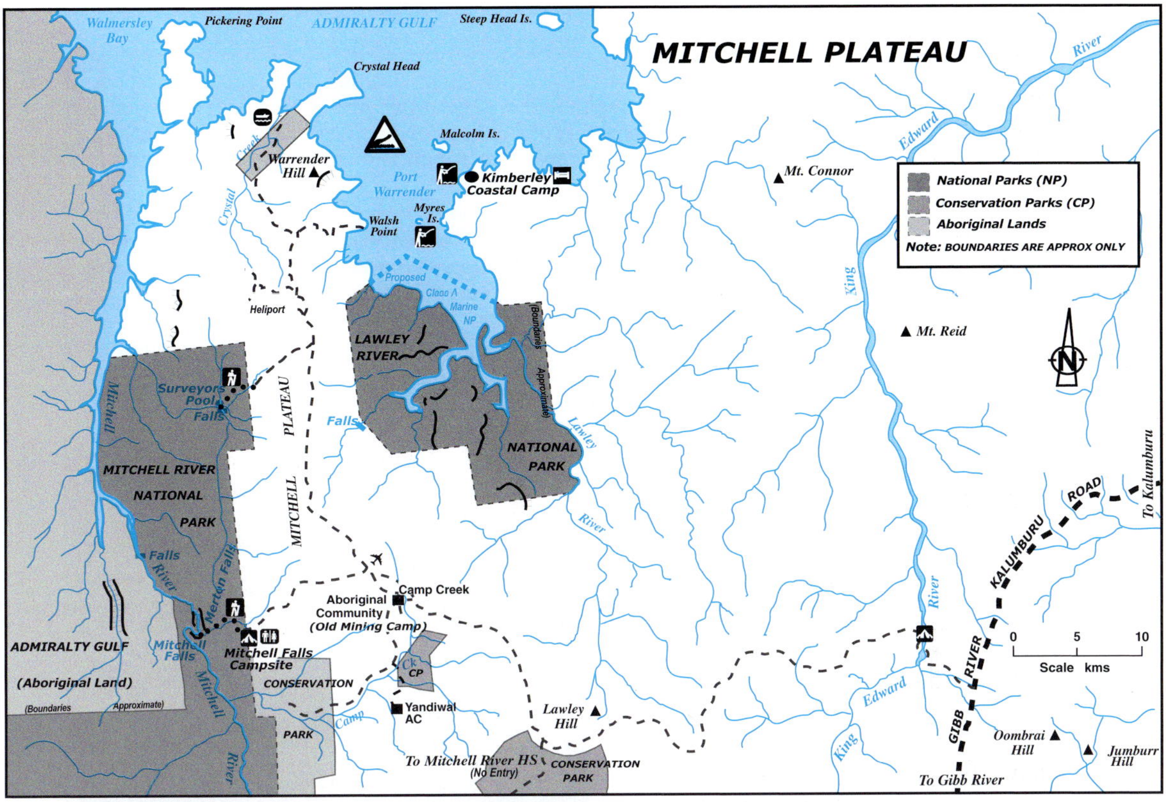

NGAUWUDU – MITCHELL RIVER NATIONAL PARK

The Mitchell River National Park is 115,300 hectares and lies in a remote part of the Kimberley where the Mitchell River, flowing northwards, drains into Walmsley Bay and Admiralty Gulf, carving gorges and waterfalls into the underlying sandstone, particularly along the margins of the Mitchell Plateau. The park abuts the northern boundary of the Prince Regent Nature Reserve, effectively creating a continuous conservation reserve of three quarters of a million hectares. **Ngauwudu** is the name the Wunambal Aboriginal people, who have lived in the vicinity for thousands of years, give to the Mitchell Plateau area, while they call the Mitchell Falls area **Punamii-unpuu**. Pets are not permitted.

HISTORY

The Mitchell Plateau region of north-west Australia contains many reminders of a significant Aboriginal link with the area. The earliest account of European contact with the region was during the second voyage of **Lt Phillip Parker King** between the years 1818 and 1822. King entered Admiralty Gulf in the 83 ton cutter *Mermaid* and anchored in a harbour at its southern end. He named the harbour Port Warrender on 12th October, 1819.

In 1921, **William Robert Easton** led a State government expedition into the north Kimberley country and was reportedly the first European to have traversed the Plateau. Easton named Mitchell River after Sir James Mitchell, the then Premier of Western Australia.

In 1954, **John Morgan** surveyed a route from Gibb River Station to the Kalumburu Aboriginal Mission. This survey provided the basis for the road links to the Mission and subsequently to the Mitchell Plateau.

The extensive bauxite deposit was discovered in 1965 by AMAX exploration team led by **Ken Malcolm**. Malcolm named the Plateau after the Mitchell River, which adjoins it. In 1979/80 bauxite interests were acquired by the Mitchell Plateau Bauxite Company Pty. Ltd.

The Plateau itself is still held under a mining claim and in recent years the Aboriginal people have shown an interest in moving back into this area after being forced out of the place during the World War 2. While the old mining camp at *Camp Creek* has been abandoned by the mining companies, a small group of Aboriginal people have now set up an outstation there.

MITCHELL PLATEAU

ABORIGINAL SITES

There is a host of Aboriginal sites throughout this region and the discerning, experienced eye will find many. All Aboriginal sites are protected under the West Australian Aboriginal Heritage Act of 1972-1980. Should you come in contact with any of these sites please do not touch the art work or damage it in any way.

The Mitchell Falls area was inhabited by the Wunambal people. Since moving to Kalumburu in the 1950s, local Aboriginal people have continued to visit the area and in the last few years have established a community there. A consultative process with Aboriginal people is underway to develop co-operative management arrangements for the park and to provide opportunities for Aboriginal enterprise and employment.

The Wunambal people refer to Wandjina as Gulingi; and the Wunggurr are creators of snakes: their winding travels through the country with Gulingi made the rivers.

GEOGRAPHY

The Mitchell Plateau is a remnant of an elevated and dissected laterite-capped eroded plain which is bordered by lower-lying, jointed sandstone plateau. The surface of the Plateau slopes over a distance of 40 km from an elevation of 430m in the south to an elevation of 290 metres at the coast to the north. A scarp, generally 5 metres high, forms the edge of the Plateau. Below the scarp, scree slopes fall away 30 metres to clay or basalt outcrops.

The sandstone plateau is rugged and jointed. It also slopes to the north and forms a low profile at the coast. The erosion of joints created narrow and deep gorges which, in places, contain waterfalls and permanent pools.

The rocky coast of Admiralty Gulf consists of basaltic headlands, low-lying sandstone, mudflats and small beaches. The headlands are escarpments which, in places, exceed 200 metres in height.

Mudflats between the headlands are of alluvial silt and are incised by meandering tidal creeks. The beaches are composed of shell fragments and fine sand.

Merten Falls has formed a spectacular chasm.

GEOLOGY

The rocks of the Mitchell Plateau are of the Proterozoic Age and basically comprise a 900 metres thick sequence of King Leopold Sandstone overlain by Carson Volcanics.

The Carson Volcanics consist mostly of submarine basalt. The basalt was folded, faulted, uplifted and finally eroded to form an elevated plain or 'plateau'.

During the last 50 million years, the surface of this basalt plain has undergone a process of weathering, or laterisation, under tropical conditions to form bauxite.

In recent times, subsequent elevations relative to sea level caused rejuvenation of the drainage system, and led to the formation of the present topography. A rise in sea level during this period resulted in drowning and silting of the river valleys.

The bauxite deposits occur in a laterite sheet that ranges in thickness from 2 to 5 metres and covers an area of about 400 sq km.

FLORA AND FAUNA

THE FLORA

The most striking feature of the vegetation on the plateau is the predominance of the fan palm *Livistona eastonii* amongst the open eucalypt forest formation of woollybutt, stringybark and Melville Island bloodwoods. This is one of the few places in WA where palms are such a dominant feature.

One of the attractions of the area is the many palms the route passes through.

Along valleys and creek lines the vegetation changes to an open woodland of *Eucalyptus tectifica* (grey box) with a large number of other tree and shrub species, including pandanus palms and Melaleucas (paperbarks) along the watercourses.

Small patches of vine thicket may be encountered on the escarpment slopes where it is thought that they receive extra moisture from ground water. A large number of what are often considered as 'rainforest' species occur in these thickets.

THE FAUNA

The mammal population of the area is rich in its variety and it is possible that up to 50 species may occur in the area, along with some 220 species of birds and 86 species of reptiles and amphibians. This area is in fact the only part of the State which still has the full range of fauna as that which occurred in pre-European times.

BIRDS

Birds are the most conspicuous of the fauna and include Brolgas, Torresian Imperial-Pigeons, Striated Herons, White-bellied Sea-Eagles, Brahminy Kites, as well as such rainforest birds as Rainbow Pittas and Cicada birds.

MAMMALS

Mammals are not nearly as conspicuous, but this area would have to be one of the best areas in Australia for seeing some of our smaller and rarer inhabitants.

The **Northern Quoll** (or North Australian Native Cat), is often seen in the evening and early morning and can even be sighted around the more popular camping sites.

The small rock-wallaby, once known as the Warabi and now called the **Monjon**, is fairly common in the region and we've sometimes fluked them as we've wandered across the rocky country on the way to Mitchell Falls. This unique animal is restricted to the Kimberley.

The **Scaly-tailed Possum** is another endemic animal that can be seen in the very rocky areas. During the day it hides deep in rock crevices and comes out at night to feed in trees.

Other wallabies, small possums and pygmy possums also inhabit this region, so it's well worth spending some time looking for animals.

REPTILES

Reptiles are very common and include large water monitors, some big snakes, plus a host of smaller lizards and snakes.

Dangerous reptiles include the Saltwater Crocodile, the Taipan, King Brown and the Northern Death Adder.

MITCHELL PLATEAU

PUNAMII-UNPUU – MITCHELL FALLS AREA

Camping

The turn-off to Punamii-unpuu - Mitchell Falls camping area is about 71 km west of the Kalumburu Road. This track can be a bit eroded in places and terminates 15 km from the turn-off close to *Mertens Creek*.

The designated camping area at the start of the walking trail to the Mitchell Falls is very popular. This is a large area with plenty of camps, large shady trees and a few long-drop 'Eco toilets'. The camping area backs onto the main walk to the falls near a shallow section of the creek. Please take all rubbish back out with you, as there are no rubbish collection facilities.

A ranger is based at this camping area from May to October, ph: (08) 9161 4172.

Helicopter Flights

Helicopter flights are operated during the peak of the tourist season when a pilot and a helicopter are located at the western end of the camping area. Operated by Heliwork WA (head office Kununurra, ph: (08) 9168 1811, web: **www.slingair.com.au/**), it provides scenic flights to and over the falls as well as around the surrounding area.

The money spent on at least a one-way trip to the falls is well worth it.

Helicopter flights are an awe inspiring way to enjoy the rugged country around the falls.

Walking into or from the falls takes you through a variety of habitats - nearly all hot during the Dry season

Mitchell Falls Walk

From the camping area a walk of 30 to 45 minutes (one way) takes you to **Little Mertens Falls**. Allow time to explore and swim in the pool below the falls. Again there is some excellent Aboriginal art in this area, the main small gallery being close to the pool on the southern side.

A half hour walk further on from Little Mertens are the spectacular **Big Mertens Falls**. These are rarely flowing in the Dry but still make for an impressive sight.

A short distance further is the top cascade of the **Mitchell Falls**. There's pleasant swimming in the pools and if the falls are running it's an unforgettable sight.

The main walk to the head of Punamii-unpuu - Mitchell Falls is a 6 km return walk, and takes about 1 1/2 hours. While the walk is moderate, it is long and hot. For the most part the track is marked with cairns of stone, but don't get caught out coming back too late in the evening – the track is hard to follow when you lose the light! If in doubt walk in close vicinity to the creek.

While access to the pools below the top fall of Mitchell Falls is possible with a rope and a guide, it is difficult and **you are not allowed to swim in the deep pools below the falls.** The lowest pools below the falls are also inhabited by Salt-water Crocodiles!.

AUNAUYU – SURVEYOR'S POOL

Aunauyu – Surveyor's Pool is an isolated pool surrounded by six metre white bluffs of King Leopold sandstone. This remote spot is worth a walk.

The present access to Surveyor's Pool is about 21 km north of the turn-off to the Mitchell Falls camping area. Access is a combination of driving 6.5 km and walking 4 km. See our 'Trek Notes' for details to get there.

Water bottles may be refilled at the pool but **no swimming is allowed**. Once again if you search around, along the cliffs lining the creek, you can find a few small galleries of Aboriginal rock art.

Allow for a walking time of about 1 hr 30 mins to 2 hrs, each way. There is little shade along the route so save it for early morning or late afternoon.

FOR FURTHER INFORMATION

Contact the CALM's Kununurra HQs, Messmate Way, PO Box 942, Kununurra, WA, 6743, ph: (08) 9168 4200, web site:
www.calm.wa.gov.au/

Surveyors Pool .

The Edward River makes for a delightful campsite.

Picturesque Steephead Island at Port Warrender.

CRYSTAL CREEK PORT WARRENDER

CRYSTAL CREEK

Crystal Creek is the northern most point in this area you can reach by vehicle. The creek flows into a small north facing bay and much of the creek near here is lined by low cliffs, however, it does have a small muddy mangrove-lined estuary. You'll quickly see the name of the area is not derived from the clarity of the water either, but from the abundance of quartz crystal found there.

The drive from the Mitchell Falls turn-off can take anything from 2 hours to a day depending on the previous Wet season and the time of the year. It varies from very rough to completely washed out. There are a number of rocky **camp sites** along the cliffs above Crystal Creek, as well as at the track's end. There is no direct access for the launching of boats in this area.

Fresh water is scarce, the sandflies are in plague proportions and there is little shade. However, the fishing is good, although big Salt-water Crocodiles are common. From the cliffs you'll see them cruising the muddy water of the creek.

WALSH POINT – PORT WARRENDER

The last 8 km to the camping area at Walsh Point on the western shores of Port Warrender takes anywhere from one hour to a day – it is not for the faint hearted! At times, this track can become badly eroded and washed out, making it basically impassable to vehicles.

Once at the coast the headland is 200 metres high in places, with mudflats, mangroves and meandering tidal creeks completing the picture. The coastal scenery in the area offers sweeping views of islands and ocean. Malcolm and Steephead are the two main islands visible.

There's six or seven camps along the rocky beach and there are no facilities. It is a fishermen's paradise and an ideal spot to put in a small tinnie. Sandflies and crocs are common.

For more detail on the fishing see the chapter, *'Fishing in the Kimberley'*.

Kimberley Coastal Camp

A remote unique, island-based permanent camp, the Kimberley Coastal Camp, is located on the eastern side of Port Warrender and can only be accessed by sea or air. Visitors can be flown from Kununurra (or by arrangement from Darwin, Broome, etc) to the Mitchell Plateau and met by helicopter for transfer to the camp.

Helicopter transfers are also available for those with their own air or 4WD access to the Mitchell Plateau. Vehicles can be left at the Heliwork's base at Mitchell Falls camping area on an unofficial basis - all care no responsibility!

Boat pick-up from Walsh Point is also available.

Stays here include all accommodation and gourmet meals, plus fully guided fishing, exploring, rock art, wildlife and birdwatching tours.

Accommodation is in twin share, gazebo-style rooms which are flyscreened and feature ceiling fans, reading lights and a great view. Showers and flushing toilets are on a share basis. There is also a swimming pool over looking Admiralty Gulf and there's only a maximum of 8-10 guests.

Open from March to October each year, you can contact the camp on ph/fax: (08) 9161 4410 (April - October only), all year ph: 0417 902 006, all year fax: (08) 9192 2903, email: kimberleycc@bigpond.com.au, or write to PO Box 3402, Broome, WA 6725. You can also log onto their web site: **www.kimberleycoastalcamp.com.au/**.

PRINCE REGENT NATURE RESERVE (633,825 ha)

Covering a vast sweep of rugged sandstone and volcanic country, the Prince Regent Nature Reserve takes in some of the most spectacular coastal scenery in Australia. The many offshore islands and the indented coastline, along with the large tidal fluctuation, causes dramatic tides, currents and whirlpools throughout the area. In fact, this area, along with the whole Kimberley coast between Derby and Wyndham, is one of the most dangerous coasts for navigation in the world.

The centre piece of the reserve is the near-straight chasm of the Prince Regent River, as it slices its way north-westward to the almost land-locked inlet of the Saint George Basin. Fairly large boats can penetrate quite a way upriver to as far as the King Cascade – a spectacular waterfall that is a highlight of any visit to this remote region.

The reserve includes many significant areas and places of scenic grandeur. Biological surveys which are still being carried out have revealed the area to be extremely rich in plant and animal life. Numerous patches of rainforest add to the natural diversity and the area contains more than half of the birds and mammals found throughout the Kimberley, while more than 500 species of plants have so far been recorded.

The region is also extremely rich in Aboriginal art, and there is still much to be discovered.

CALM have submitted proposals for the reserve to be enlarged to take in the complete water catchment area of the river, as well as the water and coast around the Saint George Basin and Prince Frederick Harbour, but this has happened yet.

Access

At present access is restricted. The reserve is declared a 'prohibited area' under the CALM Act and a permit is required to visit it. Notice is required because of the Department's agreement with the Mowanjum Aboriginal Community.

There is no road or track access into the region. The closest track comes in from Mt Elizabeth Station via the Charnley River to Walcott Inlet and to Pantijan.

Helicopter access is possible, but the most popular way is by the charter boats sailing the coast. See our chapter, *Sailing the Coast* for those commercial operators that take trips to this region.

For any further information contact the CALM Regional Office, Messmate Way, PO Box 942, Kununurra, WA, 6743, ph: (08) 9168 4200.

THE GIBB RIVER ROAD

INTRODUCTION

Without a doubt, the best and easiest way to get the feel of the magical Kimberley is to travel the Gibb River Road (GRR). Slicing diagonally through the region, it is the shortest and most spectacular way between Derby in the west and Kununurra in the east.

While the road is the shortest route between east and west, the real advantage and delight of travelling along this route is the fact that it takes you through some of the most picturesque country in the Kimberley. You pass numerous magnificent gorges, rivers and waterholes, while hidden amongst the rocky bluffs is the imposing art of the Aboriginal people – the stark space-like Wandjina figures of the Dreamtime.

HISTORY

It is only relatively recently that Europeans moved into the area beyond the King Leopold Ranges. Up until the 1930s the number of Whitemen north of the Napier Range and west of Wyndham could be literally counted on one hand.

After the end of World War II the 'furtherest out' stations were Gibb River and Karunjie, even though earlier pioneers had opened up properties closer to Kalumburu, they had failed years before. In the early 1950s Scotty Salmon and Dave Russ built a road from Wyndham to their property at Karunjie via the New York Jump-up. In 1954 a government surveying and road construction team, led by John Morgan, blazed a route from Karunjie to Gibb River then north to Kalumburu. Still by the mid 1970s the GRR was nothing more than a track and a trip to Derby from Gibb River was a two or three day run, each way!

The Mitchell Plateau, even more remote, was penetrated in the late 1950s by mineral exploration teams, but it was to be years before road access was opened up.

THE ROAD ITSELF

The graded dirt road for the most part during the Dry is pretty good. Travelling from Kununurra out as far as the Gibb River Station/Kalumburu Road the road is at its worst – and that's not particularly bad. From Gibb River south the road improves. There are a few bridges, concrete causeways and even some lengthy stretches of bitumen. Finally a narrow strip of bitumen begins and takes you into Derby.

The road is often impassable in the Wet because of the many large rivers that cut its route. Obviously if you're an early Dry season traveller you may have a little trouble. Ask at Derby, Kununurra or Wyndham Police Stations for the latest information on the condition of the road, or to check on road conditions throughout the Kimberley, contact the Main Roads Western Australia – road conditions (all hours) ph: 1800 013 314, or check out their web site: **www.mainroads.wa.gov.au/**. You could also contact the Regional offices at Derby, ph: (08) 9158 4333, or Kununurra, ph: (08) 9168 1755.

OUR TREK NOTES

Our Trek Notes describe the route in detail and the following pages give a thorough description of the many highlights to be found but describe the GRR from the Kununurra end south to Derby. In our opinion it's the best way to go as the scenery is better that way!

Be aware that differences in tyres and speedos can result in significant variations to the figures given, ie most speedos are within +/- 10%, but that can mean 10 km every 100 km!

For camping spots along the way see our Trek Notes.

REMEMBER

It should be remembered that the land on both sides of the Gibb River Road, even where it is not fenced, is private property. Please camp where provision has been made for camping – it's a privilege allowed by the station owner. Don't light fires in the open, don't trespass and don't discharge firearms. Carry your rubbish out with you.

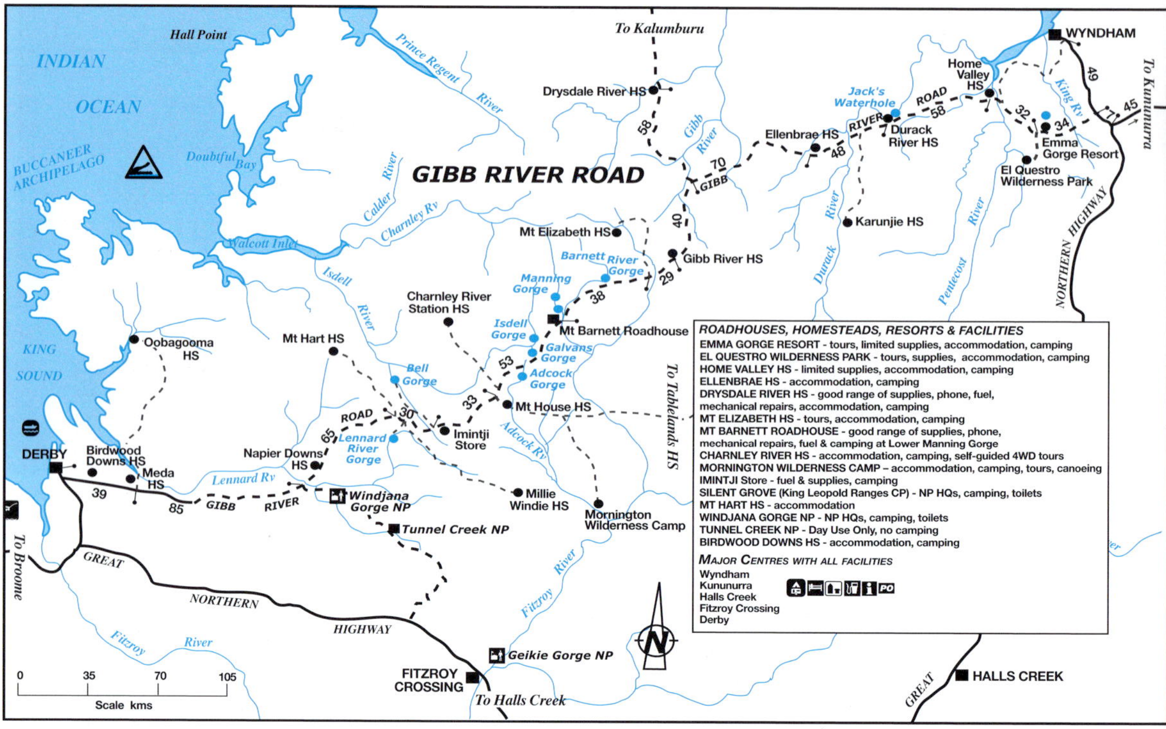

The wide causeway crossing of the Pentecost River, with the impressive ramparts of the Cockburn Range making an awe inspiring backdrop.

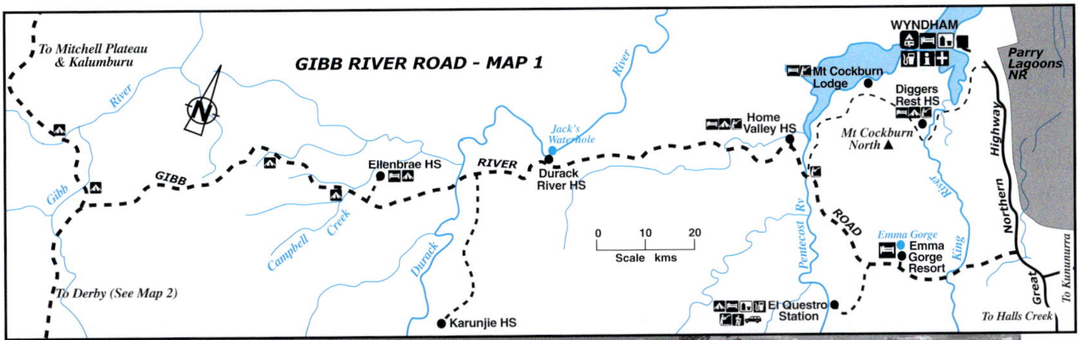

TREK NOTES

JUNCTION GREAT NORTHERN HIGHWAY & GIBB RIVER ROAD

0.0 (0.0) Track Junction *(T/J) – Great Northern Highway and Gibb River Road. Turn left onto the dirt and the start of the* ***Gibb River Road.*** *Wyndham is 49 km straight ahead and Kununurra 52 km east.*	*▲241.6 (8.4)*
8.4 (8.4) T/J – PSA*. Left-hand (LH) track (tk) leads to Aboriginal art paintings which can be found in the rocky outcrop just off the road.*	*▲233.2 (3.8)*
12.2 (3.8) T/J – PSA*. Righthand (RH) tk is the* ***King River Road*** *and leads to* ***Diggers Rest station****. (See page 101 for Trek Notes)*	*▲229.4 (4.8)*
17.0 (4.8) King River *crossing. Normally dry.* ***No Camping****. Saltwater crocodiles are possible.*	*▲224.6 (1.4)*
18.4 (1.4) T/J – PSA*. LH tk leads into Aboriginal art site.*	*▲223.2 (5.6)*
24.0 (5.6) T/J – PSA*. Right-hand (RH) tk leads to* ***Emma Gorge*** *– 2 km off road.* ***Accommodation*** *available. Part of El Questro Station.*	*▲217.6 (9.8)*
33.8 (9.8) T/J – PSA*. LH tk leads to* ***El Questro Station*** *(about 17 km from junction).* ***Camping, accommodation*** *available. There are also some lovely gorges to explore on the station, ph: (08) 9161 4318.*	*▲207.8 (3.8)*
37.6 (3.8) T/J – PSA*. LH tk leads approx 200 metres down to a group of Boabs and creek, making a possible* ***camp*** *site.*	*▲204.0 (1.0)*
38.6 (1.0) Fish Hole*. Small* ***camping*** *area with permanent water on left, marked by 3 Boab trees. This spot however is right beside the road and would be a bit dusty.*	*▲203.0 (19.2)*
57.8 (19.2) Pentecost River *– causeway. Fresh water upstream, saltwater downstream. Excellent fishing downstream. Watch out for Crocs!!* ***No camping*** *- day use area only. RH tk just before crossing on east side of river continues onwards to Wyndham along the* ***Karunjie King River Road****. See our chapter 'The Eastern Kimberley' page 101 for info and trek notes. Main road parallels river for a kilometre after crossing.*	*▲183.8 (8.7)*
66.5 (8.7) T/J – veer left *(VL) to continue on Gibb River Road. RH tk takes you to* ***Home Valley Homestead. Camping and accommodation****, ph: (08) 9161 4322.*	*▲175.1 (1.0)*
67.5 (1.0) Good views*. The Cockburn Range is dominant to the east, to the north the Pentecost and Durack Rivers and the West Arm of Cambridge Gulf.*	*▲174.1 (0.9)*
68.4 (0.9) T/J – PSA*. LH tk leads a short distance to* ***Home Valley Lookout****.*	*▲173.2 (5.9)*
The roads winds through the range.	
74.3 (5.9) T/J – PSA*. RH tk leads to camp site overlooking Durack River. No water and little shade.*	*▲167.3 (5.9)*
80.2 (5.9) T/J – PSA*. RH tk leads to small* ***camp*** *site 200mtrs from road.*	*▲161.4 (0.6)*
80.8 (0.6) T/J – PSA*. RH tk leads to small* ***camp*** *site 100 metres from road, situated on top of bank of small creek.*	*▲160.8 (4.7)*
85.5 (4.7) Bindoola Creek – O'Malley's crossing*. The first crossing of Bindoola Creek. You cross it again approx 18 km further on. Both crossings are generally dry. Wide creek bed, but no problem.* ***No camping****.*	*▲156.1 (36.0)*
121.5 (36.0) Gregory's Jump-up *– steep grade - sealed section.*	*▲120.1 (3.0)*

TREK NOTES (CONTINUED) FROM PAGE 151

JUNCTION GREAT NORTHERN HIGHWAY & GIBB RIVER ROAD	
124.5 (3.0) ***T/J - PSA***. *RH tk leads into* ***Durack River HS & Jack's Waterhole***. *No access. In the 'Wet' of 2002 the HS and facilities were washed away. This station is now Aboriginal. Contact Home Valley Station for further information.*	*▲117.1 (3.5)*
128.0 (3.5) ***T/J - PSA***. *LH tk leads to Karunjie Station.*	*▲113.6 (6.0)*
134.0 (6.0) ***Bamboo Creek***.	*▲107.6 (1.4)*
135.4 (1.4) ***Rollies Jump-up*** *- bitumen up range.*	*▲106.2 (11.8)*
147.2 (11.8) ***T/J - PSA***. *LH tk leads to* ***Karunjie Station*** *- Visits can only be organised by prior arrangement with Home Valley Station.*	*▲94.4 (4.8)*
152.0 (4.8) ***Durack River***. *RH tk just after crossing leads along river to a nice spot with plenty of shade and permanent water.*	*▲89.6 (20.5)*
172.5 (20.5) ***T/J - PSA***. *RH tk leads to* ***Ellenbrae Homestead*** *- now closed to tourists.*	*▲69.1 (3.0)*
175.5 (3.0) ***Dawn Creek***. *RH tk just after crossing leads to some reasonable* ***camp*** *spots, near permanent water. Good birdlife.*	*▲66.1 (23.4)*
198.9 (23.4) ***T/J - PSA***. *RH tk leads approx. 100 metres to a reasonable, shady* ***camping*** *area on* ***Campbell River***.	*▲42.7 (19.5)*
218.4 (19.5) ***Russ Creek.***	*▲23.2 (23.2)*
241.6 (23.2) ***T/J - turn left*** *(TL) to continue along the* ***Gibb River Road***. *Right will take you on to the* ***Kalumburu Road*** *to the* ***Drysdale River Station***, ***Mitchell Plateau*** *and* ***Kalumburu***. *Well setup roadside stop in large clearing, with information board, picnic table and shade hut .*	*▲0.0 (0.0)* *Trek cont's on page 160*

EMMA GORGE

The turn-off to Emma Gorge is approx 24 km from the Great Northern Highway and 2 km in from the Gibb River Road. Part of El Questro Station, this lovely gorge, with its diminutive waterfall, fern clothed cliffs and beautiful, clear spring water, is a lovely spot.

While there is **no camping**, **accommodation** is available in tented cabins at the **Emma Gorge Resort**, which are dotted amongst a picturesque wilderness habitat. The cabins have 240v power and fans. The more upmarket cabins have their own private facilities, whilst the standard tented cabins have use of a shared bathroom block.

There is also a fully licensed bar and restaurant, along with a swimming pool, airstrip (900m gravel strip, location: 128° 07.30'E 15° 55.30'S) and public phone, while a store offers a limited range of grocery supplies.

Day Visitors

From the car parking area and store it is only a short walk to the beautiful **Emma Gorge** itself. All guests, including day visitors just wanting to walk to the gorge and enjoy a swim need are required to purchase a **Wilderness Park Permit** - $15.00 per person, valid 1 to 7 days (children under 15 years free of charge).

All major credit cards are accepted as payment for goods and services.

For more information and bookings you can write to Emma Gorge, PO Box 909, Kununurra, WA, 6743, ph: (08) 9169 1777, fax: (08) 9169 1383, or check out El Questro's web site at:
www.elquestro.com.au/emma-gorge-resort/

EL QUESTRO WILDERNESS PARK

About 34 km from the Great Northern Highway is the turn-off to El Questro Wilderness park, which lies another 17 km off the road. While it is a working cattle station of 1 million acres, it also offers the traveller a wide range of **accommodation**, **camping,** facilities and activities.

Access

Once off the main Gibb River Road the track to the station can best be described as 'fair to good'. Early in the season the crossing of the *Pentecost River*, not all that far from the station township, can be a problem as it is often over a metre deep.

The station has a 1400 metre gravel airstrip, location: 127° 58.50'E 16° 00.30'S.

Visiting El Questro for the Day or Longer

Self Guided

Wilderness Park Permit

All visitors to El Questro Wilderness Park are required to purchase a Wilderness Park Permit upon arrival at the property.

An **El Questro Wilderness Park Permit** allows access to both the Wilderness Park and Emma Gorge. These permits are available for purchase at El Questro, Emma Gorge, or from the Reservations Office in Banksia Street, Kununurra.

A Wilderness Park Permit entitles the bearer to access many of the natural features and other attractions at El Questro. These include the Chamberlain Gorge, Zebedee Springs, the Explosion Gorge System and most fishing holes, to name a few.

The cost of the Wilderness Park Permit is, at present, $15.00 per adult, and is valid for up to seven days. Children 15 years and under free of charge.

Guided Full Day Tour

El Questro operates a full day tour of the Wilderness Park that departs from Kununurra. Accompanied by a Ranger the tour includes gorge walks, Zebedee Thermal Springs, lunch at the Steakhouse Restaurant and a boat trip on the *Chamberlain River*. Tours operate most days of the season. These can be booked at Emma Gorge Resort and the Station Store on El Questro. No forward bookings are necessary for groups under 10 persons.

Camping – Station Township & Riverside

You have a choice of a number of camping sites to choose from. The location known as **Black Cockatoo** is central to bathrooms, laundry and the Station Store. Generators are permitted, but must be turned off after 8.00 pm. For those looking for a bit of seclusion, just 10 minutes drive from the station there are a number of delightful **riverside camping** spots nestled under shady trees along the *Pentecost River*. Riverside campers have the use of the central facilities building back at the station township.

The camping season is from around the 1st April to 31st October, subject to climatic conditions. No forward bookings are required for groups under 10 persons.

Campers must purchase a Wilderness Park Permit in addition to their camping fee.

Accommodation

The Station also has a wide range of accommodation available and these include:

- **El Questro Station Township Bungalows**, situated near the heart of the station, on the banks of the *Pentecost River*, are air-conditioned with private facilities.
- **El Questro Homestead** – This fully exclusive and inclusive accommodation is a luxurious, secluded retreat.

Other Facilities

The **Station Store** supplies fuel, camping gas, road supplies and sundries. Maps and trail data sheets are also available.

The **Steakhouse Restaurant** provides meals (breakfast, lunch & dinner), while the **Swinging Arm Bar** is open in the evenings with a fully stocked bar, snacks and campfire entertainment.

Other facilities to be found include a public phone.

All major credit cards are accepted as payment for goods and services, including accommodation and camping costs.

Eftpos is also available at the store.

Fishing and exploring at the end of Chamberlain Gorge, on El Questro.

Tours

El Questro offers a diverse range of activities for the Ecotourist, Agritourist and Sportstourist alike - whether it's photographing butterflies, fishing for barramundi or 4-wheel driving.

Experience boating on the Chamberlain Gorge, or the relaxing thermal pools of Zebedee Springs. Horse trekking is a fabulous way to observe all kinds of Kimberley wildlife. While a scenic helicopter flight through canyons and gorges, past waterfalls, caves offers unrivalled views of this awesome country. Entry to Zebedee Thermal Springs closes at 12:00pm each day of the season.

Please be aware that all tours and activities are subject to availability and change due to weather conditions. Minimum and maximum tour numbers may apply.

There are a number of 4WD tracks for you to explore, such as *Explosion Gorge* and the *Salerno Gorge* & Matteo Rock Track. Alternately, you could go bushwalking, either on your own or with a guide, and explore the surrounding magnificent gorge country, such as the Gorge Trail to *Halfway Pool*, or further to *Mac Micking Pool* (6.8 km return). A little further afield is the Karunjie King River Road.

El Questro is also a birdwatcher's paradise.

For Further Information

Write to El Questro, PO Box 909, Kununurra, WA, 6743, ph: (08) 9169 1777, fax: (08) 9169 1383 (booking office), Station office, ph: (08) 9161 4318, fax: (08) 9161 4355, web site: **www.elquestro.com.au/**

HOME VALLEY STATION

Located near the junction of *Bindoola Creek* and the *Pentecost River*, the 700,000 acre Home Valley Station is owned by the Indigenous Land Corporation (**www.ilc.gov.au**) but it is managed as a tourist facility by Nick and Sarah Bradley.

Home Valley is a hub of activity that caters not only for travellers on the Gibb River Road (GRR), but for indigenous students and trainees from many communities across the Kimberley. Skills-based programmes are run continuously throughout the Dry season delivering tuition in fencing, welding, concreting, tourism, horsemanship, stock handling and other practical skills.

The property welcomes visitors and offers station style accommodation, dinner, bed & breakfast and **camping,** as well as a range of tours. It is open between April and October. For visitors there's plenty of bird life to observe, bushwalking, and of course, some great fishing.

Access

Home Valley is located just off the main GRR just west of the crossing of the mighty Pentecost River and 119km from Kununurra.

Should you wish to make arrangements for a fly-in visit, please contact the homestead. Co-ordinates for the all-weather strip are: 15° 43' 23" S 127° 49' 41" E.

The Home Valley Homestead stretches along the picturesque *Bindoola Creek* and makes a great stopover for all those travellers who are exploring the Wyndham and Kununurra area, or travelling the GRR to or from Kununurra.

Accommodation

Recently refurbished and upgraded Bed & Breakfast accommodation is available at the homestead for those who prefer their creature comforts. Guests may choose to stay in a Homestead Room or one of the 'Grass Castles', nestled along the Bindoola Creek, but also close to the homestead. These stylish and comfortable bungalows have an ensuite bathroom and air-conditioning. Guests can enjoy a drink up on their deck overlooking the creek and keep a watch out for some friendly freshwater crocs below!

Camping

The property offers a large lawn **camping** area for travellers with plenty of shade, as well as a swimming pool, BBQ facilities, hot showers and flush toilets.

For those wanting a more remote experience, **bush camping** is available at designated bush camp sites along the *Pentecost River* where ablutions and running water are also available. It is arguably one of the most scenic and idyllic locations in the Kimberley

It is best to ring and book beforehand to make sure that there is accommodation available.

Other Facilities

The Dusty Bar and Grill is open for all meals and snacks to those not only staying on the property but also passing by.

Home Valley's Reception and Store provides general items including cool drinks, snacks, ice, bait, selected groceries and personal items. EFTPOS is available but there is no cash out facility. There is also no fuel available. Minor mechanical repairs can be provided.

Tours

Home Valley offers a range of tours which can be undertaken as a passenger in their vehicle or in your own 4WD as a tag-along. The trips include:
shore or boat based fishing tours;

- 4WD tours of the station property that take in such places as Bindoola Gorge, rarely visited Aboriginal art sites, delightful Spider Springs and Ngarli lagoon;
- a bird watchers tour;
- a sunset tour which takes in spectacular views of the Cockburn Range; and,
- a range of horse riding trails.

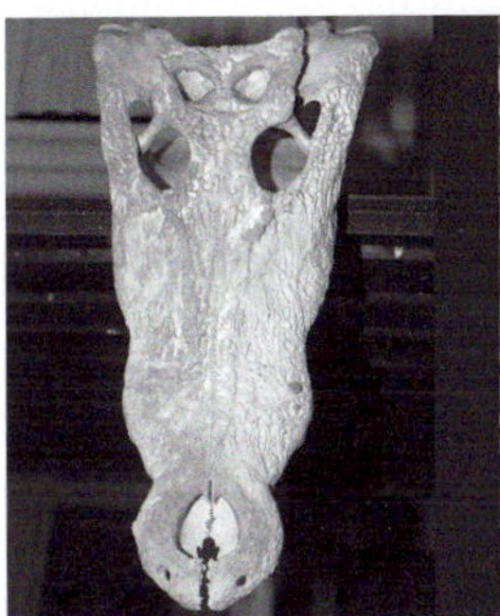

For Further Information

You can contact Home Valley by writing to PMB 15, Kimberley Downs, WA, 6728, or ph: (08) 9161 4322, fax: (08) 9161 4288, web site: **www.homevalley.com.au**

The river crossings south of Home Valley can be a little deep in the early Dry season.

DURACK RIVER STATION – JACK'S WATERHOLE

Durack River Station is another property owned by the Indigenous Land Corporation.

Situated on the *Durack River*, Jack's Waterhole is less than a kilometre off the main road and some 124 km from the Great Northern Highway. During 1986 & '87 a station homestead was built just a stone's throw from Jack's Waterhole, and over the years the facilities had been upgraded to improve the comfort and safety of travellers. Unfortunately, all that hard work, infrastructure and facilities disappeared down the Durack River in the 'Wet' of 2002.

At present there are no facilities or camping at Durack River and there is no access.. For further details contact Home Valley, ph: (08) 9161 4322.

KARUNJIE STATION

Karunjie Station is yet another property now owned by the Indigenous Land Corporation.

The turn-off to Karunjie Homestead is about 150 km from the Great Northern Highway, with the homestead some 45 km from the road. The property was once a real outpost, even by Kimberley standards and much of the surrounding country has changed little over the years.

At present the station is closed and visits can only be organised by prior arrangement with Home Valley Station, ph: (08) 9161 4322.

ELLENBRAE STATION

Ellenbrae Station is located approx 172km from the Great Northern Highway, with the homestead being reached another 5km in from the GRR. This small family run concern welcomes travellers and has swimming, bushwalking, bream fishing and bird watching to enjoy.

The station offers camping in two locations, the Ringers Camp or the Bush Camp, with the former being the better of the two. Accommodation is also available in basic eco-friendly bungalows. Evening meals and breakfasts are also available and bookings for meals and accommodation is necessary.

Basic food supplies can be procured but there is no fuel.

You can contact the station on ph: (08) 9161 4325, or write to PMB 23, Kununurra, WA 6743.

DRYSDALE RIVER STATION

This station is located 60 km north of the GRR on the Kalumburu Road, and just one km off that road. It provides a full range of services and facilities for the traveller. For complete details see the chapter, *Mitchell Plateau and Northern Kimberley. page 130.* **You can contact Drysdale River Station**, ph/fax: (08) 9161 4326. Web: **www.drysdaleriver.com.au/**.

MT ELIZABETH STATION

Mt Elizabeth Station turn-off is about halfway between Derby and Kununurra along the Gibb River Road. The homestead is 30 km in from the main road and is run by the Lacy family whose forefather helped pioneer this country.

Accommodation

Accommodation at the homestead, with dinner, bed & breakfast provided, is available for quite a moderate cost, however prior bookings are requested.

Staying at the homestead gives visitors a unique and very pleasant opportunity to spend some time with Peter & Pat Lacy and one we would thoroughly recommend.

Camping

Campers have the use of the **camping** area near the homestead with hot and cold showers, flush toilets and BBQ facilities. And, if you are sick of cooking, dinner with the Lacys' can be arranged upon request. Again, prior advice of your expected arrival is appreciated, but not essential.

Other Facilities

Visitors also have the chance to purchase locally made artifacts and souvenirs from the homestead.

At present you can only use cash or travellers cheques as payment for services and goods at the station, and we suggest that you check before your expected visit to see if the situation has changed.

The station also has its own airstrip, which during the Wet is often its only means of contact with the outside world.

Just some of the landscapes you'll encounter during your travels on Mt Elizabeth Station.

FOR FURTHER INFORMATION

You can contact Mt Elizabeth Station by writing to the station, via Derby, WA, 6728, or by ph/fax: (08) 9191 4644, web site: **www.holiday-wa.net/station.htm**.

WALCOTT INLET TRACKS

For more info see pages 158-159 for this tough trip.

TOURS – BUSHTRACK SAFARIS

The best way to explore some of the more isolated spots in the region is to join one of the 4WD safaris operated by ***Bushtrack Safaris***, based at Derby.

They specialise in bird, botany, Aboriginal art, fishing and photographic trips. On their safaris you not only get into the remote places, but also see many sites you would miss on your own. The trip follows the track to Munja, with a base camp at Bachsten Falls. Facilities include hot showers, toilets and BBQs. This tour also visits Walcott Inlet, where passengers can either board a boat and do a 6 day sea safari, flying out from Cockatoo Is back to Broome or Derby. Bushtrack Safaris also offers a 'self-contained' guided tour in your own 4WD from Mt Elizabeth, following the Guided Tour and catering for yourself.

For more information write to PO Box 7, Derby, WA, 6728, ph/fax: (08) 9191 1547, web: **www.bushtracksafaris.com.au**.

GIBB RIVER ROAD

BARNETT RIVER GORGE

About 9.5 km south of the Mt Elizabeth track is the turn-off to *Barnett River Gorge*. Keep to the right as you proceed in and you'll come to a parking area about 4 km in from the main road. The last one km or so is pretty rough and you'll get to the first parking area where a fainter track heads sharply right and along a little further.

From this second parking area, beside a large boab, it is only a 200 metre walk, upriver to the gorge. This stretch of water, although not as scenically impressive as some gorges go in the Kimberley, is still a truly delightful spot and a pleasant place to cool off. If you've got the time the birdwatching is great. On the walk in, keep a lookout on the left for the first set of markers as this will take you to another swimming spot on the gorge with sandy beaches and deep pools.

From the first car parking area it is just a short 100 metre walk across the rock slabs to some delightful small waterfalls and pools.

CAMPING

If you are looking for a pleasant **camping** spot, then take the left-hand fork back at the first track junction, 2.9 km in from the **Gibb River** road. This track will take you past some old stock yards and there are a number of tracks leading to some excellent camp sites beside the **Barnett River**. The better one is located down a sandy bank under some shady trees beside a large pool of water. There are no facilities.

Directly across the water from the end of the walking track some **Aboriginal paintings** can be found under an obvious overhang. They're extremely faded and fragile so, as with all art sites, look, but don't touch.

Delightful Barnett River near the Gorge.

WALCOTT INLET TRACKS

There are two access tracks which lead across private land leading to Walcott Inlet. One is across Mt Elizabeth station, the other is across Charnley River station. These tracks join just east of Bachsten Camp.

This is extremely remote country and the tracks are faint, sometimes non-existent as well as being very slow and rough. Rocky step-like climbs and creek crossings mean that this is not for the faint hearted. If you are the first vehicle through for the season it will be much harder as the grass makes a serious challenge of finding the track.

Good navigation skills are essential. We followed the track clearing party and the travelling times mentioned opposite are for an easy to find and follow track!

Any person wishing to travel the track must contact *Mt Elizabeth Station* or *Charnley River Station* and *Bushtrack Safaris* beforehand to get advice on areas to visit and general conditions of this track.

History

Fred Eastman was the first white man to eke out an existence in the area around Walcott Inlet – in about 1918-1920. He was taken by a crocodile and a plaque has been set-up near the old mission site to commemorate his life and death in this wild land.

The ruins of the old Munja Mission, close to the upper reaches of the Inlet was run by a Rev Love and was established in 1918. This site is obviously marked by an old galvanised water tank but in the grass there is a wood-fired baker's oven and the odds and sods of this remote settlement. Once upon a time the mission had cattle and grew a lot of peanuts, using a donkey-powered shovel to grade the ground. The old pearling luggers would come up to bring supplies to the mission and pick up the peanuts.

The Walcott Inlet Track to Munja Camp was first by established Pete Lacy (of Mt Elizabeth Station) and his brother in 1961.

Pete Lacy helped establish the Walcott Inlet Track.

Originally back in 1931 Peter's dad, Frank, had been commissioned by the government to take 1000 head of cattle from near Wyndham to the Munja Mission, which was then a feeding station for the local Aborigines. There was a fair amount of leprosy amongst the Aboriginal people at that time so the government was trying to entice them into missions for testing and treatment.

In 1961 a Bob Dowling took up the Sale River and Munja pastoral leases on condition that an access track could be built to it. After contacting Mt Elizabeth, Pete and his brother – using Frank's detailed diaries and the latest topo maps – chose a route then rode out on horses to blaze a way. With a few Aboriginal helpers, they then built a road. Over the rocky bits they manhandled boulders out of the way while digging out the creeks with picks and shovels to make them passable – no machinery was used. It took them just three weeks!

It IS NOT an 'illegal track' and has never been – as some conservation groups are want to say. All they want to do is close it!

Permits, Access and Camping

The most popular route is across Mt Elizabeth and most travellers go both in and out on this track as it is opened up each year by a party from the station and Bachsten Camp.

Permits and keys are required from Mt Elizabeth station, ph: (08) 9191 4644, for the route west of Mt Elizabeth to Bachsten Camp. Another fee is payable to Bachsten Camp (Bushtrack Safaris, ph: (08) 9191 1547) to get you to Walcott Inlet. Generally you pay one or the other both fees. To stay at Bachsten Camp, you must contact them beforehand. Hot showers, toilets and a pleasant camping area are provided.

If heading south from Bachsten Camp to Charnley River station a permit is required from the latter, ph: (08) 9191 4646.

No facilities are provided in any other bush camping areas.

This route is closed during the Wet season and generally up until May, when a team and tractor has slashed and repaired the route from Mt Elizabeth to Walcott Inlet.

Mt Elizabeth to Bachsten Camp

From near the homestead (GPS 16° 25' 6"S 126° 6' 10"E) the track heads across the sandy Hann River following fences for the first 20km or so. The route traverses fairly flat country for about 50km (2 to 3 hours driving) to the upper reaches of Drysdale River where this stream is crossed at a rocky shallow bar (GPS 16° 9' 6"S 125° 58' 18"E).

Magpie Jump-up is climbed 16.5km later and there are a number of boggy creek crossings, swamps and plains to cross. The impressive Jamieson Arch is passed another 42km further on, the arch being located high in the escarpment 200metres to the right.

Nearly 16km later the track crosses Pearson Creek and continues as before. The faint track junction to Charnley River is met 142km from Mt Elizabeth (GPS 16° 0' 5"S 125° 22' 54"E) and to this point it is about an 8 to 9 hour drive. Less than 2km later the track to Bachsten Camp is on the right. Just over 1km later you are at the camp (GPS 15° 59' 22"S 125° 19' 47"E).

This route passes a number of spectacular Aboriginal art sites.

There is some amazing art to see, as well as some swampy and rocky terrain to traverse.

Charnley River to Bachsten Camp

A pretty well maintained track from the homestead heads north for 20km passing the old Beverley Springs homestead ruins. It crosses the Charnley River and the northern boundary of the property after another 47km and a 2 to 3 hour drive from the homestead.

The next 36km to the track junction near Bachsten Camp is slow and arduous – it is often near impassable and the first through for the season has to contend with a nonexistent track, washed away gullies and creek crossings and water damaged rocky climbs. The route passes through some Aboriginal land and climbs a number of rocky jump-ups and these are very rough. This last leg, providing you are not the first, takes another 4 to 5 hours to Bachsten Camp at the best of times. A permit is required from Charnley River station to drive this route, ph: (08) 9191 4646.

Bachsten Camp to Walcott Inlet

The route from Bachsten Camp to the coast starts in rocky country which is slow to traverse. Nearly 16km from the camp you'll be in severe rock country with delightful Wren's Gorge to your right. Less than 6km later and about 2 hours drive from Bachsten Camp, you'll come to the fast flowing Calder River – be very careful with this crossing!

From here you begin to traverse river flat country and about 5km later a track on the left leads to a good campsite on Karl Lagoon. Then you'll cross Flat Rock Creek (GPS 16° 8' 49"S 125° 8' 20"E) 7.5km later and Red Bull Creek 18km further on. You'll be in hill country once again for a short while, passing a burnt out Cruiser and passing through a narrow grassy valley along a creek bed. Soon you'll be back on floodplain country again and just after a creek crossing, 66.5km from Bachsten Camp, you'll see a water tank on the left – it's the closest fresh water to Walcott Inlet. Less then 3km later you'll pass Curlew Flat (GPS 16° 18' 49"S 124° 57' 41"E) where most experienced Walcott travellers camp to stay away from the sand flies.

An old mustering camp is passed less than 2km later and then a track on the right leads to a rough airstrip. Munja Camp (16° 21' 39"S 124° 56' 48"E) on the edge of the Walcott Inlet is reached 54.5km and a 4 to 6 hour drive from Bachsten Camp. From here a track leads alongside the inlet for another few kilometres, giving access to other campsites and fishing spots.

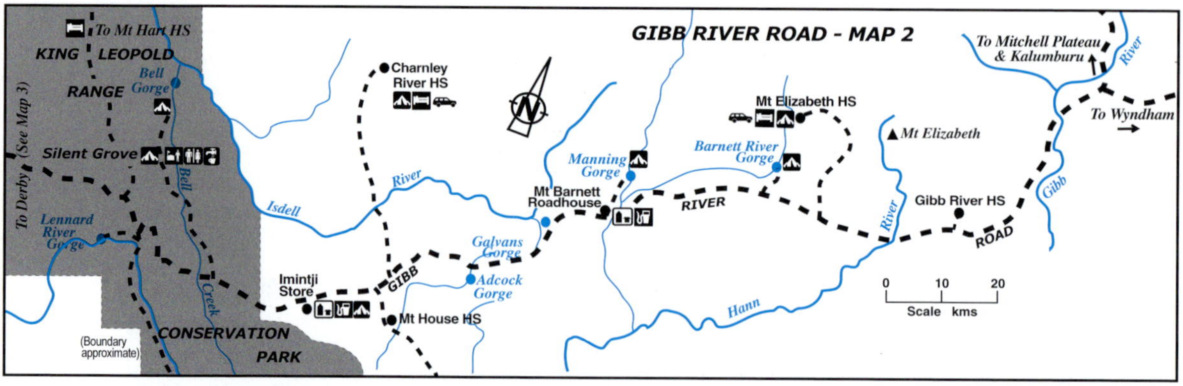

MT BARNETT ROADHOUSE – MANNING GORGE

MT BARNETT ROADHOUSE

Mt Barnett Roadhouse, situated on Mt Barnett Station, is approximately 307 km north of Derby and 32 km south of Mt Elizabeth Station and about 27 km south of the Barnett River Gorge turn-off. Manning Gorge is only accessible via the roadhouse. Since early 1988 the station has been owned and worked by the local Aboriginal Kupungarri community and the roadhouse established.

Facilities

The roadhouse is well setup, supplying all fuels to passing travellers, as well as oils, minor mechanical repairs, tyres and tubes. The store stocks a good range of groceries and frozen meals and you can even pick up some fruit and vegetables, along with hot and cold take-away food, cold drinks, ice, etc.

Toilet, shower & laundry facilities are also available.

You can also dispose of your rubbish in the central garbage trailer.

The store trades 7 days per week in the Dry season, (May to October), from 7.00am to 12.00pm and 1.00 pm to 5.00pm. Eftpos facilities available and most major credit cards accepted. It operates on restricted hours during the Wet.

You can contact the roadhouse by phoning (08) 9191 7007, or write to PMB, Derby, WA, 6728.

MANNING GORGE

Manning River Camp Site

The roadhouse is also the place to get your permit and pay your **camping** fee to stay at nearby *Manning Gorge*. The fee is quite reasonable and the camping area itself, situated 7 km from the roadhouse, is very pleasant. Situated beside the clear, cool waters of the Lower Manning Gorge, there are shady camp sites to choose from in a large camping area which is dotted with magnificent Boab trees.

There are toilet facilities, water tank and fire places, but no fire wood. If you arrive after store hours you can proceed to the camping area and obtain your permit the next day.

The Upper Manning Gorge & Manning Falls

The walk to the Upper Manning Gorge and Manning Falls is a relatively easy 1 1/2 hours each way, while speed hogs will be able to do it faster – it's around a 2 km walk. You can either cross the *Manning River* to the other side from the camping area, or walk around the pool, to begin your walk.

Beautiful Upper Manning Gorge.

TREK NOTES - GIBB RIVER ROAD JUNCTION GIBB RIVER ROAD & KALUMBURU ROAD TO SILENT GROVE/BELL GORGE TURN-OFF		Trek continues on from pg 160
0.0 (0.0)	***T-Junction*** *– veer left to continue on* ***Gibb River Road****. RH track (tk) takes you to the* ***Mitchell Plateau*** *and* ***Kalumburu****.*	▲193.3 (16.5)
16.5 (16.5)	***Creek*** *crossing – possible* ***camp*** *sites.*	▲176.8 (23.5)
40.0 (23.5)	***T/J – PSA****. RH tk leads to* ***Gibb River station*** *– no fuel available.*	▲153.3 (3.5)
43.5 (3.5)	***Bryce Creek.***	▲149.8 (1.0)
44.5 (1.0)	***Mistake Creek****.*	▲148.8 (9.2)
53.7 (9.2)	***Hann River****. Near permanent water in river.*	▲139.6 (7.0)
60.7 (7.0)	***Snake Creek****.*	▲132.6 (9.0)
69.7 (9.0)	***T/J – PSA****. RH tk goes into* ***Mt Elizabeth Homestead*** *(30 km), ph: (08) 9191 4644.* ***Camping, accommodation*** *and* ***guided safaris****.*	▲123.6 (9.5)
79.2 (9.5)	***T/J – PSA****. RH tk SP* ***Barnett Gorge*** *– veer left at first track junction on gorge track to go down to the Barnett River and a very pleasant* ***camping*** *spot, or keep veering right on tracks to reach the* ***gorge****. Parking area about 4 km from road, 300 to 400 metre walk to gorge and swimming hole. Aboriginal paintings in overhang directly opposite end of walking track.*	▲114.1 (22.0)
101.2 (22.0)	*T/J – PSA. RH tk leads to Mt Barnett Station*	▲92.1 (5.0)
106.2 (5.0)	***Barnett River*** *crossing.*	▲87.1 (1.0)
107.2 (1.0)	***T/J – PSA****. RH tk will take you into the* ***Mt Barnett Roadhouse****, 400 metres off the road, and onto* ***Manning Gorge****. Store, fuel, toilets, showers and laundry available, ph: (08) 9191 7007. You can also obtain your permit at the store to allow you to camp out at Manning Gorge, 7 km from the store.* *Aboriginal settlement on left of road.*	▲86.1 (1.5)
108.7 (1.5)	***Station Creek****.*	▲84.6 (12.5)
121.2 (12.5)	***T/J – PSA****. RH tk leads to* ***Galvans Gorge****. Parking area. It is about 1.2 km walk to the main pool and waterfall. No camping, day use only. A small Aboriginal art gallery is located near the pool. Please don't damage it in any way.*	▲72.1 (0.5)
121.7 (0.5)	**Climb up Phillips Range**. Good views to the north from crest.	▲71.6 (9.5)
131.2 (9.5)	Good views to the south.	▲62.1 (3.5)
134.7 (3.5)	***Adcock River****.*	▲58.6 (5.2)
139.9 (5.2)	***T/J – PSA****. LH tk leads to* ***Adcock Gorge*** *(SP). Access is currently closed. The track in leads 5 km from the Gibb River Road with a 100 metre walk to the main pool.*	▲53.4 (6.5)
146.4 (6.5)	***Billy Goat Springs****.*	▲46.9 (9.7)
156.1 (9.7)	***T/J – PSA****. RH tk leads to* ***Charnley River Homestead*** *–* ***accommodation, camping*** *and* ***tours****, ph: (08) 9191 4646.*	▲37.2 (3.8)
159.9 (3.8)	***T/J – PSA****. LH tk leads to* ***Mt House Homestead*** *(SP) – no access and no facilities for travellers.* *This track will also take you onto* ***Mornington Wilderness Camp*** *which offers tent* ***accommodation, camping****, fishing, swimming and canoeing.*	▲33.4 (20.2)
180.1 (20.2)	***Grave Creek****.*	▲13.2 (4.2)
184.3 (4.2)	***Saddlers Spring****. Most likely have water running.*	▲9.0 (1.0)
185.3 (1.0)	***T/J – PSA****. LH tk leads to* ***Imintji Store*** *and Aboriginal Community. The store, open 7 days, has diesel fuel only, general store, ice, limited hardware. You are welcome to camp overnight. Aboriginal arts and crafts are also for sale, ph/fax: (08) 9191 7471.*	▲8.0 (4.0)
189.3. (4.0)	***King Leopold Ranges Conservation Park****. Good views of range.*	▲4.0 (4.0)
193.3 (4.0)	***T/J – PSA****. RH tk leads to* ***Silent Grove*** *and* ***Bell Gorge****. –* ***camping*** *Precipice Range and Rifle Point can be seen to the left.*	▲0.0 (0.0) Trek continues on pg 167

You could follow the river up from the camping area, but it's a much harder walk – best to get a bit wet and cross over to the other bank – you'll soon dry. The track is faintly marked by painted rocks, rock piles and tin cans in trees – if you loose them just stick near the river

The Upper Gorge has a small sandy patch, but it's the waterfall and the huge pool surrounded by high cliffs that are the real attractions and delight of this place. Wander up in the early morning, eat lunch there, do a little exploring and wander back to camp in the evening – it's a great way to spend the day.

There's plenty of **Aboriginal art** in the area, with a painting of a large serpent under an overhang not far from the second beach in the Lower Manning George. As it's only a few hundred metres from the camp site (on the opposite bank) it shouldn't be missed. This particular painting was one of a number in the region repainted by a group of Aborigines, under an employment scheme a few years ago. The repainting by non-traditional elders caused a furore and the scheme was abandoned!

The picturesque Lower Manning Gorge.
Camping at Manning River camp site.

GALVANS GORGE

About 14 km south of Mt Barnett is the turn-off to *Galvans Gorge*. From the car parking area on the road, it is about a 1.2km walk to the main pool of Galvans Gorge.

It's a lovely swimming spot and once again some faint Aboriginal art can be found tucked under an overhang on the far right-hand side.

This is a day use area only, **no camping** is allowed.

ADCOCK GORGE

Some 19 km further south and on the east side of the road, is the turn-off to *Adcock Gorge*. The track in is about 5 km long, with the last few hundred metres being fairly rough. **Access to the track and gorge is currently closed to travellers**..

MT HOUSE STATION

Another 4 km south, on the east side of the road, is the turn-off to **Mt House Station** and **Mornington Wilderness Camp**. The Mt House Station has closed its doors to passing travellers. There are no facilities available.

Camping at *Moll Gorge* may be possible **only with permission** from the station. Phone the station on (08) 9191 4649, or (08) 9191 4703 *(see page 175)*.

MORNINGTON WILDERNESS CAMP (4WD)

The track continues past Mt House to the **Mornington Wilderness Camp**, 100 km from the turn-off. It is part of the ***Mornington Wildlife Sanctuary*** and is owned and operated by the Australian Wildlife Conservancy (AWC). It is well worth the drive, with accommodation in safari-style tents, as well as a shady, creekside campground with all amenities. It is a naturalist's paradise with prolific birdlife and a diversity of other fauna. There are spectacular gorges to explore and access to the *Fitzroy River*, *Sir John Gorge* and *Dimond Gorge*.

For full details on the track and visiting the Mornington Wilderness Camp and its facilities, see the chapter, *The Tablelands Track, page 178*. Web: **www.australianwildlife.org/**

CHARNLEY RIVER STATION

ACCESS

Once called *Beverley Springs*, the turn-off to this station is located 49km along the Gibb River Road from the Mt Barnett Roadhouse, with the station situated another 43km in from the road. While it is a working cattle station, the station also has a special licence to grow a wide range of seed crops, making its operation a little different to the normal station in the Kimberley.

ACCOMMODATION

The station also caters for specialist groups and tours, as well as general tourists travelling along the Gibb River Road, offering homestead, chalets and self-contained accommodation, with a fully equipped kitchen, toilet/shower and laundry facilities available. Alternatively, you can choose a dinner, bed and breakfast option. Please ring in advance to make sure there is accommodation available, especially during the peak season, and if you require meals, prior booking is requested.

CAMPING

For the camper, there are **camping** sites available with BBQ areas, toilets and showers, as well as laundry amenities.

Camping is allowed at Grevillea Gorge, camping limited, and a fee is payable.

At present you can only use cash as payment for services, etc, at the station, but that situation may change and we suggest that you check before your expected visit to see if it is possible to use credit cards.

THINGS TO DO

Those staying at the station can enjoy a range of activities such as fishing, swimming, birdwatching and exploring the many gorges to be found in the area. Tours can also be organised for all interests, such as fishing safaris to Walcott Inlet or special birdwatching trips. Scenic flights of the magnificent Charnley Gorge, the Synott Range & Walcott Inlet can be arranged.

Canoes are also available for hire, which are a great way to explore gorges such as Dillie and Junction Waters.

There are also self-guided 4WD trips and hiking trails, with track access to Grevillea, Daytona and Dillie Gorges, Junction Waters and Old Station waterhole.

On the way into the homestead from the main Gibb River Road you cross a creek, 6.7 km in from the junction, and 100 metres past the creek crossing is a large Boab on the right. You can't miss the blazed 'FH' on its trunk – blazed by the explorer, Frank Hann during his 1898 expedition.

Payment for services, etc, at the station can be made with credit cards via computer, or cash.

WALCOTT INLET TRACKS

For more info see pages 158-159 for this tough trip.

FOR FURTHER INFORMATION

For further information or bookings you can contact the station by writing c/- Post Office, Derby, WA, 6728, or ph: (08) 9191 4646, fax: (08) 9191 7878, web site:
www.charnleyriverstation.com.au

IMINTJI COMMUNITY ROADHOUSE

The store is run by the Imintji Aboriginal Community and is located on the east side of the road, approximately 26 km from the Mt House turn-off along the Gibb River Road, and just one km from the Saddlers Spring Crossing.

FACILITIES

The store is open all year round, with operating hours during the tourist season from 8.00am to 4.30pm. It closes for lunch.

Travellers will find a range of basic food items, cool drinks, ice creams, etc, and block ice is normally available. Diesel fuel only is currently obtainable, and we suggest that you check with the store to see if the fuel situation changes during the season.

Mechanical repairs are available.

Passing tourists can also replenish their water supply and are welcome to **camp** overnight. There is also the opportunity to purchase some locally made artifacts.

Credit cards (Mastercard, Visa and Bankcard) are accepted as payment for goods and services, and Eftpos is also available.

For any further information you can contact the store on ph/fax: (08) 9191 7471.

The Imintji Community Roadhouse can supply you with diesel fuel, food and more.

Travelling through the spectacular King Leopold Ranges.

Imintji Safari Camp – Kimberley Wilderness Adventures

Imintji Safari Camp is located near Imintji Aboriginal Community on Saddlers Creek. This is an exclusive permanent safari camp operated by Kimberley Wilderness Adventures as part of their accommodated touring program.

Travellers can purchase a Safaripass from Kimberley Wilderness Adventures before their trip and be accommodated in the camp: twin share, dinner, bed & breakfast. Safari camp features include: 240-volt lighting, twin share tent cabins with lights, beds & linen, hot showers, toilets.

Contact: 475 Hampton St, Hampton, Vic 3188, ph: 1800 655 220 or (03) 9277 8444, fax: (03) 9521 0721, web site: **www.kimberleywilderness.com.au/**

For more details see their listing in the chapter on *Tour Operators*.

KING LEOPOLD RANGE CONSERVATION PARK

The park, which includes Silent Grove, Bell Gorge, Lennard Gorge and Mt Hart Wilderness Lodge, is run by CALM, covering an area of around 370,000 ha.

This park protects some of the wildest country in the Kimberley and includes areas on both sides of the Gibb River Road from just south of the Imintji community over the crest of the range to south of Inglis Gap. At one point, south-east of Mt Bell, the road makes an abrupt turn beneath a cliff more than 50 metres high and here you can see where the sandstone face has been dramatically folded and twisted.

The park stretches west along the range to beyond Mt Hart Wilderness Lodge, but seemingly won't get to the coast unless another triangular-shaped section is included to the north along the Isdell River to Walcott Inlet.

Eastward the park will extend beyond the highest peak, Mt Ord, to near Millie Windie HS, and includes all the headwaters of the Lennard River above Lennard River Gorge as well as the gorge itself and sections of the Precipice Range.

A ranger is based at Silent Grove camping area during the Dry season, April to November, ph: (08) 9191 7058.

BELL GORGE – SILENT GROVE

Access

By turning off to Silent Grove Station some 90 km south of Mt Barnett and only about 250 km from Derby, you can head west to one of the most spectacular gorges in the whole of the Kimberley.

Nineteen kilometres in from the main road you'll come to the **Silent Grove Camping Ground** and the national park ranger base. Once an outstation run by Mt Hart Station, now, like Bell Gorge itself, it is part of the proposed new conservation park.

Continuing westward from Silent Grove on a good dirt road for about 5 km the track comes to a minor gap in the range near two large Boabs.

From the Boabs the track swings away from the range it's been following and just under 3 km from the boabs you'll begin to see the start of the **Bell Creek camping sites** on your right. For the next few kilometres there are numerous tracks leading to camping sites nestled beside the creek.

Access is only available during the Dry by 4WD, or air, and for a small camping fee, travellers can set up **camp** at Silent Grove.

Camping – Silent Grove

Silent Grove is the primary camp ground and you can choose either non-generator and generator camping areas, and use the facilities provided which include flushing toilets, showers, drinking water and BBQs. Firewood for cooking is supplied by the rangers.

Continuing westward from Silent Grove on a good dirt road for about 5 km the track comes to a minor gap in the range near two large Boabs.

From the Boabs the track swings away from the range it's been following and just under 3 km from the boabs you'll begin to see the start of the **Bell Creek camping sites** on your right. For the next few kilometres there are numerous tracks leading to camping sites nestled beside the creek.

Passing through Yammera Gap in the Napier Range. This limestone range was once a Devonian coral reef.

Trek into Silent Grove and Bell Gorge

0.0 (0.0) T/J - Gibb River Road and ***Silent Grove/Bell Gorge*** *turn-off.*

6.2 (6.2) Creek *crossing - water.*

17.5 (11.3) *Pass through old gate/fenceline.*

18.0 (0.5) T/J - PSA. *LH track just before **creek** crossing,*

18.1 (0.1) Creek *crossing - water - 'No Camping' sign on right.*

19.0 (0.9) Gate *and enter **Silent Grove camping** ground and ranger base. Toilets, water, showers.*

23.9 (4.9) *Main road veers right to gorge – on left are two large Boabs.*

26.6 (2.7) *Start of **Bell Creek camping** area sites on right - 'Water Lily Pad' camping area on right. Toilets provided.*

Track follows river.

30.0 (3.4) *Car parking area and start of walking track down to **Bell Gorge**. Boab with bell carved into trunk not far from the start of walking track.*

Camping – Bell Creek

The sites along *Bell Creek* are extremely popular, and are often all taken before lunch. There are 10 individual designated camp sites, and very early in the season you may be able to take your pick, and there are some beauties lining the edge of Bell Creek, such as *Water Lily Pad*. These camp sites operate on a **tag system**, which you must collect back near the ranger station. No tag available, no camping at Bell Creek.

Two sites have flushing toilets the rest have drop toilets. Firewood for cooking, again is supplied by the rangers, and generators are not allowed.

You can swim, paddle a canoe or fish for sooty grunters. They are delightful!

Do not use soaps or detergents in the water!

Access to Bell Gorge

Just over 10 km from Silent Grove you'll hit the end of the track. It's a one km walk from the car park to the top of the waterfall. By following the walking track you'll pass a Boab with a bell carved in its trunk and then descend the hill (the hardest bit – it gets easier after the first 200 metres or so) and then along the valley for an easy 20 minutes. You'll come out once again on Bell Creek, just above the falls. Access to the water is fairly easy near here and is about the only place you'll get to without some energetic walking and rock hopping. All up the walk should take about 30 mins.

Spend a bit of time exploring and checking out the scene. It's a reasonably easy walk along the cliff edge (not too close though!) and you'll get some great views of the gorge and waterfalls. From where the creek drops over the first fall it cascades over a number of others into a deeper and narrower gorge which continues downriver for some distance as the creek passes through the Isdell Range. It would be at least a one hundred metre drop and it's very awe inspiring.

You can get to the large pool just below the falls by crossing the creek above the falls to the north-eastern side of the stream and head downstream for a hundred or so metres to where the sheer cliff gives way to more of a sloping slab of rock and from here you can rock-hop your way down. The more energetic can head further downstream on the same side of the creek.

Activities to be enjoyed while visiting this magnificent area include bushwalking, photography and birdwatching.

For Further Information

Contact the CALM district office in Broome, Herbert St, ph: (08) 9192 1036 or the Ranger on:
ph: (08) 9191 7058
web site: **www.calm.wa.gov.au**.

__King Leopold Air__, based in Broome, offers a 'Gorgeous Gorges' flight, taking in Windjana Gorge, Bell Gorge, Mt Hart and the Horizontal Falls, incorporating escorted guided tours. You can contact them at Johnny Chi Lane, Broome 6725 ph: (08) 9193 7155, web site:

www.kingleopoldair.com.au/

LENNARD RIVER AND GORGE

Access

This 5 km long gorge was carved out by the *Lennard River* as it slashed through the surrounding range, creating spectacular sheer vertical cliffs and deep, cool, shaded pools. Lennard Gorge is narrow and deep and is a spectacular setting for those willing to drive the short distance involved.

Situated some 30 km south of the Silent Grove/Bell Gorge turn-off is the track into Lennard River Gorge, signposted 'Millie Windie'. Turn east onto this station road and then almost immediately south onto the gorge access track. The gorge proper is just over 7 km off the main road and the track conditions vary from year to year. At times it can be relatively easy, and others quite rough.

Exploring the Gorge

From the car parking area it is a short walk to the top of the gorge. From this point you can follow a trail, marked by small rock cairns, down to the centre of the gorge and a large pool of water. The track can be overgrown and the rock cairns hard to find, and it's steep and rocky, but it's an ideal swimming spot and an air bed would be a great bonus here to help explore the cliff overhangs and ledges. If you're lucky, the waterfall will still be flowing.

Another faint track leads up to the head of the gorge and is marked by a couple of rock cairns. By following the cliff top along and climbing down through the spinifex you can again reach the water.

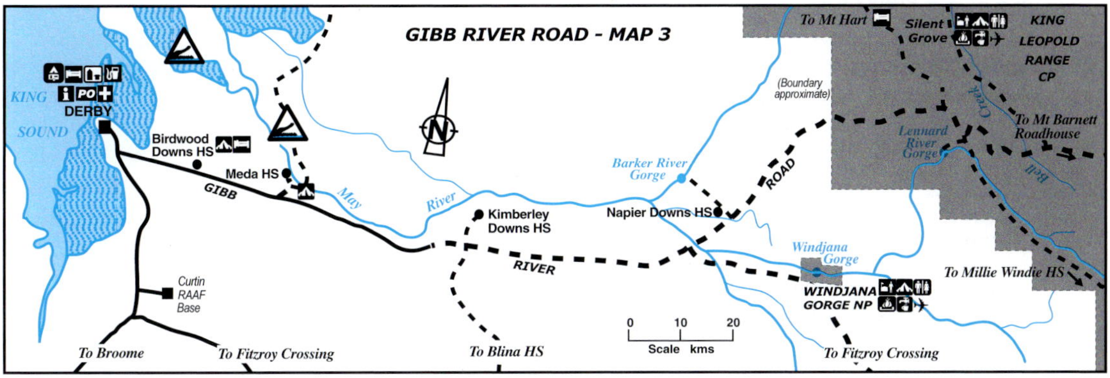

EAST ALONG THE LENNARD RIVER

East of the Gibb River Road the Millie Windie Road passes along the range crossing the Lennard River on a number of occasions. There are no facilities.

TREK NOTES – GIBB RIVER ROAD

CONTINUATION OF TREK NOTES FROM TURN-OFF TO SILENT GROVE/BELL GORGE (PG 161)

	Trek continues on from pg 161
196.8 (3.5) **Bell Creek**.	▲*215.0 (0.3)*
197.1 (0.3) ***T/J – PSA***. *RH track (tk) leads 100 metres to a pleasant spot beside the creek with plenty of large shady trees and a nice waterhole.*	▲*214.7 (0.2)*
197.3 (0.2) ***T/J – PSA***. *LH tk leads 400 metres to a spot beside the range – no water.*	▲*214.5 (0.1)*
197.4 (0.1) ***Begin to climb the King Leopold Ranges*** *– bitumen.*	▲*214.4 (1.1)*
198.5 (1.1) *Car parking area on right near the top of the range with* ***great views*** *across to the north.*	▲*213.3 (0.5)*
199.0 (0.5) *Bitumen ends at the top of the climb up the range.*	▲*212.8 (3.9)*
202.9 (3.9) ***March Fly Glen Creek*** *– water.* ***No Camping***.	▲*208.9 (2.7)*
205.6 (2.7) ***Same Creek***.	▲*206.2 (3.0)*
208.6 (3.0) ***Fern Creek***. *A nice spot on the left just before you cross the creek for a stop. It could have water in it towards the end of the Dry. There are great views of the ranges and rock faces travelling through this area.*	▲*203.2 (5.6)*
214.2 (5.6) ***Dog Chain Creek***. *A pleasant area, with plenty of shade, is on the right just before you cross the creek.*	▲*197.6 (2.3)*
216.5 (2.3) ***T/J – PSA***. *LH tk leads to* ***Lennard River Gorge*** *and* ***Millie Windie*** *(SP). Two hundred metres on from main junction veer right on track SP 'Lennard River Gorge. This gorge is spectacular. The track can be very rough and eroded and it is just over 7 km to gorge parking area.*	▲*195.3 (6.8)*
223.3 (6.8) ***T/J – PSA***. *RH tk leads to* ***Mt Hart Wilderness Lodge – accommodation****, however no camping allowed, ph: (08) 9191 4645.* ***Need to book in advance.***	▲*188.5 (0.3)*
223.6 (0.3) ***Apex Creek***. *RH tk just after crossing the creek leads to a area for a stop. Bitumen begins, just after crossing, up the range to Inglis Gap.*	▲*188.2 (1.3)*
224.9 (1.3) ***Inglis Gap*** *– top of cutting. A small parking area is on the left with good views of the valley and ranges. Bitumen ends.*	▲*186.9 (11.2)*
236.1 (11.2) ***Boundary Creek***.	▲*175.7 (2.7)*
238.8 (2.7) ***Bull Frog Hole*** *– bridged. Supposedly the camping spot for Bullfrog – an Aboriginal outlaw late last century. His lookout spot was on the nearby hill.*	▲*173.0 (6.0)*
244.8 (6.0) ***Fletcher River***.	▲*167.0 (4.6)*
249.4 (4.6) ***Yates Creek***.	▲*162.4 (3.2)*
252.6 (3.2) ***Macs Creek*** *– bridged crossing.*	▲*159.2 (3.4)*
256.0 (3.4) ***Donkey Creek***. *Good views of a large slab-like mountain to the right before Donkey Creek.*	▲*155.8 (10.4)*
266.4 (10.4) *Sign on right – '****King Leopold Ranges****'.*	▲*145.4 (0.9)*
Once south of the King Leopold Ranges the country changes and becomes flat plains with well treed creeks.	*Trek continues on pg 168.*

	Trek Continues from Page 167	*Trek continues on from pg 167.*
267.3 (0.9)	***Wombarella Creek**.*	*▲144.5 (5.4)*
272.7 (5.4)	***T/J – PSA**. LH tk leads to **Granite Mine** (SP).*	*▲139.1 (5.7)*
278.4 (5.7)	***T/J – PSA**. RH tk leads to **Napier Downs Homestead**.*	*▲133.4 (0.1)*
278.5 (0.1)	***Napier Creek**.*	*▲133.3 (0.4)*
278.9 (0.4)	***Yammera Gap** in Napier Range. Queen Victoria's Head – a rock formation – can be seen in silhouette on the right just before you enter the pass.*	*▲132.9 (9.3)*
288.2 (9.3)	***Lennard River** – bridged.*	*▲123.6 (0.4)*
288.6 (0.4)	***T/J – PSA**. LH road (SP) is the **Windjana/Geikie Gorge Road** and leads to **Fitzroy Crossing**, Windjana Gorge NP (21 km from junction), **Tunnel Creek NP** and Fairfield Homestead.*	*▲123.2 (45.4)*
334.0 (45.4)	***T/J – PSA**. RH tk takes you to **Kimberley Downs Homestead** and LH tk is SP '**Telegraph Bore**'.*	*▲77.8 (10.2)*
342.0 (8.0)	*Bitumen begins.*	*▲67.6 (1.2)*
344.2 (2.2)	***T/J – PSA**. LH road SP 'Blina Oilfields'.*	*▲66.4 (27.5)*
372.9 (28.7)	***T/J – PSA**. RH tk leads to **Meda Station** and **May River** – fishing, picnic, **camping**. Beware of Crocs.*	*▲38.9 (23.4)*
396.3 (23.4)	***T/J – PSA**. RH tk leads to **Birdswood Downs – accommodation, camping**, meals, guided tours and trail rides, ph: 9191 1275. **Prior bookings essential**. See page 193 for more details.*	*▲15.5 (7.8)*
404.1 (7.8)	***T/J – PSA**. LH tk leads to the **Mowanjum AC.***	*▲7.7 (3.0)*
407.1 (3.0)	***Information Bay** on right.*	*▲4.7 (0.6)*
407.7 (0.6)	***T-Junction – Gibb River Road** and **Great Northern Highway** – Turn right for **Derby**, 6 km. Left will take you on to **Broome** 211 km and Fitzroy Crossing.*	*▲4.1 (4.1)*
411.8 (4.1)	*Enter **Derby** township.*	*▲0.0 (0.0)*

MT HART WILDERNESS LODGE

Much of the former Mt Hart station property is managed by CALM as part of the King Leopold Ranges Conservation Park and the Mt Hart Wilderness Lodge is run as a joint management venture between Taffy Abbotts and CALM. This unique destination has an emphasis on nature based experiences, old-fashioned bush hospitality and wonderful food.

Access

The road to the old homestead of Mt Hart, some 50 km west of the Gibb River Road and 34 km south of the turn-off to Silent Grove, skirts the southern ramparts of the Leopolds, crossing a number of spring fed creeks in the process. The homestead is April to November (weather permitting), with access by 4WD or aircraft and is part of the ***Ibis Aerial Highway.***

As you head west from the Gibb River Road a large flat-topped hill will often dominate the skyline directly in front. This is Mt Humbert, one of the most westerly peaks in the King Leopolds, named by Alexander Forrest in 1879. The view from the top is excellent and is the same today as in Forrest's day.

Accommodation

The homestead is described as an 'oasis in the Leopolds', surrounded by 8 acres of lush, tropical gardens. Although there is **no camping allowed**, comfortable **accommodation** is available, for a maximum or 27 guests, in two homesteads and a 2-bedroom cottage, with dinner, bed and breakfast packages. (A number of rooms have air-conditioning.) Those flying in can arrange lunch or morning tea, as well as accommodation and all meals.

Facilities

Visitors can enjoy activities such as bushwalking, swimming, canoeing, fishing, photography, painting and just general exploring. Both ***Broome Aviation*** and ***King Leopold Air*** include a stop at Mt Hart as part of their scenic flights in the region. Check out their respective web sites at: **www.broomeair.com.au/kimbmap.htm**, and **www.kingleopoldair.com.au/** .

For Further Information

Open from mid April to mid October. Pre-booking is essential and **you can contact Mt Hart Wilderness Lodge** by writing to PO Box 653, Derby, WA, 6728, or ph: (08) 9191 4645, fax: (08) 9191 7836, web site:

www.mthart.com.au/

Birdwood Downs Station

Situated close to Derby, the station offers accommodation & camping. *See page 193 for full details.*

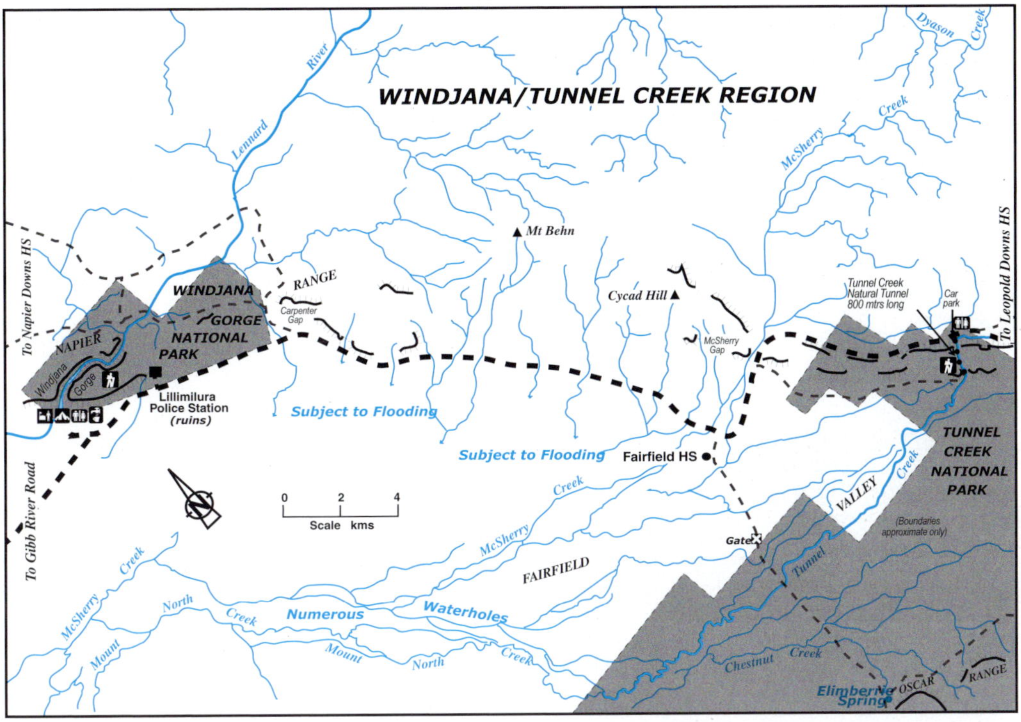

GIBB RIVER ROAD

WINDJANA GORGE & TUNNEL CREEK NATIONAL PARKS

These are parks located some distance east off the Gibb River Road, the turn-off being reached 66 km south of the Mt Hart access track, or 126 km from Derby. This eastbound road continues past these two parks all the way to Fitzroy Crossing, 165 km from the junction with the Gibb River Road. See the chapter, *Derby to Fitzroy Crossing*, for more detail on this route.

These two parks are a MUST and you can spend a day or more exploring both.

WINDJANA GORGE

GEOLOGY

Windjana Gorge is regarded by geologists as one of the classic examples of world geology. Nowhere else are the relationships between the various deposits of an ancient reef complex so well exposed as they are here. A simplified geological map of the gorge is shown in the accompanying diagram.

The gorge is a picturesque, narrow canyon cut by the Lennard River through the Napier Range, which was once a coral barrier reef. The gorge is about 3.5 km long, up to 100 metres deep, and has near-vertical walls for most of its length. The river flows for only short periods in the Wet season, and during most of the year water only occurs as isolated pools in the main channel. These pools contain a few species of fish and Freshwater Crocodiles.

The river has taken millions of years to erode out the gorge. At one stage during this process, a river gravel containing fossil remains of extinct crocodiles and turtles accumulated in a small cave on a wall of the gorge, some 40 metres above the present river level. One of the crocodiles represented among the fossil bones was a giant form about seven metres long. Another extinct animal whose bones have been found in river gravels at the gorge is the giant marsupial, Diprotodon.

The most impressive exposure of the reef and its associated deposits in the gorge is known as the ‘Classic Face’. At this spot flat-bedded back-reef and reef limestone grade into a narrow massive reef margin, which is fronted by steeply inclined marginal-slope deposits. Changes in the fossil faunas are very well displayed, passing from the back-reef through the reef to the

Halfway through Tunnel Creek the roof has collapsed.

marginal-slope deposits. The stromatoporoid Amphipora is conspicuous in the back-reef, other stromatoporoids, mainly Actinostroma, and algae were the dominant reef builders, and sponges are common in the marginal-slope deposits.

Plant and Animal Life

Trees in the gorges are mostly cadjeputs (tropical paperbarks), and river gums. Also common are native figs and the freshwater mangrove, a small tree with pendulous sprays of small red flowers.

Most native mammals here are small, nocturnal and shy, but during the day or evening you may see the Agile (or sandy) wallaby, identifiable by the pale stripe on their flanks. The more heavily built Euros also live in the area, and if you are very lucky you may spot one of the wary rock wallabies.

The Johnston (Freshwater) Crocodile lives in Windjana Gorge and can often be seen resting on sandbanks in the river. It is a fish eater, and is not dangerous to people.

History

In the recent past the gorge formed the boundaries between the Unggumi and Bunaba tribes of Aborigines. Called Windjana and Taley respectively by these people, the gorge has always figured deeply in their legends. For the Bunaba the waterholes of their tribal country had been formed by the Rainbow Serpent, Ungeroo, and the beautiful waterhole at the gorge was an important source of food and spirit children.

Spirit children were eaten by their father in the form of a fish or similar animals taken from the waterhole. Through the dreams of the father they were incarnated in the mother and when the child was born he or she took the particular animal as its totem. The totem was, and still is, an important part of Aboriginal life, guiding the person throughout his or her life.

The Dreamtime of the Aborigine was shattered with the coming of the Whiteman, with Alexander Forrest's expedition in 1879 doing the most to open up the area.

Prospectors, cattlemen and sheep herders quickly followed in his footsteps, taking up huge parcels of land in their endeavours to make it an economic pastoral reality.

By 1883 the ports of Derby and Broome had been proclaimed and white settlement had pushed out to the edge of Bunaba territory. Lillimilura homestead was located just a few hundred metres from the sheer rock faces of the Napier Range. Lennard River Station, owned and managed by William Lukin, had its homestead a few kilometres from the escarpment.

E.G. Hardman, the first of many geologists to visit the area, called the gorge, 'Devils Pass'. In 1883 he found at the western entrance to the gorge, among other things, the bones of the extinct wombat-like animal, Diprotodon australia. This animal was widespread in Australia some 10 to 20,000 years ago, inhabiting swamps and flooded lowlands. Today the area is flat savannah, rich and green during the Wet, but certainly no swamp land.

In the late 1800s **Pigeon**, or **'Jandamarra'**, a Bunaba Aboriginal, began his war against the white invaders. Stealing stock and raiding settlers' properties, Pigeon's reign culminated in the killing of Police Constable Richardson at Lillimilura in October 1894.

Later Pigeon led a large party of Aborigines, killing two white settlers who were about to drive their cattle through the gorge. A few days later a large battle took place between a police patrol and Pigeon's group. While many were killed, Pigeon and his main lieutenant escaped. Legend has it he used a cave high up in the cliffs (now called 'Pigeon's Cave') near the western entrance on the northern side of the gorge. That's pretty hard to believe. The full story of Pigeon is detailed in the chapter, *The Aborigine Heritage and The Art of the Kimberley*.

Since those days the gorge has been quiet and the area has been a park for many years.

The camping area at Windjana Gorge is very pleasant, with a magnificent backdrop.

THINGS TO DO

Camping is available in 3 camp grounds: quiet camping areas, generator camping and tour camping. The park is equipped with flushing toilets, showers, water and BBQ facilities. A ranger is in residence from April to October and a camping fee is payable for each night The park is inaccessible during the Wet season.

Canoeing is no longer allowed in the gorge.

The Gorge Walk is a 7 km return walk that skirts the Lennard River and takes you along the full length of the gorge and back. It's a very enjoyable experience as the riverine forest and the high cliffs give a cool, shaded atmosphere at times, and you get a close look at the resident fruit bats, corellas and Freshwater crocodiles. A late afternoon walk is a great time for photographs.

***Broome Aviation** offers a flight, as part of the **Ibis Aerial Highway**, from Broome including stops at Windjana Gorge. You can contact them for more details on ph: 08) 9193 5455, web site:*

www.broomeair.com.au/kimbmap.htm

***King Leopold Air**, based in Broome, offers a 'Gorgeous Gorges' flight, taking in Windjana Gorge, Bell Gorge, Mt Hart and the Horizontal Falls, incorporating escorted guided tours. You can contact them on ph: (08) 9193 7155, web site:*

www.kingleopoldair.com.au/

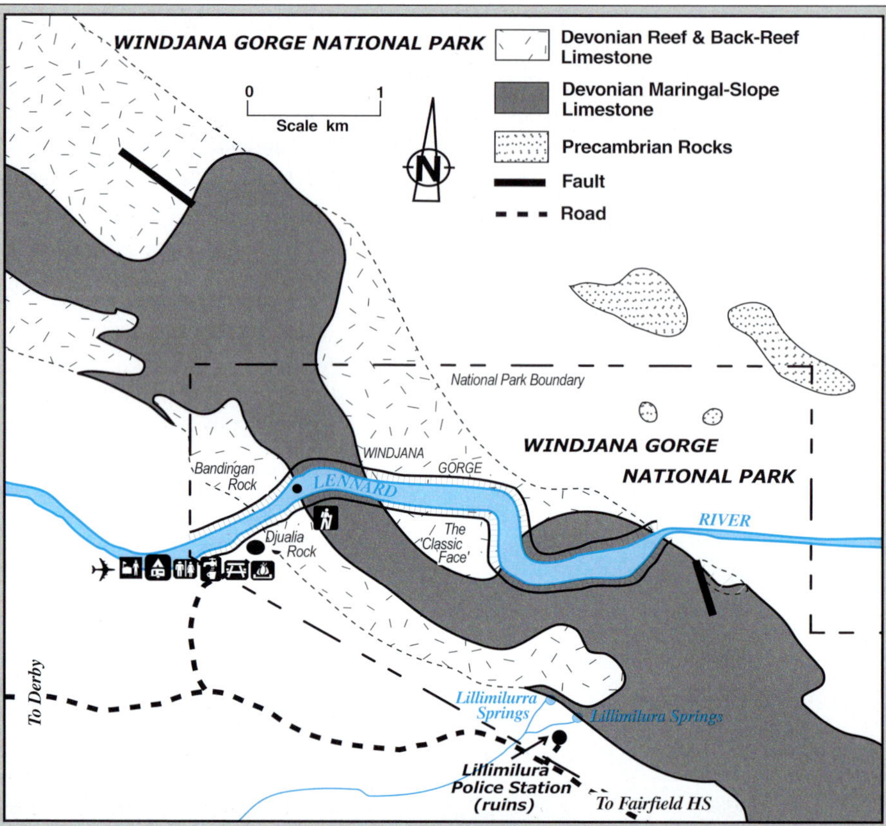

The birdwatching is also very good. While the rocky ledges hide Sandstone Shrike Thrushes, Great Bower Birds and their bowers which can be found amongst the trees, while along the water's edge spoonbills, herons, darters and cormorants congregate.

Aboriginal art can also be found in and around the gorge. They're not easy to find and keen, caring people will find the ranger the easiest way to discover them.

Lillimilura Police Station Ruins

A few kilometres east of the gorge are the ruins of Lillimilura. Established as a sheep property, it became a police outpost and the setting for the Pigeon tragedy. All that remains are the well made walls of the buildings – a poignant reminder of our early violent history. P.C. Richardson, who was initially buried here, was later reinterred in Derby cemetery.

North of the ruins, at the base of the range, is Lillimilura Springs.

For Further Information

Contact the CALM district office in Broome, Herbert St, ph: (08) 9192 1036, fax: (08) 9193 5027, web site: **www.calm.wa.gov.au/**.

TUNNEL CREEK NATIONAL PARK

Located just 30 km from Windjana Gorge is Tunnel Creek. This was Pigeon's infamous hideout and remained undiscovered for many years. You'll understand why when you visit it.

In early 1992, with the acquisition of more land, CALM took control of a swath of land to the south-east of the current small national park, the boundaries of which are yet to be proclaimed. This enlarged park includes the majority of the Oscar Range and the Oscar Plateau.

Improvements in access and facilities will be a long time coming to this region, although from personal experience we know the area contains some excellent sites for visiting and camping.

In the foreseeable future Tunnel Creek and its immediate surrounds will be the centre of any activity.

The Lillimilura Police Station Ruins. It became a police outpost and the setting for the 'Jandamarra' tragedy.

Geology

Tunnel Creek flows through the Napier Range in a remarkable natural tunnel more than 750 metres long, which has been localised by jointing in reef and marginal-slope limestones.

The tunnel contains permanent pools of fresh water, and it is possible to walk from one entrance to the other. The roof has collapsed from to the top of the range through to the creek bed near the centre of the tunnel.

It seems likely that Tunnel Creek once flowed across the top of the range when the general ground surface was higher than it is today, and it later adopted the underground course formed by water eroding along the joint fractures in the limestone. The old course is marked by a shallow valley which is still present on top of the range.

A bench in the tunnel some 8 metres above the present floor marks an older underground creek level. It coincides with the level of the plain, which is incised in a narrow channel by the creek both upstream and downstream from the tunnel.

A conspicuous feature of the algal and stromatoporoid reef limestone at the north entrance is the intense fracturing which occurred at an early stage in growth of the reef.

THINGS TO DO

This is a Day Use Area only and camping is not permitted at Tunnel Creek, however there are pit toilets and an information shelter. The area is inaccessible during the Wet season.

Walking through the tunnel is one of the experiences of visiting the Kimberley. It's only 750 metres or so and takes a leisurely one to two hours, depending how long you spend at the far end or exploring some of the side chambers.

Once inside the tunnel the walking is relatively easy, but you'll definitely get wet. You have to cross the creek at a couple of points, and the timing of your visit will determine how wet you'll get.

Obviously you need a torch for this walk. A good one such as a 'Dolphin' is ideal. Gas lanterns aren't great in deep water! Sandshoes and shorts are the other prerequisites.

Little fish and yabbies can be seen in the clear water. Bats and larger flying foxes are often seen, especially in the central area where the roof has collapsed. An early European name for this tunnel was 'The Cave of Bats'.

Stalactites, stalagmites and other features of a limestone cave can be viewed and wondered at. One of the side chambers, on the left as you head through to the southern side, does have some particularly good examples of cave formations.

Aboriginal art can be found near the northern entrance to the tunnel. The southern end of the tunnel was once used by the Aborigines as a site for stone axes and the like. It's certainly a pleasant spot to spend the hot part of the day.

See our chapter, *National Parks and Nature Reserves*, for further information on visiting these two parks.

***Bungoolee Tours** - Aboriginal tours - two day tours that include a one night stop over at a base camp near to the Biridhu community, and tours of Tunnel Creek, Windjana Gorge. For more information contact: PO Box 293, Fitzroy Crossing, WA 6765, ph: (08) 9191 5257 or 9191 5257, fax; (08) 9191 5644, or web sites:*
www.waitoc.com/malarabah.asp
or
www.aboriginalaustraliatravel.com/tour_info.cfm?id=125

For Further Information

Contact the CALM regional office in Broome, ph: (08) 9192 1036, or the Ranger based at Windjana Gorge during the tourist season on ph: (08) 9191 7076, web: **www.calm.wa.gov.au/**.

The spectacle of Dimond Gorge. There is some excellent canoeing in the placid stretches of this Gorge.

THE TABLELANDS TRACK

On the Tableland Track with the ranges near Mt House in the background.

INTRODUCTION

This route slicing through the southern heart of the Kimberley may one day become the region's next 'Adventure route'. It runs between Mt House station, 256 km north of Derby on the Gibb River Road to Springvale Station and the Great Northern Highway (Highway 1), meeting with it 66 km north of Halls Creek. From the Gibb River Road to the Great Northern Highway is around 340 km via this route, but most travellers will go to the Mornington Wilderness Camp, which will add another 100 km or so.

MT HOUSE

Mt House station takes its name from the large flat-topped mountain off to the south-east, named by Frank Hann during his 1898 expedition to the area. The station is one of the most famous in the Kimberley and one of the oldest north of the King Leopolds, taking up a million or so acres of relatively good grazing country cut by the *Hann* and *Adcock Rivers*. The homestead is located 10 km off the Gibb River Road.

There are a number of gorges on the property that are well worth a visit and are a great place to camp. **Permission to camp is essential from the homestead** and a small fee is payable.

Facilities

There are no facilities available from Mt House.

Camping on the property is allowed at *Moll Gorge*, however **campers must contact Mt House and obtain permission** and book in advance.

For further information contact the station on, ph: (08) 9191 4703 or ph/fax: (08) 9191 4703.

TREK NOTES

Gibb River Road Junction to Mornington Sanctuary Track Junction

0.0	**(0.0)**	*Road junction (R/J) – Gibb River Road / Mt House turn-off – turning to Mt House.*
8.6	**(8.6)**	*Gate/fenceline.*
9.2	**(0.6)**	*Y-junct – VR to Mornington Wilderness Camp. Left leads to Mt House. No access, no facilities.*
9.8	**(0.6)**	*Adcock River crossing – water. Continue east on main road with the bluff of Mt House to the south.*
16.2	**(6.4)**	*Bluff on right – there's a great view from the top!*
27.3	**(11.1)**	*Stumpy Creek – ford.*
32.0	**(4.7)**	*T/J – PSA to Mornington Wilderness Camp. Left leads to Moll Gorge.*

To Moll Gorge

0.0	**(0.0)**	*T/J – 32 km east of Gibb River Road, junction marked by a Telstra sign. Turn left (TL) and head north.*
8.3	**(8.3)**	*Cross headwaters of Slaty Creek.*
18.0	**(9.7)**	*T/J – VL at white sign.*
22.7	**(4.7)**	*Moll Gorge camping area.*

37.1	**(5.1)**	*Tims Yard Creek.*
53.4	**(16.3)**	*Major T/J – VR for Mornington Wilderness Camp. Straight on to Tablelands HS.*

GPS 17° 13' 25"S 126° 3' 12"E

Zero Trip Meter at this junction.

Trek Notes continue on page 179.

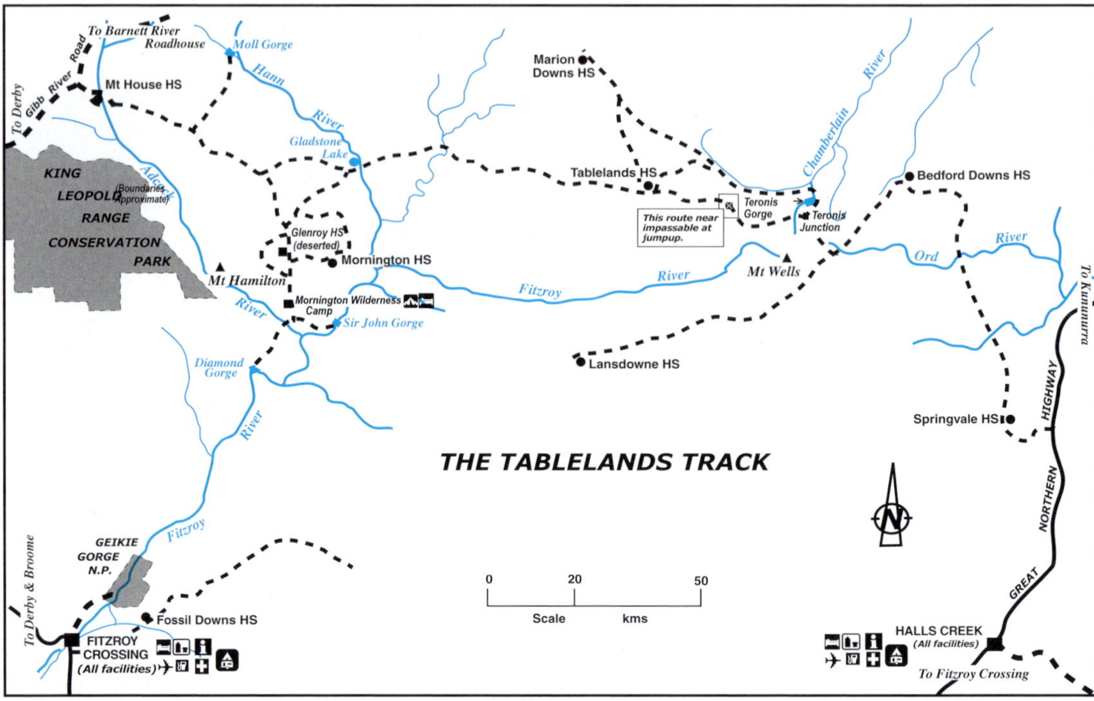

The Fitzroy River, near Dimond Gorge, at the Mornington Wilderness Camp.
The track junction of the Tablelands Track and the track to Mornington Wilderness Camp.
Swimming in the delightful Cadjeput Waterhole at the Mornington Wilderness Camp..
The Safari tent accommodation at the Mornington Wilderness Camp overlooking Annie Creek .

MT HOUSE TO MORNINGTON WILDERNESS CAMP

From the turn-off on the Gibb River Road the route to Mornington Wilderness Camp heads east. About 5 km from the Gibb River Road a track to the left leads to Mt House homestead (no access and no facilities), while the main track to Mornington Wilderness Camp and Tablelands veers right.

About 11 km from the road junction with the Gibb River Road you'll cross the Adcock River which normally has water in it, but offers no problems during the Dry.

The flat-topped bulk of Mt House dominates the horizon to the south and the main track passes to the north of the peak.

There is another lesser peak close to the main track which is relatively easy to climb and which gives good views of the surrounding country.

Another 10 km on you begin to cross the many channels of Stumpy and Mad Mile Creeks and a few kilometres later come to the turn-off to Moll Gorge.

MOLL GORGE

Located about 44 km north-east of the homestead, Moll Gorge is on the Hann River and with its back drop of cliffs is an idyllic spot to stop for a day or two.

Head out on the main Mornington Track and about 24 km east of the homestead take a minor track off to the north-east. You'll cross Slaty Creek and then about 17 km from the main track you need to veer left at another track junction. Five km later you'll be at Moll Gorge with the last section of track a little rough.

There is limited space for camping but there is plenty of shade and firewood is pretty handy. The fishing can be pretty good and if you have a canoe or a small boat the exploring and the fishing is even better.

You need permission from Mt House before stopping here.

About 45 km east of Mt House homestead, you'll come to a major track junction. Here you need to veer right to Glenroy and Mornington Wilderness Camp. The main track to Tablelands continues straight ahead.

GLENROY MEATWORKS

About 10 km further on the track to Mornington Wilderness Camp you'll pass a series of yards and tanks which were once the site of the Glenroy Meatworks.

Back in the 1950s a scheme was devised to freight whole cattle carcasses out of the remote central Kimberley by air from this site, known as the famous Air Beef Scheme. It was a fantastic scheme which operated for a few years but costs were incredible and the whole idea was really doomed to failure.

TABLELANDS TRACK

The original Glenroy Homestead.

GLENROY HOMESTEAD

The Glenroy Station buildings are bypassed about seven km later. The 'new' out station here is often used by Mt House when mustering in this region.

The original Glenroy Homestead, which was vacated back in the 1950s, still stands. There are a couple of pioneer graves close to this old homestead. Both are worth a look, but you need permission of Mt House to access the property.

As you head south the track becomes rougher and then begins to cross Annie Creek a number of times. Many of these crossings have water in them, although in the Dry they are rarely deep.

MORNINGTON WILDERNESS CAMP

After passing the track to Mornington Station and crossing Annie's Creek a few more times and some 94 km from the Gibb River Road you pass through the camping area and reach the office and resort of the **Mornington Wilderness Camp**.

MORNINGTON SANCTUARY

Mornington Wilderness Camp is part of the ***Mornington Sanctuary****. This Sanctuary covers 312,000 hectares of the Central Kimberley, including much of the upper catchment of the mighty Fitzroy River as well as sections of the rugged King Leopold Ranges. It also takes in two river gorges and four major river systems, protecting a range of ecosystems, such as tropical savanna and open woodlands, which are home to a diversity of birds, mammals and reptiles.*

FACILITIES

The Wilderness Camp provides full accommodation (with dinner, bed & breakfast) in comfortable safari tents, each with ensuite. The tents are furnished with twin or double beds, a fan and a balcony overlooking Annie's Creek.

For those **camping** there is a shady, creekside campground. Campers have access to ablutions facility, complete with flushing toilets and hot and cold showers, as well as the Redtails bar and restaurant with fully licensed bar facilities.

There is also tyre and mechanical repairs.

ACTIVITIES

- Canoeing at Dimond Gorge, Sir John Gorge and Cadjeput.
- Bushwalking, swimming and spectacular sunsets at Sir John Gorge.
- Swimming at Cadjeput Waterhole.
- Birdwatching - with over 189 species recorded, including the elusive Gouldian Finch.
- Guided ecology tours and tour to Fitzroy Bluff.
- Guided trip to Fitzroy Bluff Pools.
- Self-drive interpretive nature trails - Dimond Gorge and Sir John Gorge.
- Annie's Creek and Livistona Gully walk trails.
- Evening entertainment.

Canoes available for hire.

SIR JOHN GORGE

Just 14 km from Mornington Wilderness Camp is Sir John Gorge and the mighty *Fitzroy River*.

On the western side of the gorge the walls of the gorge are at their lowest while just across the river the walls are higher. The river sweeps away in both directions, the rocks and the walls on each side enclosing it all in spectacular fashion.

TREK TO MORNINGTON WILDERNESS CAMP *(continued from page 173.)*

0.0 (0.0) Major T/J – VR for Mornington Wilderness Camp. Straight on to Tablelands HS.

GPS 17° 13' 25"S 126° 3' 12"E

(53.4 km from Gibb River Road.)

10.8 (10.8) Old Glenroy Meatwork ruins on right. Yards and windmill nearby.

12.0 (1.2) T/J – VR to Wilderness Camp.

14.7 (2.7) Fence and T/J. VR, bypassing Glenroy HS.

18.2 (3.5) Creek crossing

19.4 (1.4) T/J - PSA. LH Tk leads to Old Glenroy HS.

23.4 (4.0 Annie's Creek crossing – water.

24.7 (0.3) T/J – PSA. Track on left leads to Mornington HS.

29.6 (4.9) Annie's Creek crossing – this stream is crossed a number of times – often has water in it.

41.3 (11.7) Enter Mornington Wilderness Camp - PSA to office. Camping area on left.

41.8 (0.5) Office. Tk on right leads to Dimond Gorge.

GPS 17° 31' 0" S 126° 6' 42"E

WILDLIFE SANCTUARY PASS

All visitors to the Mornington Wilderness Camp are required to purchase a Wildlife Sanctuary Pass upon arrival at the property.

Cost is around $20 per vehicle per visit, which allows access to designated gorges and includes comprehensive interpretive trail notes for self-guided nature trails.

Canoeing on Dimond Gorge.

The gorge stretches for over 15 km and you really only get a good idea of its vastness from an aircraft or helicopter.

There is some pleasant swimming and great canoieng. You may even see a Freshwater Croc, but they are timid and will stay out of your way.

Dimond Gorge

It's around 26km to Dimond Gorge where the *Fitzroy River* passes through the King Leopold Ranges. The placid stretches of water hemmed in by the rugged ranges are a real delight.

There is some excellent canoeing to be had and canoes are available for hire. See the manager at the Camp for details.

For Further Information

Write to Mornington Sanctuary, PMB 925, Derby, WA 6728
Ph: (08) 9191 7046, fax: (08) 9191 7419
web site: **www.australianwildlife.org**.

EAST TOWARDS TABLELANDS

THE HANN RIVER AND LAKE GLADSTONE

From the Glenroy Station/Mornington Wilderness Camp turn-off, 46 km east of Mt House, the main track to Tablelands Station continues eastward across undulating lightly timbered country.

The *Hann River* is crossed 25 km later on a rocky causeway that has seen better days. It's generally no problem in the Dry and there is normally always water along this stretch of river. It's not a great place to camp however.

Back from the river crossing, just over 3 km, a faint track heads north, winding its way through scattered lightly timbered scrub until about 6 km north of the main track you come to the shores of *Lake Gladstone* – the only natural lake in the Kimberley.

Travellers wishing to stop and camp and explore around the lake must obtain permission from Mt House Station beforehand.

The place is alive with birds – ducks, herons, Black-necked Storks, Brolgas and many more. Bird lovers will be rapt in this place and a stroll around the edge of the lake in the morning or evening is sure to bring a wealth of wildlife sightings.

Because of the shallow nature of the lake how far the water extends will depend on how late in the Dry season you are there. Generally by late July the lake is rimmed with a flat cleared area of green grass and these can be ideal to set up a **camp**.

The best spot to camp is on the eastern shore of the lake where you will find some big old Boabs. There can be a **lot of mossies** around though, so be warned!

Trek East via Lake Gladstone to Tablelands *(continued from page 175.)*

0.0	**(0.0)**	*Major T/J – Straight on to Tablelands HS. (Right leads to Old Glenroy for Mornington Wilderness Camp.)*
		(53.4 km east from Gibb River Road.)

GPS 17° 13' 25"S 126° 3' 12"E

Track from Tablelands to Bedford Downs is currently closed. *(See page 179 for details.)*

21.5	**(21.5)**	*T/J – PSA. Left leads to Lake Gladstone.*

To Lake Gladstone *- must obtain permission from Mt House Station.*

0.0	**(0.0)**	*T/J – heading north on faint track.*
2.8	**(2.8)**	*Y-junct – VL.*
3.2	**(0.4)**	*T/J – PSA. Faint RH track near large boab on left.*
5.5	**(2.3)**	*Pass through old fenceline.*
6.1	**(0.6)**	*Lake edge at SW side. Veer east around southern edge of lake – don't get bogged! Some good camping around here.*

Hann Tree at 17° 11' 12"S / 126° 14' 36"E

24.7	**(3.2)**	*Hann River crossing – water. A few places to camp but you need to look.*
45.5	**(20.8)**	*Traine River crossing.*
56.5	**(11.0)**	*Track has the Baulk Face Range to the south.*
57.9	**(1.4)**	*Major river crossing – waterhole.*
68.4	**(10.5)**	*Creek crossing.*
96.3	**(27.9)**	*Little Fitzroy River crossing*
97.6	**(1.3)**	*Gate/fenceline.*
98.1	**(0.5)**	*Track passes right beside the Tablelands HS, on left, then passes shed on right and through another gate.*
99.9	**(1.8)**	*Yards on left and LH track – TL around yards.*

Zero trip meter at this point.

Close to the lake at the eastern end and just above the high water mark, at 17° 11' 12" S, 126° 14' 36" E for those of you with a GPS, an old, large Boab can be found. On its western flank a **blaze 'FH XVI' cut by Frank Hann**, the first European explorer through the area in 1898, can still be seen. Please don't deface this tree in any way. Camp beside the lake and enjoy the scene that Hann did when he rested his horses for a day.

There is another **Hann tree** in the nearby area, this one back along the edge of the Hann River towards the causeway. A very faint, near non-existent track parallels the river (not the one detailed above) and where two creeks meet between the track and the river two large Boabs can be seen. One is blazed 'FH'. This tree takes a little finding.

TO TABLELANDS (YULUMBU) HS

Heading east the track crosses the *Traine River* about 21 km east of the *Hann Crossing* and soon after begins to parallel the sheer escarpment of the Baulk Face Range which is off to the south.

The *Little Fitzroy River* is crossed just before passing through a couple of gates before reaching **Tablelands Homestead**, 73 km east of the *Hann River* crossing. The station is now owned by an Aboriginal community and most of the time there are a few families in residence at the homestead.

The track passes inbetween the buildings at Tablelands HS so travel slowly and say 'Hi' if anybody is around.

Less than 2 km later a track on the left, near some yards, will be seen This is the track to **Marion Downs** and the route through Teronis Gorge to **Bedford Downs**. The track straight ahead, looking like the better route is the route to Bedford Downs via the Jump-up.

TREK FROM TABLELANDS HS TO TERONIS JUNCTION VIA JUMP-UP

***Note:** This route was basically impassable when we last tried to use it. It was washed out at the Jump-up.*

0.0	**(0.0)**	*Track junction (T/J) east of Tablelands HS, yards on left – PSA. Left leads via Teronis Gorge*
7.2	**(7.2)**	*Creek crossing.*
14.2	**(7.0)**	*Track is very rocky as it parallels small creek.*
21.5	**(7.3)**	*Top of range and Jump-up. Descent is very rough and can be washed out! Take care.*
22.7	**(1.2)**	*Bottom of range.*
42.2	**(19.5)**	*Teronis Junction. VR to Bedford Downs HS. VL for Teronis Gorge.*

TO BEDFORD DOWNS HOMESTEAD

VIA THE JUMP-UP

This route is extremely rough, especially at the Jump-up and is often impassable.

After leaving Tablelands the track heads directly east getting into rougher and rougher country. There is some good wildlife along here though and you'll be going slow enough to see it. About 28 km east of Tablelands you will come to the top of the range and the jump-up. The track is rough and basically impassable when we last saw it. There are some great views from the top of the range overlooking what is the Fitzroy River valley, across to Mt Wells and Mt Bedford, marking the north-eastern limit of the King Leopold Ranges.

The track winds down the escarpment in a southerly direction and then turns eastward again before crossing a small creek and arriving at a track junction, 21 km from the top of the jump-up. We call this junction, Teronis Junction.

Right leads to Bedford Downs, left takes you to Teronis Gorge.

TREK FROM TABLELANDS HS TO TERONIS JUNCTION VIA TERONIS GORGE

0.0	(0.0)	*Yards on left and LH track, just past Tablelands HS – TL around yards.*
5.2	(5.2)	*Old fenceline and Y-junct at 17° 14.5'S / 126° 56.1'E. – VR.*
8.5	(3.3)	*Track follows creek on left and then passes through a grassy area which could be quite boggy when wet.*
18.6	(10.1)	*Y-junct – VR. Left is main access to Marion Downs.*
19.8	(1.2)	*Y-junct – VR past old yards on right, located at 17° 13.9'S / 126° 3.8'E. Track follows range on left.*
31.2	(11.4)	*Major creek crossing.*
32.6	(1.4)	*Major creek crossing.*
45.1	(12.5)	*Old yards on right – Teronis Yards.*
47.0	(1.9)	*Track enters Teronis Gorge with creek on left. The creek is crossed three times in next 2 km or so. Some small but pleasant camp sites in gorge.*
49.7	(2.7)	*Last creek crossing and exit gorge.*
50.3	(0.6)	*T/J – VR on main track to Bedford Downs HS. Faint LH track.*
52.2	(1.9)	*Teronis Junction – TL. Track coming in on right is from Tablelands HS via Jump-up.*

Teronis Gorge /Bedford Downs Track

The track through Teronis Gorge to Bedford Downs is currently closed with a locked gate by Bedford Downs Station. Contact the station for possible permission to use this track, ph: (08) 9167 8829.

Via Teronis Gorge

From the track junction east of Tablelands, this route heads north-east and then close to the headwaters of the *Chamberlain River* meets with a track junction 20 km from Tablelands. Left at this junction leads to Marion Downs HS, while right leads to the gorge and Bedford Downs. The track begins to parallel the river, which is off to the north and 26 km east of the track junction you pass a set of old yards on the right and less than 2 km later the track enters Teronis Gorge.

This is a delightful place with a few palms and Boabs dotting the scene and always at least a trickle of water running through the length of the gorge. There are a few spots to **camp** within the gorge but they are pretty small.

Once out of the gorge, only about 2 km from where you entered it, keep to the main track and a few km later you will come to where the jump-up route joins with the main track, at what we call Teronis Junction, veer left. About 8 km later the track begins to pass between ranges – the Durack Range to the north and the King Leopolds to the south. Mt Bedford dominates the scene.

Once through this major range complex and about 15 km from the exit from the gorge a track junction is met and here you need to veer left, staying on, what is now a main station track.

About 28 km north of the junction you'll pass the Bedford Downs HS on your left.

BEDFORD DOWNS TO THE HIGHWAY

From Bedford Downs the track leaves the rugged range country behind and crosses the vast undulating plains that border the headwaters of the Ord River. About 23 km from the homestead you cross that stream and then winds its way through a low range of boulder strewn hills before passing Springvale HS on the right, about 79 km from Bedford Downs.

Just 16 km later you arrive at the Great Northern Highway. Halls Creek is 66 km to the south and you are something like 330 km east of Mt House HS.

Remember there are no supplies or fuel along this route.

Driving through Teronis Gorge.

Trek from Teronis Junction to the Great Northern Highway

0.0	**(0.0)**	*Track Junction (T/J) – Teronis Junction – VR to Bedford Downs if coming via Jump-up. VL if via Teronis Gorge. Track begins to improve. Left leads to Teronis Gorge.*
6.0	**(6.0)**	*Track begins to pass through range country.*
11.7	**(5.7)**	*Dam & windmill on left – Mt Bedford on right.*
13.6	**(1.9)**	*T/J – VL. RH tracks leads to Landsdowne station. Good station track from now on. There are a few gates along here – leave them as you find them.*
41.0	**(27.4)**	*T/J – PSA. LH track leads into Bedford Downs HS which is only 100 metres or so away.*
42.6	**(1.6)**	*T/J – VL – airstrip on right. RH track SP 'Cattle Creek Bore'. A number of gates and tracks off to bores as well as some creek crossings in next 22 km.*
65.7	**(23.1)**	*Ord River crossing.*
75.2	**(9.5)**	*Creek crossing & small gorge on left. Track begins to wind through low range. There are a few gates along this section and a couple of creek crossings. A couple of faint station tracks off to each side as well – stick to main track.*
121.1	**(45.9)**	*Gate/fenceline and pass into Springvale Station. Main track veers left.*
121.4	**(0.3)**	*T/J – PSA.. RH track leads to homestead.*
137.2	**(15.8)**	*T-junct – bitumen – Great Northern Highway. TR to Halls Creek, 66 km south.*

TABLELANDS TRACK

DERBY TO FITZROY CROSSING

INTRODUCTION

This sweep of country centres around the great southern arc of the *Fitzroy River*, taking in the barrier of ranges to the north of that great river and the azimuth of near desert country to the south.

This region was where the first Europeans settled in the Kimberley region and today it is the gateway to the magnificent gorge country of the central Kimberley, as well as the maze of islands that dot the Kimberley's rugged indented coastline.

HISTORY

Opening Up The Land

When **Alexander Forrest** blazed his way through this region in 1879 he started a land rush that quickly saw the land along the *Fitzroy River* taken up in huge pastoral properties. Earlier, in 1866, **Alexander McRae** had explored the mouth of the Fitzroy River and the surrounding country, but little followed this venture.

George Patterson took the first sheep to the Kimberley and established Yeeda Station in 1880. Soon afterwards the port of Derby was established and proclaimed officially in 1883, by the then Surveyor-General, **John Forrest** (Alexander's brother). That year bales of wool lying on the mud flats awaiting shipment were damaged by a freak tidal wave caused by the explosion of Krakatoa in far away Indonesia. It must have been some wave to penetrate that far into King Sound!

The discovery of gold at far away Halls Creek in 1885 had many hopeful gold diggers passing through the new port and, while the rush was short-lived and not particularly rich, it helped establish Derby as a major port.

Alexander Forrest arrives at the Fitzroy River.
Pic courtesy of the J.S.Battye Library of WA History.

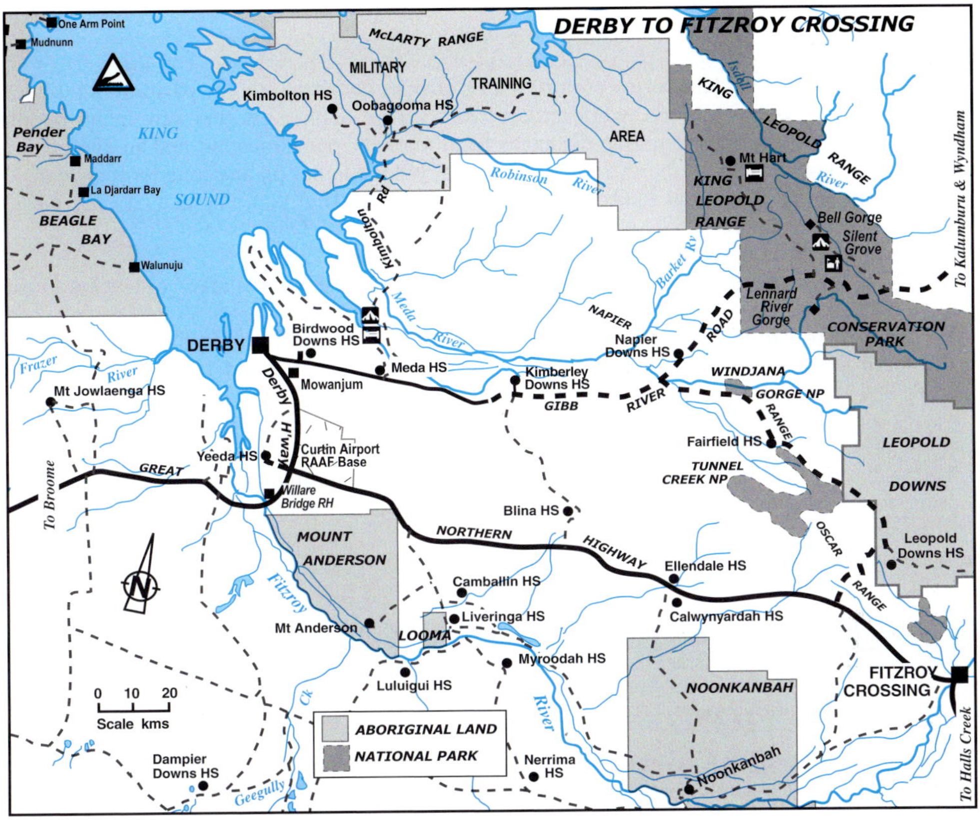

Sheep, Cattle and Problems

While cattle were the backbone of the East Kimberley pioneers, in the West Kimberley, along the banks of the Fitzroy, the first pastoralists brought sheep. While their numbers waxed and waned, viable populations of sheep continued to graze the country until the 1960s, when cattle took over completely.

By 1885 the port of Derby supported a Resident Magistrate and a police force, but because Derby had no jetty it wasn't used very much by local pastoralists. In that year the government constructed a jetty and just a couple of years later over 790 bales of wool were shipped from the port.

The population of the Kimberley was, by 1891, less than 1500. That didn't include Aborigines, but did include the nearly 800 people based in Broome and on the pearling fleet. It didn't leave many people for the rest of the region – by all accounts only 62 were women!

Around this time many European landholders were reporting large numbers of sheep and cattle being speared by Aborigines. You could hardly blame the Aborigines; their tribal lands along the *Fitzroy River*, once rich in wallabies, were now swarming with domesticated animals that made an easier target! Some properties reported up to 7000 sheep speared in one year.

Pigeon, or **Jandamarra** as he was called by his people, was one of the most notorious Aboriginal rebels and was still to make his mark along the Fitzroy, but already the problems were becoming untenable.

In 1894 a police post was established at a spot on the *Fitzroy River* called 'The Crossing'. We know it today as Fitzroy Crossing. A couple of years earlier the Overland Telegraph Line had reached this point from Derby and this was extended, in stages, to Halls Creek and finally to Wyndham.

A young **Constable Pilmer,** who was to later gain fame in the Pigeon affair and in the investigation of the spearing of Shoesmith and Thompson on the Canning Stock Route in 1912, was one of the two policemen at the isolated post at Fitzroy Crossing.

After a brief reign of terror which began with the killing of **Police Constable Richardson** (now buried in the **Derby Cemetery**) at Lillimilura Station near Windjana Gorge, Pigeon was killed on the 1st April, 1897. The news reached Derby, the main police headquarters, on 6th April, 1897. It was met with much rejoicing in the area as well as big headlines in the newspapers in far away Perth.

The Last 90 Years

The fortunes of the West Kimberley region, with Derby as its base, rode the pastoral big dipper. Some years were boom periods, while others were severe depression that saw many people come and go. Two World Wars, long distances from markets, poor transport and an even worse road network, not to mention the extremes of climate, put the halter on any long term growth.

It was during the 1950s that roads began to be improved. Mind you, Highway 1 only got its full complement of tar in 1987, so it was a fairly slow process. Tourists also started to appear around this time and the search for minerals began to build up.

In 1951 BHP loaded its first iron ore from Yampi Sound as the 'Iron Islands' of Cockatoo and Koolan gave up their wealth.

Western Australian Petroleum (WAPET) commenced searching for oil in the Canning Basin to the south and south-east of Derby in 1953. Earlier, between 1919 and 1923, four wells had been drilled with little success. Between 1953 and 1975 WAPET drilled some 59 wells, but it wasn't until 1979 that Home Oil drilled its first well at Blina, 100 km east of Derby, and a payable field was discovered.

Today that oil is piped to the Erskine Terminal near the main highway where it is trucked to Broome for loading onto ships heading for the Kwinana refinery near Perth.

Mineral wealth, tourism, a better pastoral industry and a number of defence establishments are today, changing the face of Derby and its hinterland.

DERBY

INTRODUCTION

The townsite of Derby, located on *King Sound* north of the mouth of the *Fitzroy River*, was gazetted in 1883. It is named after Edward Henry Stanley, Lord Derby (1826-1893), Secretary of State for Colonies 1882-1885. The town was established to service the growing Kimberley cattle industry, and grew rapidly following the discovery of gold in the Kimberley in 1885.

Australia's first air mail service arrived at Derby in a WA Airways Bristol Tourer piloted by Major Norman Brearley and Charles Kingsford Smith, then 1922 Australia's first scheduled air service commenced between Geraldton and Derby.

Derby is the seat of the Local Authority, being the Shire of Derby/West Kimberley. The main part of town is set on a peninsula of slightly elevated land above the surrounding flat, tidal marshland. While the town may lack the glamour of Broome, an ongoing campaign has seen Derby sporting a new, clean image, which is attracting more and more people.

As it caters for a vast hinterland, most supplies and repair facilities are available.

ACCESS

Derby is located on King Sound, near the mouth of the *Fitzroy River*, approximately 2366 km by road from Perth and just 220 km north of Broome. Wyndham is some 914 km away by the blacktop of Highway 1. By the scenic Gibb River Road it is just over 690 km.

THINGS TO SEE AND DO

Derby is often called the 'Gateway to the Gorges', however there are a number of attractions around Derby itself to keep the visitor's interest.

PLACES OF INTEREST

Boab Prison Tree

Located 7 km south of Derby just off the Great Northern Highway. The story goes that this giant, hollowed out Boab tree, with a girth of 14.7 metres, was used by policemen as a holding cell until prisoners could be transported into Derby. Pigeon was supposedly amongst those who spent a night in this lockup. The Boab is said to be over 1500 years old.

Myall's Bore & Frosty's Pool

This bore can be found on the left just as you turn onto the road to the Boab Prison Tree. This lengthy cattle trough, built in 1911, is thought to be the longest in the southern hemisphere at 120 metres. It was originally filled from an artesian bore and in its heyday it supplied water to a thousand cattle at a time while they were being driven to the Derby jetty for shipment.

Frosty's Pool was built during the Second World War in 1944 and was used as a bathing area for the troops stations near Derby.

Old Derby Goal & Police Yard

Located adjacent the present day Derby Police Station, off Loch St, the police station and depot for the Police Horse Patrol was originally located halfway between the original town of Derby and Derby Point. Now restored, it is one of the oldest buildings in the town, circa 1906. This is where Pigeon was an inmate, having previously been employed as a tracker.

Wharfingers House Museum

Built in the 1920s for the local harbour master, this house is a design typical of the tropics. Located on the corner of Loch and Elder Streets, it now houses a museum outlining the communications, shipping and aviation history of the region as well as displaying items made by patients of the former Derby Leprosarium. Open on request. You'll need to contact the *Derby Visitor Centre* for the key.

Royal Flying Doctor Service

The RFDS base, in Loch St (cnr Ashley St), ph: (08) 9191 0200, is open to visitors Monday to Friday (except holidays) 9.00 am, 11.00 am and 2.00 pm for video and souvenir sales. Visitors can help support this service by leaving a donation or by purchasing some souvenirs. For more information on the RFDS check out their web site: www.flyingdoctor.net/. Donations can be made on their web site.

Derby Pastoral Trail

This trail tells the story of the last day of the travel for drovers with their herds from Myall's Bore to the jetty. Stage one starts at the One Mile dinner camp at the corner of Mimosa St and Rowan St and ends at the Centenary Pavilion at the jetty.

Botanical Gardens; Joon Joo Botanical Trail

- The **Botanical Gardens** features a variety of exotic palms and fruit trees, as well as native species.
- The **Joon Joo Botanical Trail** is a 3 km easy walk on the outskirts of Derby, with descriptions of the plants and animals of the Wanganut Land System and their use by the Nyikina people of Derby.

Pidgeon Heritage Trail

The Pigeon Munnda Heritage Trail is part of the Heritage Trails Network. This self-guiding tour is divided into two sections.

The first begins at Derby and features sites significant to Pigeon's life and creates an image of the town and region before the turn of the century.

The second section begins at Windjana Gorge and finishes 30km from there at Tunnel Creek. A brochure is available and can be downloaded from the Heritage Council of WA, web site: www.trails.heritage.wa.gov.au/.

Wetland

Derby (waste water) Wetland, access via Conway Street. Birdwatchers can make use of an observation tower provided by the Water Corporation near the waste water ponds to view a great variety of ducks, waders and other water birds that use the area as a day time roost.

Library

The **Library**, adjacent to the Botanical Gardens features displays of Aboriginal artifacts and works by local Kimberley artists.

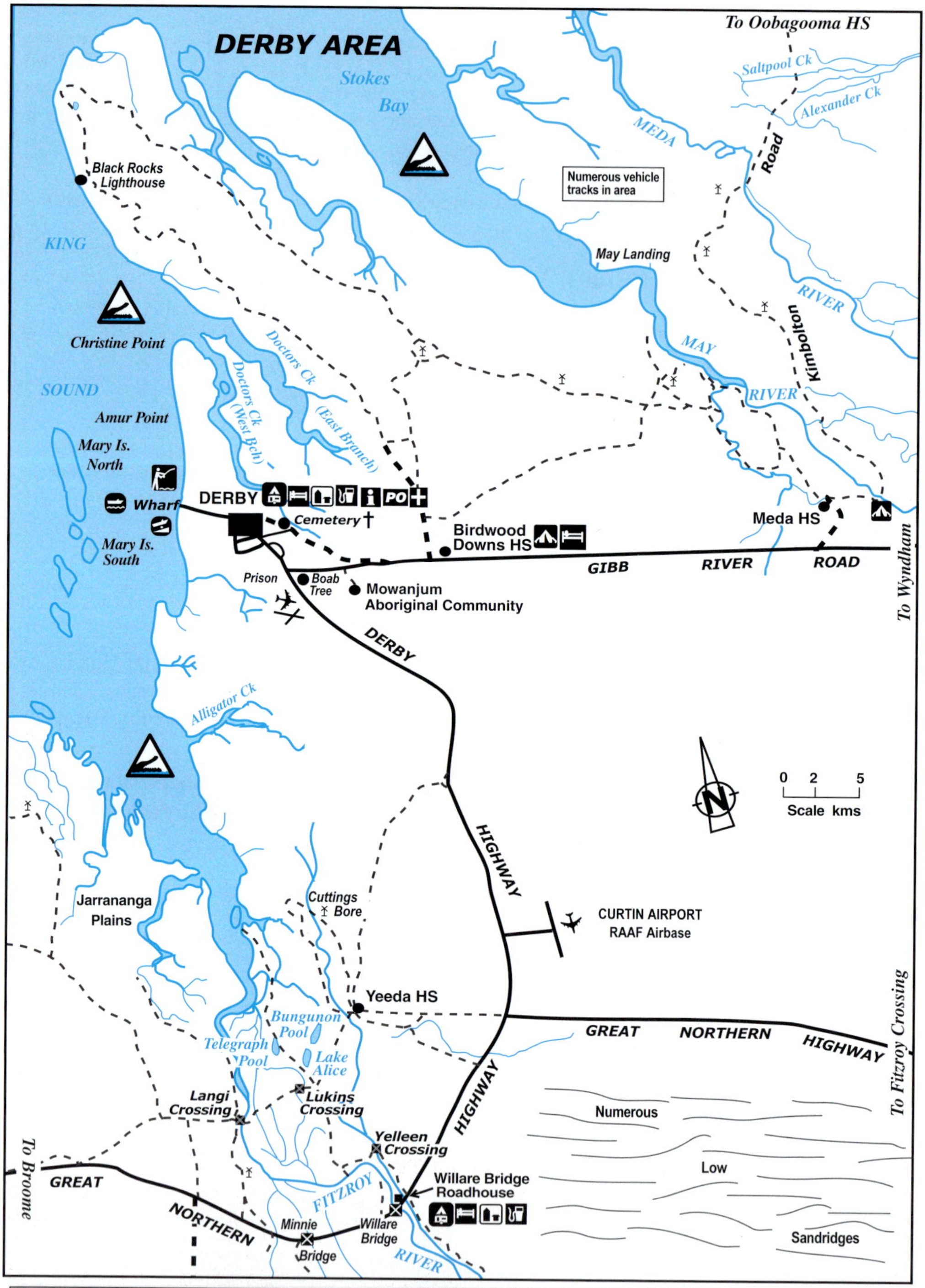

The Derby Jetty or Wharf & Boat Ramp

The jetty (or wharf), reached by a long causeway across the mudflats that separate the town from the waters of King Sound, is the Derby Export Facility for shipping lead and zinc, as well as tourist and pleasure craft. The stumps of the old original jetty, built in 1894, can still be seen at low tide.

A meal of fish and chips from the *Wharf Restaurant*, near the entrance to the jetty should be tried. Dine indoors or out (bookings essential), or takeaway.

Beside the jetty is the boat ramp which offers access to the sea. Access however is dependent on the tide. At times of low spring tides the jetty and boat ramp are completely out of water. Derby, in fact, has the highest tidal range in Australia at 11.8 metres, and one of the highest tides in the world. While the fishing is good, spectacular even, you've got to watch the tides and the currents they produce! See our chapter, *Fishing in the Kimberley*, for more details.

Mangroves crowd the jetty on both sides and while the sandflies call anyone a friend, the fishing here can be quite good. In fact, it must be the only town in Australia where you can catch mud crabs off the local jetty. The jetty if also the place to view the beautiful sunsets.

At the approach to the wharf is the **Centenary of Federation Pavilion**, with its magnificent 28 square metre **mosaic tile floor**, the work of 370 children and adults from the community.

PLACES OF INTEREST FURTHER AFIELD

MAY RIVER

A little closer to Derby, the *May River* flows into King Sound 30 km north of the town. Meda Station owns this area and the river is popular with locals who want to dangle a line and catch a barra, as well as have a go at catching some cherabin.

To reach the picnic/**camping** area, take the dirt road at the May River/Meda Station junction with the Gibb River Road (approx 40 km from Derby). Travel 6 km along this dirt road, veering right where the road forks to reach the picnic area.

Please do not intrude on the Meda Station homestead and beware of Salt-water crocodiles which definitely inhabit this area.

POINT TORMENT

A circuitous 4WD track leads to Point Torment, about 50 km north of Derby and a good fishing spot. This track should not be used during high tides (10 metres or above) and a detailed map is required. Contact *West Kimberley Guns n Ammo*, Fitzroy Street, Derby, ph: 9191 1490, for more details and directions.

THE GORGES

All the gorges, such as Windjana, Tunnel Creek, Adcock, Bells, Lennard's and Galvans are accessible from Derby. See the chapter, *The Gibb River Road*, for more detail on these gorges.

YAMPI MILITARY TRAINING AREA

The Yampi Military Training Area takes in a huge swath of land to the north of Derby. It is centred on Kimbolton and Oobagooma Stations which the Commonwealth Government acquired back in 1979. Basically, access to this remote area is prohibited, with permission only being granted for scientific research.

Relaxing in the Lennard River, not far from the road junction to Windjana Gorge.

THE FITZROY RIVER

The *Fitzroy River* is one of Australia's greatest rivers. Unlike the *Ord River* whose catchment area of 54,000 sq km has created WA's biggest irrigation project, the Fitzroy River remains undammed with a huge catchment area of 85,000 sq km. In normal flood it could fill the Serpentine Dam (outside Perth) in just over 5 hours, or even more spectacularly, in times of peak flood (an average of one every 3 years) it would fill Sydney Harbour in just 21 hours!

The Fitzroy is a popular river with anglers in pursuit of the magnificent barramundi. The females spawn in the saltwater estuaries and young fish migrate up the Fitzroy as far as Geikie Gorge, near Fitzroy Crossing. Another edible treat to be found in the Fitzroy River is the cherabin, or freshwater prawn. At the end of each Wet cherabin can be seen towards evening and at night climbing the barrage at Camballin in large numbers

WILLARE BRIDGE AREA

The Fitzroy River is crossed by the Great Northern Highway 57 km south of Derby.

Just north of the bridge is Willare itself. Consisting of just a roadhouse, which dispenses fuel and limited supplies. Some repairs are available (although you're better off getting to Derby) and there is also a small shady, caravan/**camping** area with powered sites, and rooms available, ph/fax: (08) 9191 4775.

On the southern bank are some great picnic spots set amongst large shady trees, and it is also a great place to do some birdwatching. Camping is not allowed. Day use area only.

Barra frequent the deep pools up and down the river, while cherabin can also be caught. Remember this is Salt-water crocodile country, **don't swim**.

Gill netting in the rivers and estuaries of the Shire of Derby/West Kimberley is prohibited and substantial fines apply to offenders.

LANGI CROSSING

Langi Crossing is where the old, unsealed, Northern Highway once crossed the **Fitzroy River** south of Derby, about 75 km south of Derby. It's another good fishing spot and cherabin (fresh water prawns) abound here. You can find your way down to this area along the southern or northern banks, although the southern bank of the Fitzroy River takes you into some good **camping** spots. Langi Crossing itself is a little desolate for a good camp.

This is private property and permission must be obtained from Yeeda Station for access and camping. Respect the owners' roads, stock and any buildings. Remember it's also Salt-Water crocodile country.

TELEGRAPH POOL

A little further downstream is *Telegraph Pool* (approx 80km from Derby) and the wide sandy river bed makes a good **camp** and there's some good fishing.

This is private property and permission must be obtained from Yeeda Station for access and camping. Respect the owners' roads, stock and any buildings. Remember it's also Salt-Water crocodile country

Further downstream still are the wide flats of the river mouth. Take care down here as you are fairly remote and the tide often comes in as a virtual wall of water. People who have experienced it say it's one of the scariest episodes they've ever had! There is a fair amount of sand and gravel extraction going on downstream of Langi Crossing and many tracks into the river end in sand pits.

PELICAN POOL

Also along the same track as Langi Crossing, approx. 95 km from Derby, is *Pelican Pool*, another fishing spot. A detailed map is essential.

This is private property and permission must be obtained from Yeeda Station for access and camping.

MYROODAH CROSSING

Langi Crossing on the Fitzroy river, south of Derby

To reach Myroodah Crossing you need to take the main road from Derby towards Fitzroy Crossing. Approx 83 km from Derby, turn right onto the dirt road heading towards Camballin. Travel another 33 km along this road to reach the crossing, situated 116 km south-east of Derby.

This crossing on the *Fitzroy River* makes a very pleasant picnic and **camping** spot. Part of the **Noogoora Burr Quarantine area**, access is permitted upstream on both sides of the river for a short distance, while downstream access is only permitted on the northern bank. (See the maps on the *Noogoora Burr Quarantine Area* page 188 for details.)

CAMBALLIN

Camballin is the centre of a huge, potential irrigation area on the Fitzroy River, about 130 km south-east of Derby. This irrigation area has been in development for many years, but while it promises much, problems always crop up that hold it back, and today the area is fairly quiet..

For visitors the area is in a **quarantine area** (as is the whole *Fitzroy River* downriver from Fitzroy Crossing to Willare Bridge) because of **Noogoora Burr**. (See details on page 189 *Noogoora Burr Quarantine Area* for access and quarantine details.)

There are some excellent areas for camping and fishing along this stretch of river, so it's definitely worth a look see if you have the time.

SPECIAL EVENTS & FESTIVALS

These are just some of the events to be held in Derby throughout the year. For exact dates check with the ***Derby Visitor Centre*** or log onto their web site and check out the Events Calendar, **www.derbytourism.com.au/**.

April: **Buccaneer Classic Fishing Event** – Usually held over the Easter period. A classic fishing competition held in the waters of the Buccaneer Archipelago.

May: **Derby King Tide Day** – held on the jetty to celebrate the day of the highest tides in Australia. Family, fun, art, games and fishing. Lots of unique local entertainment

June: **Moonrise Rock Festival** – held among the boabs under the full moon at the Derby Racecourse with fireworks!
Derby Races – June/July

July: **Bush Poets Breakfast –** Bush poetry, verse over a country style breakfast.
Mowanjam Festival – Art & cultural festival at Mowanjam Community over 2 days.
Boab Festival – is the town's premier event which runs for two weeks, featuring a combination of art and culture and lots of fun. Mud football, crabbing competition and races, float parade, speedway, mardi gras and marsh party, to name just a few of the happenings of the Boab Festival.

Aug: **Outback Rodeo** – 3 day event with the excitement of the traditional Rodeo, including camp draft, gymkhana and bucking bull and bronco events.

Sept: **Country Music Talent Quests**.

Oct **Races.**

The jetty at Derby is the place to be to celebrate the 'Derby King Tide Day'.

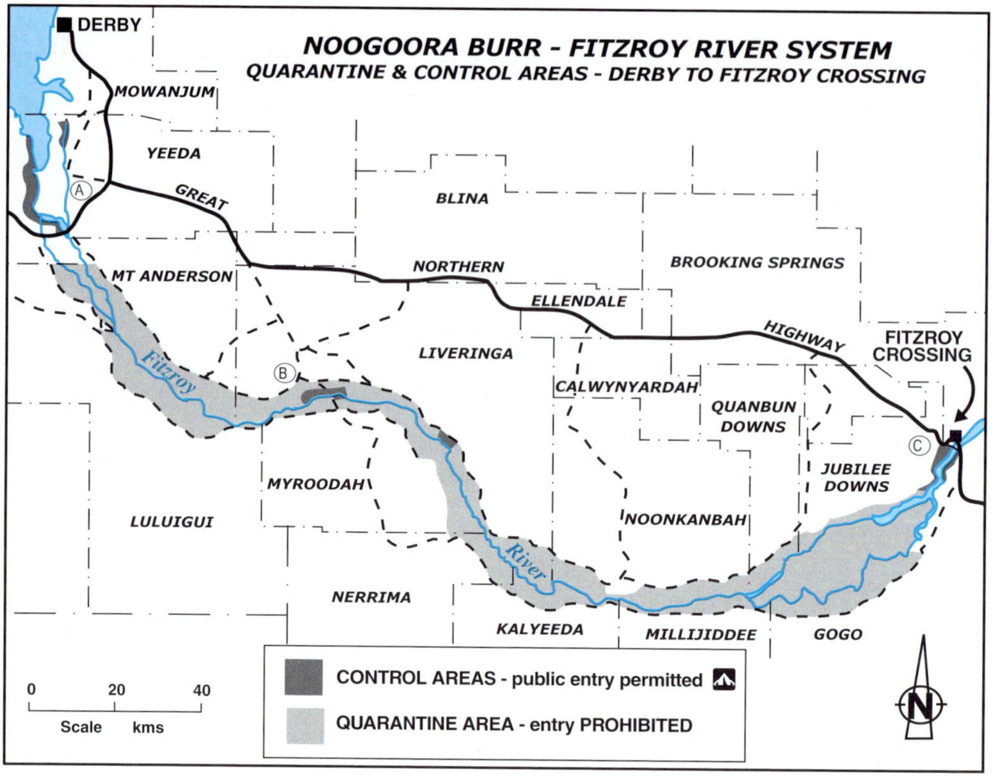
NOOGOORA BURR - FITZROY RIVER SYSTEM
QUARANTINE & CONTROL AREAS - DERBY TO FITZROY CROSSING
DERBY
MOWANJUM
YEEDA
GREAT
NORTHERN
HIGHWAY
BLINA
BROOKING SPRINGS
MT ANDERSON
ELLENDALE
LIVERINGA
CALWYNYARDAH
QUANBUN DOWNS
FITZROY CROSSING
JUBILEE DOWNS
MYROODAH
LULUIGUI
NOONKANBAH
Fitzroy
River
NERRIMA
KALYEEDA
MILLIJIDDEE
GOGO
A
B
C
0
20
40
Scale kms
CONTROL AREAS - public entry permitted
QUARANTINE AREA - entry PROHIBITED
N

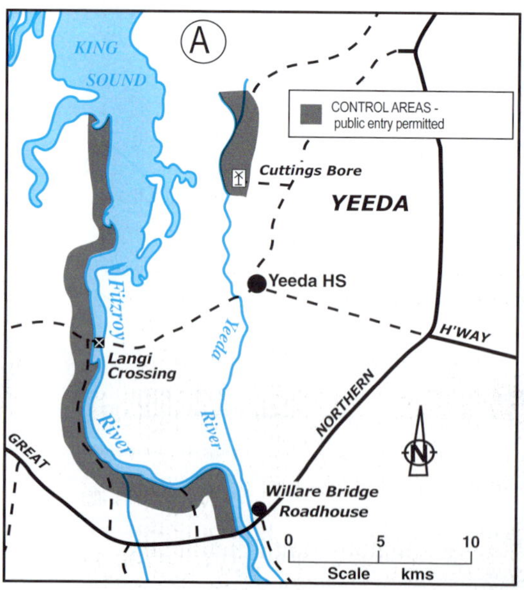
A
KING SOUND
CONTROL AREAS - public entry permitted
Cuttings Bore
YEEDA
Yeeda HS
Fitzroy
Langi Crossing
Yeeda
River
River
H'WAY
NORTHERN
GREAT
Willare Bridge Roadhouse
N
0
5
10
Scale kms

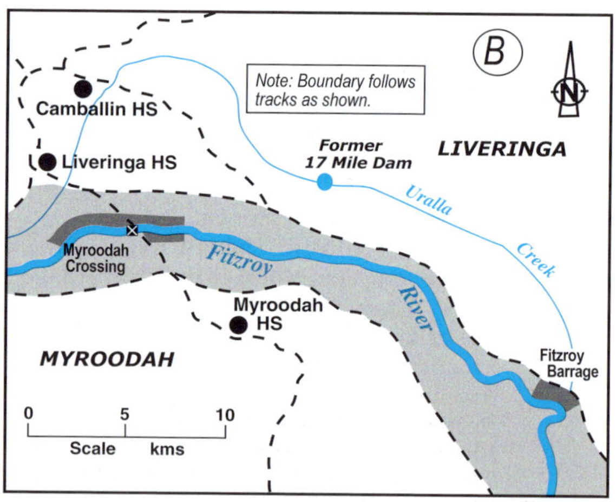
B
Note: Boundary follows tracks as shown.
Camballin HS
Liveringa HS
Former 17 Mile Dam
LIVERINGA
Uralla
Creek
Myroodah Crossing
Fitzroy
River
Myroodah HS
MYROODAH
Fitzroy Barrage
0
5
10
Scale kms
N

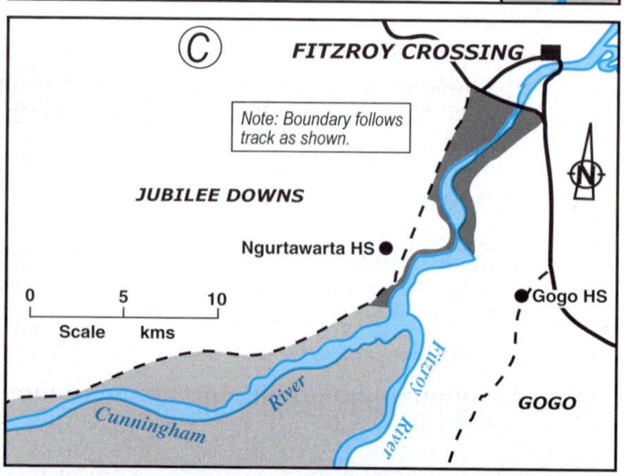
C
FITZROY CROSSING
Note: Boundary follows track as shown.
JUBILEE DOWNS
Ngurtawarta HS
Gogo HS
0
5
10
Scale kms
GOGO
Cunningham
River
Fitzroy
River
N

NOOGOORA BURR QUARANTINE AREA

Upstream from Willare Bridge, to Fitzroy Crossing itself, the whole area surrounding the river is a Quarantine Area because of Noogoora Burr, which is one of Australia's most destructive weeds.

Things to Do

- Don't go into quarantine areas unless you're visiting a station homestead and, in that case, always stay on gazetted public roads. Don't forget, you need permission to camp from the landowner.
- Before leaving or taking anything off a station in the quarantine area, inspect all vehicles,
- machinery, etc.
- Pull out and destroy any Noogoora Burr plants you find. Burn the plants in the campfire if they have burrs on them.
- Check all your clothing, camping equipment and fishing gear, especially throw-nets before leaving the river. Burn any burrs found in the campfire.
- Only go to the Public Access Areas detailed below. Signs indicate these areas and are located at main road parking bays and river access tracks.

Public Access Areas

See the maps showing quarantine and access areas.

The following four areas have been nominated for public access:

Area A – downstream of Willare Bridge to the river mouth on the western side of the Fitzroy River, and portion of the Yeeda River known as the 'Cuttings'.

Area B– area around the Fitzroy Barrage on the north side of the river, and the stretch of river around Myroodah Crossing. Up stream from Myroodah Crossing includes both sides of the river, while downstream only includes the northern bank.

Area C – stretch of water down stream from Highway 1 crossing of Fitzroy River at Fitzroy Crossing on both the east and west banks and small area on west bank continuing down from Ngurtawarta.

For more information contact:

Dept of Agriculture, Western Australian Quarantine and Inspection Service (WAQIS), Loch St, PO Box 278, Derby, WA, 6728, ph: (08) 9191 0333, fax: (08) 9191 0334; or at Kununurra, Durack Dve, PO Box 19, ph: (08) 9166 4000, fax: (08) 9166 4066, or Broome, 27 Hunter St, PO Box 5502, Broome, 6725, ph: (08) 9194 1400, fax: (08) 9192 2946.

You an also find information on their web site: www.agric.wa.gov.au/.

The Kimberley Development Commission web site also has some info on the Noogoora Burr and the quarantine area along the Fitzroy River, web: www.kimberley.wa.gov.au/index.cfm?menu=285&page=vk_quarantinenog

Crossing the Fitzroy River at Myroodah Crossing, part of the Noogoora Burr Quarantine Area.

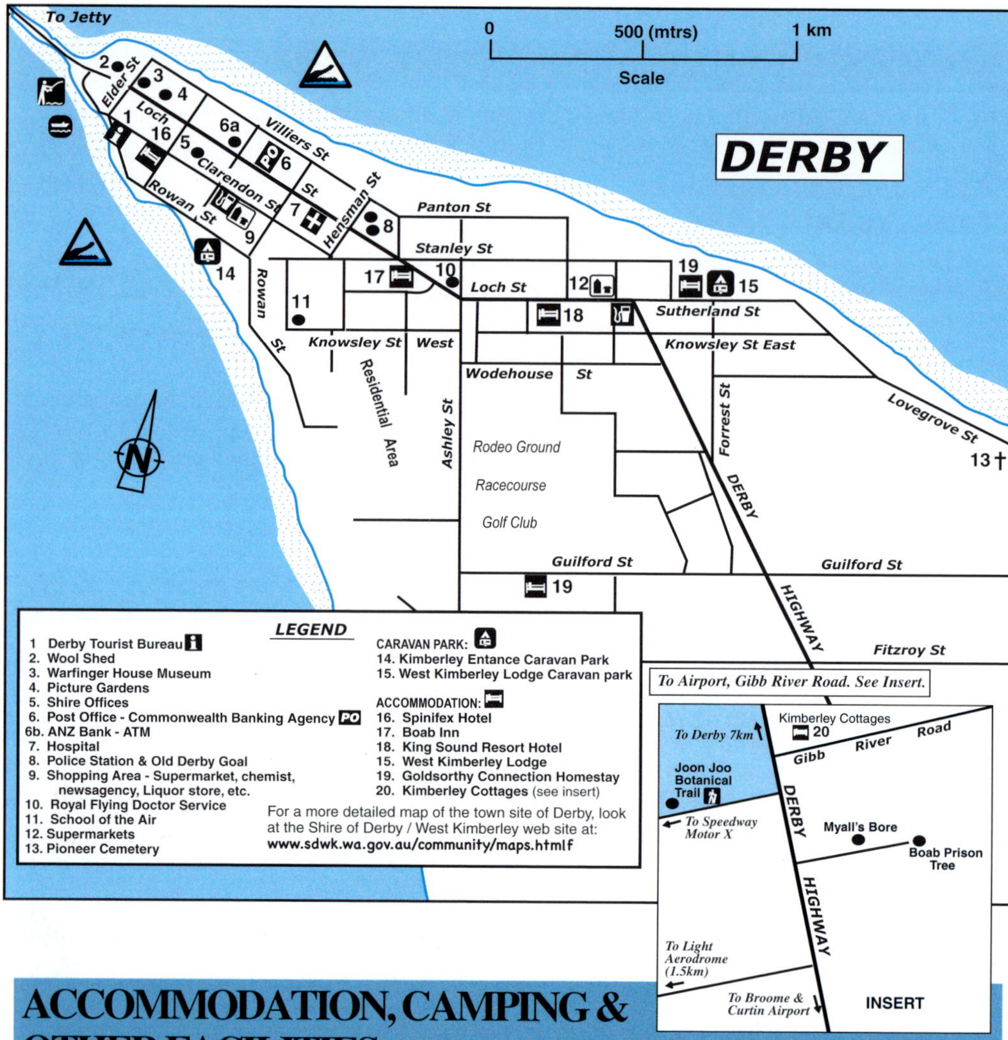

ACCOMMODATION, CAMPING & OTHER FACILITIES

Accommodation

Derby Boab Inn, Loch Street, ph (08) 9191 1044.
Goldsworthy Connection, Guilford St, ph/fax: (08) 9193 1246.
Kimberley Cottages, 18 Windjana Road, ph: (08) 9191 1114.
King Sound Resort Hotel, Loch St, ph: (08) 9193 1044 web: **www.kingsoundresort.com.au.**
Spinifex Hotel & Derby Backpackers, Clarendon St, ph: (08) 9191 1233.
West Kimberley Lodge, Cnr Sutherland & Stanley Sts, ph: (08) 9191 1031.
You'll find details of the above accommodation on the Derby Visitor Centre web site: **www.derbytourism.com.au**

Caravan Parks/Camping

Kimberley Entrance Caravan Park, Rowan St, ph: (08) 9193 1055 – shady tent sites with BBQs and all amenities. Disabled facilities. Chemical toilet disposal facilities. Web: **www.kimberleyentrancecaravanpark.com/.**

West Kimberley Lodge Caravan Park, Lot 100 Sutherland St, PO Box 390, ph: (08) 9191 1031 – Shady area for powered sites plus overflow. Fully equipped laundry, Barbecue area. Within walking distance to Supermarket No Pets allowed. Disabled facilities. Web: **www.bookeasy.com.au/website/accom_result1.asp?code=18617.**

Accommodation & Caravan Parks in Surrounding Area –

The following facilities are available close to Derby:–

Willare Bridge Caravan Park/Roadhouse – near the Fitzroy River, about 57 km from Derby on the Great Northern Highway, PO Box 888, Derby, ph: (08) 9191 4775. Facilities include shady tent sites (with power), BBQs and all **camping** ground facilities. Pets allowed under control. Air-conditioned accommodation is also available, as well as dine-in or take-away meals from the roadhouse. The roadhouse also supplies all fuels, limited stores and repairs – open 7 days a week from 6.00 am to 10.00 pm.

Birdwood Downs Station, Gibb River Road, via Derby, WA 6728, ph: (08) 9191 1275 – Situated 16km along the Gibb River Road and 1km in, Birdwood Downs is a working station. Savannah Huts in bush setting with shared ablutions. Trail rides and Guided tours available. Dinner, Bed & Breakfast or room only. Camping also available. No Domestic Pets. **Prior bookings essential**. Web: **www.birdwooddowns.com/**.

FACILITIES

Derby can supply all requirements for the traveller. Those not available can be flown up from Perth within a day or so.

Some of the facilities readily available are :–

Hospital, Clarendon Street (access), ph: (08) 9193 3333
Dental Clinic, ph: (08) 9191 1340
Ambulance, ph: (08) 91 93 3333
Police, Loch Street, ph: (08) 9191 1444
Fire, ph: (08) 9193 1194
Veterinary Clinic, Cnr Rowell & Marmion Sts, ph: (08) 9191 1471
Shire of Derby/West Kimberley, Loch St, ph: (08) 9191 0999, web: **www.sdwk.wa.gov.au/**
Royal Flying Doctor Service, Clarendon St, PO Box 52, ph: (08) 9191 0200
Post Office (full postal services & Commonwealth keycard banking facilities), Loch Street, ph: (08) 9191 1350.
Main Roads of WA – Kimberley Regional office Derby, Wodehouse St, PMB 959, ph: (08) 9158 4333, web: **www.mainroads.wa.gov.au**
CALM, Derby Ranger's Office, ph: (08) 9193 1411, web: **www.calm.wa.gov.au/**
Banks
ANZ, Loch St – ATM
National – City Centre
Commonwealth Bank – Agency Post Office – Keycard facilities
Derby Telecentre, Clarendon St, (opposite newsagency)
Supermarkets – trading 7 days a week with Eftpos facilities:
Rusty's One Stop Shop, 52 Clarendon St – supermarket open 7 days ph: (08) 9191 1210, liquor store 6 days per week, web: **members.westnet.com.au/rustys/**.
Woolworths, Loch St, open 7 days. Liquor Store reduced opening hours, ph: (08) 9191 1055, web: **www.woolworths.com.au/storelocator/index.asp**.
West Kimberley Guns Ammo & Fishing Tackle – Fitzroy St, ph: (08) 9191 1490 – for all your fishing & hunting needs, bait, trailer parts, ice, eskys, throw nets, swags and more.
Big Barra's One Stop Shop, 18 Nevill St, ph: (08) 9191 2111 - sports, fishing & camping.

Derby Tourist Information

DERBY VISITOR CENTRE

2 Clarendon Street, PO Box 48, Derby, WA, 6728.
Ph: (08) 9191 1426, fax: (08) 9191 1609
Free Call: 1800 621 426
Email: info@derbytourism.com.au
Web site: **www.derbytourism.com.au/**
Open April, May & September - Mon to Fri 8.30 am to 4.30 pm, Sat/Sun & Public Holiday: 9.00 am to 1.00 pm.
Open June/July/August: Mon to Fri 8.30 am to 5.00 pm, Sat/Sun & Public Holiday: 9.00 am to 4.00 pm.
Open October to March, Mon to Fri 8.30 am to 4.30 pm, Sat 9.00 am to 12.00 noon.
The Centre can organise all your accommodation, local and interstate travel needs, as well as local and Kimberley tours and accommodation. The Centre can also arrange air & coach transport.
Visitors can also purchase a range of guide books, souvenirs, gifts and maps, with major credit cards being accepted.
There is also email access available.

ABC Regional Radio - Derby	
Local Radio	873 AM
Radio National	107.5 FM

Other stores include:

Boab Pharmacy & Newsagency, 48 Clarendon St – open 7 days week, Eftpos facilities, ph: (08) 9191 1160.

Cafes	Butchers	Bakery	Bait & Fishing Gear
Hardware	Restaurants	Swimming Pool	

Service Stations:

Derby Tyre & Exhaust Centre, 31 Clarendon St, (08) 9191 1020 – repairs, tyres, batteries, etc.

BP Colac Roadhouse & Service Station, 84 Loch St (just as you come into town), ph: (08) 9191 1429 or Roadhouse ph: (08) 9191 1278 – open 7 days week – all fuels and autogas, mechanical repairs & servicing, tyres, batteries, auto accessories, ice and gas, fishing gear and bait. Eftpos and credit card facilities.

Numerous automotive & caravan/trailer repairs, panel beaters and service facilities including –

Boab Spares & Repairs/Kimberley Towing Services, 717 Brearley St, ph: (08) 9191 1311, a/h ph: (08) 9191 1075.

Derby 4x4 & Marine, 20 Wells St, ph: (08) 9193 1919 – servicing, repairs & parts, all vehicles, boats & outboards. 4WD repair specialist and parts.

Derby Auto Electrical & Air-conditioning, Lot 17, Derby H'way, ph: 0419 931 917 – trucks, cars and marine.

Derby Auto Parts, 72 Clarendon St, ph/fax: (08) 9193 1775.

Derby Welding, Cnr Waycott & Stanley Sts, ph: (08) 9191 1911 – caravan and trailer repairs.

Derby Weldall & Radiator Service, 20 Wells St, ph: 0419 917 075 – radiator repairs & recores, aluminium welding.

Kimberley Automotive Centre, Lot 919 Wells St, ph: (08) 9193 2222 – repairs & service to all makes and models & 4WDs; tyre & exhaust sales & service.

CRUISES & TOURS

The following is a list of locally based operators who run a variety of tours from Derby. Tours can also be organised through the **Derby Visitor Centre**.

Local Day Tours from Derby

Air Tours

Bush Flights, PO Box 1330, Derby WA 6728, ph: (08) 9193 2680, web: **www.bushflight.com** - scenic, seaplane and charter bookings - around Derby, Horizontal Falls, etc.

Derby Seaplanes, Derby Airport, ph: (08) 9192 6208 – fly/cruise Horizontal Falls, web: **www.derbyseaplanes.com.au/**

Golden Eagle, 44 Villiers St, ph: (08) 9191 1132, web site: **www.goldeneagleairlines.com/kimberley.html** – operates high wing aircraft – Thousand Is Coast tour and Cape Leveque Thousand Is Coast tour. Also offers charter flights and flies the Mail Plane run north & south of Kununurra to cattle stations & Aboriginal communities.

Kimberley Seaplanes, ph: (08) 9191 1760, web: **www.horizontalfalls.com.au/derbyflights.html** - 1/2 day fly/boat Horizontal Falls.

Reef Flight, ph: (08) 9192 3028, web: **www.reefflight.com** - 1/2 and full day Buccaneer fly tour. Also available for charter.

4WD Tours

Derby Bus Service – **Windjana Tours & Derby Discovery Tour**, Fitzroy St, ph: (08) 9193 1550, web: **www.westkimberleytours.com.au** – day tour to Windjana Gorge and Tunnel Creek with local guides. *Derby Discovery Tour* – Discover Derby and its history by taking this tour which includes Bungarun (the old Leprosarium), Mowanjum Community (aboriginal art), Birdwood Downs (station property). Bookings are essential for both tours. For information or bookings, contact the *Derby Visitor Centre*.

Fishing Tours – See Fishing Safaris

Aboriginal, Bushwalking & Camel Tours

Bush University - JBAC Bush Adventures, PO Box 1776, Broome, 6725, ph/fax: (08) 9191 7467, 0417 922 335 – **Mt Anderson Cattle Station**, situated 1 1/2 hours drive from Derby. *Harry Watson's Camel Adventures* of half-day, full-day or overnight starting at the community. The Nyikina/Mangala people, the indigenous owners, guide you through the surrounding country. Meals and camping gear are included and tours, or you can opt for cabin accommodation. Run from May to October. Check out the web sites:
www.wedgetailstours.com.au/
www.jarlmadangah.com/camtour.htm

Extended Tours

4WD Safaris

Bushtrack Safaris, 171 Knowsley St, ph/fax: (08) 9191 1547 – specialise in bird, botany, Aboriginal art, fishing and photographic trips. Tours explore the remote north-west Kimberley area with guides that have an intimate knowledge of this area. Self or fully catered, with plenty of opportunity for fishing, photography and wildlife observation. They also offer self drive guided tours on all their safari routes. Check out their web site: **www.bushtracksafaris.com.au/.**

Gibb River Road Bus Services, 3 Cocus Way Kununurra WA 6743, ph: 1800 197 262 or (08) 9169 1880 - drops off freight, tourists or visitors at station access roads along the Gibb River Road, from Kununurra to Derby. Web site: **www.gibbriverbus.com.au.**

Wedgetails Tours, Leonard Rd, Hahndorf, SA, 5245, ph: (08) 8388 7246 – The Aboriginal Bush University is the initiative of the Ngarinyin Aboriginal Corporation aimed at providing visitors with a genuine Aboriginal cultural experience. Visitors are taken on expeditions to incredible rock art galleries by the custodians of those sites, who explain the stories and meaning of these special places. Participants have close interaction with the Ngarinyin people as they learn about Ngarinyin law, spirituality, bush medicines and foods, language and early history, ceremony and songs. Web: **wedgetailstours.com.au.**

West Kimberley Tours (Derby Bus Service), Fitzroy St, ph: (08) 9193 1550 – 3 day camping tour visiting numerous gorges along the Gibb River Road. Extended tours from 2 to 5 days. Web: **www.westkimberleytours.com.au.**

Windjana Tours (Derby Bus Service), Fitzroy St, ph: (08) 9193 1550 – 2 day tour of Windjana Gorge & Tunnel Creek, King Leopold Ranges and Bell Gorge, also 3 day tour (as for 2 day) including Manning Gorge .

Fishing Safaris

Big Barra's Fishing Adventures, 18 Nevill St, ph: (08) 9191 2111 - fishing adventures around Derby with a local.

Buccaneer Sea Safaris, 40 Villiers St, PO Box 532, ph/fax: (08) 9191 1991, mob: 0419 917 797, web site: **www.buccaneerseasafaris.com** – runs 4 to 12 day sea safaris exploring areas such the Buccaneer Archipelago, Prince Regent River and Walcott Inlet. Caters for all groups: photographers, bushwalkers, artists, botanists, birdwatchers, fishing enthusiasts, etc. Charters also ex Broome.

One Tide Charters, Greg Prouse, PO Box 1241, Derby, ph: 08 9193 1358, Mob: 0417 977 038, web site: **www.onetide.com/** – Buccaneer Archipelago Eco Adventure tours depart from Derby weekly. With smaller group numbers, tours can be customized to suit individual client preferences. Extended scheduled tours 5 to 22 days exploring the Buccaneer Archipelago.

Unreel Adventure Safaris, PO Box 116, Derby, 6728, ph: (08) 9193 1999, mob: 0417 180 463, web: **www.unreeladventures.com** – Extended fishing safaris from 2 to 20 days. Safaris can cover the coast from Derby to Wyndham.

See our chapter, *Tour Operators, Lodges and the Like*, for further details.

Information and reservations can be made through the *Derby Visitor Centre*, ph: (08) 9191 1426.

TRANSPORT: TO AND FROM

AIR

Derby Airport (terminal ph: (08) 9191 1570, is located 10 km from town.

Golden Eagle Airlines provides flights six days per week between Derby and Broome where passengers can link with jet services. Golden Eagle Airlines and Amity Aviation are the major charter operators at the Derby Airport. Contact 44 Villiers St, ph: (08) 9191 1132, web site: **www.goldeneagleairlines.com/kimberley.html**

The **Derby Visitor Centre** can also organise flights.

BUS/COACH SERVICES –

Derby is serviced by the following bus companies –

Derby Bus Service, 1 Sutherland St, Derby, ph: (08) 9193 1550 – Derby/Broome/Derby, Mon, Wed & Fri. Depart Derby Mon 5.00am, Wed & Fri 6.00am. Web site: **www.derbybus.com.au.**

Greyhound Australia (ph: 13 14 99), web site: **www.greyhound.com.au/** runs regular services to Derby.

HIRE 4WDS

There are a number of hire car companies in Derby where you can rent anything from sedans to 4WDs. These include:

Avis, Loch St, ph: (08) 9191 1357, web: **www.avis.com.**

Budget Rent A Car, Terminal Building Kununurra Airport, ph: (08) 9168 2033, web: **www.budget.com.au.**

Travelling through a magnificent forest of Boabs following the Fitzroy River.

Derby is reached at the western end of the Gibb River Road.

DERBY TO FITZROY CROSSING

FITZROY CROSSING

INTRODUCTION

Once a sleepy little hamlet on the banks of the mighty *Fitzroy River*, Fitzroy Crossing's main claim to fame was its reputation as a watering hole for travellers either about to brave the river bed or who were stranded by floods. With the construction of a bridge across the Fitzroy in 1974, a new town grew up to the south.

The town has all the important facilities (fuel, stores and repairs) for travellers, and even if you're in a hurry you should check out the Crossing Inn – the sprawling pub near the original crossing place.

For many people the 'Crossing' is mainly used as an overnight stop or as a stepping off point for nearby Geikie Gorge National Park. See further on in this chapter for details.

ACCESS

Fitzroy Crossing is a small settlement on Highway 1. It's some 255 km east of Derby and 290 km west of Halls Creek.

VIA HIGHWAY 1 – THE GREAT NORTHERN HIGHWAY

Via the main blacktop, from either direction, it is hardly a scenic route and most take just a few hours from the closest towns to get to the Crossing. You're in cattle country, so take it carefully, especially at night!

There are a number of 24 hour Roadside Rest Areas to be found along the highway if you are looking for an overnight stop.

Ellendale is 87km west of Fitzroy Crossing – toilets, tables & fireplaces.

Ngumban Cliff is 98km east of Fitzroy Crossing - toilets, tables & fireplaces.

Mary Pool is 117km west of Halls Creek – toilets, tables & fireplaces.

LAARRI ART GALLERY

The Laarri Art Gallery is passed 120km from Halls Creek, and 170km from Fitzroy Crossing on Highway 1. The Yiyili Aboriginal Community has set up this indigenous art gallery where you can meet the artists and see them at work painting and carving. You can purchase paintings, artefacts and books from the gallery, and light refreshments are also available. It is open June, July and August from 9.00am to 4.00pm Monday to Thursday, or by appointment, ph: (08) 9191 7195, (closed school holidays). Visitors are welcome. Check out their web site at:
www.aboriginalart.org/

VIA THE WINDJANA GORGE ROAD

This road leaves the Gibb River Road 126 km east of Derby. For the most part it is a good dirt road during the Dry, but becomes impassable during the Wet.

It passes Windjana Gorge National Park and then the ruins of the Lillimilura Police Station, for much of the way skirting the sheer rock face of the Napier Range, before passing through McSherry Gap and coming to the parking area for the Tunnel Creek NP. See the chapter, *The Gibb River Road*, for more details on these two parks.

The road stays in the valley of Tunnel Creek, before swinging south-westerly and passing the turn-off to the Leopold Downs HS. The Brooking Gorge Conservation Park is located on this property, but access, at this stage, is not permitted. See further on in this chapter for more details.

You meet with the bitumen of Highway 1, 38 km west of Fitzroy Crossing and 127 km east of the Gibb River Road.

THINGS TO SEE AND DO

PLACES OF INTEREST

THE HISTORIC CROSSING INN

Situated on the banks of the *Fitzroy River*, the historic Crossing Inn was built by Joseph Blythe in the 1897 as a shanty inn and trading store. It served not only the local people, but passing prospectors, bullock team drivers and cattle drovers. The Inn has been flooded out on numerous occasions, with the highest flood level recorded in 2002. The Inn offers travellers a cold beer, basic meals, as well as accommodation and a caravan/**camping** ground.

THE CROSSING INN ART

View over 20 magnificent pieces of art by the students from Fitzroy Crossing District High School. Inspired by the success of the High School winning the 2000 Olympic Art Competition, the Crossing Inn sponsored and challenged the local youth to do paintings for the outside walls of the 100 year old hotel. The results are amazing - outstanding in both artistic merit and their local content. So the walls of this popular and historic hotel are a wonderful museum of local heritage, culture and art. Check out the Crossing Inn web site for more info: **www.kimberleyhotels.com.au/crossinginn/**.

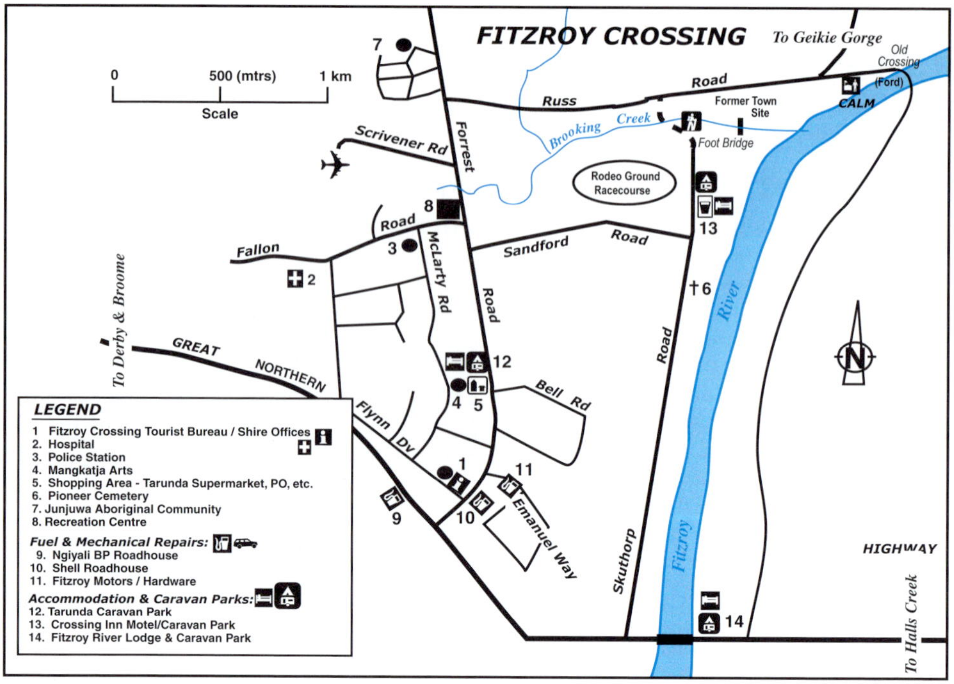

Pioneer Cemetery

Many of the early pioneers of the Kimberley are buried in this cemetery, on Skuthorp Road, with graves dating back to the 1890s.

Old Town Site

The Crossing Inn is situated at the old town site near the ford crossing of the river, and it is not the only building of that era still standing. The former post office and police station are still reminders of a past era, while an avenue of Boab trees and a footbridge across the *Brooking Creek* link the Inn and the original cemetery to the old town.

Mangkaja Arts

The Mangkaja Arts Resource Centre is located in the town centre at Shop 5 Tarunda Supermarket Complex in Fitzroy Crossing, ph: (08) 9191 5272. It is a community based art centre and gallery which services artists from the Fitzroy Valley. You can also look at the artworks and purchase them from their web site at: **www.mangkaja.com/index.html**

SPECIAL EVENTS & FESTIVALS

July **Fitzroy Rodeo** – a real Kimberley rodeo with all its excitement and spills.

Oct: **Garndywa Amboorny Wirnan Festival –** collection of song, dance & sporting events featuring young people of the Kimberley region.

Nov: **Barra Splash** – a weekend fishing competition with great prizes to be won and with real local flavour.

BROOKING GORGE

North-west of Fitzroy Crossing is Brooking Gorge where the *Brooking Creek* has slashed its way through the barrier of the Oscar Range.

The surrounding area is to be proclaimed a conservation park. However, even though the permanent water makes it an ideal place to visit and swim and nearby canyons contain caves with Aboriginal paintings, the park will not be open to travellers.

Pastoral lease surrounds the park and there is no access until CALM formalises management and access arrangements. Don't hold your breath!

MIMBI CAVES

The Mimbi Caves are located on Mt Pierre Station, 109 km east of Fitzroy Crossing. The station is Aboriginal owned and is managed by the Dolby family, their supporting staff and the Gooniyandi people from Galeru Gorge. Excised from the neighbouring Go Go station in 1989 and handed over to the traditional owners, many of them live on the station at the Galeru Gorge and Mimbi communities.

At the Mimbi Caves, limestone fractures have created more than 50 cavernous entrances while stalactites hang over clear pools. Tours are run by the Mimbi Gooniyandi people to the caves and the area is set to become a conservation reserve and a management plan is being developed. Tours are run during the Dry, between March and October. Contact the Mimbi Gooniyandi Aboriginal Community for further information and details on their tours: c/- Mt Pierre Station, Fitzroy Crossing, 6765, ph: (08) 9191 7137, fax: (08) 9191 7437.

A number of tour operators work in conjunction with the Gooniyandi community and their tours also visit the caves, such as *Bungoolee Tours,* ph: (08) 9191 5355, web:
www.diversetravel.com.au/experiencesAboriginal/BungooleeTours.htm

Northwest Regional Airlines, ph: (08) 9192 1369, has a fly/drive package from Broome to Geikie Gorge and Mimbi Caves. For more info look at their web site:
www.northwestregional.com.au

Contact the *Broome* or *Derby Tourist Centres* for more information on tours.

GEIKIE GORGE NATIONAL PARK

Geikie Gorge National Park is situated 21 km north-east of Fitzroy Crossing, where the *Fitzroy River* has cut a gorge through the limestone formations of the Geikie and Oscar Ranges. These Ranges are part of a fossilised tropical reef that once ran around what is now the Kimberley area in the north of Western Australia. It is very appropriate that in 1883 the gorge should have been named after the renowned British geologist, Sir Archibald Geikie.

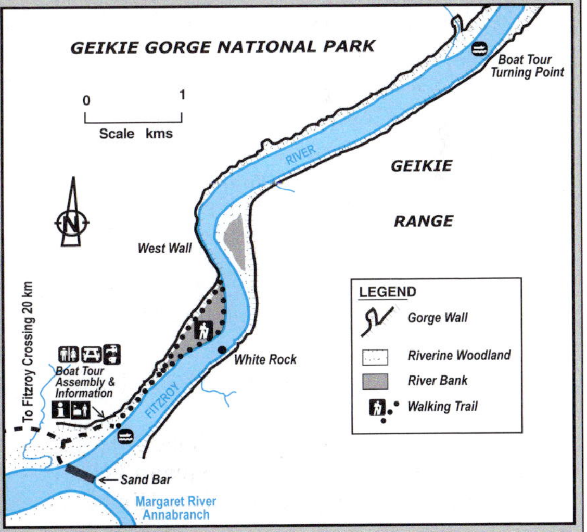

The Park was originally relatively small, just 8 km long and 3.2 km wide (3136 ha), until early 1992 when it was greatly enlarged. The new additions saw the park extended along the west bank of the Fitzroy River both above and below the small parcel of land that includes both banks of the river and the spectacular gorge itself.

Today the park is managed by CALM and the Darlngunaya Aboriginal Corporation, representing the traditional owners of the area. Public access will remain unchanged to what it is at present.

The Fitzroy River

The *Fitzroy River* flows through Geikie Gorge down the centre of the older section of the Park.

The Fitzroy River, beginning in the Hann Range and winding over 1000 km to the Indian Ocean just south of Derby, drains an area of 88,980 sq km (slightly larger than half the State of Victoria). The average annual rainfall over the catchment area varies from 300 mm to 700 mm, giving the Fitzroy a discharge rate of 29,000 cubic metres per second, or the capacity to fill Canning Dam, one of Perth's water supply dams, in less than 20 minutes.

During the Wet season the river rises in the gorge by up to approximately 16.5 m. The high water line can be seen on the faces of the gorge. However, in the Dry season the river ceases to flow and transforms itself into a series of beautiful water holes.

History

Geikie Gorge, with its permanent water, figured prominently in the legends of the Aboriginal people. The tradition owners, the Bunaba, call the gorge 'Darngku'. The gorge got its unusual European name 'Geikie Gorge' in 1883, from Sir Archibald Geikie, the Director General of Geological Survey for Great Britain and Ireland.

In the early 1880s the area was taken up by pioneer pastoralists and Brooking Springs and the police outpost, at nearby Fitzroy Crossing, featured in the Pigeon saga.

It was during the early 1960s that the area we now know as the park was resumed from the surrounding pastoral leases, including the very well known Fossil Downs station.

Geology

Geikie Gorge, cut by the Fitzroy River through the Geikie Range, exposes an excellent section through the Devonian 'Great Barrier Reef'. The gorge is some 14 km long, and is divided into two sections of approximately equal length by the eastern end of Copley Valley, near Sheep Camp Yard. Several atoll-type reefs are present in the Copley Valley and on Fossil Downs station, adjoining Geikie Gorge.

The walls of the gorge are generally about 30 m high. They are cleaned white by flood action to a height of about 10 to 12 m above the normal Dry river level, and internal features of the limestone, including the contained fossils, are clearly visible on these clean surfaces.

Most of Geikie Gorge in the southern part of the national park is cut through back-reef deposits which, together with the narrow reef, were constructed almost entirely by algae, with only minor contributions by stromatoporoids. The contact between steeply inclined marginal-slope deposits and horizontally bedded reef and back-reef deposits is well seen 2 km south of the Sheep Camp Yard. The marginal-slope deposits in this area contain some conspicuous bivalve shell fossils.

Vegetation

The trees along the gorge are mostly cadjeputs (tropical paperbarks) and river gums. Of three species of cadjeput here, the most common and the largest is *Melaleuca leucadendron* which has pendulous branches and long, bright green leaves. Smaller in size is the Silver Cadjeput, *Melaleuca argentea*, which has silvery foliage. The River Gum, *Eucalyptus camaldulensis*, is also common.

Native figs with smooth, dark green foliage and small, round yellowish fruit also grow in the gorge.

The Freshwater Mangrove, *Barringtonia acutangula*, is a small tree or shrub found along the banks, bearing pendulous sprays of small red flowers. There are also Leichhardt Trees, *Nauclea orientalis*, with dark green shady crowns of large leaves borne in opposite pairs, and round heads of yellow flowers which are followed by rough, spherical fruit.

The common Screw Pine along the river is *Pandanus aquaticus*, a widespread species with clusters of fruit-like small pineapples.

Scrambling over trees and shrubs is a wild passionfruit vine, *Passiflora foetida*, with bright green, furry leaves, white flowers with purple on the inner crown and dry but edible fruit. Clumps of a tall grass grow in open areas on the banks. This is the tropical reed, *Phragmites karka*.

Fauna

Geikie Gorge abounds in wildlife of all sorts. The Johnston Crocodile is common and easily seen as it rests on sandbanks. It is normally a fish eater and is not a danger to man. Other reptiles include tortoises, lizards and snakes.

The fish of the gorge are most interesting. Among the species present are sawfish and stingrays, both of which are usually marine or estuarine, but here they are cut off from the sea. Both the rare Freshwater Sawfish and the Dwarf Sawfish are species that are found here.

Another fascinating fish is the Archer Fish, which shoots down insects from foliage above the river with a jet of water. They may be seen in large numbers near the surface of the water where their silver colour, six or seven black marks on the upper side and tapered snout easily identify them.

The most common kangaroos are the Agile (or Sandy) Wallaby, usually identifiable by a pale stripe on the flank, but you may see the more heavily built Euro, or if you are very lucky, a Short-eared Rock Wallaby. There are many more mammals, but they are mostly small, nocturnal and unobtrusive.

The Fitzroy River flows through magnificent Geikie Gorge.

Birds abound and the rangers have compiled a list of over 100 species. You can be sure to see ibis, herons, sea eagles, darters, cormorants and many more. Brolgas, Black-necked storks and spoonbills have been recorded, but to the avid birdwatcher the numerous smaller species will be most rewarding. Space does not permit a full list, but these may whet the appetite – Lilac-crowned Wrens, Red-backed Kingfishers, Blue-winged Kookaburras, Great Bower Birds, Red-winged Parrots.

Things to Do

The park is only open during the Dry season, between April and November, from 6.30 am to 6.30 pm for day visits. Entry is closed during the Wet season (Dec-Mar) when the Fitzroy River floods.

Camping is not permitted at Geikie Gorge.

Activities beside the tours include: sightseeing, photography, walking and nature observation.

The nearest caravan/camping facilities can be found in Fitzroy Crossing.

Facilities

Toilets, water, gas BBQs, information shelter and tours, as well as access for disabled people.

The Sanctuary

The east bank along the river has been declared a sanctuary zone. This means that there is no unsupervised access. See the ranger regarding access.

Walking

Reef Walk: The walk along the west bank to the west wall, known as the Reef Walk, is most rewarding. It's a 3 km return walk of moderate difficulty – allow an hour or so. Best early morning or late afternoon. Take your camera to catch the reflections as the sun is setting.

River Walk: An easy 20 minute walk from the info centre to the sandbar near the junction of the Fitzroy and Margaret Rivers. A popular fishing and swimming place. Swimming is at your own risk. Beware of submerged snags and logs and avoid diving into the water.

Most of the rest of the park is rugged and inhospitable to walkers.

Tours

Boat tours operated by **CALM** take visitors for a cruise up the best section of the gorge – a distance of a few kilometres. There's a small charge made and the boats leave at 8.00 am, 9.30 am and 3.00 pm daily during the peak of the tourist season, April/May to September/November.

At other times contact the ranger in Fitzroy Crossing on ph: (08) 9191 5121 or (08) 9191 5112 for tour times. Tickets are available on site 20 minutes before departure. You can contact the ranger at Geikie Gorge on ph: (08) 9191 5112. No bookings are required for individuals. Group bookings needed.

The **Darngku Heritage Cruises** depart 8.00 am, Monday to Friday, April to October. This half day tour, is given by Darlngunaya Aboriginal guides and will take you along the waters of Geikie Gorge, with a climb up Banbara lookout, the Larrawani Walk and lunch beside the Fitzroy River. A 2 to 3 hour guided walk is also run from 8.00am to 2.00pm daily in season. Enjoy a guided walk along the ancient reef to the West Wall of Geikie Gorge, transported by boat.

For ticket bookings, details or information on any of the Darngku tours, you can contact the *Fitzroy Crossing Tourist Bureau*, ph: (08) 9191 5355 or the *Derby Visitor Centre*, ph: (08) 9191 1426.

Private Boats

Private boats and canoes can be used on the river only after 4.30 pm from April to November. You must notify the rangers before launching your boat.

For Further Information

Information on this park can be had from CALM, Regional Office, Messmate Way, Kununurra, 6743
ph: (08) 9168 4200
or the District Office,
Herbert Street, Broome 6725
ph: (08) 9192 1036
web site: **www.calm.wa.gov.au/**.

ACCESS TO THE FITZROY RIVER

Below the bridge at Fitzroy Crossing most of the river bank is out of bounds to travellers. However, there is an area where public access is allowed and people can bush camp.

See the section on *Noogoora Burr and Area 3*, along with the relevant maps at the beginning of this chapter for more details.

ACCOMMODATION, CAMPING & OTHER FACILITIES

Accommodation

Fitzroy River Lodge, 102 Great Northern Highway (2 km east of PO), ph: (08) 9191 5141 – situated on the banks of the Fitzroy River amongst 50 acres of natural bush with shady trees and landscaped gardens. The Lodge offers accommodation in studios, SC rooms, hotel rooms, as well as tented safari lodges. Lots of facilities, including restaurant, bistro, swimming pool, tennis & volley ball courts, golf course, BBQ area, internet access, etc.
Web: **www.kimberleyhotels.com.au/fitzroylodge/**

Tarunda Caravan Park, Forrest Road, ph: 9191 5330 – 6 units available with air-conditioning and some kitchen facilities. Web: **www.accommodationguide.com.au.**

The Crossing Inn, Skuthorp Rd, ph: (08) 9191 5080 – one of the 'original' Kimberley hotels on the banks of the Fitzroy River. This historic inn offers a variety of motel units, all with air-conditioning, as well as barbecue and outdoor eating facilities. Web: **www.kimberleyhotels.com.au/crossinginn/**

Caravan Parks/Camping

Fitzroy River Lodge Caravan Park, 102 Great Northern Highway, ph: (08) 9191 5141, fax: (08) 9191 5142 – situated on the banks of the Fitzroy River amongst 50 acres of natural bush with shady trees and landscaped gardens. The Lodge has an extensive camping area with all facilities. Web: **www.kimberleyhotels.com.au/fitzroylodge/** – situated on the banks of the Fitzroy River, the Lodge offers shady tent sites, wood BBQs and all facilities, with partial wheelchair access. Dogs on application.

Tarunda Caravan Park, Forrest Road, ph: 9191 5330 – centrally located adjacent to the shopping complex in Fitzroy Crossing, it has all facilities, including BBQs and a campers kitchen. Dogs are allowed on a leash at the park's discretion. Web: **www.accommodationguide.com.au.**

The Crossing Inn Caravan Park & Camp Ground, Skuthorp Rd, ph: (08) 9191 5080 – adjacent to the Inn, the caravan park has shady sites and there are several wood-fired barbecues available for guests. Pets are welcome under supervision. Web: **www.kimberleyhotels.com.au/crossinginn/**

FACILITIES

Most facilities are readily available –

Hospital, Fallon Road, ph: (08) 9166 1777
Dental Clinic (Hospital), ph; (08) 9191 5075
Police, McLarty Rd, ph: (08) 9191 5000
Fire, ph: (08) 9191 0050 – emergency only ph: (08) 9191 5111
Shire of Derby/West Kimberley, Loch St, PO Box 94, ph: (08) 9191 0999, fax: (08) 9191 0998, web: **www.sdwk.wa.gov.au**
Post Office, Forrest Rd, ph: (08) 9191 5060
Banks:
ANZ Agency – Tarunda Supermarket
Commonwealth Bank Agency – Post Office – keycard facilities.
Tarunda Supermarket & Newsagency, Tarunda Shopping Cntr Forrest Rd, ph: (08) 9191 5004 – open 7 days a week during peak tourist season – full range of groceries, frozen goods, fruits & vegetables and more.

A number of automotive repairs and service facilities, including –

Fitzroy Motors & Hardware, Main Street, ph: (08) 9191 5050 – sales & service, supply parts, Toyota & Suzuki. General store and firearms dealer.

FX Mechanics, ph: (08) 9191 5538.

Ngiyali BP Roadhouse, Great Northern Hwy, ph: (08) 9191 5366 – open 7 days a week offering all fuels, autogas, towing service, workshop repairs, oils, tyres, batteries, etc. Travellers can also get a meal in the restaurant, take-aways, groceries, drinks, souvenirs, as well as a shower.

Shell Roadhouse, 6 Forrest Rd, ph: (08) 9191 50050.

Wyatt Welding Works & Fencing, 94 Emmanuel Way, ph: (08) 9191 5058 – caravan repairs.

ABC Regional Radio - Kununurra	
Local Radio	106.1 AM
Radio National	107.7 FM

FITZROY CROSSING TOURIST INFORMATION

FITZROY CROSSING TOURIST BUREAU

Flynn Drive,
PO Box 101, Fitzroy Crossing, WA, 6765.
Ph: (08) 9191 5355, fax: (08) 9191 5085
Email: fxinfo@sdwk.gov.au

Open 7 days a week
April-September 8.00am to 5.00pm,
Oct to Mar Mon-Fri 8.00am to 4.30pm

The Bureau acts as agent for Greyhound buses and can also arrange any tours and accommodation, both in and around Fitzroy Crossing, or throughout the Kimberley. You'll find a large range of Kimberley interest books and souvenirs available. The Bureau also houses two Aboriginal art galleries.

CRUISES & TOURS

The following local tour operators are based at Fitzroy Crossing –

AIR

Geikie Air Charter, Fitzroy Crossing Airport, Fitzroy Crossing, 6765, ph: (08) 9191 5068, a/h ph: (08) 9191 5193 – scenic flights over the Dimond & Geikie gorges, Bungle Bungle, St George Range, Prince Regent River, Fossil Downs Homestead, or flights can be arranged to suit your needs. Also available for general charter.

Fitzroy Helicopters, Fitzroy Crossing, 6765, ph: (08) 9191 5034 – Aircraft Charter & Rental Services

Colourful and impressive art adornes the outside walls of The Crossing Inn.

Vehicle Tours

Bungoolee Tours – Aboriginal tours with local guide Dillon Andrews – one to three day tours that include a one night stop over at a base camp near to the Biridu community. Tour includes Tunnel Creek, Windjana Gorge and follow in the footsteps of Jandamarra, a Bunuba freedom fighter, and explore and Mimbi Caves. Includes all meals, guiding & camping equipment. If you have your own 4WD you can tag-along behind the tour. For more information, ph: (08) 9191 5355, web: **www.diversetravel.com.au/experiencesAboriginal/BungooleeTours.htm**

Fitzroy River Nature Walks

Take a leisurely walk along the mighty Fitzroy River with an experienced informative local guide who knows about all the local flora and fauna. You also visit The Crossing Inn and view local aboriginal art. The walking tour departs from the *Fitzroy River Lodge* daily at 6:30am and takes approximately 1.5 hours. For more info contact the ***Fitzroy River Lodge***, ph: (08) 9191 5141, web: **www.kimberleyhotels.com.au/fitzroylodge/abouttown_naturewalk.html**

Boat

Geikie Gorge Boat Tours – operated by CALM. See *Geikie Gorge National Park*, page 202.

Darngku Heritage Cruises - 3 & 5 hour guided walk and a tranquil boat trip in Geikie Gorge. Ph: (08) 9191 5552 or book through the *Fitzroy Crossing Tourist Bureau*, ph: (08) 9191 5355 or the *Derby Visitor Centre*, ph: (08) 9191 1426. See *Geikie Gorge National Park*, page 202.

Fishing

The *Darngku Heritage Cruises* offers fishing trips up the gorge to do a spot of barramundi fishing. See the section on the *Geikie Gorge National Park* for full details.

TRANSPORT: To and From

Air

Fitzroy Crossing Aerodrome is located approximately 3.5km from Fitzroy Crossing township. The access road from the township to the aerodrome is sealed. The airport terminal can be contacted on ph: (08) 9191 5193.

Geikie Air Charter, Fitzroy Crossing Airport, ph: (08) 9191 5068, a/h ph: (08) 9191 5193 1 – provide flights to/from Derby, Broome or Kununurra.

Golden Eagle Airlines provides flights six days per week between Broome/Fitzroy Crossing/ Halls Creek where passengers can link with jet services. For more info ph: (08) 9191 1132, web site: **www.goldeneagleairlines.com/kimberley.html**.

Bus

Greyhound Australia (ph: 13 14 99), web site: **www.greyhound.com.au/**, runs regular services to Derby. Information and reservations can also be made through the *Fitzroy Crossing Tourist Bureau*, ph: (08) 9191 5355.

The Geikie Gorge Boat Tour, operated by CALM, is a great way to get a close look at this spectacular gorge.

BROOME AND ITS SURROUNDS

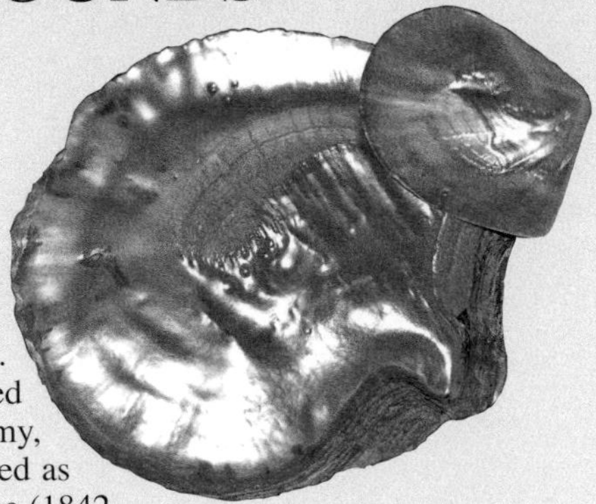

INTRODUCTION

Broome has a fascinating history and a unique cosmopolitan feeling about it which originates from its early pearling days when over 400 luggers plied the coast as part of its pearling fleet. Although pearling still plays a major role in Broome's continued development, tourism is playing an even bigger part in its economy, making it one of WA's most popular tourist destinations. Gazetted as a townsite in 1883, it is named after Sir Frederick Napier Broome (1842-1896) who was the then Governor of Western Australia. He took office in June 1883 and in September 1890 was appointed Acting Governor of Barbados.

ACCESS

Broome, the southern gateway to the Kimberley on the coast in the south-western part of the region, is 2213 km north of Perth. Derby, the next closest town, is 220 km to the north-east and Port Hedland is 613 km to the south, all joined by a ribbon of tar that is Highway 1.

North of Port Hedland

North of Port Hedland the main highway skirts the mighty Eighty-Mile Beach to the west and the Great Sandy Desert to the east. While **Port Hedland** and surrounding mining towns have all you ever require, northwards habitation is pretty thin on the ground.

One of our favourite **camps** is on the north banks of the **De Grey River**, about 100 km north of Port Hedland. It's a popular spot, but there's plenty of room and shade and the water is lovely.

Pardoo Station, 13 km off the road towards the coast, has cottage and budget accommodation as well as powered and unpowered sites for vans and **campers**, ph: (08) 9176 4930.

The **Pardoo Roadhouse and Tavern**, nearly 160 km north of Port Hedland, and 440 km south of Broome, has basic amenities, powered and unpowered caravan/**camping** sites and a small shop, ph: (08) 9176 4916.

The **Cape Keraudren Coastal Reserve**, 14 km off the main road with the turn-off near the roadhouse, has an excellent beach and good fishing. There is some nice camping here, but facilities are basic with just pit toilets and no fresh water and you must bring in your own firewood. Vehicle entry fee and camping fees are payable. A caretaker Ranger is present, and dangerous dogs are not permitted. For more info check out the web site: **www.eastpilbara.wa.gov.au/tourism/ck.htm.**

Eighty-Mile Beach is Karajarri and Nyangumarta country and has been designated a Ramsar listed wetland, a feeding ground for migratory birds.

The **Eighty-Mile Beach Caravan Park & Cabins** can be reached 10 km off the Great Northern Highway, by taking the signposted turn-off some 45 km south of Sandfire. There's a range of accommodation, along with powered and unpowered caravan/**camping** sites. There's good fishing and relaxing to be had. The mini - supermarket / bakery is open 12 hours a day, 7 days a week, April to October. Phone: (08) 9176 5941, web: **www.eightymilebeach.com.au**. It's a lovely spot and very popular!

There are some great camping spots to be found north of Port Hedland.

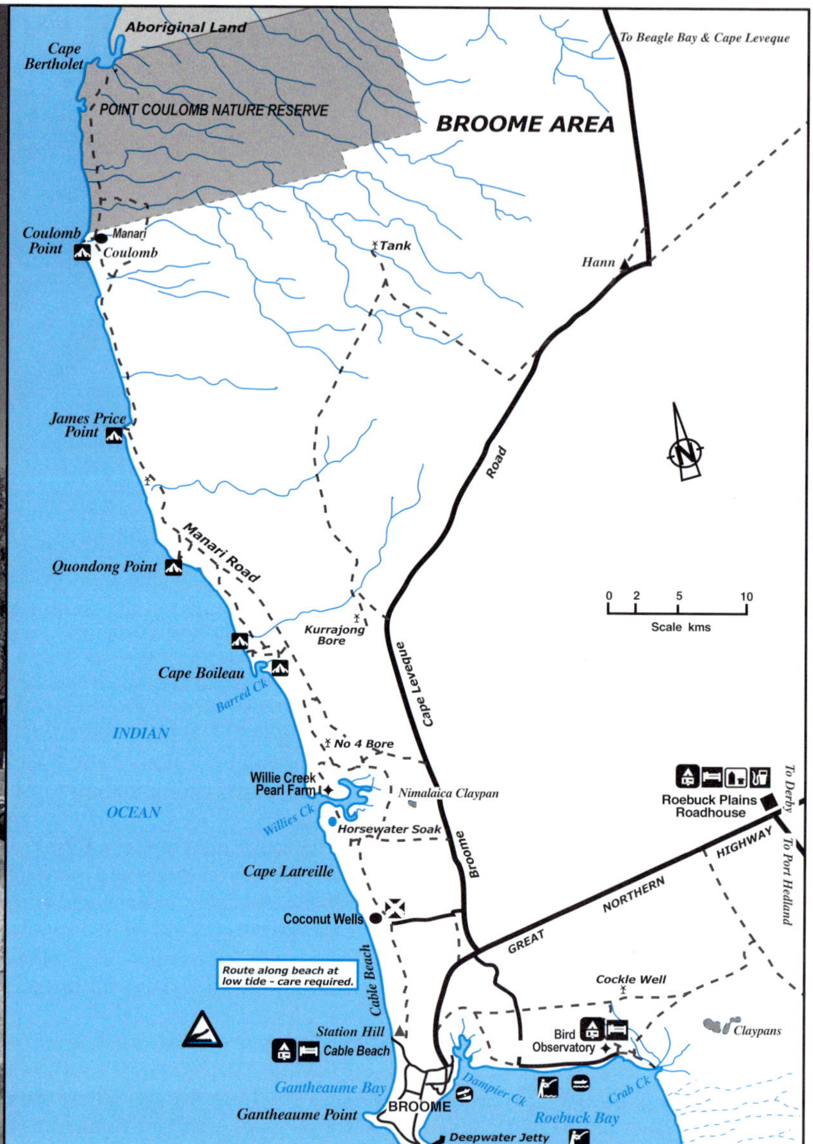

Sandfire Roadhouse and Caravan Park, 290 odd km north of Port Hedland, has changed greatly since it was founded nearly 30 years ago. Nearly everyone stops here, if not for fuel, then for a cold drink or an ice cream. The Roadhouse also has motel units and powered and unpowered caravan/**camping** sites, ph: (08) 9176 5944. Pets allowed on leash.

The **Stanley 24 hour roadside stop** is located on Highway 1, 106km north of Sandfire. Here you'll find toilets, tables and fireplaces.

Further north and right on the coast 140 km south of Broome, in Roebuck Bay in a naturally protected lagoon, is **Port Smith Caravan Park**. Here, the fishing is great, plus there's an interesting bird park, a 9-hole golf course and garden and you can take your dog by arrangement – they must be on a leash and a bond is required. Accommodation is available in bunkhouse style rooms and SC units and there are plenty of shady camp sites.The park has all the normal facilities along with essential foodstuffs and supplies, basic fishing tackle and ice. Eftpos facilities available. Phone (08) 9192 4983.

The **Barn Hill Beachside Station Stay**, on the Eighty-Mile Beach, has also opened its doors to tourists, ph: (08) 9192 4975. It is situated 130 km south of Broome and 9 km off the highway, right on the coast. There are three self-contained cabins and caravans and **campers** are welcome to take up a patch of shady lawn. Dogs are allowed.

HISTORY

Prehistory and European Discovery

Aboriginal people have lived along this section of coast for thousands of years existing mainly on the rich bounty of the sea and the coast.

Almost definitely Malays and Macassars plied this coast well before the coming of Europeans, collecting beche de mer, turtles and possibly even oyster shell. Both Matthew Flinders (1801) and Phillip King (1818-1821) reported seeing large fleets of boats sailing and fishing the northern coast of Australia.

The first European to sail this coast was **William Dampier** in 1688. This swashbuckling buccaneer so impressed the Admiralty that in 1699 they gave him command of HMS *Roebuck* and sent him back on a voyage of discovery. His report of the land and the people wasn't all that favourable so the region was forgotten until 1821. In that year **Phillip Parker King**, on one of his four voyages to the Kimberley coast, named Roebuck Bay.

The first jetty was built in 1897 and the pearling fleet continued to grow. By that time Broome had become a racial melting pot with Europeans, Aborigines, Malaysians, Chinese and Filipinos brushing shoulders along the busy wharfside. The pioneer pearling firm of Streeter and Male had already built their store and the Roebuck Bay Hotel.

Between 1900 and 1914 Broome was at its height, but the First World War saw trade in pearl shell suspended and the town never again rose to its pre-war heady heights, even though pearling began again in earnest once the war finished.

In 1917 one of the greatest pearls ever discovered, the 108.8 grain *Star of the West*, was found, but the price paid was high. In the seven years before then over 140 divers had lost their lives, most to the dreaded 'bends', its cause not completely understood in those days.

Pearling and the Rich Beginnings of Broome

Pearling started in WA during the 1850s and by the 1870s had moved as far north as the Kimberley coast. Cossack, near Roebourne, was the main base, with about 80 boats working from it.

As the rich beds of pearl shell were discovered off the Kimberley coast, more and more boats moved north. By 1880 a settlement had grown up near the mouth of Dampier Creek.

In 1883 the town was officially proclaimed and named after Sir Frederick Napier Broome, the then Governor of WA.

As the pearling fleets plied the coast in ever increasing numbers, pioneer pastoralists were opening up the inland.

In 1889 Broome became connected to the Overland Telegraph Line from the south. As well, a submarine telegraph cable was laid between Broome and Banjawangie in Indonesia. Suddenly Broome found itself to be a major centre of communication.

Early pearling operations offshore from Broome. *Pic courtesy of the Latrobe Library of Victoria*

During the 1920s Broome had a population of 5000; of these 3500 were employed in the pearling industry, while over 400 luggers, producing 80% of the world's mother-of-pearl shell, plied the coast from this port. In that decade, the first regular air service to the region began.

In 1935 a cyclone sunk 20 luggers in the Lacepede Channel with only one person out of over 140 surviving. Another 16 boats sheltering up and down the coast from Broome managed to survive, even though all received some damage.

World War 2

In 1939 Broome got its first meatworks, but pearling was well in decline by then. With the internment of over 500 Japanese divers and crew in 1941, the pearling industry closed down for the duration of World War 2. Many of the luggers were sailed south or burnt on the beaches so they could never fall into enemy hands.

By early 1942 Broome was a staging post for people being evacuated out of Malaya, Singapore, the Philippines and Indonesia in front of the advancing Japanese army. In one month over 7000 soldiers and refugees passed through Broome and there was a continual shuttle of aircraft coming to and leaving from Broome. Many of those were flying boats and so it was on the 3rd March, 1942, with 16 flying boats at anchor on Roebuck Bay and a few bombers and other transport planes on the airstrip, that 10 Japanese fighters pounced. Only one small plane escaped and the death toll was probably in the hundreds – nobody will ever really know! The wrecks of some of those flying boats can still be seen, at very low tides, today.

Story has it, that at that time, a fortune in diamonds went missing and those diamonds have never been found *(see page 219).*

With that attack the authorities evacuated the town and only a small military garrison remained.

After the War

Record prices for mother-of-pearl had Broome booming again just after the war, but the bubble burst when plastic buttons became the norm and in weeks pearl shell went from a record price to being near worthless.

In 1956 the cultured pearl centre of Kuri Bay, 400 km north of Broome, was established. By the 1970s Broome was producing over 60% of the world's cultured pearls. Today, the pearling fleets, made up of faster boats than the traditional lugger, collect pearl shell for Kuri Bay and other cultured pearl centres in the Kimberley, maintaining the region as one of the best places in the world for pearls.

In 1962 a good source of water was found to supply the town and the following year the Broome meatworks was enlarged, followed in 1966 by the opening of the deep water port. During that decade and the 1970s the meatworks, along with a growing tourist trade, were the major employers.

Today, tourism is the driving force in and around Broome. While that isn't necessarily bad, many feel the old time charm of Broome has been lost in the almighty clamour for the tourist dollar.

THINGS TO SEE AND DO

Broome has many fine old buildings, both colonial and oriental in style. Along with its long history and multi-racial community, it offers visitors a host of fascinating places to discover, some of which are listed as follows.

PLACES OF INTEREST

Japanese Cemetery

The Japanese played an important role in Broome's and the pearling industry's development. Their cemetery, with headstones dating back to 1896, is on Port Drive, on the way to Cable Beach. Over 900 graves lie in this little enclave, with most of the headstones being made out of large sandstone rocks, inscribed in Japanese. Many lost their lives from either drowning, the bends (the dreaded diver's accident), or during cyclones.

Pearl Luggers

This display features the restored 1957 Broome built pearling lugger, the 'Sam Male', which has recaptured and brought to life the essence of Broome's pearling history.

Daily tours, from April to November, cover the evolution of pearling and pearl diving in Broome. They are presented by pearl divers who spent many years living aboard pearling luggers and diving for Mother of Pearl shell.

31 Dampier Tce, Broome, ph: (08) 9192 2059, web: **www.broomecam.com/gold/pearlluggers.htm**

An old Pearling Lugger.

Pioneer Cemetery

Located near the old jetty at the end of Robinson Street and close to Town Beach and Apex Park, this cemetery is the resting place for many of the early pioneers and settlers, dating back to 1880.

Broome Historical Society Museum

The old Customs House that now houses the museum is regarded as one of the best regional museums in Australia. You'll get an idea of how it was in Broome's early days with displays on the pearling industry, guns, a fine shell collection, old photograph albums and lots more.

Located at 67 Robinson St, the museum is open June - Nov 10.00am - 4.00pm Mon-Fri, 10.00am - 1pm Sat - Sun & Nov - June 10.00am - 1.00pm every day. There is a small entrance fee payable. Phone (08) 9192 2075, web: **amol.org.au/guide/instn.asp?ID=W146.**

Other Buildings & Places of Interest

The **Courthouse**, Cnr Hamersley St & Frederick St, was built in the distinctive 'Broome style' and dates back to the turn of the Century. It is open Mon to Fri 8.30 am to 4.30 pm. **Captain Gregory's House**, built in 1917 for Captain A.C. Gregory, again is a fine example of early Broome architecture and has now been converted to an art gallery. Situated on the corner of Hamersley and Carnarvon Streets in the same grounds as **Matso's Gallery** and **Broome Brewery**. Phone (08) 9193 5811 for opening hours and exhibition details.

The original **Broome Lock-up** dates back to 1895 when in the chain gang era it was used to hold prisoners of the day.

Matso's Store was the first Union Bank built in 1900 which later became a general store before being moved to its present location in Hamersley Street, overlooking Roebuck Bay.

There's also the **Cultured Pearl Monument**, located in Carnarvon St in Chinatown, which commemorates the pioneers of the cultured pearling industry in Broome, while adjacent is a life size statue of the **Hard Hat Pearl Diver**. The **Horrie Miller Memorial** in Weld Street is the site one of Australia's most historic aircraft.

The **Broome Heritage Trail** is a 2 km walk which features buildings and places of historic interest. Details are available from the *Broome Visitor Centre*.

Manbana Aquaculture Hatchery & Discovery Centre

This Aboriginal owned Centre, located in the Port area, explores the theme of water & Aboriginal life - from the creation stories through traditional Aboriginal fishing practices, to the arrival of European settlers and involvement of Aboriginal people in the development of the commercial pearling and Trochus industries. Located at Lot 6 Murakami Rd, Broome, ph: (08) 9192 3844, web: **www.manbana.com.au.**

Between April and September, the Broome town bus service operates a service to the port area each day, stopping at the Aquaculture Park. The Centre is open daily, with one hour guided tours held Mon to Sat at 10.30 and 1.30pm. During the low season (Oct to March) opening hours and tour times may vary.

Malcolm Douglas Wilderness Wildlife Park

Malcolm Douglas is currently developing a commercial Crocodile Farm and is working within the Crocodile Specialist Group to ensure the survival of endangered species around the world.

The crocodile farm continues to grow, and the Park will give visitors the opportunity to see rare and endangered Australian animals. For more info on the new park. The Park is located 16km from town on the main highway, ph: (08) 9192 1489 or visit the web: **www.malcolmdouglas.com.au/**.

Shell House

Located at 76 Guy St, ph: (08) 9192 1423, this collection exhibits over 6000 shells as well as pearl jewellery, mother of pearl and pearls. Open Mon to Sat 8.30 am to 5.00 pm.

Chinatown

Once a mix of pearl sheds, Japanese boarding houses, saloons and hotels, today Chinatown is a hive of business centred on the commercial pearling industries. Many of the old pearling sheds in Dampier Terrace have been transformed into pearl emporiums where visitors can purchase magnificent pearls and jewellery, or just look. Pearl shell displays can also be seen at the Historical Museum.

Of course, no trip to Broome would be complete unless you took a look at the packing sheds at the foot of Streeters Jetty. While you're down that way, take the opportunity to check out the jetty itself, the original for the pearling luggers. The only pearling lugger still operating from Broome today can sometimes be seen tied up to the jetty.

Pearling Luggers Display & Tour

(See page 209) for details.

Sun Pictures

Believed to be the world's oldest open air picture garden, this theatre, classified by the National Trust, still operates today in Carnarvon Street. It was officially opened in 1916 and is still showing current movie titles each day of the week. The foyer houses some interesting old movie posters, along with a display of original projectors used in the early years, ph: (08) 9192 1077, web: **www.sunpictures.com.au**.

Buccaneer Rock

This navigational beacon, situated in Roebuck Bay at the entrance to Dampier Creek, has become a landmark. Dampier was reported to have careened his ship, *Roebuck*, at this spot.

Flying Boat Wrecks

The remains of three Royal Dutch Air Force flying boats can be seen half buried in the sand at extreme low tide in Roebuck Bay, about a kilometre from Town Beach. These planes, loaded with women and children who had been evacuated from Java during World War 2, were sunk at their moorings by Japanese aircraft as they awaited re-fuelling in 1942. If you'd like to know more about the history of these boats, then check out the Western Australian Museum web site: **www.museum.wa.gov.au/collections/maritime/march/treasures/zerohour/doco_a.html**

Hovercraft tours to the wrecks are available when they are visible.

Sun Pictures, believed to be the oldest open air picture theatre in the world.

Gantheaume Point – Dinosaurs Footprints & Anastasia's Pool

At the red, craggy cliffs at Gantheaume Point, 6 km from town, you can check out the tracks left behind some 130 million years ago by a carnivorous species of **dinosaur**. The tracks are only visible at low tide, so for those that don't want to climb down or get their feet wet, cement casts of the tracks can be viewed near the automatic warning beacon on the cliff top.

On the north side of the point is a small man-made rock pool, **Anastasia's Pool**, built by a former lighthouse keeper for his wife who was crippled with arthritis.

Staircase to the Moon

This natural phenomenon occurs from March to October for three days each month and is caused by a full moon reflecting off exposed mud flats at Roebuck Bay at extremely low tide. As the moon rises a beautiful optical illusion of a staircase occurs. Generally there is a ***Staircase Market*** held at the Town Beach in conjunction with the 'Staircase to the Moon' occurrence, with plenty of local fare and entertainment. The *Visitor Centre* can let you know the exact dates it happens. Dates are also on the web site: **http://broomewa.com/cam/StaircasetotheMoon.htm**.

Bush Camping

There are some excellent bush camping areas around Broome, although none could be called real handy to the town. See our section, *The Dampier Peninsular*, in this chapter for more details.

Boat Launching Ramps

These ramps are situated at the end of Robinson Street at the Town Beach (next door to the Roebuck Bay Caravan Park) and at Entrance Point (near the jetty).

Willie Creek Pearl Farm

Approximately 38 km from Broome, Willie Creek was originally a sheltering place for pearling luggers during cyclones. Today visitors can observe a pearl farm at close quarters and learn how cultured pearls are grown. Self-drive tours are available, or join one of the daily half day or full day tours. The farm caters for private vehicles and coach tours, however bookings are essential. Contact Willie Creek Pearls, Old Zoo Complex, 2 Challenor Drive, Broome, 6725, ph: (08) 9192 6300, web: **www.williecreekpearls.com.au/**.

Shell collecting

Shell collecting is a favourite pastime in Broome and shells can usually be found on most beaches. A good spot to look for shells, at low tide, is Coconut Beach (take the Beagle Bay Road for 2 km, turn left at the road junction and continue for another 10 km). There are however, prohibited shelling areas and you should contact the Dept. of Fisheries in Broome for more details.

Picnic and Fishing Spots

There are lots of areas to explore close by to Broome for the day and some great picnic and fishing spots to discover such as Deep Water Point, Crab Creek, Barred Creek, Willie Creek, Fisherman's Bend, Prices Point, Quondong and Manari.

Access to the beaches north of Broome are detailed in the Trek Notes at the end of this chapter. For Crab Creek, see below.

Crab Creek

This road gives access to the Broome Bird Observatory and continues for some distance past the observatory to the shores of Crab Creek.

This dirt road, via Fisherman's Bend, leaves the main road into Broome about 4 km north of the town. The road for the most part is pretty good, but can be a little slippery when wet, especially where it crosses Dampier Creek.

For the most part the road skirts the coast and often gives great views of the rich red cliffs and a strip of beach that becomes hundreds of metres wide at low tide.

There's good fishing and crabbing along this stretch of coast. See our chapter, *Fishing in the Kimberley*, for more details and information on closed areas, contact the Dept. of Fisheries in Broome for more details.

CABLE BEACH

Cable Beach takes its name from the cable which linked Broome with what is present day Indonesia. There aren't many good beaches to be found in northern WA. Cable Beach, with its miles upon miles of clean white sand and turquoise blue sea, offering safe swimming, is a gem along this coastline. Remember that marine stingers are present in these waters from November to March.

North of the vehicle access ramp onto the beach is a declared nude bathing beach.

There is always something going on along Cable Beach; para sailing, surf cats, water skiing, jet skis and a lot more. Camel treks along the beach in the evening are popular and are a delightful way to end a day.

A short nature trail exists between Gubinge Road and the last roundabout, just before the vehicle access ramp to the beach. Opened in 1992 by CALM and the local botanical society, it features information signs identifying many of the interesting plant species found along this section of coast.

Enjoying the experience of watching the sun go down on Cable Beach, on the back of a camel.

DRIVING THE BEACH

It is possible to drive your vehicle onto Cable Beach, although vehicles are not permitted south (left) of the access ramp which leads onto the beach. However, by heading north (right) once off the ramp you can drive along the beach for around 10 km. Northern access is via Coconut Wells. There are a few tricky spots on the run north, especially where a couple of small creeks cut across the beach. A permit system with an access fee may soon be introduced.

Take care when driving and watch the tides at all times – it comes in extremely quickly! While travelling along the beach, do not drive into or on the dunes, or the lagoon at Coconut Wells.

At **Gantheaume Point** it is also possible to drive onto the beach, however vehicles are only permitted to travel 300 metres from the access road.

Maximum speed limit on all beach areas is 15 km/hr. No trail bikes, road bikes, beach buggies, three or four wheel motorcycles are permitted on either Cable Beach of Gantheaume Point Beach.

OTHER BEACHES

For those who don't want to tackle the surf at Cable Beach you can head for Reddell Beach, Front Beach and Gantheaume Point for some swimming.

REDDELL BEACH

This spectacular stretch of beach is an ideal place to observe the red pindan cliffs of Broome's peninsula coastline. It was named after Captain Reddell, who was murdered by his mutinous crew in 1899. Great for swimming and picnicking. Located 8 km from the town centre.

BROOME BIRD OBSERVATORY

Over 250 species of birds can be found in the area around Broome, with many of these migrating from as far away as Siberia. These waders congregate in their thousands and with such a wealth of birds arriving and visiting Broome, it's no wonder that *Birds Australia* has established one of its bird observatories at Roebuck Bay – recognised as one of the top five wader bird viewing locations in the world.

The Observatory was opened in 1988 as a research base and is situated 25 km east of Broome on Crab Creek Road. An unsealed road gives easy access, except in extremely wet conditions, to both 2WD and 4WDs.

The greatest number of waders occur from September to April, but birdwatching around the area, at any time of the year, is interesting and rewarding.

Tour and Courses

Various guided and self drive tours are available. Bookings are essential, ph: (08) 9193 5600.

Ornithological courses are run during the year and are designed to provide an unforgettable experience as well as educate participants about the birds of Broome, focusing on the migratory shorebirds of Roebuck Bay. All meals and accommodation included. Linen provided but please bring your own towel. Contact the Wardens for details.

There's also a variety of interesting walks and excursions available along the beach, mangroves, plains and bushlands.

Accommodation and Camping

The Observatory is open all year round and offers seclusion and peaceful surroundings in acacia woodland for those wanting to stay. Facilities include a natural history library, video and slide room, display panels and marked trails.

Accommodation includes single, bunk and double rooms, all air-conditioned with shared amenities along with a large kitchen and dining area. There is also a fully self-contained, air-conditioned chalet which sleeps up to 6 and has a fully equipped kitchen.

The **camping** area set amongst woodland has powered and unpowered sites, toilets, hot showers, BBQs and a screen shade house, as well as access to a well equipped kitchen/dining room area.

It is advisable to book beforehand between June to September. No pets allowed.

Transport can also be arranged for a small charge for pickup and return to Broome.

Day visitors are welcome and for those who take the time to drop into the Observatory, a wealth of information is made available, making the small entrance fee charged well worth it!

For those interested, a book has been written by Peter Collins, a past Assistant Warden at the Observatory, titled '*The Birds of Broome – An Annotated List*'.

Keen birdwatchers can also get a ***Local Bird Guide*** from *Birds Australia* for Broome, as well as other areas in the Kimberley. Check out their web site:

http://birdswa.iinet.net.au/.

For Further Information

Contact the Wardens at:
PO Box 1313, Broome WA 6725
Ph: (08) 9193 5600, fax: (08) 9192 3364
Email: bbo@birdsaustralia.com.au
Web: **www.broomebirdobservatory.com**

Cable Beach is popular but you can always find your own piece of sand.

BROOME & SURROUNDS

SPECIAL EVENTS & FESTIVALS

For more information on any of the following festivals and events contact the *Broome Visitor Centre*, ph: (08) 9192 2222, web: **www.broomevisitorcentre.com.au** -

Mar to Oct: **Staircase Market** – Coincides with the '**Staircase to the Moon'** phenomenon which occurs over a few evenings each month between March and October. These evening markets are held on Town Beach where you can sample local fare and be entertained.

Courthouse Markets – Held in the courthouse gardens every Saturday morning, May to October, with a melange of stalls displaying goods such as local produce, plants and arts/ crafts for sale.

April: **Broome Arts & Music Festival - Art Exhibition.**

May/June: **Broome Arts & Music Festival - Music Festival.**

June/July/Aug: **Broome Race Rounds**.

Aug: **Opera Under the Stars,** features an outstanding cast of Australian stars, ph: 0414 791 935 or (08) 9192 1303 web: **www.operaunderthestars.com.au**

Shinju Matsuri – Festival of the Pearl – This festival is held each year over 10 days during August and pays tribute to Broome's pearling industry and its multicultural community. This festival has become one of Australia's best known and most popular and one not to be missed by any visitor who happens to be in the area at this time. Festivities include a float parade, art exhibitions, pearl jewellery competition, Shinju ball, mardi gras, sporting events, dragon boats and much more. Web: **www.whinjumatsuri.com.**

November: **The Mango Festival**

THE DAMPIER PENINSULA

The Dampier Peninsula, north of Broome, features miles of great coastline, secluded bays, red pindan cliffs, blue waters and some great fishing, as well as a good variety of bird and animal life. Access is pretty good, but it is definitely 4WD country. A number of Aboriginal communities have opened their doors to travellers. No dogs are allowed.

Road upgrades are constantly on the agenda, so road conditions can vary considerably.

At present, various groups are working on the management of the proposed **Dampier Peninsula Conservation Park** on Waterbank Station. The Project is managed by the Kimberley Land Council and it involves local Aboriginal interests.

Aboriginal Communities

Ardyaloon (One Arm Point) Communities	(08) 9192 4930
Bardi & Jawi (One Arm Point) Communities	(08) 9192 4930
Beagle Bay Community	(08) 9192 4913
Djugarargyn Community	(08) 9192 4980
Djarindjin Community	(08) 9192 4940
La Djardarr	(08) 9192 4896
Lombadina Community	(08) 9192 4936
Kooljaman Resort (Cape Leveque)	(08) 9192 4970
Middle Lagoon (Nature's Hideaway)	(08) 9192 4002
Maddarr	(08) 9192 4371
Mudnunn	(08) 9192 6070

ACCESS TO BEAGLE BAY AND CAPE LEVEQUE

The main road to Beagle Bay and Cape Leveque is a reasonable dirt road that can be, a times, a little broken up. After rain though it's definitely 4WD country. The track to Point Coulomb, the Manari Rd, leaves this main road and sticks close to the coast giving access to some fine fishing and **camping** spots.

While you don't need permits to travel the main road or the track to Point Coulomb, once you leave them you need the permission of the relevant land owner. See our map of the peninsula and the phone numbers following to help you get where you're going to.

Dampier Peninsular Travellers Guide

*The **Mamabulanjin Aboriginal Corporation** (ph: (08) 9192 1662) produces an excellent little booklet titled the **Dampier Peninsula Travellers Guide** with details on all the Aboriginal Communities, access, camping, accommodation, tours, and more. For just a few dollars it is good value and you should be able to pick up a copy at the **Broome Visitor Centre** or they can tell you where to get one.*

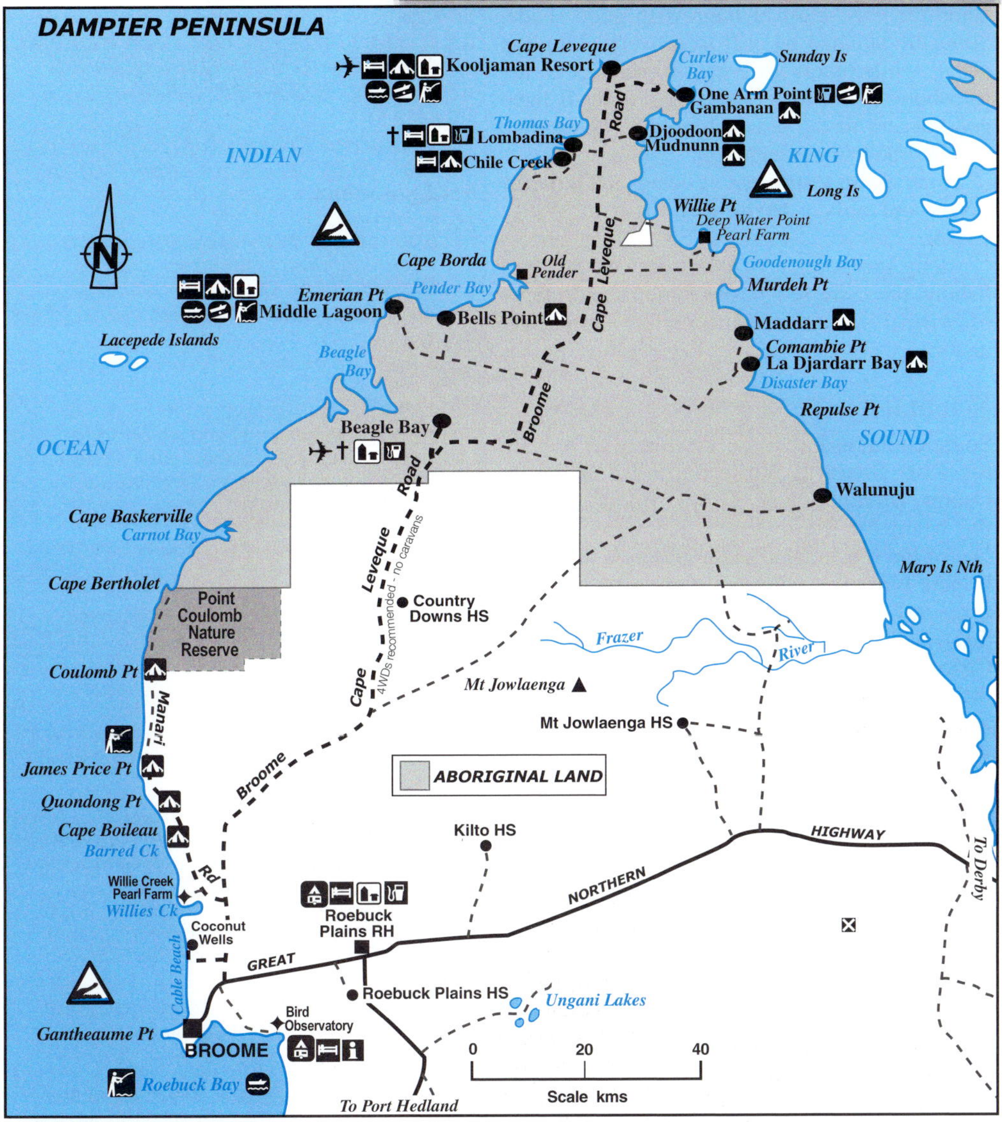

BROOME'S NORTHERN BEACHES

North of Broome are some of the best beaches you'll see in the Kimberley region. Not only that, but it is the closest area you can bush **camp** to Broome.

Access and Camping (4WD)

The Manari Road leaves the main Beagle Bay Road and parallels the coast giving reasonable access for four wheel drives to the beach for camping and fishing.

Some sections of the track are covered by bad corrugations and in places the verges have been eroded. Some of the creek beds will have to be checked out before crossing, especially if there has been a high tide or rain. Some creek sections can also be very muddy It is advisable to obtain a tide chart before venturing north. The track north of Prices Point deteriorates with many tidal creeks and obscure tracks. Travellers should take extreme caution.

This track runs as far as Cape Betholet in the far north of the Point Coulomb Nature Reserve.

There are plenty of good camping sites along the way, most of them with good shade. Some are situated on cliff tops overlooking the ocean, while others are right on the edge of the foreshore. A lot have fireplaces, and all have good access to the sea or beaches. Please take all your rubbish out with you.

There is **no camping** allowed at **Coconut Wells** and only a **three day limit** at **Willie Creek**.

Along this section of coast as well as good fishing, there are beaches to explore and plenty of wildlife for those interested in natural history.

Wildlife

Some common birds you are likely to see are the Kori Bustard, White-bellied Sea-Eagle, Osprey, Brahminy Kite, Brown Booby, herons, the beautiful Blue-winged Kookaburra, and one of the most magnificent gliders – the Least Frigate bird. You will also come across flying foxes and bats in the evenings, and don't forget that you are in recognised Estuarine (Saltwater) Crocodile country. You only need to observe a little common sense and you won't experience any problems with these animals.

Lurujarri Heritage Trail

This walking trail starts at Minarriny at Point Coulomb and heads south, along the beaches and across the headlands to Yinara or Entrance Point just outside Broome. The trail retraces an Aboriginal song cycle that took in all of this coast, passing many points of interest such as old camps, middens and Dreaming sites.

In all it's about a six day walk of fairly easy stages but you do need to cross a few creeks and these need to be done at low tide.

A brochure is available from the *Broome Visitor Centre*, or contact the Mamabulanjin Aboriginal Resource Centre, Dora St, Broome, ph: (08) 9192 1662. You can also download a copy direct from the Heritage Council of WA, web site: www.trails.heritage.wa.gov.au/.

Our Trek Notes take you to some of the points of interest.

The Northern Beaches Trek

0.0 (0.0) Broome township*. Head north/north-east out of town on Broome–Derby road.*

10.0 (10.0) Road junction *(R/J) – turn left (TL) onto* ***Broome Cape Leveque Road****. Corrugations quite bad on this road.*

24.5 (14.5) R/J *– TL onto* ***Cape Betholet****, or* ***Manari Road****. Note water tank on left.*

27.9 (3.4) R/J – PSA*. Left leads to* ***Barred Creek****.*

To Barred Creek –

0.0 (0.0) Track junction *(T/J) on Cape Betholet Road – TL for* ***Barred Creek****.*

0.8 (0.8) T/J *– take lefthand (LH) track. Righthand (RH) track goes to* ***Barred Creek Outcamp*** *(disused).*

1.4 (0.6) T/J *– veer left.*

1.9 (0.5) Barred Creek *– good* ***camp*** *site on low cliff overlooking the creek.*

Turning right at the 0.8 km mark will take you to the river mouth and the coast. Some good ***camp*** *sites closer to the coast, but watch the soft sand. As you head towards the* ***coast*** *keep left as there are a number of tracks. Finally, after 3 to 4 km you will get to the mouth of the* ***creek****. Some low cliffs border the lagoon just back from the ocean and this would make the best* ***camp*** *in this area and a spot to launch a boat. There's plenty of soft sand.*

Retrace steps back to road junction on main Cape Betholet track for continuation of Northern Beaches Trek.

Zero trip meter *at this junction to Barred Creek*

7.7 (7.7) R/J – PSA. *LH track (tk) leads to* ***Quondong Point****. 3 km from signpost (SP) are various tracks to some good* ***camp*** *sites.*

21.6 (13.9) R/J *– PSA. LH tk leads to* ***James Price Point****. Some excellent areas around here to* ***camp*** *and some great tidal pools for the kids to explore. The fishing is good too!*

The track north begins to deteriorate after James Price Point becoming quite narrow, closely fringed by trees in places, with fallen trees over the road. It is very sandy and badly corrugated in some spots. There are a few creeks to cross and the condition of these crossings will depend on tidal movement. Low tide is obviously the best. 4WD should be used as the sand is very soft.

37.2 (15.6) R/J – PSA*. LH tk leads to* ***Coulomb Point****.*

41.1 (3.9) R/J – PSA*. LH tk leads to* ***'Manari'****. The track follows a seasonal creek bed.*

43.3 (2.2) Camp *sites on left. Beware – very sandy.*

55.4 (12.1) Cape Betholet*. Camp site is at end of track.*

A Word of Warning

The Point Coulomb Nature Reserve extends from Coulomb Point to Cape Betholet. The rest of the land through which you travel belongs to Waterbank Station, and there are plenty of cattle, so drive carefully.

On the coast are extensive areas of the reef exposed at low tide, with very interesting rock pools. The kids will love paddling around, but make sure you have on heavy footwear as *Stonefish* also like these tidal pools. The *Blue-ringed Octopus* is also resident.

If you intend swimming in the ocean, be careful of strong rip-tides and long-shore currents caused by the big tidal differences in the north-west.

Apart from these few points, you will enjoy the location, as not many people come up the Peninsula and you will find the camping nice and quiet.

POINT COULOMB NATURE RESERVE

This Nature Reserve lies some 70 km north of Broome and extends from Coulomb Point to Cape Betholet. The surrounding land belongs to Waterbank Station. The Reserve was originally founded to preserve an area of Pindan shrub and its characteristic fauna. It is planned to increase the area of the reserve sometime in the future.

For most visitors it's the coast, blue water and good fishing that attracts them.

See our chapter, *National Parks and Nature Reserves of the Kimberley*, for more information, or CALM in Broome, ph: (08) 9192 1036.

If it rains, the Peninsula's roads become interesting, and your vehicle the colour of 'pindan' red.

NORTH TO BEAGLE BAY (4WD)

The main road north, the Broome Cape Leveque Road, continues much as before with the occasional sandy section and washout to keep you on your toes.

BEAGLE BAY

Access & Facilities

Just 2 hours drive (120 km) north of Broome on the Dampier Peninsula, Beagle Bay is renown for its spectacular church and is well worth a visit.

A scattering of old buildings, including the church, dormitories and hospital provide reminders of the days when Beagle Bay was the focus of Catholic Church missionary activities in the north of WA.

Visitors must contact the administration/office on arrival and small fee is charged for entry to the community and this money is used for the upkeep of the historic church, office ph: (08) 9192 4913. If nobody's there, try the store which is right beside the church.

Access is by 4WD only. Tours are available from Broome – contact the *Broome Visitor Centre* for more information.

The **store** (ph: 08) 9192 4831) has basic supplies and is open Mon to Fri, 8.00 am to 12.30 noon and 2.00 pm to 4.00 pm, Sat 8.00 am to 12.00 noon.

Fuel (unleaded and diesel) is available during office hours.

Office hours are Mon to Thur 8.00am to 12.00 noon and 1.00pm to 4.00pm; Fri 8.00am to 3.00pm.

History

Beagle Bay Mission was established by Trappist Monks in 1890, however it fell into disrepair and passed to the Pallottine Pious Society of Missions in 1901. The church was built by the Pallottine Monks during and after World War 1 from local stone and decorated with shells. The three altars are works of art and are inlaid with pearl shell and cowries.

Following heavy rains in early 2000, part of the building collapsed, but restoration work has since brought it back to its former glory.

For more information on the Dampier Peninsula Parish, the Beagle Bay and Lombadina Churches, and their history, look at the Catholic Diocese of Broome web site:

www.broomediocese.org/beaglebay.html

Beagle Bay's beautiful Church, adorned with shells.

To the Coast

Getting to the coast from the village is a little difficult, but is possible. You will **need permission** and once you have it, get some directions and head west. Take care with driving on any of the beaches – stories of vehicles being lost, especially just after the Wet season, are legendary – and common!

Our mud map will give you an idea of one way – a safe way – to get to the shores of Beagle Bay itself. There's no freshwater readily available out here and little shade, however, the fishing can be good and the exploring interesting.

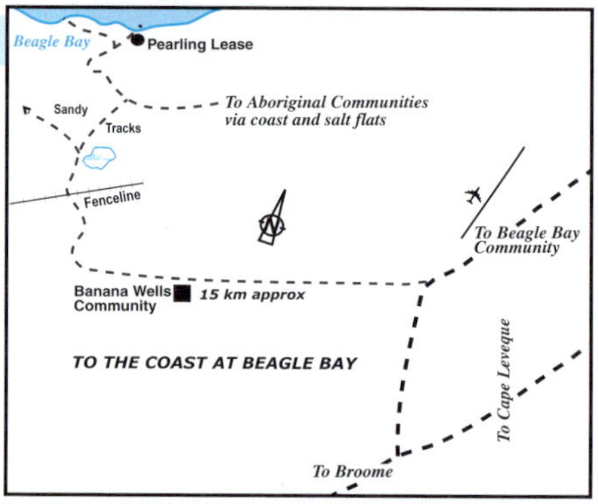

Camping & Accommodation

Accommodation is available at units run by the Sacred Heart Church (ph: (08) 9192 4917). Camping is available at Bobieding (ph: (08) 9192 4082) and Billard (ph: (08) 9192 9208). Both are outstations located about 4km from Beagle Bay.

For Further Information

For further information write to the: The Chairman, Beagle Bay Aboriginal Community, PO Box 326, Broome, W.A. 6725, ph: (08) 9192 4913. Web site: **www.beaglebaycommunity.com/**

CAPE LEVEQUE & AROUND

If you intend going north of Beagle Bay you really need to take more than just a day. The far northern coast is fantastic and the **camping** at the Kooljaman Resort absolutely fantastic.

MIDDLE LAGOON Nature's Hideaway

Access & Facilities

Just 146 km north of Broome, past the turn-off to Beagle Bay, and then another 33 km to the coast, is the idyllic spot of ***Nature's Hideaway Middle Lagoon***.

This tranquil coastal retreat offers visitors the chance to swim, snorkel and fish, or just walk along vast stretches of secluded beach.

Fishermen can launch their boat from the launching ramp on the front beach.

A Day Visitor Fee per vehicle is payable.

Limited supplies, bait, ice, souvenirs and drinks are available from the office.

Office hours are 8.00am to 12.00noon & 1.00pm to 5.00pm.

No pets or spearguns allowed.

Carnot Bay's Diamond Legend

In March 1942 a lone Royal Dutch East Indies Airlines DC-3 heading for Broome was shot down by Japanese fighters. This aircraft had earlier left Java with 11 people on board, but what made this Dutch aircraft so different from the hundreds of others evacuating people from the threat of the Japanese, was a plain brown paper parcel that had been given to the pilot, Ivan Smirnoff, just as he had taken off.

The pilot crash landed the plane on the sands of Carnot Bay, just south of Beagle Bay and four of the survivors died over the next five days before the rest were rescued. Ivan was quickly questioned about the 'parcel' and was surprised to learn that it contained a fortune in diamonds, worth over $20 million today! Government sponsored searches quickly followed and while the brown wrapping paper and seals were found no sign of the box or its contents has ever been turned up.

Legend has it that a beach comber come fisherman, Jack Palmer, forever afterwards known as 'Diamond Jack' found the wrecked plane and the important package. Court cases followed and a number of people were implicated in the diamonds' loss, but nothing was proven and only a few of the diamonds were ever recovered.

There have been a number of expeditions to try and find the diamonds over the last 60 years and it is possible that they still lie scattered in the mud of Carnot Bay. What does mark the spot though is one of the wings of the DC-3 that can still be seen at low tide.

The only track access to the bay is via Aboriginal land and permission is required.

More details, check out the Museum of WA web site at:
www.museum.wa.gov.au/collections/maritime/march/treasures/zerohour/carnotbay.html

There are some great camping spots to choose from at Middle Lagoon, close to the water.

Bookings are essential during the peak season, it's a popular spot.

Camping & Accommodation

Accommodation is available in a fully self contained cabin overlooking the beach with private facilities, or in semi contained cabins. For those looking for something a bit more basic, then the beach shelters on the beachfront are ideal. Guest utilise a shared ablution and there's a BBQ for cooking.

There are also a large **camp** ground with powered and unpowered sites and two ablution blocks with hot and cold freshwater showers and flushing toilets.

For Further Information

For further information write to: Middle Lagoon, PO Box 182, Broome, 6725 Ph/fax: (08) 9192 4002, web: **www.waitoc.com/kullarri.asp#nhml**

Salt-Water Crocodile Warning

Salt-water Crocodiles inhabit this peninsula – its beaches, mangroves, estuaries and around the islands, so please take heed of any warning signs and be aware of their possible presence.

BELLS POINT

Access & Camping

Bells Point is located 175km from Broome, north of Middle Lagoon on the shores of Pender Bay, with access off the Middle lagoon road. A camping ground has been established at this outstation, with limited facilities. For more information, ph: (08) 9192 4006 or mobiles 0437 317 823 or 0428 552 517.

DJUGARARGYN

Walking Tours

Deborah Angadoo Sibosado is a Bardi woman from the Dampier Peninsula living on the family block at Djugarargyn commonly known as 'lower blok'. This is about 170km north of Broome. Walking tours are offered showcasing native flora and fauna on the Dampier Peninsular. For more info contact Debbie at:

Djugarargyn Aboriginal Corporation, PO Box 1908, Broome, WA 6725, ph: (08) 9192 4980.

LA DJARDARR BAY

Access & Camping

The turn-off to La Djardarr is located 150 km north of Broome, and from there is it another 40 km east along a narrow and sandy track to the camp ground on La Djardarr Bay. Here a **camp** ground has been established with basic facilities, no power.

Guided walks, mud crabbing, history and culture walk and other activities can be arranged, as can 2 and 3 day packages which include fishing and mud crabbing. Activities can also be organised for day visitors.

There are launching facilities for small boats. Remember this is Salt-water crocodile country.

> **For Further Information**
>
> **For further information** contact the Community on ph: (08) 9192 4896, web: **www.waitoc.com/kullarri.asp#nhml**

MADDARR

Access & Facilities

Located 197 km from Broome, it is 150 km to the turn-off (look for the access road 4km north of the turn-off to Middle Lagoon), and then another 47 km into a small community called Maddarr Aboriginal Corporation, home of ***Barramundi Moon***. Owned by the Manado Family, the property is located on the coastline of the eastern side of the Dampier Peninsula, overlooking King Sound.

Visitor numbers are limited to a maximum of 10 people at a time, so the service and experience is personal. Packages include fully escorted 2 night/3 day package, as well as overnight self-cater camping and day visits with activities available, May to October.

You will enjoy magnificent scenery, eco tours, reef walks and bird watching. Learn about local family history, view old stone tidal fish traps, catch delicious Mangrove Crabs and fish. Family guides will take you on a journey into their lifestyle and beliefs of traditional Aboriginal people. Accommodation comprises simple beach shelters with fold out camp beds.

Access to Maddarr is restricted to prearranged bookings. **Visitors cannot make their way into the community unannounced.**

> **For Further Information**
>
> Contact *Barramundi Moon:*
> PO Box 1828, Broome, 6725
> Ph: (08) 9192 9100
> Web: **www.waitoc.com/kullarri.asp#bm**

LOMBADINA

Access

The turn-off into Lombadina is around 192 km from Broome, and then it is just 3 km west to the small community. Situated in a picturesque setting with shady mango trees and spreading palms, it is a pretty spot, while the sand dunes provide the backdrop to an endless expanse of sandy beach and warm blue waters.

Visitors can drive (4WD advised), cruise by boat or fly to Lombadina. 4WD transfers are available by arrangement.

The Lombadina Mission, with its unique construction, is well worth a visit.

The Mission

The Lombadina Mission was, like Beagle Bay, established by Trappist Monks in 1892. The present **church** was built in 1934 and is considered an architectural masterpiece. Built from mangrove wood with a paperbark roof, it also has corrugated iron on the outside, a lining of paperbark and supports made from bush timber, and is well worth a look.

Facilities

Facilities include a general store, bakery and a craft shop where locally produced Aboriginal artifacts and jewellery can be purchased. Refreshments are also served at the craft shop. Operating hours 8.00am to 4.00pm, weekdays, 9.00am to 3.00pm weekends. The **general store** is open Mon to Fri 8.00am to 11.00am and 1.30pm to 4.00pm, closed Sat & Sun. **Fuel** (diesel and unleaded) is available Mon to Fri (closed 11.00am to 1.00pm) and there is no fuel on the weekend.

A **day pass** is available for travellers wishing to visit the community at a cost of $5.00 per vehicle. It can be obtained from the Community office, ph: (08) 9192 4936, which is open Mon to Fri 8.00 am to 11.00 am and 1.00 pm to 4.00 pm, or from the craft shop on weekends. The entry fee is used to help maintain the roads, grounds and church and allows visitors the opportunity to experience the community and get access to the most beautiful beaches on the Peninsula.

If travellers advise the community beforehand of their visit, tours and meals can be organised.

The units are surrounded by lawns and lush vegetation.

Tours

Lombadina Aboriginal Adventures can organise a wide range of **tours** and activities which include bushwalking, whale watching (May to Oct), 4WD day tour, 1/2 and full day fishing charters and mud crabbing. The *Shakari*, a 33ft charter boat, takes tours to the Buccaneer Archipelago and further afield, as well as fishing trips around Lombadina.

Accommodation

Accommodation is available in fully self contained units which sleep 4 and all linen and cooking utensils are provided. Or you can choose the backpacker style units with shared bar fridge, a fully equipped kitchen and laundry facility. Bed linen and towels are again provided.

There is **no camping** at present in Lombadina, but that may change in the future. Give them a ring to see what the current situation is.

For Further Information

Contact the **Lombadina Community**, Dampierland Peninsular, PO Box 372, Broome 6725, ph: (08) 9192 4936.
A detailed **brochure** on the Community can be downloaded from their web site: **www.lombadina.com.au**

DJARINDJIN

Right beside Lombadina is the Djarindjin Aboriginal Community. While you can't camp or stay at Djarindjin, it does have a reasonably stocked store.

All correspondence to:
The Chairman, Djarindjin Aboriginal Community, via Broome, W.A., 6725, ph: (08) 9192 4940.

CHILE CREEK

Access

The small Chile Creek community is located just 7km from Lombadina and is set in a bush setting less than 2km from the Indian Ocean. Activities include fishing, bushwalking and birdwatching.

Accommodation & Camping

For campers Chile Creek has unpowered camping sites and basic bush style shelters. There is also a rustic camp kitchen and wood fuelled BBQ. There is also accommodation available in two rooms in the main community house.

For Further Information

Contact **Chile Creek Aboriginal Corporation**
PO Box 2208, Broome WA 6725
Ph/Fax: (08) 9192 4141
Web: **www.waitoc.com/kullarri.asp#bm**

MUDNUNN

Access, Tours & Facilities

Mudnunn Outstation is located 230km north of Broome on the King Sound side of the Dampier Peninsula. The Angus family, who are part of the Bardi people of One Arm Point, owns Mudnunn, and with their family business ***Baniol Tours,*** provide visitors with a unique opportunity to share an indigenous lifestyle and learn of local history and heritage, of traditional hunting, collecting and survival skills, as well as the special relationship that Jawi and Bardi people share with the sea.

A **camp** ground has been established within walking distance of the secluded beaches of King Sound. It is the home base for cultural excursions that include bush tucker walks, fishing, oyster collecting and mud crabbing in the nearby tidal creeks.

Visitors need to be self sufficient as there are few facilities. Remember this is Salt-water crocodile country.

The **Camping** ground facilities are basic but include an ablution block. No power.

For further details on Mudnunn and ***Baniol Tours***, contact Rosanna & Vincent Angus, c/- Bardi Aborigines Corporation, One Arm Point, via Broome, 6725, ph: (08) 9192 4930 or 9192 4121, web: **www.waitoc.com/kullarri.asp#mt**.

DJOODOON

Access & Facilities

Djoodoon is situated 1km further on from Mudnunn, using the same access road. Unpowered camping sites are available. For more details ph: (08) 9192 4858.

ARDYALOON – ONE ARM POINT COMMUNITY

One Arm Point, 221 km from Broome, is the home for the Bardi and Jawi Aboriginal people and it is a pleasant friendly village where access to the coast can easily be achieved. The Ardyaloon community at One Arm Point was established when the mission at Sunday Island closed and its residents moved to the mainland.

Access & Facilities

All visitors should report to the administration/office, which can be found on the left-hand side as you enter the community, just past the community store. A small **entry fee** per vehicle is payable. The Community Office can be contact on ph: (08) 9192 4930.

The Community **Store** (ph: (08) 9192 4803) is open Mon to Fri 8.30 am to 12.00 noon and 1.30 pm to 4.00 pm; Sat 9.00 am to 11.00 am. **Fuel** (diesel, unleaded and outboard) is also available, but you must purchase a **fuel card** from the store before you can access the fuel bowsers.

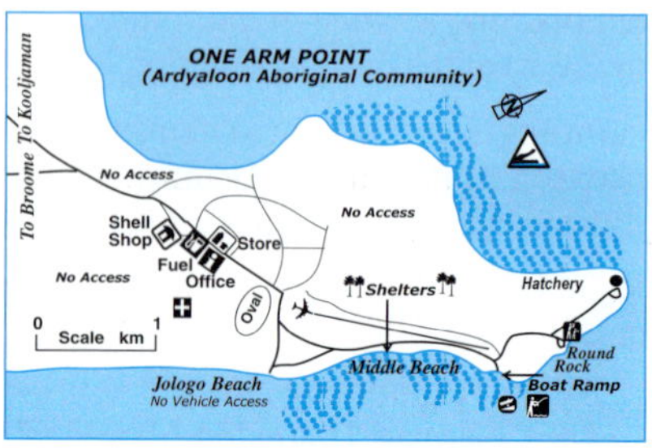

Trochus shell jewellery is a speciality of the Bardi people and artifacts are for sale.

There is no accommodation or camping available. *(See 'Gambanan' below for camping near One Arm Point.)*

There is a pretty good **boat ramp** located close to the very tip of the point. When the tide is running this is a very impressive place – read dangerous place, so be warned!

The view at One Arm Point across the strait to the offshore islands.

For Further Information

Contact the Community Office:
One Arm Point Community, via Broome
Ph: (08) 9192 4930

Things to See & Do

At the Community Office you can purchase, for around $5, a copy of the ***One Arm Point Community Map***, which details the places of interest for you to see and visit, such as:

Round Rock: A good spot for swimming & fishing.
Middle Beach: A good spot for fishing, swimming & spearing amongst the mangroves.
Jologo Beach: Swim, fish and try the oysters on the rocks.

Goombading Cultural Scenic Boat Tour

A local aboriginal family operates a full day spectacular scenic charter to ***Sunday Island*** *that includes swimming, snorkelling, reef walking, exploring the old mission ruins and learning about local culture. The itinerary varies daily dependent on the tidal movements. Tours can also be organised through Kooljaman at Cape Leveque. Web:* **www.kooljaman.com.au/**

GAMBANAN

Access & Facilities

The small camping ground at Gambanan is run by a well known Bardi family. It is located 1.5km off the main access road to the Ardyaloon community at One Arm Point. It offers the opportunity for fishing and leisurely exploration of the coastline and you can learn more about the Bardi culture. For more details, phone (08) 9192 4220 or 9192 4171.

KOOLJAMAN AT CAPE LEVEQUE

Access

The ideal base to explore the area around the Cape is at the site of the Cape Leveque lighthouse, some 240 km north of Broome, now known as *Kooljaman at Cape Leveque*. **Bookings are essential** before you go. The resort is very popular and is often full. The road is suitable for 4WD off-road camper trailers only. NO caravans. Dogs are not allowed.

The resort has its own dirt strip nearby where you can land and get picked up for your stay.

Air transfers are available, ex Broome April to Nov. **Road Transfers** with various tour operators are available April to October. Contact the *Broome Visitor Centre* for details.

Facilities

Jointly owned by the Djarindjin and One Arm Point communities, the *Kooljaman Resort* offers **camping** and accommodation. Facilities include a **Restaurant** (unlicensed) – open for dinner between April and mid-October, as well as take-away lunches. A **kiosk** sells basic food items, ice and bait and operates on limited hours. Fresh fruit and vegetables are not available. BYO alcohol.

Fuel is not available, however **Fuel cards** are usually available from the Kooljaman office or can be purchased direct from the communities of One Arm Point or Djarindjin/Lombadina. These cards can be used to access fuel (24hrs) from the bowsers located at One Arm Point & Djarindjin Communities.

Activities & Tours

Activities include swimming, snorkelling, fishing, mud crabbing, beachcombing, or just relax and enjoy the surroundings.

There are a host of **tours** you can do: tours with local aboriginal guides, scenic flights, island tours and whale watching. The ***Goombading Cultural Scenic Boat Tour*** to Sunday Island is run by a local aboriginal family. (See pg 223 for more detail.)

A 4WD track heads along the eastern coast to Hunters Creek, about 7 km away from the resort. Stay off the dunes and keep to the track. There's good fishing along the way. Watch out for Salt-water Crocs in the creek.

If you have your own boat there is endless scope for fishing. Launching the boat over the soft sand may be a bit of a hassle though, with the best spot to launch about 1.5 km along the Hunters Creek track. If you don't have a boat, you can **hire a 4.3 metre dinghy**, with 25hp outboard motor, licensed to carry 4 passengers.

Accommodation & Camping

Fully self-contained *safari tents* are built on raised timber decking high on the hillside, while the *cabins* come with mosquito nets, ceiling fans, fridge/freezer, tea making and outdoor setting and gas BBQ, with shared amenities. The *units* are located within the camp ground with similar facilities as the cabins. The *beach shelters,* which are a pole framed structure with palm frond roof and walls, and sand floor, have a picnic table and wood BBQ and freshwater shower. The toilet and shower block are a short walk away.

There are 30 powered and unpowered **camping** sites located in a grassed area with some shade cover and wood BBQs are situated through the camp ground. Ablutions are nearby, but there are no laundry facilities.

Cape Leveque to Highway 1 (Broome–Derby Road)

0.0 (0.0) Cape Leveque office*. Head out of resort and south along main road to Broome. Ignore roads to One Arm Point (to left) and Lombadina (to right).*

83.2 (83.2) T/J *- Turn left (TL). This T/J can easily be missed. An old Falcon wreck about 1 km before turn is best landmark.*

116.5 (33.3) T-junct – TL*.*

127.0 (10.5) T/J – TR*. Junction hard to see - small black & white striped sign on right. Track can be rocky in places.*

146.0 (19.0) *Small sandhill*

150.0 (4.0) *Small sandhill*

161.0 (11.0) *Area of termite mounds. Follow track along fence line to right.*

167.0 (6.0) Creek *and cattle yards.*

170.5 (3.5) Creek *- steep banks.*

172.0 (1.5) *Rocky gap.*

173.5 (1.5) *Water tank on right. Follow track left through gate.*

179.0 (5.5) Creek *Crossing.*

179.5 (0.5) Creek *Crossing.*

180.7 (1.2) Creek *Crossing.*

184.7 (4.0) *Gate on right, drum on left - PSA.*

187.5 (2.8) *Gate.*

193.0 (5.5) T/J – PSA*. Track on left.*

194.0 (1.0) T/J – PSA*. Track on left.*

197.5 (3.5) *Gate.*

198.5 (1.0) *Gate and creek.*

199.0 (0.5) Highway 1*. Turn left for Derby 110 km; turn right for Broome, 111 km.*

For Further Information

Contact '*Kooljaman at Cape Leveque*', PMB 8, Cape Leveque via Broome, WA, 6725
Ph: (08) 9192 4970
Web: **www.kooljaman.com.au**

Spectacular scenery and great camping can be found at Cape Leveque.

BROOME REGION

ACCOMMODATION, CAMPING & OTHER FACILITIES

ACCOMMODATION:

There is a very wide range and variety of accommodation available in Broome as detailed. For bookings and more details you can also check out the Broome Visitor web site at:
www.broomevisitorcentre.com.au/accommodation.asp#.

Hotels & Resorts: Cable Beach

Bali Hai Resort, 6 Murray Rd, ph: (08) 9191 3100, web: **www.balihairesort.com**/.
Blue Seas Resort, 10 Sanctuary Rd, ph: (08) 9192 0999, web: **www.blueseasresort.com.au**/.
Cable Beach Club Resort Broome, Cable Beach Rd, ph: (08) 9192 0400, web: **www.cablebeachclub.com/**.
Seashells Resort Broome, Challenor Drive, ph: (08) 9192 6111, web: **www.seashells.com.au/.**

Hotels & Resorts: Broome

Mangrove Hotel, Carnarvon St, ph: (08) 9192 1303, web: **www.mangrovehotel.com.au/.**
Mercure Inn - Continental, Weld St, ph: (08) 9192 1002, web: **www.accorhotels.com.au**.
Roebuck Bay Hotel/Motel, Carnarvon St, Chinatown, ph: (08) 9192 1221, web: **www.kimberleyhotels.com.au/roebuckbay/.**
Tropicana Inn, Cnr. Saville & Robinson Sts, ph: (08) 9192 1204, web: **www.tropicanainnbroome.com.au/.**

Accommodation: Motels

Broome Apartments Park Court, 7 Haas St, ph: (08) 9193 5887.
Broome Motel, Frederick St, ph: (08) 9192 7775, web: **www.broomemotel.com.au.**
Mangrove Resort Hotel, 47 Carnarvon St, ph: (08) 9192 1303, web: **www.mangrovehotel.com.au.**
Ocean Lodge, 1 Cable Beach Road, ph: (08) 9193 7700, web: **www.oceanlodge.com.au.**

Accommodation: Self-contained Apartments / Bungalows / Suites / Cabins / etc

Bamboo Retreat, Old Broome, ph: 0417 457 802, web: **www.windramart.com.au/bamboo.htm.**
Bayside Holiday Apartments, Cnr Carnarvon & Anne Sts, ph: (08) 9193 6026, web: **www.bha.broomeaccommodation.com.au/.**
Broome Beach Resort, 4 Murray Rd, Cable Beach, ph: (08) 9158 3300, web: **www.broomebeachresort.com.**
Broome Caravan Park (see listing under Caravan Parks).
Broome Motel, Frederick St, ph: (08) 9192 7775, web: **www.broomemotel.com.au.**
Broome Vacation Village Caravan Park (see listing under Caravan Parks).
Cable Beach Caravan Park (see listing under Caravan Parks).
Cable Beachside Resort, Murray Rd, Cable Beach, ph: (08) 9193 5545, web: **www.cablebeachside.com.au**.
Cocos Beach Bungalows, 6 Sanctuary Rd, Cable Beach, ph: (08) 9194 1000, web: **www.cocosbeach.com.**
Frog Hollow Bungalow, Coconut Wells, ph: 0410 696 187, web: **www.froghollowbungalow.com.**
Habitat Resort, Port Drive, ph: (08) 9158 3520, web: **www.habitatbroome.com.**
Ocean Lodge, 1 Cable Beach Road, ph: (08) 9193 7700, web: **www.oceanlodge.com.au.**
Palm Grove Holiday Resort (see listing under Caravan Parks).
Quality Suites Moonlight Bay Apartments, Carnarvon St, ph: (08) 9193 7888, web: **www.mlb.broomeaccommodation.com.au/.**
Raintree House, 6 Mary St, ph: (08) 9192 1348, web: **www.raintreehousebroome.com/.**
Rendezvous Sanctuary Resort, Lot 997, Lullfitz Drive, Cable Beach, ph: (08) 9192 8088, web: **www.rendezvoushotels.com/broome/.**

Accommodation: Backpackers

Broome's Last Resort, 2 Bagot St, ph: (08) 9193 5000, web: **www.broomeslastresort.com.au.**
Cable Beach Backpackers, 12 Sanctuary Road, Cable Beach, ph: (08) 08 9193 5511, web: **www.cablebeachbackpackers.com/**.
Kimberley Klub Broome, Frederick St, ph: (08) 9192 3233, web: **www.kimberleyklub.com.**
Roebuck Bay Backpackers, Napier Tce, ph: (08) 9192 1183, web: **www.kimberleyhotels.com.au/roebuckbay/contact.html.**

Accommodation: Bed & Breakfast / Guest Houses

Captain Kennedy's House & Cottage, Herbert St, ph: (08) 9192 3886, web: **www.mcalpinehouse.com.**
Baxter's B&B, Cable Beach, web: **http://broome.stays.com.au/19263.**
Broome Town B&B, 15 Stewart St, ph: (08) 9192 2006, web: **www.broometown.com.au/.**
Coco Eco Nature Retreat, Lot 9 Williams Rd, Coconut Well, ph: (08) 9192 3103, web: **www.cocoeco.com.au.**
Demco Bed & Breakfast, 61 Demco Drv, ph: (08) 9192 6688, web: **www.demcobnb.com.au.**
Gwen's Place, Taylor Road, Cable Beach, ph: (08) 9192 2874 web: **www.gwensplace.com.au/.**
Old Broome Guest House, 64 Walcott St, ph: (08) 9192 6106, web: **www.oldbroomeguesthouse.com.au.**
The Bungalow, 3 McKenzie Road, ph: 0417918420, web: **www.thebungalowbroome.com.au.**
The Court House B&B, 10 Stewart St, ph: (08) 9192 2773, web: **www.thecourthouse.com.au.**
The Lounging Lizard, 528 Broome Rd, ph: (08) 08) 9193 7439, web: **www.lounginglizard.com.au.**
Reflections B&B, 69 Demco Drv, ph: (08) 9192 6610, web: **www.reflectionsbnb.com.au/.**
The Temple Tree B&B, 31 Anne St, ph: (08) 9193 5728, web: **www.templetreebnb.com.au.**
Waterfront B&B, Demco Dve, ph: (08) 9192 6661, web: **www.broomebb.com/pages/home.**

Caravan Parks/Accommodation/Camping

Broome Caravan Park, Cnr Great Northern Highway & Wattle Drv, ph: (08) 9192 1776 – nestled amongst bushland, 4kms from Broome's centre. All amenities, self-contained cabins with ensuite and on-site van accommodation. Dogs allowed on a leash at manager's discretion.
Broome Vacation Village Caravan Park, Port Drive, ph: (08) 9192 1057 – shady park with all amenities. Facilities include Shop/Fuel/Pool/Laundry, web: **www.broomevillage.com.au.**
Cable Beach Caravan Park, Millington Rd, Cable Beach, ph: (08) 9192 2066 – all facilities and large shady sites. On-site accommodation and eftpos. No dogs allowed
Palm Grove Holiday Resort, Cnr Cable Beach & Murray Rds, Cable Beach, ph: (08) 9192 3336 – all facilities, with park homes, caravan and tent sites. No pets, web: **www.palmgrove.com.au.**
Roebuck Bay Caravan Park, Walcott St, ph: (08) 9192 1366 – set amongst a shady park right on Town Beach. No Pets. All facilities and on-site van accommodation, web: **www.roebuckbaycp.com.au.**
Tarangau Caravan Park, Millington Rd, Cable Beach, ph: (08) 9193 5084, shady sites, just 10 minutes stroll to Cable Beach, ph: (08) 9193 5084.

Accommodation and Camping Facilities in Surrounding Area

Barn Hill Beachside Station Stay, on the Eighty-Mile Beach, ph: (08) 9192 4975. *(See page 206 for lots more details.)*
Broome Bird Observatory, 25 km east of Broome on Crab Creek Rd, ph: (08) 9193 5600. *(See page 213 for lots more details.)* Web: **www.broomebirdobservatory.com.**
Eco Beach – Cape Villaret, 130km south of Broome, by the sea on Roebuck Bay, ph: (08) 9193 5050, 1800 631 414, web: **www.ecobeach.com.au/**.
Port Smith Caravan Park, 140 km south of Broome, in Roebuck Bay, ph: (08) 9192 4983. *(See page 206 for more details.)*
Roebuck Plains Roadhouse & Turn Table Tavern, Cnr Great Northern Highway & Northern Coastal Highway (34 km east of Broome), ph/fax: (08) 9192 1880 – cabin accommodation, caravan sites and **camp** ground with all facilities – animals allowed.

Dampier Peninsula

For a full listing of accommodation and camping on the Dampier Peninsula, *see the section* ***Cape Leveque & Around*** *on pages 218 to 224 for all details.*

FACILITIES

Broome can supply most of the travellers needs and again those not readily available can be flown up from Perth within a day or so. A brief outline of facilities available is mentioned below –

Hospital, Robinson St, ph: (08) 9192 9222
Ambulance 000
Police, Cnr Frederick & Hamersley Sts, (08) 9194 0200
Dental Clinic, 6 Barker St, ph: (08) 9192 1624
Broome Veterinary Hospital, Cnr Port Drive & Cable Beach Rd, ph: (08) 9192 1319

Banks –
ANZ, Carnarvon St, Chinatown (ATM)
BankWest, Carnarvon St, Chinatown (ATM) & Frederick St (ATM)
Westpac, Carnarvon St, Chinatown (ATM) & Boulevard Shopping Centre (ATM)
Commonwealth, Hamersley St, (ATM)
Post Office, Carnarvon St, Chinatown, ph: (08) 9192 1380.
Broome Shire Council, Cnr Haas & Weld Sts, ph: (08) 9191 3456, web: **www.broome.wa.gov.au.**
CALM – Dept. of Conservation and Land Management, Herbert St, ph: (08) 9192 1036.
Shopping Centres / Supermarkets – there are a number of shopping centres and supermarkets in Broome, open 7 days a week, with Eftpos facilities, such as –
Paspaley Shopping Centre – large shopping centre & supermarket.
Streeter & Male, Short St, Chinatown.
Fong's Store, 29 Saville St.
Yuen Wing Store, 19 Carnarvon St, Chinatown.
Boulevard Shopping Centre – large shopping complex and supermarket.
Cable Beach Shopping Centre – 49 Reid Road, Cable Beach.

Other Stores include:

Pearl Sea Laundromat – Shop 13 Boulevard Shopping Centre, Frederick St, ph: (08) 9192 1611.

Pharmacies

Amcal Chemist, Shop 12 Broome Boulevard Shopping Centre, ph: (08) 9192 1866.
Chinatown Pharmacy, Shop 2, Paspaley Plaza Shopping Centre, ph: (08) 9192 1399.

Bookshops

Kimberley Bookshop, 4 Napier Tce, ph: (08) 9192 1944 – has a great range of books on the Kimberley.
Woody's Book Exchange, Shop 13 Johnny Chi Lane, ph: (08) 9192 8999.

Outdoor Supplies

Kimberley Caravan & Outback Supplies, 65 Frederick St, ph: (08) 9193 5909 – full range of camping gear – for sale or hire.
Norwest Tackle & Sport, Shop 2/32 Dampier Tce, ph: (08) 9192 1669, fax: (08) 9193 6073 – all your fishing needs and diving gear.
Workline Dive & Tackle, ph: (08) 9192 2233 web: **www.workline.com.au/** – fishing, diving, charters, tours.

BROOME TOURIST INFORMATION

BROOME VISITOR CENTRE

Cnr Broome Highway & Bagot St,
PO Box 352, Broome, WA, 6725.
Ph: (08) 9192 2222, fax: (08) 9192 2063
Toll Free 1800 883 777
Web: **www.broomevisitorcentre.com.au/**
Open 7 days a week. Expert advise on Broome and the Kimberley, as well as handling all your travel requirements – airline, coach, tours and accommodation bookings.
The Centre stocks a huge range of brochures covering the Kimberley, and supplies not only information, but also maps, history books and guides and information leaflets, plus lots more.

ABC Regional Radio - Broome	
Local Radio	675 AM
Radio National	107.7 FM

Photographic shops can be found at the Paspaley & Boulevard Shopping Centres.

Service Station & Fuel Outlets

There are quite a few to choose from in Broome, as well as the *Roebuck Plains Roadhouse,* Cnr Great Northern Highway & Northern Coastal Highway (34 km east of Broome), ph/fax: (08) 9192 1880 – open 7 days a week – fuel, meals, etc.

VEHICLE/CARAVAN/TRAILER/BOAT – SERVICE, REPAIRS, PARTS & ACCESSORIES

The following are just a selection of the wide range of outlets in Broome that offer the above services & facilities –

Auto Electrical, Air-conditioning and Batteries

Field Air-conditioning & Auto Electrical, Blackman St, ph: (08) 9193 5322.

Caravan Repairs

Overall Constructions, 5 Glenister Loop, ph (08) 9193 5434.

Marine

Moby Dick Marine, Cnr Clementson & Hunter Sts, ph: (08) 9192 2479.
Steve's Marine, 6 Penbroke Rd, ph: (08) 9193 5775 – boating accessories, trailer repairs & spares.
Total Marine Maintenance, 42 Anne St, mob: 0417 270 198 & 0407 788 057

Motor Service Centres

Broome Automotive Spares, 4 Minilya, ph: (08) 9192 5551.
Broome Diesel & Hydraulic Service, 1788 De Castilla St, ph: (08) 9192 1330 – diesel repairs.
Broome Toyota – **RAC Agency**, 7 MacPherson St, ph: (08) 9192 1277 – 4WD repairs, parts, service, tyres, batteries, towing, etc.
Broome Windscreens, Lot 2707 Tanami St (cnr Coghlan St), ph: (08) 9193 6494.
Shinju Motors, Walcott St, ph: (08) 9192 1250 – agents for Ford, Mitsubishi, Rover & Nissan.
Tropical Motors, Minilya Rd, ph: (08) 9192 2595.

Towing

Broome Towing & Salvage, 135 Reid Rd, ph: (08) 9192 3009, mob: 0417 223 009.

Tyres

Beaurepaires, Lot 28 Napier Tce, ph: (08) 9192 1644.
Broome Discount Tyres, Gregory St, ph: (08) 9193 6293.
Broome Tyre Centre, McPherson St, ph: (08) 9192 1277.
Kimberley Tyres, 6 Port Drv, ph: (08) 9192 1711.

Boarding Kennels

Broome Boarding Kennels, Cnr Cable Beach Rd & Frederick St,, ph: (08) 9192 1319, fax: (08) 9193 7394.
Broome Pet Motel, 15 McDaniel Rd, ph: (08) 9193 5384, mob 0417 935 384.

Hire Camping Equipment

Kimberley Camping & Outback Supplies, 65 Frederick St, ph: (08) 9193 5909, fax: (08) 9193 6878 – open 7 days a week – camping packs available, web: **www.kimberleycamping.com.au**
Kimberley Camping Hire, Shop 3/ 65 Frederick St, ph: (08) 9193 5354 – hire camping & Leisure Equipment

CLUBS OF SPECIAL INTEREST

Broome Fishing Club, PO Box 1957, Broome, 6725, phone Clubhouse: (08) 9193 6623 or 9192 8122.
Broome Historical Society Museum, Lot 271 Saville St, Broome, 6725, ph: (08) 9192 2075. (08) 9192 2075, web: **amol.org.au/guide/instn.asp?ID=W146**

CRUISES & TOURS

You can contact the ***Broome Visitor Centre*** for information on any of the following local tours and the Centre can also organise any bookings for you. You can also check out their extensive wet site at: **www.broomevisitorcentre.com.au/tours.asp.** All the listed tour operators work out of Broome.

Local Day Tours from Broome

4WD Tours

Aussie Off Road Tours, ph: (08) 9192 361, web: **www.aussieoffroadtours.com.au.**
Australian Pinnacle Tours, ph: (08) 9192 8080, web: **www.pinnacletours.com.au/.**
Broome Eco Adventures, ph: (08) 9193 7997.
Chomley's Tours, ph: 9192 7307, web: **www.chomleystours.com.au.**
Kimberley Getaway Safaris, ph: (08) 9193 7139, web: **www.kimberleysafaris.com.au.**
Kimberley Wild Expeditions, ph: (08) 9193 7778, web: **www.kimberleywild.com.**
Over The Top Adventure Tours, ph: (08) 9192 5211, web: **www.4wdtourswa.com.**

Aboriginal Tours

Kimberley Wild Expeditions, ph: (08) 9193 7778, web: **www.kimberleywild.com.**
Larwarrdu Aboriginal Cultural Tours, ph: (08) 9192 5067, web: **www.waitoc.com/kullarri.asp#lact.**
Mamabulanjin Aboriginal Tours, ph: (08) 9192 2660, web: **www.waitoc.com/kullarri.asp#mat.**

Also check out the listings under the section ***'Cape Leveque & Surrounds'*** on page 218 for a full range of indigenous tour operators on the Dampier Peninsula.

Air Tours – Scenic

Broome Aviation, ph: (08) 9192 1369, web: **www.broomeaviation.com.**
Broome Trike Flights, ph: (08) 91935697.
King Leopold Air, ph: (08) 9193 7155, web: **www.kingleopoldair.com.au/.**
Reef Flight, ph: (08) 9192 3028, web: **www.reefflight.com.**

Astronomy Tours

Astro Tours of the Kimberley, ph: 0417 949 958 or (08) 9193 5362, web: **www.astrotours.net/.**

Ballooning

Outback Ballooning, ph: 1800 809 790, web: **www.outbackballooning.com.au/** – June to Sept.

Camel Rides

Broome Camel Safaris, ph: 0419 916 101, web: **www.bushwalks.com/broomecamels/.**
Cable Beach Camel Safaris, ph: 0414 457 788, web: **www.maddenscamels.com/.**
Red Sun Camel Safaris, ph: (08) 9193 7423, web: **www.redsuncamels.com.au.**
Ships of the Desert, ph: 08) 9192 6383 or 0419 395 206.

Coach Tours

Broome Day Tours & Charters, ph: (08) 9192 1068, web: **www.broomedaytours.com.au.**
Broome Sightseeing Tours, ph: (08) 9192 5041, web: **www.broomesightseeingtours.com.**
Broome Top Deck Tours, ph: 0427 850 559.
Salty Dogs Broome Tours, ph: (08) 9192 1651, web: **www.saltysbroometours.com.au.**
Willie Creek Pearl Farm, ph: (08) 9192 6300, web: **www.williecreekpearls.com.au/.**

Photographic Tours

Red Dirt Photographic Tours, ph: 0418 917 078, web: **www.reddirtphoto.com.au/.**

Sea Kayaking Tours

Turtle Bay Kayak Adventure, ph: 1300 665 888, web: **www.broomeadventure.com.au.**

Wildlife, Birdwatching and Natural History Tours

Broome Bird Observatory (*see page 213 for full details*).
Kimberley Birdwatching, 32 Hopton St, ph: (08) 9192 1246, web: **www.kimberleybirdwatching.com.au.**
Leveque Wilderness Fishing & Adventure Charters, ph: (08) 9193 6836.
Turnstone Nature Discovery, ph: (08) 9192 8585, web: **www.turnstonenaturediscovery.com.au/.**

Boat Tours & Cruises

Broome Pearling Lugger Experience, ph: 9192 7321, web: **www.broomelugger.com.**
Broome Hovercraft, ph: (08) 9193 5025, web: **www.broomehovercraft.com.au.**
Dampier Creek Boat Tours, ph: (08) 9192 2050.
Kimberley Discovery Cruises, ph: 1800 185 960, web: **www.kimberleydiscoverycruises.com.au.**
Willie Pearl Lugger Cruises, ph: 0428 919 781, web: **www.williecruises.com.au/.**

Fishing & Diving Tours

Broome Billfish Charters, ph: (08) 9192 2127, web: **www.broomebillfish.com.**
Broome Fishing & Dive Charters, ph: (08) 9193 6339.
Broome Time Charters, ph: (08) 9192 2458.
Fad Game Fishing Charters, ph: (08) 9192 3998, web: **www.fadcharters.com.au.**
Kimberley Fishing, ph: (08) 9193 5689, web: **www.kimberleyfishing.com/.**
Leveque Wilderness Fishing & Adventure Charters, ph: (08) 9193 6836.
North Cape Fishing Charters, Cable Beach, ph: 0419 046 035.
Sentosa Fishing Charters, ph: (08) 9192 8163, web: **www.sentosafishingcharters.com.**
Workline Dive & Tackle, ph: (08) 9192 2233, web: **www.workline.com.au/.**

Extended Tours from Broome

There is a multitude of 4WD, fishing and dive charter, scenic flight and coach tour operators to choose from who operate extended tours from Broome. Contact the ***Broome Visitor Centre*** for information or bookings. Also there are a number of other ***specialists travel agencies*** in Broome who can organise and book tours for you, such as:

Best Of The Kimberley, ph: 1800 450 850, web: **www.kimberleytravel.net** – "One Stop Shop" of advice, expertise and booking service. Specialised tour packages as well as accommodation.

Broome & the Kimberley Holidays, ph: (08) 9193 5790, web: **www.broomekimberley.com/** – specialist travel agent for accommodation and tours throughout the Kimberley.

Broome Visitor Centre, ph: (08) 9192 2222, web: **www.broomevisitorcentre.com.au/**- can help you with all your bookings for tours, accommodation and much more.

Kimberley Cruise Centre, ph: 1800 677 830, web: **www.kimberleycruises.com** – boats, charters, diving, fishing and tour packages.

Air

Broome Aviation, ph: (08) 9192 1369, web: **www.broomeaviation.com.**

4WD Safaris

All Terrain Safaris, ph: (08) 9295 6680, web: **www.allterrainsafaris.com.au.**
APT Kimberley Wilderness Adventures, ph: 1800 675 222, web: **www.kimberleywilderness.com.au.**
Aussie Off Road Tours, ph: (08) 9192 3617, web: **www.aussieoffroadtours.com.au.**
Australian Adventure Travel, ph: (08) 9248 2355, web: **www.safaris.net.au.**
Australian Pinnacle Tours, ph: (08) 9192 8080, web: **www.pinnacletours.com.au/.**
Broome Safari Treks, ph: (08) 9376 1419, web: **www.safaritreks.com.au/broome_safari.html.**
Chomley's Tours, ph: 9192 7307, web: **www.chomleystours.com.au/**.
Discover The Kimberley Tours, ph: (08) 9193 7267, web: **www.bunglebungle.com.au.**
Kimberley Getaway Safaris, ph: (08) 9193 7139, web: **www.kimberleysafaris.com.au.**
Kimberley Wild Expeditions, ph: (08) 9193 7778, web: **www.kimberleywild.com.**
Kimberley Wilderness Adventures, ph: (03) 9277 8444, web: **www.kimberleywilderness.com.au/.**
Over The Top Adventure Tours, ph: (08) 9192 5211, web: **www.4wdtourswa.com.**
Wilderness 4WD Adventures, ph: (08) 8941 2161, web: **www.wildernessadventures.com.au**

Aboriginal Tours

Bush University - JBAC Bush Adventures, Broome, ph/fax: (08) 9191 7467, 0417 922 335 – **Mt Anderson Cattle Station**, web: **www.wedgetailstours.com.au/**. (*See Derby Chapter, page 195 for full details.*)
Sacred Earth Safaris, ph: (08) 8981 8420, web: **www.sacredearthsafaris.com.au**.

Astronomy Tours

Astro Tours of the Kimberley, ph: 0417 949 958 or (08) 9193 5362, web: **www.astrotours.net/.**

Sea Kayaking Tours

Turtle Bay Kayak Adventure, ph: 1300 665 888, web: **www.broomeadventure.com.au.**

Wildlife, Birdwatching and Natural History Tours

Kimberley Birdwatching, ph: (08) 9192 1246, web: **www.kimberleybirdwatching.com.au.**

Cruising & Fishing Safaris & Charters

Broome Billfish Charters, ph: (08) 9192 2127, web: **www.broomebillfish.com.**
Broome Fishing & Dive Charters, ph: (08) 9193 6339.
Buccaneer Sea Safaris, ph: (08) 9191 1991, web: **www.buccaneerseasafaris.com.**
Fad Game Fishing Charters, ph: (08) 9192 3998, web: **www.fadcharters.com.au.**
Freshwater Cove, ph: (08) 9193 6836, web: **www.freshwatercove.com.**
Kimberley Birdwatching, ph: (08) 9192 1246, web: **www.kimberleybirdwatching.com.au.**
Kimberley Catamaran Cruises, ph: (08) 9192 8668, web: **www.shorething.com.au.**
Kimberley Discovery Cruises, ph: 1800 185 960, web: **www.kimberleydiscoverycruises.com.au.**
Kimberley Fishing, ph: (08) 9193 5689, web: **www.kimberleyfishing.com/.**
Kimberley Fishing Charters, '*Simara III*' – Kimberley Cruise Centre, ph: 1800 677 830, web: **www.kimberleycruises.com.**
Leveque Wilderness Fishing & Adventure Charters, ph: (08) 9193 6836.
North Cape Fishing Charters, ph: 0419 046 035.
North Star Charters, ph: (08) 9192 1829, web: **www.northstarcruises.com.au.**
One Tide Charter, Broome, ph: (08) 9193 1358, web: **www.onetide.com.**
Pearl Sea Coastal Cruises, '*Kimberley Quest*', ph: (08) 9193 6131 web: **www.kimberleyquest.com.au.**
Red Sky Cruises, ph: 0407 739 738, web: **www.redsky.com.au.**
Sentosa Fishing Charters, ph: (08) 9192 8163, web: **www.sentosafishingcharters.com.**
The Great Escape Charter Company, ph: (08) 9193 5983, web: **www.kimberleyescape.com.**
Willie Pearl Lugger Cruises, ph: 0428 919 781, web: **www.williecruises.com.au/.**
Workline Dive & Tackle, ph: (08) 9192 2233, web: **www.workline.com.au/.**

TRANSPORT: To and From

You can arrange all your travel needs through the ***Broome Visitor Centre,*** ph: (08) 9192 2222, web: **www.broomevisitorcentre.com.au/,** or travel agents in Broome at:

Best of the Kimberley, ph: 1800 450 850, web: **www.kimberleytravel.net.**
Broome & The Kimberley Holidays, ph: (08) 9193 5790, web: **www.broomekimberley.com/.**
Harvey World Travel, Paspaley Plaza, ph: (08) 9193 5599.
Jetset, Shp 21 The Boulevard Shopping Centre, ph: (08) 9192 1199.
Terri's Travel, 2 Carnarvon St, ph: (08) 9192 2992.
Travelworld, Shop 9 Johnny Chi Lane, ph: (08) 9193 7233.

Air:

Broome Internatoinal Airport

This is the region's air hub and supports air transport operations that link Broome to other Australian cities, the remote Kimberley outback and foreign destinations. Contact: PO Box 68, Broome 6725, ph: (08) 9193 5455, Air/ground radio (MBZ): 126.00 MHz, ATIS: 126.55 MHz. Comprehensive web site listing flight info, facilities, history and tourism. Web site: **www.broomeair.com.au**.

Domestic Scheduled Flights:

Air North, reservations ph: 1800 627 474, web: **www.airnorth.com.au.**
QantasLink ph: 13 13 13, **www.qantas.com.au/flightinfo.**
Skywest, 1300 66 00 88, web: **www.skywest.com.au/.**
Virgin Blue, 13 67 89, web: **www.virginblue.com.au/.**

Regional Scheduled Flights:

Air North, reservations ph: 1800 627 474, web: **www.airnorth.com.au** - daily scheduled regular public transport services between Broome, Kununurra and Darwin.

Golden Eagle Airlines, Derby Airport, ph: (08) 9191 1132, web: **www.goldeneagleairlines.com** – scheduled regular public transport services between Broome/Derby, and Broome/Fitzroy Crossing/ Halls Creek.

In addition to remote airstrip access, Broome has a fleet of float planes that service the islands of the Buccaneer and Bonaparte Archipelagoes and the offshore pearling industry.

Ibis Aerial Highway

*The **Ibis Aerial Highway** is the network of airstrips located at remote communities, homesteads, national parks and other places of interest to facilitate air access throughout the region. For details check out the web site:* **www.broomeair.com.au/kimbmap.htm.**

Bus/Coach:

Between April & Sept, the **Town Bus Service r**uns an hourly service from 7.10am to 6.30pm - 7 days a week. All buses go to Chinatown and Cable Beach. For more info and a timetable, check out their web site: **www.broomebus.com.au.**

Derby Bus Service, 1 Sutherland St, Derby, ph: (08) 9193 1550 – Derby/Broome/Derby bus service, Mon, Wed & Fri. Depart Broome Mon, Wed 10.30am, Fri 2.30pm. Web site: **www.derbybus.com.au.**
Greyhound, ph: 13 14 99, web site: **www.greyhound.com.au** – runs regular services to Broome.

Freight

Broome Freightlines, Port Drv, Broome, ph: (08) 9193 6322.

Hire Motorcycles

Exclusive Motorcycle Hire, Dawn Way, Broome, ph: 0418 951 943 – motor cycles hire & tours

Hire Camping Equipment (see page 229)

Hire Boats

Coastal Catch Boat Hire, ph: 0417 176 648 – boat charter services & hire.

Hire 4WDs/Campervans/Motorhomes

Avis Car Rentals, Cnr Frederick & Walcott Sts, Broome, 6725, ph: (08) 9193 5980, web: **www.avis.com.au**.
Britz, 10 Livingstone St, Broome, ph: (08) 9192 2647, web: **www.britz.com/**.
Broome Broome Car Rentals, 7/6 Hamersley St, Broome, ph: (08) 9192 2210, web: **www.broomebroome.com.au**.
Broome Topless Rentals, 25 Hunter St, ph: (08) 9193 5017.
Budget, Broome Airport, ph: (08) 9193 5980 or 1300 794 344, web: **www.budget.com.au**.
Europcar, Broome Airport, ph: (08) 9193 7788, web: **www.deltaeuropcar.com.au**.
Four Wheel Drive Hire Service, 5 Lucas Street, Broome, ph: 08 9192 8854, web: **www.4wdhire.com.au**.
Hertz *Wheels Over The Kimberley*, Broome Airport, ph: (08) 9192 1428, web: **www.hertzcampervans.com**.
Just Broome Car Hire, Cable Beach, ph: (08) 9192 6636.
KEA Campers, 5 Lucas Street, Broome, ph: 08 9192 8854, web: **www.keacampers.com/**.
Maui Rentals, 10 Livingstone St, Broome, ph: (08) 9192 2647, web: **www.maui-rentals.com/**.
South Perth 4WD Rentals, Hunter St, Broome, ph (08) 9193 7946, web: **www.sp4wd.com.au/**.
Thrifty, Broome Airport, ph: (08) 9193 7712, web: **www.thrifty.com.au**.
Trailmaster Campervan Rentals, PO Box 72, Guildford WA 6935, ph: 1800 651202 or (08) 9228 0012, web: **www.trailmaster.com.au/**.
Tru Blu Rentals, 2 Coghlan St Broome, ph: (08) 9192 5177.

self-drive.com – Campervan Rental and Car Hire Specialists, ph: 1300 305 505 or (03) 9879 0511, web: **www.self-drive.com** - offers Britz & Maui campervans throughout Australia.

Top: The spectacular rocky coastline of the Dampier Peninsula.

An old diver's helmet on display at the Pearl Luggers.

Bottom: The Japanese Cemetery in Broome is the resting place of many pearl divers.

A unique phone box in Broome.

The jetty in Broome is a well known fishing spot.

THE NATIONAL PARKS & NATURE RESERVES

INTRODUCTION

The National Parks and Nature Reserves so far proclaimed within the Kimberley protect some of the most outstanding areas of the region. Many areas proposed by the Environmental Protection Authority back in 1980 in the *System 7 Red Book of Recommendations* have yet to be proclaimed - if they ever will be. We've included some of those recommended areas on the map, for information only. This does not imply any right of entry as many of the areas are still owned and operating cattle leases.

More recently the Department of Conservation and Land Management (CALM) published a book called Nature Conservation Reserves in the Kimberley, where once again they had a large 'wish list' of areas within the Kimberley that could be - should be - reserved. We haven't included these areas on the map as it really is a wish list!

In late 1991, early 1992, with the demise of one of the regional cattle empires, a number of stations came up for sale. Mt Hart was procured by CALM, along with parcels of land in the Napier and Oscar Ranges to the east of Tunnel Creek National Park. While the areas are managed as parks, they are yet to be opened to the public.

While some of the parks in the Kimberley are spectacular and relatively accessible, sadly many are not. Limitations on access and prohibited areas abound.

THE PARKS AND RESERVES

BROOKING GORGE CONSERVATION PARK

North-west of Fitzroy Crossing is Brooking Gorge where the Brooking Creek has slashed its way through the barrier of the Oscar Range.

No access is permitted and no facilities exist. Ranger contact: Ranger-in-Charge, Fitzroy Crossing.

See the chapter, *Derby to Fitzroy Crossing*, page 198, for more detail.

DRYSDALE RIVER NATIONAL PARK (448,264 ha)

This is the largest national park in the Kimberley region. It's also extremely remote and for the most part completely inaccessible.

No facilities exists within the park, but **camping** is allowed in one place.

Ranger contact: Regional Office, Kununurra.

See our chapter, *The Mitchell Plateau and Northern Kimberley,* pages 138 to 140 for more details.

GEIKIE GORGE NATIONAL PARK (3136 ha)

Geikie Gorge National Park is situated 21 km north-east of Fitzroy Crossing, where the Fitzroy River has cut a gorge through the limestone formations of the Geikie and Oscar Ranges.

Camping is not permitted but boat tours are very popular and a great way to see the gorge.

Ranger contact: Ranger in Charge, Fitzroy Crossing, or District Office in Broome.

See the chapter, *Derby to Fitzroy Crossing*, pages 199 to 202, for more detail.

KING LEOPOLD RANGE CONSERVATION PARK (370,000 ha)

The park, which includes Silent Grove, Bell Gorge, Lennard Gorge and Mt Hart Wilderness Lodge, is run by CALM. A ranger is based at **Silent Grove** during the Dry season.

Camping is provided for in a couple of places and there is accommodation at the old Mt Hart homestead (bookings essential).

Ranger contact: Ranger base Silent Grove, or Ranger-in-Charge at Derby, or District Office, Broome.

See the chapter, *The Gibb River Road*, pages 164 to 166, for more detail.

VISITOR INFORMATION AND CONDITIONS

CONDITIONS

All components of the natural environment, both living and non-living, are protected in national parks, nature reserves and conservation parks. *This includes birds, mammals, snakes, lizards, frogs and invertebrates, all vegetable matter, from the largest tree to individual fruits, flowers, seeds, leaves and even minute mosses and lichens, along with soil, rocks, Aboriginal artifacts and paintings. These are not to be disturbed or interfered with in any way at any time!*

Note: *Fish and fishing doesn't fall into the above categories. In a rather strange twist you can still fish many of the rivers that flow through these parks, e.g. Geikie Gorge. However, at other places, such as Windjana Gorge, fishing is definitely frowned upon as many birds, as well as the small population of crocs, depend on the fish and the fish stocks are definitely limited.*

Dogs, cats and other domestic animals must not be taken *onto or kept in national parks or nature reserves.*

Firearms are not permitted *in national parks or in nature reserves.*

Restrict using your vehicle in the national park to constructed roadways *and designated four wheel drive tracks.*

Take extreme care with fire at all times. *Light campfires only in constructed fireplaces. In regularly maintained camping or picnic areas fires must only be lit on the ground in approved fire places. Never leave a fire unattended and make sure that your fire is extinguished before leaving camp.*

Remove all rubbish *from the national park or place it in bins where these are provided. Leave your camp site clean and hygienic.*

The local Park Ranger can advise of any special precautions and on availability of sites for camping. *National parks with facilities are usually equipped with tables, fireplaces and toilets. Firewood is provided wherever possible, but travellers are encouraged to carry their own cooking fuel or camping stoves.*

Show due consideration *for the right of other park visitors to enjoy peaceful and quiet conditions at all times. Disorderly, improper, indecent or unseemly conduct is not allowed.*

While in the national park you are required to ***obey any reasonable instruction given by an officer*** *of the Dept of Conservation and Land Management (CALM).*

NATIONAL PARK PASSES

Visitors fees apply to some WA NPs and a range of passes are available.

DAY PASS - covers entry into one or more parks on any one day. Passes are available from rangers in the parks. Needed for **Purnululu** and **Mirima**.

ANNUAL LOCAL PARK PASS – applicable if you live near a NP and visit frequently.

HOLIDAY PARK PASS – this pass entitles you to as many visits to as many parks as you wish for any four-week period.

ANNUAL ALL PARKS PASS – This pass entitles you to visit any park throughout Western Australia as many times as you wish for a period of 12 months.

GOLD STAR PASS is an *Annual All Parks* Pass that includes a one-year subscription to CALM's wildlife magazine, *Landscope*.

CONCESSIONS – Drivers who hold a Seniors' Card, aged pension card or Dept of Veterans' Affairs Card are entitled to pay a concession price for Day Passes.

Park Passes do not include camping fees.

For further details on fees, and where to obtain passes, contact your nearest CALM office.

Wolfe Creek Crater National Park.

Surveyor's Pool on the Mitchell Plateau.

CALM District & Regional Offices

Executive Office:
Hackett Drive,
Crawley WA 6009
Ph: (08) 9442 0300

State Operations Office:
17 Dick Perry Ave,
Kensington WA 6151
Ph: (08) 9334 0333

East Kimberley Regional Office:
Messmate Way,
PO Box 942,
Kununurra WA 6743
Ph: (08) 9168 4200,
Fax: (08) 9168 2179

West Kimberley District Office:
Herbert Street,
Broome WA 6725
Ph: (08) 9192 1036
Fax: (08) 9193 5027

Regional CALM Offices:

Fitzroy Crossing Office:
PO Box 37,
Fitzroy Crossing, WA 6765
Ph: (08) 9191 5121
Fax: (08) 9191 5165

Derby Office:
Delaware St,
Derby, WA 6728
Ph: (08) 9193 1411
Fax: (08) 9193 1415

MIRIMA NATIONAL PARK (2068 ha)

Just on the outskirts of Kununurra, approximately 3 km from the centre of town is Mirima National Park, previously known as Hidden Valley.

There is no camping permitted. Visitors need to purchase a **Day Pass.**

Ranger contact: Regional Office, Kununurra.

See our chapter, *The Eastern Kimberley*, page 111, for more detail.

(NGAUWUDU) MITCHELL RIVER NATIONAL PARK (115,300 ha)

The Mitchell River National Park lies in a remote part of the Kimberley where the Mitchell River, flowing northwards, drains into Walmsley Bay and Admiralty Gulf, carving gorges and waterfalls into the underlying sandstone, particularly along the margins of the Mitchell Plateau. The park abuts the northern boundary of the Prince Regent Nature Reserve, effectively creating a continuous conservation reserve of three quarters of a million hectares.

Camping is possible in a few places, with limited facilities.

Ranger contact: Ranger base Mitchell Plateau, or Regional Office, Kununurra.

For more information about this fabulous area see our chapter, *The Mitchell Plateau and Northern Kimberley*, pages 143 to 147.

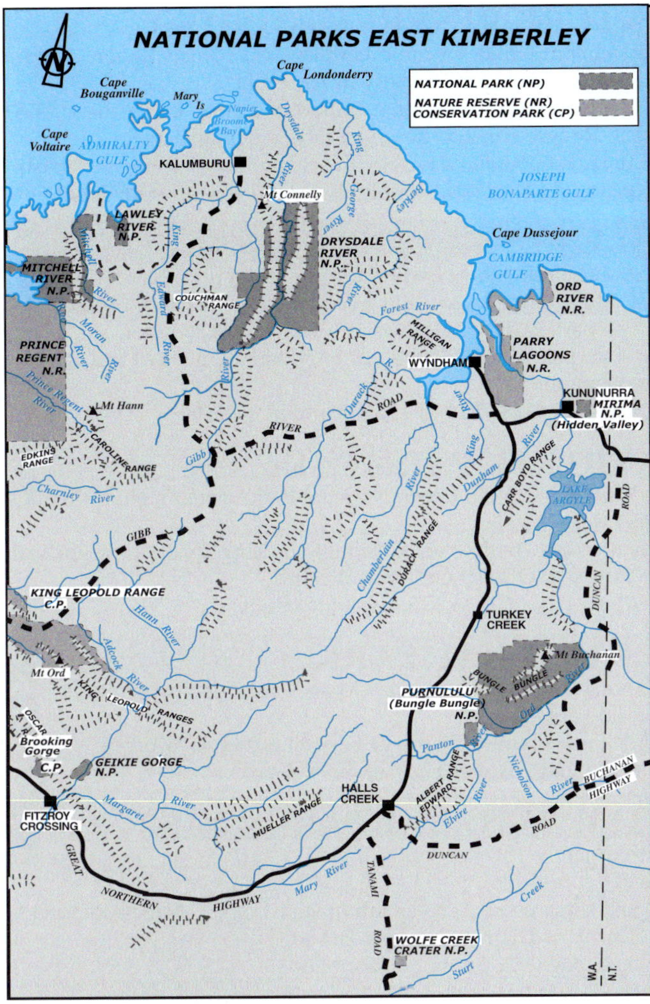

CALM

Dry Season Ranger Bases

During the Dry season rangers are also based at:

Geikie Gorge
Ph: (08) 9191 5112

Mirima
Ph: (08) 9168 4200

Mitchell Plateau
Ph: (08) 9161 4172

Purnululu
Ph: (08) 9168 7300

Silent Grove
Ph: (08) 9191 7058

Windjana Gorge
Ph: (08) 9191 7076

Web Site

CALM has an Internet site called 'Nature Base'. There is a large amount of information on everything from facilities in parks, to tours in parks, passes and expeditions run by CALM.

You can visit them at:

www.calm.wa.gov.au/.

PARRY LAGOONS NATURE RESERVE (36,000 ha)

The Parry Lagoons NR and its wetlands are located about 15 km south-east of Wyndham and not only takes in Parry Lagoons, but also Marlgu Billabong, Police Hole and the extensive flood plains of the Ord River. The birdlife in the area is incredible.

Camping is not allowed. Ranger contact: Regional Office, Kununurra.

See our chapter, *The Eastern Kimberley*, page 102 for more details.

POINT COULOMB NATURE RESERVE

This nature reserve lies some 70 km north of Broome.

To get there see our Trek Notes (page 217) detailed in the chapter, *Broome and the Dampier Peninsula.*

POINT SPRINGS NATURE RESERVE

This is a small reserve located 50 km north of Kununurra along the Weaber Plain (or Legune) Road. The Reserve surrounds a patch of rainforest at the base of the Weaber Range escarpment and contains a lagoon fed by natural springs.

There are no facilities and no camping allowed. Ranger contact: Regional Office, Kununurra.

See our chapter, *The Eastern Kimberley*, page 110, for more details.

PRINCE REGENT NATURE RESERVE (633,832 ha)

Covering a vast sweep of rugged sandstone and volcanic country, the Prince Regent Nature Reserve takes in some of the most spectacular coastal scenery in Australia.

At present access is restricted. The Reserve is declared a 'prohibited area' under the CALM Act and a permit is required to visit it. Ranger contact: Regional Office, Kununurra.

Helicopter access is possible, but the most popular way is by the charter boats sailing the coast.

See the chapter, *The Mitchell Plateau and Northern Kimberley*, page 148, for more detail.

PURNULULU (BUNGLE BUNGLE) NP (320,000 ha)

The Purnululu (Bungle Bungle) National Park is best known for its spectacular tiger-striped, beehive-shaped domes but there is much more to see and experience in this large remote park, 250 km south of Kununurra. The park is only open between April & September.

Camping is allowed and facilities are provided. Visitors need to purchase a **Day Pass**.

Ranger contact: Regional Office, Kununurra.

See our chapter, *The Eastern Kimberley*, pages 124 to 1281, for more details.

TUNNEL CREEK NATIONAL PARK (91 ha)

Located just 30 km from Windjana Gorge is Tunnel Creek National Park, which includes the majority of the Oscar Range and the Oscar Plateau.

Camping is not allowed here, day use only, but the walk through the range is not to be missed.

Ranger contact: Ranger's Office Derby or District Office in Broome.

See the chapter, *The Gibb River Road*, page 172 to 173, for more detail.

WINDJANA GORGE NATIONAL PARK

This small park is located north-east of Derby and Windjana Gorge is regarded by geologists as one of the classic examples of world geology.

Camping facilities are provided. Ranger contact: Derby or District Office in Broome.

See the chapter, *The Gibb River Road*, page 169 to 172, for more detail.

WOLFE CREEK CRATER NATIONAL PARK (1460 ha)

Wolfe Creek Crater is located approximately 150 km south of Halls Creek on the very edge of the Great Sandy Desert and is easily accessible.

Facilities include a parking/picnic and camping area and an information board. There is no water.

Ranger contact: Ranger's Office Derby or District Office in Broome.

See the chapter, *Around Halls Creek*, page 90, for more information.

THE OFFSHORE ISLANDS

A number of islands off the Kimberley coast have been proclaimed either a national park, a marine park or a reserve. Most are either already classified as nature reserves or as Aboriginal reserves.

The inshore islands include the islands of the Buccaneer and Bonaparte Archipelagos, along with the Admiralty Gulf Islands and Pelican Island in the Joseph Bonaparte Gulf.

The oceanic islands include the Lacepedes north of Broome, Adele Island, Browse Island, Ashmore Reef and Scott Reef.

Rowley Shoals and the three major reefs that make up this complex are the first to be declared marine national parks. Situated nearly 200 km offshore from Broome they are becoming popular for diving expeditions.

Access is limited to charter boats operating from Derby or Broome.

Ranger contact: Regional Office, Kununurra, or District Office in Broome.

CANOEING & BOATING

GENERAL

We would always recommend that some form of boat or canoe be carried on any trip to the Kimberley. Even the smallest car-top tinnie or single kayak gives travellers another opportunity to experience a completely different and interesting aspect of the Kimberley. It's a pleasant way to see places and the only way to see many spots that can't be reached by vehicle.

The great dams on the Ord River and the long stretches of water that stay all year on the other mighty rivers are where anyone can enjoy a day's paddling or boating. However, none of the rivers stay navigable for anywhere near their whole length during the course of the Dry season. The Ord, below the dam, is the only one that flows at a near consistent height all year. Even the mighty Fitzroy River dries to a series of ponds and stretches of still water.

Access is another problem that limits canoeing or boating on any of these streams. For the most part the rivers are inaccessible and to run anywhere near their length is a major expedition. In fact, many of the rivers have never been canoed for that very reason.

THE ORD DAMS

Both Lake Argyle and Lake Kununurra offer a wide expanse of water for boating and canoeing.

LAKE KUNUNURRA

Lake Kununurra has a number of boat launching ramps near the town. The fishing is reasonable, the wildlife amongst the backwater (the Everglades) excellent and because of its size is a relatively safe place for a canoe or small boat.

LAKE ARGYLE

Lake Argyle, with its vastness, can be likened to an inland sea. It's not the place to be if a storm blows up.

Lake Argyle has a boat ramp not far from the Village and while the boating and fishing are excellent, canoeing, because of the Lake's vast size, isn't so brilliant.

The Ord River, just below the dam wall.

THE ORD RIVER

The Ord River, between the dam wall of Lake Argyle and Kununurra, would be the easiest and one of the most enjoyable canoeing experiences (and boating for that matter) in the Kimberley. The river is suitable for anyone, including novice canoeists. The trip takes an easy three days for the whole length and two days if you pull out at the tiny settlement of Crossing Falls. Below the settlement the canoeing is a long slog over the still waters of Lake Kununurra.

Camping sites aren't all that common along the river, mainly because the near constant height of the water has allowed thick vegetation to grow on many old sandbars. The first decent sites are just after you enter **Carlton Gorge**, on your left, about 16 km from the start point. There's not much firewood around and the mossies can be thick!

Other good camp sites occur near Pelican Rock and at the Fig Tree, 23.5 km and 30.0 km respectively from the start. At around 32.0 km, Spillway Creek joins the Ord on the right. There are a number of good camp sites just a short distance up this stream – the water is crystal clear and there's a bit of timber around.

The pickup points down river are at Crossing Falls, at *Kona Lakeside Tourist Park*, or just 250 metres above the dam wall at the boat ramp. You can get to *Kimberleyland Holiday Park* by entering Lily Creek on the right above *Kona Tourist Park*. The entrance is marked by a large dead tree about 1 km upriver from Kona and is the second major entrance. Basically once in the backwaters keep going left until you see *Kimberleyland* in front of you. This area of everglades is a real delight to paddle, especially in the early morning and evening.

You can do this trip in a small tinnie. Once a year the locals even have a *Dam to Dam Dinghy Race* where they race down the river in a variety of craft.

The ***Canoe Trek*** detailed below is based on a map that was published by the WA Department of Sport and Recreation, with many of our own additions. Site numbers 1 to 30 refer to points marked on our map ***Kununurra Area & Ord River Canoe Trail***, detailed in the chapter, The *Eastern Kimberley,* page 109.

Downriver from *Lake Kununurra* to **Ivanhoe Crossing** is good canoeing and boating. Further downstream the river really becomes boating only territory. Remember the closer you get to the sea the more likely you are to see **Salt-water Crocodiles**. We'd hate to see a big one when we are in a canoe. Get our drift!

For more information on canoeing down the Ord, or hiring your own canoe, or even joining one of the tour operators who run canoe trips, contact the following in Kununurra.

Big Waters Kimberley Canoe Safaris & Go Wild Adventure Tours.

For full address, phone contact details, etc, see the chapter, The *Eastern Kimberley,* page 117.

EXPLORING THE ORD RIVER

ORD RIVER CANOE TREK

No.		
1	*0.0*	***Ord River Dam Wall****. Launching spot for canoes 100 metres downstream on left, just upriver from picnic grounds.*
2	*1.0*	*Banks heavily vegetated with Paperbark trees and Pandanus Palms. Cave visible in the hills on the right.*
3	*1.5*	*Hill on the left is home for some Cycad Palms.*
4	*3.0*	*Paperbarks hug the bank as the river narrows.*
5	*4.0*	*River widens.*
6	*5.0*	*Bank along this stretch lined with Kebungi Reed. River narrows.*
7	*6.0*	*Veer right of the trees in the water.*
8	*7.0*	*Small creek on left.*
9	*9.0*	*Two small creeks enter Ord on left. Surrounded by Coolibah trees and River Gums it makes a pleasant spot for a break.*
10	*9.2*	*Creek on left.*
11	*11.0*	*Creek on left and Cycad Palms on hill to the left.*
12	*12.0*	*River narrows and divides with Coolibahs on the righthand bend. Take the righthand channel.*
13	*13.0*	*Dead paperbarks just before a bend in the river.*
14	*15.5*	*Begin to enter the spectacular* ***Carlton Gorge****.*
15	*16.0*	*Reasonable camp sites on lefthand bank, before second bluff. There is another camp site - the last in the gorge, just after the second bluff.*
16	*23.5*	*Major creek on left. You'll find a good camp site at this junction with* ***Pelican Rock*** *just ahead.*
17	*25.5*	*Large Boab on the right.*
18	*26.5*	*Dead trees in the middle of the river and small creek on left.*
19	*30.0*	*'****The Fig Tree****' or '****The Swimming Pool****' on left situated on a wide pool on bend in river with* ***Echo Point*** *visible just ahead. Good camp site.*
20	*32.0*	***Spillway Creek*** *joins the river on the right. There are some good camp spots available just a short distance up this creek. From here the river widens.*
21	*33.0*	*Small cliffs. Upper reaches of Lake Kununurra begin soon after this point.*
22	*42.5*	*Backwater of '****everglade****' area to the right.*
23	*43.5*	***Packsaddle Pump Station*** *on the left. Crossing Falls settlement on right. Small jetty/landing gives access to the settlement. Possible pickup point.*
24	*48.0*	***Everglades*** *area and* ***Elephant Rock*** *on right.*
25	*50.0*	*Race Club buildings on right.*
26	*52.0*	*Everglades area on right with access to KimberleyLand Caravan Park. It's difficult to find your way though if you don't know the area.*
27	*53.0*	***Kona Caravan Park*** *and Pump Station on right.*
28	*55.0*	*Everglades area on left.* ***Ski club*** *and* ***Yacht club*** *on right with boat ramp a short distance further down. Pickup point.*
29	*55.5*	***Ord River Diversion Dam****. During the wet season or after heavy rain use extreme caution as the Diversion Dam gates can open automatically.*

GEIKIE GORGE

Geikie Gorge on the Fitzroy River, offers excellent boating and canoeing, however there are a number of restrictions placed on boat and canoe owners by the National Parks. See the chapter, *Derby to Fitzroy Crossing*, page 200, for more information.

THE FITZROY RIVER

The mighty Fitzroy offers many long waterholes for canoeing or boating. Most people visit these places for fishing, but there's more than just fishing along these stretches. The bird and animal life will keep any nature lover fully engrossed. Canoeists however must also be aware that Salt-water Crocodiles inhabit this river.

THE GREAT GORGES

Mornington Wilderness Camp, ph: (08) 9191 7046, gives access to Dimond Gorge where the Fitzroy River cuts its way through the King Leopold Ranges. You can hire a canoe or boat from the Camp and enjoy yourself for a day or a week. For more details see our chapter, *The Tablelands Track, page 178*. Web site: **www.australianwildlife.org/mornington4.asp**.

DOWNSTREAM FROM FITZROY CROSSING

Remember, downstream from Fitzroy Crossing you need a permit from the Dept. of Agriculture in Derby (see page 189) before you can enter any of the land along the river. You also need permission from the land owner. While it's a pretty long paddle from Fitzroy Crossing down to the mouth, there is access to the river at Myroodah Crossing, much further downstream. It would make a good run from here to the Willare Bridge – river heights being suitable of course!

Use caution if paddling this section of the river as it is definitely Salt-water Crocodile territory. See our chapter, Derby to Fitzroy Crossing, for more details.

TERRY BOLAND – KIMBERLEY CANOEIST

Probably the most experienced canoeist as far as the Kimberley region goes is Terry Bolland, a Perth based canoe instructor and owner of Paddle Sports business 'Canoeing Downunder'.

In 1982 he set out on a 100 day solo trip from Broome paddling north along the coast in a Nordkapp Sea Kayak to Cape Leveque across the top of King Sound to Collier Bay. Chased by crocs a couple of times he passed across the entrance to Walcott Inlet pushing north along the coast to Brecknock Harbour and entering the St George Basin, paddling up the Prince Regent River to near King's Cascade, where he was again chased by a big croc. He continued north along the coast finally ending his trip at Port Warrender.

In 1983 he was back again, this time to paddle his kayak from Wyndham to Port Warrender, this time taking 54 days and once again on his own.

In 1985 he led a trip down the Drysdale and Carson Rivers and in 1987 he was back at sea with a mate paddling north from Derby. This trip took him to Hanover Bay where he retraced George Grey's 1838 expedition inland before returning to his kayak and paddling south to Broome.

In 1988 with a couple of mates, he cycled, walked, ran and canoed his way 3500km from Broome to Derby, onwards to Windjana Gorge, Fitzroy Crossing, Halls Creek, and finally to Wyndham. From there he headed bush, overland to Forrest River and north to the coast crossing the great rivers of the Berkeley and King George before arriving at Kalumburu. From there it was to the Mitchell Plateau and the remote western coast around the Moran River mouth, before cycling to Derby and finishing off with a run to Broome!

Want to know more about canoeing the Kimberley, or read more of Terry's canoeing exploits, then check out his web site:

www.canoeingdownunder.com.au/

LAKE GLADSTONE

This small natural lake is found close to the Hann River just north of the Tablelands Track, east of Mt House station. It's a pretty shallow lake but makes for a pleasant spot to paddle a canoe. The birdlife is great. Travellers wishing to stop and camp and explore around the lake should obtain permission from Mt House Station beforehand. See our chapter, *The Tablelands Track*, page 178, for more detail.

JACK'S WATERHOLE

Located on the *Durack River*, Jack's Waterhole and the station is presently closed to travellers.

At present there are no facilities or camping at Durack River. Should it reopen, the fishing is good and the birdlife superb. For more information contact Home Valley Station and see our chapter, *The Gibb River Road*, page 155, for more detail.

CHAMBERLAIN GORGE

This spectacular gorge is on the river of the same name on El Questro Station. Camping is allowed (fee payable) and the highlight of a camp here is to paddle or take a small boat up the gorge to the far end. The scenery is superb, the fishing good and there is some Aboriginal art at the far end.

Canoeists be aware that Salt-water Crocodiles have been known to frequent this stretch of water. See the chapter, *The Gibb River Road*, page 154, for more detail.

PENTECOST RIVER / WEST ARM CAMBRIDGE GULF

Downriver from where the Gibb River Road crosses the *Pentecost River* there is ample opportunity for boating, as there is along the whole of the Cambridge Gulf.

Wyndham sports a boat ramp for easy access to the sea. The fishing is good, but watch the tides and don't venture near the area called 'The Gut' – a narrow constriction in the western arm of Cambridge Gulf.

We wouldn't go canoeing around here! Besides the dangerous tides, there are plenty of Salt-water Crocodiles around.

The Delights of Kimberley Canoeing

In 1985 Terry Bolland lead a small group of canoeists down the Drysdale River. In the end they walked out but not before many tough days of paddling and dragging their canoes.

On day 5 of their trip in a place they called Pandanus Palm Alley they had some fun ...

"Good progress was made on a long pool that morning. After another portage the pool continued, until the river suddenly stopped at a sandy beach. We couldn't believe it, the water had disappeared! It seemed impossible that we could lose a river, but we did. We walked around in all directions crossing several dried up gullies until we came to a narrow stretch of stagnant water thickly lined with pandanus palms. It was hard to believe that this piece of stagnant water was the river, but we had no choice but to try it.

The task of carrying our kayaks 150 metres across to the channel, up and down slimy, muddy gullies was a major exercise in itself. The water had filtered through the palms a few metres before the river stopped. This was a constant problem, the palms allowed water to pass but their roots were too thick to negotiate our kayaks through."

Extracted with kind permission from Terry Bolland's book, Kimberley Challenge.

DERBY

Derby has a boat ramp near the jetty that gives good access (when the tide is in) to King Sound. Once again remember the tide and don't venture too far unless you're properly equipped. This isn't the place for canoeing either!

BROOME

There are plenty of boating opportunities (normally for fishing) around Broome. See the chapter, *Broome and Its Surrounds*, page 205.

THE UNTOUCHED RIVERS

Of all the other rivers in the Kimberley only a few have ever been paddled – and in each case only once or twice before.

In the early 1980s Malcolm Douglas took a canoe down the *Prince Regent River*, shooting a film along the way.

In 1985 Terry Bolland led a small canoe group that spent much of their time walking down the *Drysdale River* from near Drysdale Station to a point where they crossed to the *Carson River* and walked down to just past Carson River Station. They airlifted their kayaks out at a later date.

Two years later, Project Raleigh navigated the Drysdale in rubber boats.

In 1993 Peter Treseder and a small group walked and paddled rafts down the *Manning* and *Isdell Rivers*, and then back up the *Charnley River* to their start point at Mt Elizabeth Station.

Boating or canoeing, there are some great spots in the Kimberley to explore.

The many other rivers remain untouched. The Durack, King George, King Edward, Mitchell and many others await the adventurous and well equipped paddler.

THE COAST

North of Derby is a great stretch of uninhabited coastline. Power boats and yachts do make the run, but it needs a fairly large boat, well equipped and with people who have the experience to handle the ferocious conditions of this coast. Small tinnies and canoes are definitely out, unless you are in the Terry Bolland league of adventurers!

Of Whirlpools and Tidal Rips

In 1987 Terry Bolland set out on his third major sea kayaking trip, this time from Broome, up along the Dampier Peninsula coast, across King Sound, passed Koolan Island to Walcott Inlet and beyond. Near Walcott Inlet he and his partner nearly met disaster. The following account is of just one of the many hazards that will be met when paddling the wild Kimberley coast.

".... it wasn't long before we reached the swift tidal stream rushing out of Walcott Inlet. We entered the fast running current that was riddled with eddies, boils and whirlpools. The sun had just risen giving us glowing glimpses of the fiery rays trying to escape from behind the clouds. We moved across the current carefully, with our rudders in full action trying to control our craft. A large boil started to form. It's sides opened up like a developing earthquake. It became bigger and started to erupt. The boiling water lifted at least a metre above the rest of the sea. I was struggling to prevent myself from being dragged into it, but it subsided in the nick of time.

Without warning another formed, first the outside crater and the hole and then the eruption. We seemed surrounded as one more formed on my right side. Ken was directly in it's path. There would be no chance of him keeping upright in such a destructive force of water so he desperately back paddled to escape its violent eruptions. Relief was in sight as we escaped the powerful tidal effects, but in the long days ahead the turbulent seas produced many more anxious moments.

What a pleasure it was when we surfed on a following sea into the pearling settlement of Kuri Bay. Nothing could please us more than to have a short rest, collect our food packs and receive the hospitality of the management."

Extracted with kind permission from Terry Bolland's book, Kimberley Challenge.

FISHING IN THE KIMBERLEY

GENERAL

Fishing is one of the favourite pastimes of visitors to the Kimberley. While both freshwater and sea fishing are better than reasonable, a lack of access to many places means most travellers are limited in their choice of places to go. For those with the time and inclination to reach some of the more out of the way places, the Kimberley can be a fishing paradise. Big barra abound in many of the tidal rivers, while further upstream Sooty Grunters and big Forktail Catfish can provide plenty of sport.

Along the coast and in the estuaries fish such as Mangrove Jack can provide dynamite action, while further out Spanish Mackerel and a host of other open water pelagics can put on a great show. Reef fishing for Coral Trout and other delectables can also be had on the offshore reefs.

MORE INFORMATION ON FISHING THE KIMBERLEY

Guides & Pamphlets

The guidelines and regulations are constantly changing. Fishermen should contact the Department of Fisheries of WA for current fishing rules. The Dept also publishes a range of excellent booklets, and the ***Recreational Fishing Guide – Pilbara/Kimberley Region*** covers all you need to know and can be download direct from their web site: **www.fish.wa.gov.au/.**
If you have any questions or concerns about fishing, call or write to the Dept of Fisheries.

Internet

Also on the internet you will get heaps of fishing info, as well as details on charter boat operators, fishing safari operators and the like. Regular reports on the fishing scene in the Kimberley are also featured. A couple of the best sites to visit are ***Fishing Western Australia***, at, **www.fishingwa.com**, and *Fishnet*, at, **www.fishnet.com.au**.

FISHING REGULATIONS

RECREATIONAL FISHING LICENCES

Recreational licences are not required for prawning, crabbing or saltwater angling in Western Australia at the present time. However gear restrictions, bag limits, size limits and seasons may still apply.

You must have a Recreational Fishing Licence from the Dept of Fisheries if you wish to **net** fish (gill net, haul net or throw net) or take **Rock Lobsters**, **Abalone** or **Marron**, as well as **Freshwater Angling**.

Licenses are valid for 12 months from the date the licence is issued.

The following are particularly relevant for those fishing in the Kimberley region –

- **Rock Lobster fishing – Licence cost $31**
- **Net fishing (gill, haul & throw) – Licence cost $26**

You may apply for a licence from any Dept of Fisheries office, and Licence application forms can also be obtained from Australia Post outlets. You can also vary your existing licence or renew your licence on line at: **www.fish.wa.gov.au/**.

A Gear Registration Number for the identification of rock lobster pots and fishing nets will be issued with each Recreational Fishing Licence.

The following guidelines on fishing in Kimberley waters should help you on your fishing forays. **However, we would suggest that you contact the Dept of Fishers for further details and copies of the excellent guides and pamphlets that they produce**.

Department of Fisheries of WA
3rd Floor, The Atrium
168-170 St George's Terrace
Perth WA 6000
Ph: (08) 9482 7333
Fax: (08) 9482 7389
Email: headoffice@fish.wa.go.au
Web: **www.fish.wa.gov.au/**
Locked Bag 39
Cloisters Square
Perth WA 6850

Department of Fisheries of WA
Broome Regional Office,
401 Port Dve,
Broome, WA, 6725.
Ph: (08) 9193 8600
Fax: (08) 9193 8699.

If you observe illegal fishing or fish sales, please call the Dept of Fisheries on the 24 hour Fishwatch number:
1800 815 507

Fishing off the coast around Kalumburu.

SALE OF FISH

It is illegal for recreational fishers to sell any of their catch.

LEGAL FISHING GEAR

The following fishing gear can be used –

- Lines & hooks – limit to maximum of three hooks or three gangs of hooks per line.
- Shore based recreational anglers may use a maximum of two fishing lines.
- Rods & lines must be attended.

ILLEGAL FISHING GEAR

The following fishing methods are banned –

- Unattended lines, either on boat or shore.
- Explosives, firearms, fish poisons or jagging.
- Nets using finer than 6kg (0.35mm diameter) monofilament line.
- Crab and cobbler pots.
- Fish traps and dredges.
- It is illegal for recreational fishers to use commercial fishing gear such as purse-seine nets, trawls, longlines, droplines, etc.

NETTING

A licence is required to use net fish – gill, haul and throw.

Recreational throw netting is permitted in all ocean waters not specifically closed to netting and all inland waters of the Pilbara/Kimberley region for the taking of cherabin and baitfish.

Recreational set and haul netting is prohibited in all waters of the Pilbara/Kimberley region, with the exception of haul netting in the waters of the Dampier Archipelago (between Cape Preston and Cape Lambert), with restrictions.

Please refer to the ***Recreational Net Fishing Guide*** available from the Department's web site for all the info on net fishing.

SPEARFISHING

Spearfishing in all rivers, dams and tributaries is prohibited, with the exception of estuarine cobbler, which may be taken by hand spears only.

Free-diving spearfishing is generally permitted in ocean waters, except marine parks and reserves where all types of fishing is often prohibited.

BARRAMUNDI

Special bag limits and regulations have been set for Barramundi:

- Bag limit – 2 legal-size fish per angler.
- Minimum legal size: 550 mm (this applies in all waters across the state). Note: A maximum size limit of 800 mm applies in both the Ord River and King Sound – Fitzroy River areas.
- A person may only fish for barramundi by means of a single rod and reel or a single hand line.

There are also three special BARRAMUNDI CONSERVATIONAL AREAS where different rules apply. These are:

- **Ord River**
  - Maximum size limit of 800 mm.
  - Bag & Possession limit of one (1) legal sized Barramundi per person per day. This includes the lower section of Dunham River which flows into the Ord River, and the Ord River all the way to the Cambridge Gulf.
  - No filleting on water – all barramundi must be landed whole.
- **Fitzroy River & King Sound**
  - Maximum size limit of 800 mm (all waters upstream of 17º 27' South latitude – lower reach of King Sound).
  - Bag & Possession limit of two (2) applies per person per day.
  - No filleting on water – all barramundi must be landed whole.
- **Broome Area**
  - Minimum legal size 550 mm.
  - Daily bag limit of one (1) legal-sized barramundi per person per day. This applies to all waters from Cunningham Point (east of Cape Leveque) to 19º South latitude (northern end of Eighty Mile Beach).
  - Bag & Possession limit of two (2) applies.

Please refer to the ***Recreational Fishing Guide – Pilbara/Kimberley Region*** available from the Department's web site for all the info barramundi fishing.

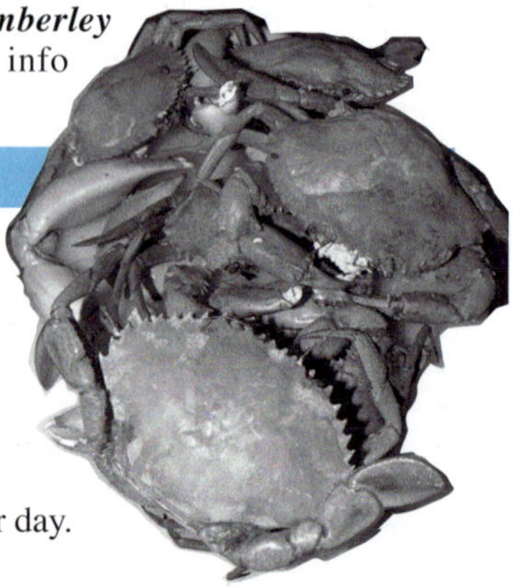

CRABS

No licence is needed to fish for swimmer or mud crabs.

BLUE CRAB (SWIMMER)

- Minimum legal size 127mm (carapace).
- Bag limit - 20 crabs per person/per day. Boat limit 40.

MUD CRABS – GREEN AND BROWN

- Minimum legal size 150 mm Green/120 mm Brown (carapace).
- A combined bag limit of 5 green/brown mud crabs per person per day.

- A combined boat limit of 10 mud crabs (all species combined) may be carried or held aboard a vessel. A separate boat limit of 20 applies to the waters of King Sound and its tributaries.

The following regulations apply to both Green and Brown Mud Crabs –

- It is legal to use drop nets, scoop nets and non-piercing metal hooks to catch mud crabs.
- Not more than 10 drop nets per person or 10 drops nets per boat, regardless of how many people are on board the vessel.
- Drop nets must not exceed 1.5m in diameter.
- Scoop nets must be constructed of rigid mesh with an internal diameter of no bigger than 375mm.
- Metal hooks must not be capable of piercing the crab and are used held in the hand.
- Spawning or berried females and undersized crabs not to be taken – they must be returned immediately to the water.
- **It is illegal to use crab traps, pots or any dilly nets which entangle the catch. These are strictly prohibited in WA waters.**

ORNATE (TROPICAL) ROCK LOBSTER

A **Recreational Fishing Licence required**. This licence allows fishers to catch legal sized lobsters by diving or potting and is valid from 12 months from date of issue.

- **Minimum legal size (Tropical Cray) 76 mm carapace length**. Undersize crays must be returned to the water immediately. (No maximum.)
- **A daily bag limit is 8 lobsters per day per licensee** (any specie). If there is more than one licence holder on a boat, you may carry no more than 16 lobsters per day/per boat. Special bag limits may apply in marine conservation areas.
- **Bag limits for waters to the east of 114°50' east** longitude (north of Ashburton River). Combined bag limit of 4 (all species), with a possession limit of 2 days bag limit outside permanent place of residence. Within this limit you may have a maximum of 2 Ornate (painted) and 2 Western Rock Lobster – boat limit of 8 (all species).
- **Spawning or berried females not to be taken** – they must be returned within 5 mins of capture to the water.
- Maximum number of pots per licensee – 2. Minimum escape gaps must be at least 54 mm high and 305mm wide. You must brand your floats and pots with your gear ID number.
- Closed season: **No closed season applies** for painted or green tropical rock lobsters north of 21°44'S latitude (the line runs about one nautical mile south of South Muiron Island near the Exmouth Peninsula).
- Divers may only catch lobster by hand, or by using a hand-held snare or blunt crook. Spears and similar devices that puncture or damage the lobster are illegal.
- The tail fan must be clipped (the hole must be more than 10mm wide) within 5 minutes of taking the lobster out of the water and Lobsters must be kept whole until you get them home.

Special restrictions apply to the catching of tropical rock lobsters as well as haul netting in the Marine Conservation Area which exists within the Dampier Archipelago between Cape Preston and Cape Lambert..

> ***Hide Bait Banned from Recreational & Commercial Rock Lobster Fisheries***
>
> *A total ban on the use of hide baits in both the commercial and recreational rock lobster fisheries has been introduced after concerns about threats to overseas markets.*
>
> *The ban extends to both commercial and recreational fishers to ensure that no rock lobster taken by a commercial operator has previously been exposed to bovine, hide or hair-covered baits.*

Please refer to the ***Recreational Fishing Guide – Pilbara/Kimberley Region*** available from the Department's web site for more information on other regulations pertaining to Western and Tropical Rock Lobster.

PRAWNS – KING AND SCHOOL

- No licence required.
- Bag limit – 9 litres (approx 1 standard plastic bucket) per fisher/per day.
- No minimum legal size applies.
- Closed prawning seasons do not apply in the Kimberley.

CHERABIN

- No licence required.
- Bag limit – 9 litres (approx 1 standard plastic bucket) per person/per day.

MOLLUSCS AND OTHER REEF ANIMALS

- No licence required.

Cockles, Pipis, Clams and Other Edible Molluscs

- Bag limit – 2 litres per person/per day.

Mussels

- Bag Limit – 9 litres per person/per day.

Oysters

- Bag Limit – 9 litres per person/per day.

Razorfish

- Bag Limit – 20 per person/per day.

Sea Urchins

- A daily bag limit of 20 per person/per day.

Squid, Octopus, Cuttlefish – Combined

- A combined bag limit of 15 per person/per day.
- Boat limit of 30.

All other species of edible mollusc not mentioned – Combined

- A combined bag limit of 2 litres person/per day.
- **Trochus – M**inimum legal size 65mm.

NET FISHING, TRAP FISHING, LONGLINES

Haul & Set Netting

All waters of the Pilbara/Kimberley region are closed to haul and set netting at all times with the exception of haul netting in the waters of Dampier Archipelago (see the map on the *Recreational Net Fishing* guide from the Dept of Fisheries).

Throw Netting

Throw nets are permitted in all inland waters of the Kimberley region north and east of Onslow for the take of cherabin and baitfish of the sardine, bony herring, hardyhead, anchovy, mullet and garfish families

- **A Recreational Fishing Licence is required** for net fishing, whether that is a set (gill) net, cast (or throw) net or haul net.
- Only **one net** can be used by a person at a time, and you are required to stay with your net at all times.
- The **daily bag and size limits** of fish caught by set, haul and cast netting, where permitted, are the same as for recreational angling.
- A few fish species, such as some baitfish, do not currently have daily bag and size limits.
- There are a number of fish species that recreational net fishermen are **forbidden** to catch, or attempt to catch, which include **Barramundi** and **Blue Swimmer Crab**.

Restrictions on types, sizes, meshes and closed or restricted areas are too numerous to publish here. Refer to the Dept of Fisheries in Perth or their Broome office for further information, and a copy of their booklet, *Recreational Net Fishing*, or check out their web site:

www.fish.gov.au

OTHER RULES AND REGULATIONS

Obstruction of Fisheries Officers

The obstruction of any Fisheries Officer acting in the course of his duty, the refusal to produce a licence or give a name and address, or the giving of a false name and address are serious offenses under the Fisheries Act and can lead to heavy fines and, in some cases, imprisonment.

Identification of Fisheries Officers

All Fisheries Officers carry an appointment authority and identification card. Police officers are also Fisheries Officers.

COASTAL DATA CENTRE - TIDAL PREDICTIONS

Part of the Dept of Planning & Infrastructure, the Coastal Data Centre can give you predictions of the time of high and low waters for every day of the year and waves for the Kimberley. Check out their web site:

www.dpi.wa.gov.au/imarine/coastaldata

Fishing on the lower Ord River.

SPECIES BAG POSSESSION LIMITS

There is a limit on the quantity of recreationally-caught finfish you may possess in WA. Daily bag limits, for specific groups of fish that a person may take in any 24 hour period, have been set by the Department of Fisheries and apply throughout Western Australia, unless other limits for special areas, such as Marine Parks and for the special Barramundi Conservational Areas, have been specified.

Minimum legal size limits also apply.

Remember, only someone actively fishing, not just watching, is entitled to a bag limit.

Each person may have a maximum of:

20 kilos of fillets or pieces of fish; or

10 kg of fillets or pieces of fish plus one day's bag limit of whole fish; or

Two days' bag limit of whole fish.

These limits only apply to finfish. For full details check the Dept of Fisheries web site or their *'Recreational Fishing Guide'* brochure.

PROCESSING YOUR CATCH AT SEA

The Dept of Fisheries has divided fish into a number of categories and the rules regarding processing of your catch at sea vary, depending on the type of fish caught *(see table below)*. We've detailed only a brief summary, for full details check the Dept of Fisheries web site or their *'Recreational Fishing Guide'* brochure.

Category One *(highest risk)* **and Two fish** *(medium risk)* can be filleted or trunked at sea provided the fillet/trunk length is longer than 30cm and the skin and scales are attached.

Category Three fish *(low risk)* may be filleted or trunked at sea provided the skin is attached to the fillet/trunk. A minimum fillet length does not apply.

An angler who has been at sea, or staying on any island, for more than one day, may accumulate up to the possession limit of whole (or trunked) fish or filleted fish.

TRANSPORTING & STORING YOUR FISH

There are strict rules on all recreationally-caught fish which are being transported or stored and they must be packaged and labelled correctly. *For full details check the Dept of Fisheries web site or their 'Recreational Fishing Guide' brochure.*

SAFETY

Fishing from the rocks, or from small craft fishing inshore, can be hazardous. Don't forget, many areas of the Kimberley record a tidal rise and fall of up to and over 10 metres during King Tides. Places such as the flat sandy mouth of the Fitzroy River are particularly noteworthy and dangerous. The tide there can come in nearly faster than you can run! It's unbelievable!!

Such big tides can produce tidal currents exceeding 8 knots (faster than a small tinnie and outboard) and, in places, dramatic waterfalls off the edge of reefs, as well as standing waves and whirlpools. The area around the mouth of the Prince Regent River is especially noted for these dramatic occurrences.

Volunteer Sea Rescue Groups use VHF channels 16 and 67, 27MHz channel 88 and HF channel 2182.

Before you leave, tell someone about your boating plans and always let them know when you return. Also notify them immediately if your plans change..

CATEGORY ONE – HIGHEST RISK

Mixed daily bag limit of 7 per angler.

Fish	Minimum Legal Size (mm)	Bag Limit
Amberjack / Yellowtail Kingfish / Samson fish – combined	600	2
Barramundi *(see page 246 for details)*		
Billfish (sailfish, swordfish, marlins)	N/A	1
Cobia	750	2
Cods – combined (no more than 2 Rankin, estuary or Malar cod		4
Cods over 1000 mm in length or 38kg are protected.	Estuary 400	
Coral Trout or coronation trout combined when taken north of the De Grey River	Coral - 450	1
Emperors and seabream - combined (including nor' west snapper and Robinson's seabream.	Spangled - 410 Blue-lined (black snapper - 320 Other emperors - 280	4
Mackerel – Shark	500	4
Mackerel – Spanish, broad-barred	750	2
Mackerel – Spanish, narrow-barred	900	2
Mackerel – wahoo	900	2
Mahi Mahi (dolphinfish)	500	4

Category One – HIGHEST RISK cont'd ...

Fish	Minimum Legal Size (mm)	Bag Limit
Mangrove Jack	300	2
Northern Mulloway	700	2
Red emperor	410	2
Sharks and rays - combined (all species except Whale Shark and Great White Shark)	N/A	2
Scarlet (saddle tail) and crimson sea perch - combined	N/A	4
Threadfin salmon - giant	450	2
Tripletail	300	1
Tuna - southern & northern bluefin, yellowfin, bigeye & dogfish	N/A	2
Wrasse (including blue bone, baldchin, groper & tuskfish)	Baldchin groper, blackspot & blue tuskfish - 400	2

CATEGORY TWO – MEDIUM RISK

Mixed daily bag limit of 16 per angler.

Fish	Minimum Legal Size (mm)	Bag Limit
Barracuda	N/A	4
Bream - north-west black and yellowfin - combined	North-west - 250 Yellowfin - 350	8
Catfish - all species - combined	N/A	8
Dart	N/A	8
Javelinfish & Sweetlips	300	8
Mackerel - Queensland school & spotted - combined	500	4
Queenfish	N/A	4
Snooty grunter	250	8
Threadfin salmon - all species other than giant threadfin salmon	N/A	4
Trevally combined	N/A	4
Tropical sea perch and snappers - other *Lutjanus* spp. including fingermark, Chinaman fish and job fish - combined	Stripey sea perch & fingermark - 300	4

CATEGORY THREE – LOW RISK

Mixed daily bag limit of 40 per angler.

Fish	Bag Limit
Garfish Longtom Milkfish Mullet, sea and yellow-eye Whiting	You can only take a combined maximum of 40 Category Three fish. No size limits apply.

All other unlisted species of fish in the *Recreational Fishing Guide* (except baitfish and feral freshwater species).

Baitfish: A combined daily bag limit of 9 litres applies to baitfish of the sardine, anchovy and hardyhead families.

PROTECTED SPECIES

The following species are totally protected –

Potato cod;
Humphead Maori wrasse;
Queensland groper;
Sawfish (all species);
Speartooth shark;
Great white shark
Grey nurse shark
Whale shark
Leafy Seadragon
Corals

FISHING

MARINE CONSERVATION AREAS

Rowley Shoals

These reefs located north-west of Broome are pristine coral atolls which have great conservation value. Made up of a number of separate reefs, Imperiuse and Clerke Reefs are Marine Parks, while Mermaid Reef is a Commonwealth Marine Nature Reserve.

All shellfish, corals, cods, wrasse, gropers and coral trout are protected within 1.6 km of the lagoons. For more information about Rowley Shoals see the chapter, *National Parks*

Dampier Archipleago

A Marine Conservation Area exists within the Dampier Archipelago between Cape Preston and Cape Lambert. **Special restrictions apply to the catching of tropical rock lobsters as well as haul netting.** Contact the local Dept of Fisheries office for more details.

Salt-water Crocodile Warning

Don't forget Salt-water Crocodiles! They are all along the coast and inhabit all the major rivers, its beaches, mangroves, estuaries and around the islands, so please take heed of any warning signs and be aware of their possible presence. See our chapter, Safety and Medical Aspects, for more information on crocodiles. Don't become lunch for a reptile!

THE SOUGHT AFTER FISH

BARRAMUNDI

There is probably no better known tropical fish than the famed barra. While the WA angling record is only around 15 kg, we know for a fact that a lot bigger have been caught and the Kimberley is the place. Across the border in the Northern Territory fish up to 40 kg have been landed, so there is no reason why the Kimberley coast can't and won't produce fish of that calibre.

It is important to note that there are **special bag limits and regulations for Barramundi** in the **Ord River, Fitzroy River-King Sound,** and **Broome Area**. For more details see page 246.

Best Baits and Rigs

In the Kimberley, as elsewhere, live baiting with small fish is regarded by those in the know to be the best method of getting into the big ones.

While live baits may be considered the best way of catching barra, most travelling fishermen prefer to use artificial lures. Don't forget barra are ambush feeders, so basically everything from surface poppers to chrome spoons and rubber jig-heads are all in the running. Talk to the locals and the fishing stores in the towns for the best ones to have.

Everything from heavy hand lines to sturdy bait casters, or threadline reels, can be used to fish for barra, but you should use a short wire trace to stop the fish hacking through the line.

Best Time

Without a doubt, the best time to catch a barra is during the Wet season, with the prime time early in the Wet, and even though the weather is hot, the fishing is fantastic. From March to early June the fishing can also be spectacular, depending on the length and severity of the Wet season. During the Dry (May to November), the barra may have gone off the bite completely. At this time of the year the best chance for a fish is in the estuaries of the larger rivers.

During the Wet, barra are easier to catch and can be caught well upstream – as long as they have access to the sea! Inland, (such as Geikie Gorge), the fish prefer deep pools and hide near the banks under overhangs or around snags and collapsed trees.

Barra caught in saltwater tend to be tastier and have a firmer flesh with less fat than those taken from freshwater. No matter which though, both taste great and fight well. Have fun!

SOOTY GRUNTERS

There are at least four species of fish that are commonly called 'Sooty Grunters' (sometimes Black Bream) – all are closely related and provide equal sport for their size.

Growing to around 2 kg maximum, sootys can be found virtually in any stream or waterhole throughout the region. Those living in fast flowing water tend to take a bait or lure more readily than those in deeper, stiller water and put up a better fight to boot.

Best Baits

Sootys take a wide variety of bait, including red meat, insects, shrimps and worms. They are also frequently hooked on a whole host of lures, including the wobbling-minnow type and surface-popper varieties.Most of the grunter group of fish are good eating, with the quality improving if the fish is bled and cleaned properly.

CATFISH

Catfish are easily caught with just about any sort of bait. They can grow larger than 30 kg, so you'll need a heavy line to catch them. Catfish make a good table fish, but are difficult to skin and prepare because of three large spines which can inflict a painful wound.

LONGTOM

These are a long and slender fish and for their small size and are a good sporting fish. They are excellent to eat while fresh and grow to about 60 to 70 cm long and a weight of up to 1 kg.

MULLET

Mullet are mainly used for strip baits and a cast net is the most widely used method of catching these fish. Attaining a length of 50 cm, they are best cooked on a BBQ if you decide to eat them. Catching them on a line requires a very small hook, some slime from river reeds, bread, mincemeat or something similar. Their eating qualities aren't very high.

STRIPIES

These little fish make excellent bait for big Black Bream, Barramundi and Catfish and are easy to catch with a cast net if you put some red meat into the water to concentrate the fish in one spot. They are extremely abundant in all freshwater streams throughout the Kimberley.

TARPON

Growing to about 3 kg, this fish is the power house of freshwater fishes. Once hooked, it leaps and tail walks giving more than an adequate display for its relatively small size. However, they are very bland to eat.

THREADFIN SALMON

There are three species of fish that are generally classified under the term Threadfin Salmon. Growing up to over 25 kg in weight, they are an excellent fighting fish and make great eating. Threadfin Salmon love steaks (crosswise slabs) of bony bream or wolf herring. These fish are only caught in saltwater, but the method of capture is similar to that of the Barramundi. When preparing Salmon for the table, take a rough fillet off both sides, leaving a good amount of meat on the backbone. The sweetest meat is also next to the backbone, so cook that as well.

FISHING FOR OTHER SPECIES

There are a whole host of other fish to delight recreational fishermen, so we'll only mention a few here and what we've heard or experienced to be the best bait.

Bluebone Groper go crazy over hermit crabs.

North-west Snapper have a definite preference for fresh squid.

Queenfish and the many species of trevally have a preference for chrome spinners or surface popper type lures.

WHERE THE ACTION IS

BROOME'S FISHING SPOTS

Situated on Roebuck Bay, Broome has some excellent fishing around it and in recent years has gained acclaim as one of the most prolific sailfish grounds in the world. The Broome Sailfish Tournament began in 1988, while in 1994 533 Sailfish and three Marlin were tagged and released by just 171 anglers fishing from 51 boats! Contact the *Broome Visitor Centre* for details and dates on fishing events and competitions.

For those not into such glamour fish, Broome can still turn on some great action with a variety of reef fish, giant pelagics and lure munching stream dwellers. For those with a small tinnie, or those people who just dangle a line from shore or wharf, Broome has much to offer.

Boat fishing will generally produce better fish, but care should be taken with the tides and the tidal rips generated by the large rise and fall. Around Broome the tidal movement ranges from – 0.6 low to 9.7 metres high, so take care – especially with vehicles on the beach!

Boat ramps are located at Town Beach and Entrance Point.

See our chapter, *Broome and Surrounds*, to give you detailed information on access to the areas listed below.

Roebuck Bay is probably best known for its catches of Threadfin Salmon. May to August are the peak salmon months and salmon are best taken on 'making' spring tides at the mouth of creeks in little more than a metre of water. Skipjack appear about June, with Trevally being common throughout the year. Queenfish, catfish and shark can also be caught in this area.

The **Jetty** has an Australian wide reputation for its great fishing. The main fish are Queenfish, Trevally and Bluebone Groper, with the occasional Mulloway, Spanish Mackerel, Red Emperor, Coral Cod and Barracuda. About 150 metres out from the jetty the *Big Hole* is a top spot for big Black Dufish.

Entrance Point to Buccaneer Rock can produce good catches of Whiting, Mullet, Flathead, Catfish, the occasional Barra and of course, Salmon. The *Roebuck Deep*, a channel that parallels the coast about 1.5 km south-west of Entrance Point, is a good spot for Black Dufish, shark and Fingermark.

Dampier Creek is probably better known for its mud crabs, but they are not as plentiful as they once were. 'Drop Nets' are probably the best way to crab this creek, as the deep mud banks make hooking the crabs particularly adventurous. Don't forget that both this creek and Crab Creek are closed to set netting.

Fishermen's Bend to *Crab Creek* is a popular area, particularly the stretch of coast back from Crab Creek to Dog Rock. Salmon, Sharks, Mullet, Skipjack, Bream and the occasional Mulloway make this area very productive. There are plenty of 'muddies' when the tide is out.

Entrance Point to Reddell Beach and Gantheaume Point offers top rock or reef fishing for a host of species, especially an hour either side of high tide. The area takes a heavy toll on gear and, with tidal currents of 6 to 8 knots, can be dangerous for the unwary boat fisherman.

Willie Creek, about 20 km north of Broome, produces good catches of Trevally, Barracuda, Bream, Cod, Flathead, Salmon, the occasional Mangrove Jack and Barra. Best fished during neap tide or on the slack water. 4WD recommended.

Barred Creek is 4WD country, but there is some good fishing at the end of the track, especially across the sand at the mouth. Here, fish off the high rock ledge into the sea or off the rocks into the creek – there are a heap of fish that can be caught. Fishing at the 'windmill' before you cross the sand can produce Trevally, Bream and Salmon at high tide.

Quondong Point offers Queenfish, North-west Snapper (east coast fishermen will know this fish as Sweetlip Emperor), Bluebone and Trevally. Fishing out of a tinnie you'll take all these, plus Spotted Cod and Coral Trout.

Prices Point further north offers similar fish to Quondong. Manari and Coulomb Point offer excellent fishing for Queenfish and Trevally. The south side of the reef produces reef species such as Cod, Coral Trout and Bluebone.

The **Offshore Reefs** north and south of Broome offer excellent fishing for the complete range of pelagic and reef fish. Mackerel, Tuna, Queenfish, large Trevally and even Sailfish are not uncommon. Reef fish include Sea Perch, Sweetlip, North-west Snapper, Cod and beautiful Coral Trout. **Disaster Rock**, 13 km south-west, is one such spot.

Further afield you can head north along the coast to Cape Leveque, taking in **Cape Bertholet**, **Cape Baskerville**, **Beagle Bay**, **Pender Bay** and **Lombadina Point**. Much of the access to these places is across Aboriginal land so you need the Community's permission before entering. There's good Spanish Mackerel, Queenfish, Trevally, cod and Spangled Emperor to keep the lines tight.

The **Lacepede Islands**, more easily reached by a charter boat from Broome than the nearby coast, lie about 35 km west of the Beagle Bay community. There's good Coral Trout on the reefs and a host of pelagics out in the open water. The trick with most of these places is to get the catch aboard before it falls to a feed by the numerous sharks that are around. They can be a pain at times!

Kooljaman at Cape Leveque is a top spot as a base for fishing the nearby coast. There's good land-based fishing for reef species, salmon, trevally and mackerel, while with a boat the scope of territory and the fishing available is unreal. This can be treacherous water though with tidal surges and very strong currents – make sure you and your boat are suitable and up to the encounter!

BROOME VOLUNTEER SEA RESCUE GROUP

- *27MHz Channel 88*
- *HF Channel 2182*
- *VHF Channel 16*
- *24 hours a day, 7 days a week*
- *Phone (08) 9192 8202 or 9193 5935*

Point St, PO Box 2558, Broome WA 6725

FOR FURTHER INFORMATION

For more information on fishing or diving around Broome*, contact:*

Norwest Tackle & Sport*, Shop 2/32 Dampier Tce, ph: (08) 9192 1669, fax: (08) 9193 6073. They can also help you out with all your fishing needs and diving gear.*

Workline Dive & Tackle*, ph: (08) 9192 2233, web:* **www.workline.com.au/**

You can also contact the local fishing clubs:

Broome Fishing Club*, PO Box 1957, Broome, 6725, phone: (Clubhouse) (08) 9192 8122.*

DERBY'S HOT SPOTS

Derby is built on a slight rise of land that juts into King Sound, north of the Fitzroy River mouth. See our chapter, *Around Derby* for information on access to the fishing spots in the area.

The **Wharf** is the only wharf (town jetty) in Australia where, in the 1990s, we've seen people catch mud crabs. From the jetty you'll also catch the occasional barra, some good Threadfin Salmon, catfish and Golden Grunter (a type of Mulloway). As well, there have been some huge cod and groper caught, along with the occasional shark. The most popular baits are mulies, squid, octopus and mullet. For **mud crabs**, you can't go past the numerous small creeks north and south of the wharf. These are accessible by dinghy (10ft or bigger). Other areas in the **King Sound** should only be travelled to in boats l6ft or bigger.

Langi Crossing, Yeeda, Telegraph Pool and the **Willare Bridge** (all on the mighty Fitzroy River) are better barra spots and can really turn it on at times. Trolling a lure or live bait from a boat is the best way to go but land bound fishing people should try mullet or frogs from the bank. To gain access to **Langi Crossing, Yeeda** and *Telegraph Pool* you need to obtain **permission** from **Yeeda Station**.

Pelican Pool, a saltwater inlet on the *Fitzroy River*, approx 95 km from Derby, is accessible only by 4WD along the same track as Langi Crossing. Good barra, salmon, catfish, sharks and mud crabs are often caught here. The best baits are live mullet, mulies and squid. This is private property and you need to obtain **permission** from **Yeeda Station**.

Cherabin are in plentiful supply during the Wet season and the best way to catch them is by using red meat or chook pellets in drop nets.

Upstream from the **Willare Bridge** the river becomes a chain of large, deep pools during the Dry. Barra, Oxeye Herring, catfish and other surprising species such as Sawfish can be caught in these pools.

At **Camballin** the irrigation barrage stops all but big barra moving upstream. In the dam behind the wall there are plenty of Sooty Grunters and large catfish.

There is another gourmet's delight that at times can be had by the bucketful at Camballin. This is the Cherabin. At the end of the Wet, Cherabin can be seen at night climbing the barrage wall in extremely large numbers. When the 'run' is on (normally April/May) you can catch hundreds.

The *May River*, north of the town, is a good spot for Barra, especially just after the Wet, and Threadfin Salmon. Sawfish and catfish are common in the tidal reaches, while further upstream you'll start to get into Sooty Grunters again. Around the mouth and wherever there are a few mangroves you'll get some good mud crabs. Don't forget you'll need **permission** to go to this area from **Meeda Station**.

Point Torment, about 50 km north-west of Derby, is accessible via a 4WD track that does flood at high water. Mud crabs, barra, mulloway, catfish and Fingermark Perch are often caught, and once again the best baits include mulies, squid, octopus, and live mullet. A detailed map is required to reach this spot, and you can get advise from *West Kimberley Guns Ammo & Fishing Tackle,* in Fitzroy St, Derby.

Other good fishing spots include **Blue Hole** and **Tumble Goodie**, which is a great camping spot.

Further **north** the coast is a fisherman's paradise. It is also extremely remote and hard to get to. Boat trips need to be well organised and the boat at least 7 metres and well equipped. For the visiting fisherman a charter boat trip or a visit to Cockatoo Island is probably the best way to go.

For 4WDs the coast between here and Kalumburu has only very limited access. Only a few rough tracks actually reach the coast and the going is slow. Needless to say any vehicle trip needs organisation and top equipment.

DERBY VOLUNTEER MARINE RESCUE GROUP (DVMRG)

EMERGENCY CALLOUT NUMBERS

In Order of Priority:

Derby Police Station, *ph: 9191 1444 - (Emergency Rescue Coordinator)*

Derby Base Radio Centre, ph: 9191 1316 - *The Radio base is not always manned. Please telephone to arrange coverage prior to leaving - the answering machine will advise you of the contact number to call.*

Radio Operator, *ph: (08) 9191 1100*
After Hours, *ph: 0419 959 376*

Information required at time of launch -

- *Boat's name and callsign.*
- *Boat's specification.*
- *Estimated time of departure and point of departure.*
- *Estimated time of arrival and point of arrival.*
- *Number of people on board.*
- *Fuel carried.*
- *Any other special requirements, ie radio schedules.*

DVMRG Details

Station Call sign: Derby Rescue on VHF/27mhz
VMR694 (spoken as 'Victor Mike Romeo Six Nine Four') on MF/HF

Frequencies as follows:

VHF - Ch 16 Calling
27 mhz - Ch 88 calling, move to Ch 90 / Ch 96
MF/HF - 2182, 4620, 4856

FOR FURTHER INFORMATION

For more information on fishing around Derby, *contact:*

West Kimberley Guns Ammo & Fishing Tackle *- Fitzroy St, ph: (08) 9191 1490 - for all your fishing & hunting needs and more.*

Big Barra's One Stop Shop, *18 Neville St, ph: (08) 9191 2111 - sports, fishing & camping.*

Along the coast a good boat is required, but for the keen fishing person the rewards are well worthwhile.

The **Derby Volunteer Marine Rescue Group (DVMRG)**, based in Derby, was formed to assist the boating public, as well as providing a number of services such as radio communications coverage, weather information and recovery facilities in the event of minor breakdowns. It is manned completely by volunteers.

KUNUNURRA & WYNDHAM FISHING

Kununurra, on the banks of the Ord River and near the diversion dam, offers a good choice of fish and fishing spots.

The **diversion dam** or *Lake Kununurra* is not particularly brilliant, with only Sooty Grunter and catfish to be had.

The *Ord River* below the diversion dam wall is the better area for fishing and it's particularly good during the Wet season. While there aren't many large fish at this spot, big bags of up to 70 to 80 fish (which is illegal) have been taken in the past. It's also a top spot for collecting bait, especially prawns and small fish such as mullet, stripies and Black Bream. Barra can be caught here and in the *Dunham River* which enters the Ord less than 2 km down river.

Remember that there are three special ***Barramundi Conservational Areas*** *in the Ord River, Fitzroy River – King Sound, and Broome with special bag limits and regulations for Barramundi. For more details see page 246 under Barramundi. Please also refer to the* ***Recreational Fishing Guide – Pilbara/Kimberley Region*** *available from the Dept of Fisheries web site for all the info barramundi fishing.*

The fishing improves below the **Ivanhoe Crossing**, which in itself is a good spot to drop a lure and one of the most popular fishing spots in the area. Ivanhoe Crossing is the first big obstacle that barra encounter on their yearly migration to freshwater. This normally occurs at the start of the Wet season, around December. Deep holes below the Crossing trap the fish until the river level is high enough to allow the barra to continue upstream. At such times the fishing can be very productive, however the Crossing itself is very slippery and extreme care must be taken. Salt-water Crocodiles also inhabit this spot, so beware!

Bullocks Crossing, accessible through the Frank Wise Institute of Tropical Agricultural Research, is a popular spot for fishing and camping. It also provides access to a good section of the Ord River.

Fords Beach is found between the Dunham River mouth and the Ivanhoe Crossing on the Ord. Consisting of a stretch of rapids with a number of large pools, it provides good fishing for Black Bream and barra. Access is via Ivanhoe Road and River Farm Road.

Valentines Creek enters the Ord River at Fords Beach and once again is a good spot for Black Bream and Barramundi. Access is through Ivanhoe Station, on the Wyndham side of the Ord River. This is along Parrys Creek Road.

Upriver from the diversion dam to the dam wall of Lake Argyle the fishing is better than the diversion dam itself, improving as you get closer to the outflow of the huge lake behind the main wall. Once again Sooty Grunters, catfish and the sporty Longtom are the main fish caught. A small boat with a 10 hp outboard will take about four hours and 20 litres of fuel to travel the stretch of water one way. See our section on *Canoeing* for more details.

A nice estuary cod, caught off the beach at Kalumburu.

The ***Wyndham Jetty*** *occasionally produces big catfish, sawfish, golden grunters, salmon and barra.*

The ***mudflats*** *north of the jetty are crossed by a number of tracks leading to Parry Creek where threadfin salmon, cod and catfish can be caught. The King River, south of Wyndham, is also another good barra stream.*

With a boat the range of fishing is endless and can include top barra spots along the East and ***West Arms of Cambridge Gulf*** *or out into the productive open water around* ***Lacrosse Island****.*

The large estuaries of the Keep, Pentecost and King Rivers produce some good fishing when conditions are right. Winds, tides and phases of the moon all play an important part. Barra, mangrove jack, threadfin salmon and shark make for exciting fishing.

Access to the coast is difficult and there's only one patch of blue-water fishing. Access is through Carlton Hill Station and permission, as before, is necessary. Allow about three days for this trip as the four wheel drive tracks ensure slow going. A large selection of blue-water fish, including Queenfish and Spanish mackerel, as well as trevally, mangrove jack, salmon, barramundi and shark can be caught along this section of coast. Self-sufficiency is the name of the game for any fishing trip along this stretch of water.

FISHING

Lake Argyle offers good fishing and big catches of Forktail Catfish can almost be assured, along with large Longtoms. Beware though, the lake is a large expanse of water and big waves are not uncommon during high winds and storms.

Carlton Crossing, House Roof Crossing, Yellow Waterhole and **Wild Goose Creek** are all good spots for barra, but access is difficult because of the Quarantine restrictions.

Tarrara Bar is about 40 km from Kununurra and because of the many big fish caught there it's highly favoured by locals. Tracks lead to the upper, middle and lower reaches with the lower section being accessible through Carlton Hill Station. Permission must be sought before entry.

Sandy Beach is another pleasant camping and fishing spot on the Ord River, about 50 km from Kununurra, and once again is accessible through Carlton Hill Station.

Keep River is a top fishing area that is accessible through Legune Station and is by 4WD only. Permission is essential. Because much of the river is in the Northern Territory, fishing laws applicable to that State apply.

Crocodile Hole**,** Parry Lagoons and the other billabongs and waterholes bordering the Ord and its many tributaries offer reasonable fishing, but are easily fished out – especially for barra.

South of Wyndham, and accessible via the Gibb River Road, are the top rivers of the **Chamberlain, Pentecost, Durack** and **Forrest.** These can all produce good barra, especially in their lower reaches. As the Dry season wears on, these lower reaches are the only place to fish for barra. Upstream, especially above the influence of the saltwater, big Forktail Catfish and some nice size Sooty Grunter are the order of the day.

PORT WARRENDER & KALUMBURU REGION

Crystal Creek, near Port Warrender, is probably the easiest (but still slow going), most accessible spot you'll find in this region and good size barra can be caught from the high rock ledges bordering the river. Mangrove Jack, Queenfish, Salmon, Catfish and Sharks can also turn it on around here. And, while it is out of the national park, part of the area is now within a small section of designated Aboriginal land that covers part of this northern area. (See our chapter on *The Mitchell Plateau and Northern Kimberley* for access details.)

Port Warrender itself is a fisherman's paradise, however at times the track to Walsh Point and Port Warrender can become badly eroded and washed out, making access extremely difficult. (See our chapter on *The Mitchell Plateau and Northern Kimberley* for access details.) Once there, it's an ideal spot to launch a small tinnie off the rocky beach area. A good variety of reef fish, along with pelagic fish such as Queenfish, Trevally, Mackerel and Tuna can be caught, as well as Fingermark Bream. Crystal Head is easily accessible by boat from Port Warrender and offers superb fishing. In the Lawley River area good catches of barra can be had. The **Kimberley Coastal Camp** is located on the eastern side of Port Warrender and can only be accessed by sea or air. See page 148, *The Mitchell Plateau and Northern Kimberley*, for access details.

The Mitchell, King Edward, Carson and **Morgan Rivers** will all produce barra in their lower reaches. In their upper reaches you'll have to make do with sootys and catfish!

The many beaches and bays **north of Kalumburu** and around Pago can produce good catches of a whole host of fish, including barra, Cod, Threadfin Salmon, Queenfish and much more! There are now a couple of fishing guides operating from camping areas north of Kalumburu. See the page 138 in the chapter, *The Mitchell Plateau and Northern Kimberley,* for more details on access.

FISHING TRIPS, GUIDES & BOAT CHARTER

For many travelling fishermen the only real method to catch a barra or to experience top fishing is to hire a guide or go to a place set up for fishing. Below are listed just some of the operators. You'll find more detailed information in the various chapters under *'Fishing Trips* and *Safaris'*.

Australian Pinnacle Tours, ph: (08) 9417 5555, web: **www.pinnacletours.com.au**
HotSpot Fishing Tours, ph: (08) 89832167, web: **www.alexjulius.com.au**
Track Air Adventures, ph: 0417 551 373, web: **www.trackairadventures.com**

Fishing Trips from Kununurra/Wyndham

Alligator Airways, ph: (08) 9168 1333, web: **www.alligatorairways.com.au/**
Argyle Expeditions, ph: (08) 9168 7040, web: **www.ozhorizons.com.au/wa/kimberly/argyle/home.html.**
Diggers Rest Station, ph: (08) 9161 1029, web: **www.diggers-rest.com**
El Questro, ph: (08) 9169 1777, web site: **www.elquestro.com.au/**
Kimberley Coastal Camp, ph: (08) 9161 4410, web: **www.kimberleycoastalcamp.com.au/**
Kimberley Fishing, ph: (08) 9193 5689, web: **www.kimberleyfishing.com.**
Kimberley Sportfishing, ph: (08) 9169 2752.
Lake Argyle Cruises, ph: (08) 9168 7361, web: **www.lakeargyle.com/english/tours.htm.**
Look Sea Tours, ph: (08) 9161 1775, web: **www.lookseatours.com.au**
Lower Ord Cruises, ph: (08) 9168 2144.
Mackas Barra Camp, ph: (08) 9169 1759, web: **www.mackasbarra.com.au/**
Ultimate Adventures, ph: (08) 9168 2310, web: **http://members.westnet.com.au/web/ultimateadvent/welcome.htm**

Fishing Safaris Derby

Big Barra's Fishing Adventures, ph: (08) 9191 2111.
Buccaneer Sea Safaris, ph: (08) 9191 1991, web site: **www.buccaneerseasafaris.com**
Bushtrack Safaris, ph: (08) 9191 1547. Web: **www.bushtracksafaris.com.au/**
One Tide Charters, ph: 08 9193 1358, web: **www.onetide.com/**
Unreel Adventure Safaris, ph: (08) 9193 1999, web: **www.unreeladventures.com**

Fishing & Diving Tours Broome

Broome Billfish Charters, ph: (08) 9192 2127, web: **www.broomebillfish.com.**
Broome Fishing & Dive Charters, ph: (08) 9193 6339.
Broome Time Charters, ph: (08) 9192 2458.
Coastal Catch Boat Hire, ph: 0417 176 648 – boat charter services & hire.
Dampier Creek Boat Tours, ph: (08) 9192 2050.
Fad Game Fishing Charters, ph: (08) 9192 3998, web: **www.fadcharters.com.au.**
Freshwater Cove, ph: (08) 9193 6836, web: **www.freshwatercove.com.**
Kimberley Birdwatching, ph: (08) 9192 1246, web: **www.kimberleybirdwatching.com.au.**
Kimberley Catamaran Cruises, ph: (08) 9192 8668, web: **www.shorething.com.au.**
Kimberley Discovery Cruises, ph: 1800 185 960, web: **www.kimberleydiscoverycruises.com.au.**
Kimberley Fishing, ph: (08) 9193 5689, web: **www.kimberleyfishing.com/.**
Kimberley Fishing Charters, ph: 1800 677 830, web: **www.kimberleycruises.com.**
Leveque Wilderness Fishing & Adventure Charters, ph: (08) 9193 6836.
North Cape Fishing Charters, ph: 0419 046 035.
North Star Charters, ph: (08) 9192 1829, web: **www.northstarcruises.com.au.**
One Tide Charter, Broome, ph: (08) 9193 1358, web: **www.onetide.com.**
Pearl Sea Coastal Cruises, ph: (08) 9193 6131, web: **www.kimberleyquest.com.au.**
Red Sky Cruises, ph: 0407 739 738, web: **www.redsky.com.au.**
Sentosa Fishing Charters, ph: (08) 9192 8163, web: **www.sentosafishingcharters.com.**
The Great Escape Charter Company, ph: (08) 9193 5983, web: **www.kimberleyescape.com.**
Workline Dive & Tackle, ph: (08) 9192 2233, web: **www.workline.com.au/.**

A nice salmon caught with a handline off the beach.

FISHING

BUSHWALKING AND CYCLING THE KIMBERLEY

BUSHWALKING

GENERAL

The bushwalking opportunities the Kimberley has to offer are near endless and range from easy strolls along the Napier Range to wilderness extravaganzas taking in the untracked expanses that stretch from Walcott Inlet to the Carson Escarpment and beyond.

There are a number of day walks and shorter forays included in the pages of this book, but for the experienced, well equipped bushwalker there are a host of tracks and trails and vast areas of untracked country calling out to be explored.

In the wilder rockier range country you'll probably need to carry a short rope and have a bit of experience with rock scrambling and abseiling.

Don't forget your insect repellent and always carry water. Many areas away from the rivers and creeks are totally devoid of water during the Dry and the heat reflected from the rocks is debilitating.

TOUGH WALK, LITTLE WATER ... THEN PARADISE

Well known Kimberley adventurer, Terry Bolland has had numerous experiences in the region during his many canoeing and walking trips through the area.

On one trip when he was canoeing, cycling and walking around the Kimberley in a 3500 km 91 day marathon, he and three companions were retracing the route of Bertram and Klaussman's 1932 trek in very remote country to the south-west of Cape Londonderry when things began to go wrong. This extract from his book, ***Kimberley Challenge****, gives you some idea of the extremes that are part and parcel of any walking adventure.*

"...Our journey to Forrest River, via Emergency Bay, the Atlantis's forced landing site, became a nightmare. We were tormented by the heat and heavy backpacks and the meagre freshwater supply along our route had been fouled by cattle dung and urine. The water was boiled and filtered through Dennis's hat (which never smelled the same again). Our plight through the tick infested scrub and dry creek beds turning into a hellish trip.

We were getting quite desperate when the semi-arid area suddenly turned into a lush valley with pandanus palms, creepers and tall grasses bordering a beautiful sweet running stream. A paradise, where birds probed the flowers of silky grevilleas ..."

PURNULULU NATIONAL PARK

This is a favoured area for overnight walks, with the walk out to Piccaninny Gorge being the most popular. The scope for other adventures, taking in the extremity of the Plateau and the many different gorges is great.

THE MITCHELL PLATEAU

The plateau, with its many scenic highlights, is another favoured area for some longer bushwalks. Here, once away from the tracks, you could well be forced to do some scrambling and climbing, especially if you wish to follow the **Mitchell River** or cut across country between the Mitchell Falls and Surveyor Pool.

FOLLOWING THE RIVERS

During the Dry season the rivers offer a route through the region that can be ideal for the remote area bushwalker. The *Drysdale, Regent* and the *Chamberlain Rivers* are just a few that give access to some wild and wonderful land.

GEORGE GREY'S ROUTE

A number of parties, including a group led by Terry Bolland have followed the 1838 route of the explorer Charles Grey from Hanover Bay south into the rock wilderness of the range country to the south.

Charter boats can provide the access but only skill, determination and good equipment will get a party through.

A CIRCUIT OF THE WESTERN KIMBERLEY

In August 1992 a 500 km circuit of the southern Kimberley was successfully completed by Peter Treseder, Tony Gavranich, Ken Wilson and Keith Williams.

The team set out from Mt Barnett Station on the Gibb River Road to make the first complete descent of the Isdell River from source to mouth.

The team became the first to paddle the magnificent Isdell Gorge and after reaching Walcott Inlet ascended the Charnley River to its source. The team thereby became the first people to follow the whole length of the Charnley. The Manning River led them back to Mt Barnett Station to complete the circuit.

Norforce (Australia's Northern Army Reserve Force) assisted the expedition with placement of strategic food dumps and travel to and from the remote Mt Barnett Station.

Peter Treseder on his circuit of the Western Kimberley.

CYCLING

GENERAL

The rugged terrain of the Kimberley limits bike trips to the roads and tracks of the region. Elsewhere the steep-sided rocky mountains and ridges hem you in and limit what you can do on a bike.

Once again no matter where you are riding, carry ample water. Passing traffic is always pretty thin on the ground and could be non-existent on some days, depending on the track you are on. There can be long distances between water points on many trips, so plan accordingly.

LONG TRIPS

All of the major routes described in this book that cut across the heart of the Kimberley or around its southern extremity lend themselves to long distant cycling trips.

The Gibb River Road and the Tablelands Track are two that would be ideal bike trips.

SHORT JOURNEYS

Shorter forays from a base camp are also possible, once again mainly taking in many of the routes previously described in this book.

Such adventures would include the trip out to Walcott Inlet from Mt Elizabeth Station, or the trip to the gorges from the camping area at Mornington Wilderness Camp. The coastal trip north from Kalumburu would also be a good one.

PEDALLING THROUGH THE KIMBERLEY

Friends of ours, Alex and Jacky Sklenica, travelled through the Kimberley on push bikes back in 1954. Here's what they had to say in a letter to us about it in 1990, after they had just completed a similar return trip in their trusty 4WD.

"Repacking our push bikes, we were considering possible routes from Wyndham to Derby. A shorter but very rough 700 km on the Durack and Gibb River track, confusingly crossed by stock routes petering out in the bush and no supply points along the way. Or the 1000 km via Turkey Creek, Halls Creek, Fitzroy Crossing. This longer way, still rather a bush track than road in 1954, was used mainly by drovers and station vehicles. A decisive advantage was, that food supplies would be available from shops at Halls Creek and Fitzroy Crossing.

The Wyndham Police and locals in the pub offered advice, wished us luck and one grinned: "You know what I am thinking".

The main highway, east of Derby, in 1954.

We had to travel light and lived mostly off the land. A limited amount of basic food supplies were brought in Wyndham. Water, still remaining after the previous 'rainy' and some edible plants would have to be found on the way. Not a beginner in the Australian bush, I carried also a few fishing hooks and a line and a single shot .22 rifle. We hoped to catch fish, but knew that our main food source would consist of pigeon, ibis meat, ducks, galahs and wallabies.

We were unable to ride our bikes over the frequently sandy or rock strewn stretches, but had to walk, pushing the bikes or sometimes ride on firmer surfaces parallel to the road.

There were no camping grounds, National Parks or tourists there. During four months, we met only one car with two Melbourne tourists and one Frenchman riding a motorcycle around Australia. When, on rare occasions, we met with station people, we stopped to boil a billy and to exchange news.

Once a passing stockman from Bohemia Downs stopped his truck near our little camp fire for a bit of a talk, sharing with us a billy of tea. Looking our scanty outfit over: "On bikes ... but how ... what do you eat?". Pointing to our saddle bags I replied: "We have some flour, tea, sugar and such here and there is plenty of game around waterholes".

When leaving our camp, he dropped an apparently empty plywood tea-chest: "Perhaps you can use this as a table". Inside the tea-chest was his present. A loaf of bread and a pound of butter wrapped in sheets of newspaper. Fresh bread and real butter. Immediately, we boiled another billy, spread slices of buttered bread on the tea-chest and read every scrap of newspaper, adverts including. This was indeed a happy camp, still vivid in our memory.

There were no marked tracks through spear grass and spinifex leading to Geikie or Windjana gorges. Near Tunnel Creek, overhanging rock shelters were still periodically inhabited by nomadic natives. We found and left undisturbed spears, stone knives and scrapers.

We met a mounted police patrol and sat till midnight smoking and talking, listening to natives singing around a camp fire near the billabong.

A period in our life when we were not tied to conventions and restrictions of crowded civilisation. A time when we were free to walk over the horizon. A slice of damper and roasted wallaby washed down with Bushel's was a repast. A shady tree, the warmth of a small fire on cool nights, bright stars our roof. Unforgettable memories of an unfenced land, of outback people and times past.

Just such a short time ago and much has changed. Yet so much remains the same."

Alex Sklenica. 18.12.1990

FOSSICKING AND DETECTING FOR FUN AND FORTUNE

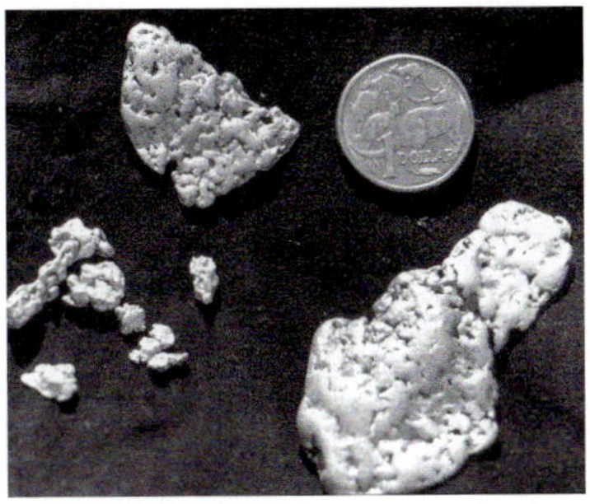

INTRODUCTION

Fossicking is a great way to spend a holiday, and for some it's more a way of life. And the Kimberley is one of the most fascinating areas for collectors and lapidary enthusiasts in all of Australia. While diamonds may be the gem and the lure of the present, gold can still be found, along with such significant gemstones as agate, zebra rock, malachite, garnet and jasper, to name just a few.

THE LEGAL REQUIREMENTS

Unless you are well acquainted with prospecting, fossicking and mining in WA, it would be advisable to contact the Department of Industry & Resources, Mineral & Petroleum (DoIR), 100 Plain St, East Perth, WA, 6004, phone general enquiries: (08) 9222 3333, fax: (08) 9222 3862, web: **www.doir.wa.gov.au/mineralsandpetroleum/index.asp.**

Basically in WA before you can search for minerals you require a **Miner's Right** which may be obtained for a fee of $25.00 from the DoIR. An Application form can be downloaded from the Department's web site, or you can apply at any Mining Registrar's Office.

Once you have a **Miner's Right** you are **authorised to**: prospect on Crown land which is open for mining; prospect for minerals (including gold); conduct geological mapping; conduct tests for minerals; undertake limited sampling using hand held equipment and to remove samples up to 20 kilograms; mark out mining tenements; fossick for rocks, gemstones, etc.

Possession of a Miner's Right does not authorise these activities on private land or Reserve land (except for the purposes of Common, Mining or Public Utility).

Prospecting can be carried out for all minerals including gold and a metal detector can be used. Prospecting cannot be carried out on a mining tenement unless the tenement holder's consent is obtained and if a pastoral lease is affected the pastoralist should be notified.

Fossicking authorises the collection of mineral specimens (excluding gold and diamonds) for lapidary work or hobby interests. Use of a metal detector is not permitted. In addition the written consent of any mining tenement holder and the pastoralist is required.

There are a host of other requirements laid down in the Act, but basically there are a few points you need to know.

- Unless you have written government permission you are not allowed to prospect in National Parks, State Forests, Aboriginal or any other designated reserve.
- **A Miner's Right does NOT give right of entry to privately held land or leasehold land; you must have written consent of the occupier**. Also, the holder of a Miner's Right is legally responsible for any damage that may be caused by his or her prospecting activities.
- The holder of a Miner's Right is authorised to search for and remove samples from Crown land, however he is not permitted to carry out activities such as "strip mining" (ie. the use of front-end loaders and bulldozers or similar machinery to strip the surface of soil or vegetation).

> ***This information is to be used as a guide only.***
>
> You should contact the DoIR for current regulations. The DoIR also has pamphlets available which lay down the requirements quite clearly, such as Prospecting the Right Way; Code of Conduct *for Mineral Exploration on Pastoral Leases, and Prospecting, Exploring, Mining on Pastoral Leases.*

WHAT TO LOOK FOR

DIAMONDS

Once it was gold that made people tramp off to the Kimberley, now it's diamonds.

The Kimberley of Western Australia was given its name sometime last century because the geology was thought to be much the same as the fabulous diamond bearing region of South Africa. However, it took until the 1970s to prove how right the geologists of old were. In 1979 a diamond bearing kimberlite pipe was discovered south of Kununurra, near Lake Argyle. In 1986 the mine began production and 13.3 million carats were recovered during the first six months. While most of these were industrial diamonds, some were of gem quality, while a small percentage were rare, gem quality pink diamonds.

Now the Argyle Diamond Mine is the single biggest producer of diamonds, by volume, in the world and while it's the major success story of the Kimberley, it's not alone in the diamond stakes.

Tours of the Argyle mine are available through *Slingair Heliwork WA*, Kununurra, ph: 1800 095 500 or ph: (08) 9169 1300, web: **www.slingair.com.au/**.

OTHER DIAMOND FINDS

In the early 1980s, alluvial diamonds were found in the gravels of Limestone and Smoke Creeks. Commercial sampling of the Bow River produced even more.

There was extensive exploration for diamonds following the discovery of Argyle, and again since 1991. Exploration was concentrated in the Kimberley, bob onshore and offshore, and new occurrences have been indicated in the Forrest River, Mt Elizabeth and Ellendale areas.

On the *Lennard River*, about 130 km east of Derby, nine alluvial diamonds led to the discovery of a cluster of kimberlite pipes on Ellendale Station, two of which proved to be diamond bearing.

Beta Creek, 180 km north-west of Wyndham, also produced some small diamonds around this time. Since then other finds have been made and the searching still goes on. Maybe there is another Argyle deposit out there waiting.

It should be noted that in terms of the 1979 Argyle Act the general public (that's you and me) and prospectors are forbidden entry, and the right to fossick, in the designated areas of the Argyle Mine and the Ellendale area.

GOLD

It was the discovery of gold at Halls Creek in 1885 that was much of the impetus for the settlement of the region. While the original rush didn't last long, modern mining and detecting techniques have paved the way for a new rush.

Around Halls Creek a number of larger mines have started operation and there are, as well, a handful of full time fossickers working with metal detectors. Part timers, mainly visitors from down south, are also finding a little gold and having a lot of fun doing it. You could be amongst them. Here's a few places to start looking.

The old crusher & mining relics at the Ruby Queen battery complex.

BROCKMANS AND THE GOLDEN CROWN

South-east of Old Halls Creek is the area known as Brockmans. The Golden Crown mine, situated to the east of the main Duncan Road about 15 km south of Old Halls Creek, is approximately in the centre of this rich gold bearing area. Nuggety Gully, a short distance to the north of the Golden Crown, is also worth a look see.

See map and more info in chapter, *Around Halls Creek*.

The Twelve Mile Digging

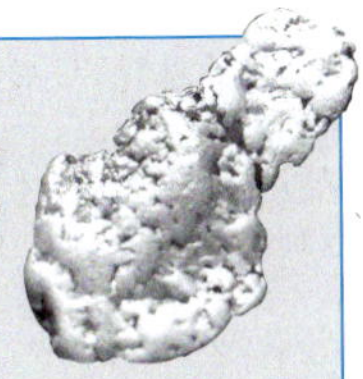

Further east, around the Elvire River, are Saunders Gully, Poverty Gully and other gold bearing areas. All of these places, once worked by the early prospectors, have more than a good chance of still holding a few nuggets.

See map and more info in chapter, *Around Halls Creek*.

The Ruby Queen and Surrounds

Gold was discovered in this area in January 1888 and a rush soon set in. Little alluvial gold was found, but the reef gold was extensive and rich. The two most important mines were the Ruby Queen and the Saint Lawrence. The Ruby Queen battery is located about 28 km south of the Old Halls Creek township. *For all the details, see page 86, Around Halls Creek.*

Grants Creek and Places North of Halls Creek

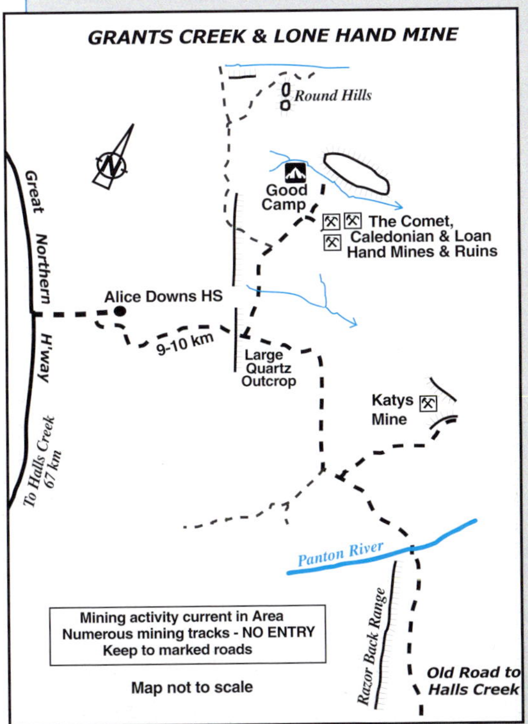

Grants Creek, situated approx 10 km east of Alice Downs HS (itself some 60 km north from Halls Creek) has a number of small mines and alluvial fields scattered over a wide area. The Lone Hand mine and its nearby allies of the Comet and the Caledonian were the most productive in the area.

South from here, to well over the Panton River, small gullies and alluvial fields, including Katy's Patch, have been worked in the past and still produce some nuggets.

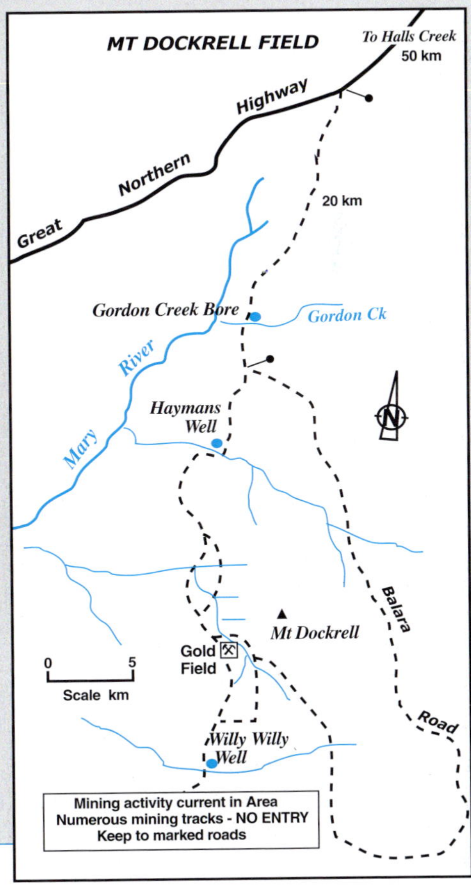

Other Areas Around Halls Creek

There are many other gold mining areas around Halls Creek.

The **Mt Dockrell field** is over 100 km south-west of the town and while the original rush to the field didn't last long, it still produced some good finds of gold. Although the alluvial diggings were patchy and scattered, the two mines of note, the Victoria and McNeils, produced a small amount of very rich ore.

In recent times, using detectors, there have been some fine nuggets, up to 12 ounces, found in the field.

The **Mary River field** is centred on the headwaters of the river of the same name and is spread over a large area on both sides of the Tanami Road, about 20 km south of its junction with the Northern Highway. There are many gold bearing creeks and gullies, all worth a good look at.

See the chapter *Around Halls Creek*, pages 87 & 88, and the map on page 80, for more details

Mt Broome Gold

Mt Broome, one of the highest mountains in the Kimberley, is a remote peak in the King Leopold Range, situated some 40 km north-east of Windjana Gorge. It is the only other area where gold has been found in the Kimberley.

Around 3 km west of the peak in the gullies of Mt Broome Creek and the Richenda River, a number of alluvial areas have been worked. A couple of small reefs have also been mined, with the shafts and the mullock heaps visible in aerial photos of the area. This area is still very remote and no roads or tracks lead there – it's a hard walk over steep, rugged range country! Certainly, with modern detectors and a bit of effort the chances of finding a nugget or two are pretty good.

OTHER GEMS TO FIND

Malachite/Azurite

Specimens of these two copper ores can be found widely throughout the Kimberley.

Malachite can be found near Narlarla (east of Napier Downs), Barker Gorge and throughout the Napier Ranges. Around Halls Creek it can be found near Water Point and it occurs along the length of the Ord River, Dunham River and on Speewah pastoral station. Both Azurite and Malachite are found along the Pentecost River, south-west of Wyndham.

Jasper

Jasper occurs in a large range of colours and can be found along the Lennard, Fitzroy and the Margaret Rivers.

Agate

There is a vast range of different agates, many known by different names. Agate occurs along the Lennard River, the Fitzroy River, at Mount Herbert north-west of Mt Broome, as well as on the Antrim Plateau south-east of Halls Creek.

Prehnite

Prehnite is mainly pale green in colour and occurs in vesicles and joints in basalt rock in the east Kimberley region. It's most commonly found as water worn pebbles in creek beds between Halls Creek and Kununurra.

Fluorite

Colourless to amber specimens of fluorite come from Speewah Station, south of Wyndham, while other varieties (white and green) come from near Turkey Creek, halfway between Wyndham and Halls Creek.

Zebra Rock

Zebra Rock is a distinctive rock that is mainly found south of Kununurra in the Ord River area. At one time it was thought all this stone would be drowned under the waters of the dam, but deposits do occur throughout the region, especially on Argyle Downs Station.

Fossils and Other Gems

Fossils can be found on Fossil Downs Station. Petrified wood is fairly common in the Poole Range.

Other gemstones that can be found in the Kimberley include garnets, calcite, corundum, tourmaline and many others. As one of the managers of the diamond mine said to me one day "We're only just beginning to find out what's here!"

SAFETY AND MEDICAL ASPECTS

MEDICAL ASSISTANCE

BEFORE YOU GO!

The Kimberley is a remote region and the number of doctors and medical facilities can almost be counted on one hand.

Before you go you should be in reasonable health, know your limitations and be conversant with first aid procedures and especially, expired air resuscitation (mouth to mouth resuscitation). You should also have in your vehicle, as a very minimum, a good basic first aid kit, plus any special medication that you or your family requires.

It is recommended that people attend a St. John's Ambulance First Aid Course, or better still, a dedicated remote area first aid course, before they venture into any remote region, not only the Kimberley. Always carry a copy of the St. John's First Aid Manual – the latest one or something similar!

While you're exploring this remote area of Australia, you are in Royal Flying Doctor Service (RFDS) country and they can be contacted by telephone or radio from most homesteads in the area. Also most of the commercial travel operators carry a HF radio transmitter suitable to contact the RFDS, or the commercial radphone service.

With the recent advent of affordable satellite phones many commercial operators are now using these as well.

Medical and/or hospital facilities are located :

Broome, ph: (08) 9192 9222
Fitzroy Crossing, ph: (08) 9166 1777
Kununurra, ph: (08) 9166 4222
Derby, ph: (08) 9193 3333
Halls Creek, ph: (08) 9168 6003
Wyndham, ph: (08) 9161 1104

HF RADIO LICENCES & OPERATION

The Outpost Licence for HF radio, issued by the Australian Communication Authority (ACA), is no longer required unless you want to use the designated RFDS channels for general chit chat, ie., on 2020 or the frequencies not being used after a RFDS base closes down for the day.

If you are not registered with the ACA you will need to be registered by one, or more, of the service providers that are now in operation, so you can access their frequencies and thereby legally use your HF radio.

Emergency use of the RFDS channels is still provided, even though you're not registered with the ACA.

ROYAL FLYING DOCTOR SERVICE (RFDS)

The RFDS no longer offers a radphone service, although they still provide 24 hour HF radio medical and emergency services. For more info you can also check out their web site on:

www.flyingdoctor.net/default.htm.

DERBY RFDS BASE

The RFDS base, in Loch St (cnr Ashley St), ph: (08) 9191 0200, is open to visitors Monday to Friday (except holidays) 9.00 am, 11.00 am and 2.00 pm for video and souvenir sales. Visitors can help support this service by leaving a donation or by purchasing some souvenirs. For more information on the RFDS check out their web site: **www.flyingdoctor.net**.

Contacting the RFDS

You can still use the RFDS network not only for emergency calls (only in an emergency!), but also for medical diagnosis and treatment.

The **Derby Base** of the RFDS, Loch St (cnr Ashley St), can be contacted for general enquiries on ph: (08) 9191 0200.

The **Alice Springs base** can be contacted on ph: (08) 8952 5355.

For all medical and emergency calls (24 hours) you should phone 1800 625 800 (freecall).

RFDS Medical Chest

Most homestead properties have a comprehensive RFDS Medical Chest for use with the RFDS radio/phone service. These chests are provided for the free use of all, but remember, they are the residents only source of medication and they are really not meant for wayward travellers.

Frequencies

You can check out the Frequencies on the RFDS web at: **www.flyingdoctor.net/hfradio.htm**

Frequencies and Call Signs for Derby and Alice Springs

CallSign	Station	Pref Freq KHz	Alt Freq KHz
VJB	**Derby** ph: (08) 9414 1200	5300,	2792(n) 5360(d)(n)
VJD	**Alice Springs** ph: (08) 8952 5355	5410(d)(n)	6950 2020(n)

(d) frequency (day) (n) frequency (night)

COMMUNICATIONS

Phonecalls Via the HF Radio

Telstra has now closed all its bases and got out of the HF radphone business. A number of private operators have cranked up a variety of replacement RDD (Radphone Dial Direct) HF radio telephone services to replace the loss of the Telstra operator connected Radphone and the auto RDD systems.

There's a range of new frequencies for these service providers and they are all single channel and Selcall accessed, so old HF sets will need to be reprogrammed to handle the new channels, depending on who you use. Most HF radio outlets will insist that you have a licence for one of the networks detailed, before this is carried out.

Costs for the service will vary depending on the service provider, but expect around a $120/year registration and access fee and $1 or so a minute for a call.

Reids Radiodata has **BushTelephone+Network**, with bases located in Perth, Alice Springs, Woomera, Melbourne, Cowra, Charters Towers and Brisbane. This service gives you the ability to make telephone calls using your HF Radio. All bases are only accessed by a direct dial service utilising the telcall format. Their bases and frequency can be found on their web site. They can be contacted on ph: (02) 6341 1154 or fax: (02) 6342 4397, web site: **www.reidsradiodata.com.au/**.

RadTel HF Radio Network, another service provider, has bases in Perth, Derby, Newcastle, Ti-Tree north of Alice Springs and Charters Towers. Selcall only access is provided for RDD calls to anywhere in Australia. Their bases and frequency can be found on their web site. For more info on the Radtel network, ph: (02) 4943 1745, web: **www.radtelnetwork.com.au**.

Australian National 4WD Radio Network

The Australian National 4WD Radio Network, more commonly know as **VKS 737**, is another designated service provider with base stations around Australia, but they do not operate a RDD network. These stations are located in Adelaide in SA, Swan Hill in Victoria, Alice Springs and Darwin in the NT, Cairns and Charters Towers in Qld, Perth and Derby in WA, Newcastle in NSW and St Marys in Tasmania.

Weather, road conditions, safety logging, message handling, emergency telephone calls and general communications, including car-to-car, are all features of the VKS 737 Network. Regular skeds take place from stations around the country, which assist travellers in making the right travelling decisions when in the outback. The Network also offers a calling service to pre-set telephone numbers and limited Direct Dial and operator connected call services.

For more information on the VKS 737 Australia Wide HF Radio Network phone (08) 8287 6222, or email: info@vks737.on.net, or check the web site: **www.vks737.on.net**.

Bush Telegraph

The Bush Telegraph is a similar HF radio network to the 4WD Network, using the same frequencies on the radio, but bases do not talk to those registered with the other service. BT bases are located at Derby, Woomera, Adelaide, Maryborough, Cowra and Charters Towers.

This network is much smaller than the 4WD Network, but it costs less to join. For more info on the Bush Telegraph, ph: (02) 6341 1544. Also get more information on the Reids Radiodata web site: **www.reidsradiodata.com.au/bushtelegraph.htm.**

Hiring or Buying a HF Radio

The cost of a HF radio, suitable to contact the RFDS or Telstra, is in the vicinity of $3000 to $4000. You can hire one from a number of commercial radio outlets in capital cities (try Telstat in Melbourne, ph: (03) 9786 9422, web: **www.telstat.com.au/**). Also check out the RFDS web site for details on hire outlets and contacts, **www.flyingdoctor.net/hfradio.htm**.

The hire for a HF radio is around $50 to $200 per week, depending on the model and the company involved, plus fitting and any extra frequencies if required, as well as a booking deposit of $100 to $300 or so. You need to book well in advance to ensure you get a radio when you want it.

No matter which way you go you'll need to be registered with one of the service providers.

SATELLITE PHONES

Satellite phones may be the go for many people, but while they are cheaper to buy than a HF radio they are expensive to operate and you can't talk car-to-car and you don't get free weather or road reports and the like.

Their are 3 types of Satphone systems available in Australia – ***Inmarsat***, ***Globalstar-Australi*** and ***Iridium***.

Telstra Countrywide (Mobile Satellite) has a range of hand-held sat phones, powered by the *Iridium Satellite System*. Check out their web site for more info at:

www.telstra.com/countrywide/telstramobility/

For more information on **Iridium**, the pioneers of the hand-held sat phone system, check out the web at: **www.stratosglobal.com.**

Globalstar offers an Australia wide service with a hand-held phone with access to Cellular and Satellite networks. For more info on Globalstar, ph: 1300 882 448, or check out the web at:

www.globalstar.com.au.

Telstat, 52 Brunel Rd, Seaford, Vic 3198, ph: (03) 9786 9422, can also help you with any questions on any of the above phones. They also sell many types of Satellite phones. Check out their web site at:

www.telstat.com.au/.

Satellite phones are a great way of staying in touch.

POLICE ASSISTANCE

All Police Stations in the Kimberley have 4WD vehicles which are equipped with radios capable of communicating with the RFDS or Telstra.

Police Stations can be contacted by phone at the following places, but only contact them for assistance in an emergency –

Broome, ph: (08) 9194 0200
Fitzroy Crossing, ph: (08) 9191 5000
Kununurra, ph: (08) 9166 4530
Derby, ph: (08) 9191 1444
Halls Creek, ph: (08) 9168 6000
Wyndham, ph: (08) 9161 1055.

FIRST AID KIT

You can either buy a suitable kit or make up your own. Kits can be purchased from the ***St John Ambulance*** (**www.stjohn.org.au/**) or from ***Survival Emergency Products***, ph: (02) 4385 6889, web: **www.survival.net.au/**. They also produce an excellent *First Aid Emergency Handbook* ideal for the traveller or for home.

First Aid Kit Should Include

First Aid Manual/Pencil/Note Book/
Triangular Bandages (Qty 6)
Crepe Bandages –
  Qty 2 to 3 of each width size –
  2.5cm, 5cm, 7.5cm, 10cm & 15cm
Bandaids (1 pkt)
Eye Pads (6 or so in individual packs)
Butterfly Closures (1 pkt)
Surgipad Combination Dressing
  4 or 5 – 20cm x 20cm)
Non-Adherent Dressings (Qty 5)
Adhesive Tape
SAM Splint – available from *First Aid Training & Supplies*
Antiseptic Cream (eg Savlon)
Antiseptic Liquid (eg Dettol)
Antiseptic Powder
Cotton wool/buds
Eye Drops (eg Visine, etc.)
Calamine Lotion/Metho 'Stop Itch'
  (or whatever works on insect bites for you)
Water soluble burn gel
Headache tablets
Diarrhoea tablets
Nausea tablets.
Gastrolyte
Something for toothache –
Dentist in a Box, ph: 1800 670 261, isn't bad
Sheers
Small scissors
Tweezers
Splinter probe
Thermometer
Safety pins
Disposable gloves

TROPICAL BITES AND STINGS

There are a number of animals and insects in the Kimberley that can bite or sting. Most of the life-threatening ones are easily avoided, so the first point is TAKE CARE – prevention is far better than cure! Others, generally the myriad of insects can, at times, drive you nearly mad. First and foremost, take an effective repellent.

Snake Bite

Venomous snakes found in the Kimberley region that are considered dangerous to man include the King Brown, Western Brown Snake and Death Adder. Active in warm weather, people should be wary when they are walking through long grass or along the water's edge. Wandering through these areas in thongs is definitely not recommended.

Remember that the use of tourniquets for snake bite is no longer recommended and a far better method, of a firm bandage and splinting the limb, is now used. If nothing else, a first aid course will teach you the latest method.

Marine Stingers

Many different types of stingers or jelly fish are found in the sea and beaches of Northern Australia, including the Kimberley. Of most concern are those from the large **box jellyfish** *Chironex fleckeri*. These stings leave big welt marks and cause immediate and severe pain, sometimes resulting in death.

While most marine stingers are only around over the summer months, Box Jellies can be found all year round. However the numbers increase dramatically over summer, during the Wet season.

The **Box Jelly can kill** and is not only a danger for swimmers but also people using a net or the like. They're also extremely hard to see in the often muddy waters of the inshore beaches and bays.

The symptoms can include severe generalized pain, abdominal cramps, nausea, vomiting, headaches, severe back pain and a feeling of impending doom. Rarely victims can also have heart and breathing difficulties. Together, these symptoms are referred to as **Irukandji Syndrome.**

About the best way not to get stung is not to go into the water in the first place!! You can wear panty hose or the like for protection if you are not self-conscious about it.

> ***If somebody is stung***
>
> 1. *Keep him calm and cool, and lay him down.*
> 2. *The area of the body on which any jellyfish sting has occurred should immediately be flooded with vinegar to stop the remaining stinging cells from firing.*
> 3. *Sustain respiration and circulation.*
>
> ***DO NOT RUB THE AREA OR TRY TO REMOVE THE TENTACLES.***

The ***Tropical Australian Stinger Research Unit*** of the James Cook University in Queensland has an excellent brochure on **Irukandji Syndrome,** which you can download from their web site at:
www.jcu.edu.au/interest/stingers/irukandji%20brochure1.pdf

SANDFLY BITES AND OTHERS

Winged biting creatures abound in the Kimberley. Mosquitoes, Sandflies and annoying Bush Flies are common, so take an effective repellent.

Mosquitoes in the Kimberley

Mosquitoes in the Kimberley are responsible for the transmission of a number of diseases. These diseases include Ross River virus, the potentially fatal Murray Valley encephalitis (MVE) and Barmah Forest virus.

Mosquitoes are most active just before sunset until mid-evening, so if you are outside cover up as much as possible and use a protective personal insect repellent containing diethyl toluamide (DEET) or picaridin, and reapply regularly.

Sandflies

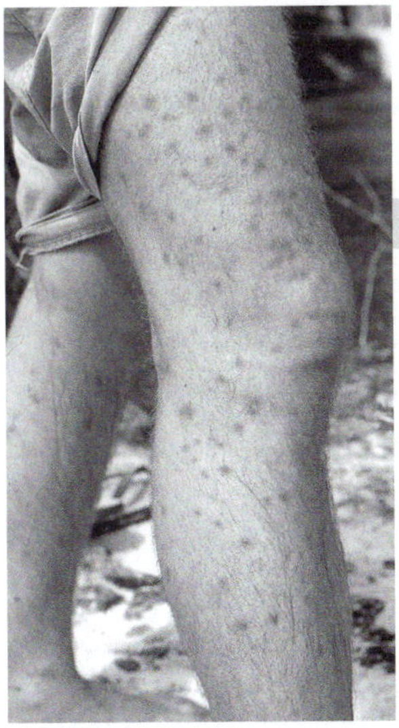

Sandflies can be a real curse and most people do not feel them bite. A few hours later (or next day) an itchy sore can develop.

> ***A Special Mix for Sandflies***
>
> *For Sandflies we use a special mix of equal quantities of Baby Oil and Dettol. You can add 1 part metho as well for that little bit extra, along with some citronella and/or lemon juice. Keep exposed parts liberally coated with the mixture and it should not only help you not get bitten, but soothe any previous bites as well.*
>
> ***Lavender Oil***
>
> *Is known as an anti-infection agent and has significant pain relieving properties as well. Great for bites, stings, burns, perfume, headaches, stress and if you have trouble sleeping. Worth a try!*

Other Nasties

Native Wasps and their nests are also commonly seen. Their honeycomb nests often house thousands of small insects and if you annoy them, you'll know all about it, with the best repellent in the world being of little use.

Believe us, their sting is like a mini-hypodermic needle hitting you at high speed!! Unless you are allergic or stung a multitude of times, the stinging will slowly abate.

A sandfly victim - they can make life miserable!!

> *More details on these animals that bite and sting and the recommended first aid can be found in the* ***St. John's First Aid Manual*** *and the* ***First Aid Emergency Handbook*** *published by Survival Emergency Products* *(see page 270).*
>
> ***Aids to Survival*** *is a 112 pg booklet produced by the* ***WA Police Dept*** *- An excellent guide. Available free from any WA police station, or from the web at:* **www.police.wa.gov.au.**

CROCODILES

Two species of crocodiles live in the waters of the Kimberley.

The small **Freshwater Crocodile** (Johnstoni Crocodile) lives in the freshwater streams, rivers and waterholes and grows to a maximum of 3 metres, though any specimen over 2 metres is big. This shy and inoffensive animal normally flees from humans and as such is harmless – he'd only bite you if you were silly enough to corner and provoke him, and then he'd flee!

The **Salt-Water or Estuarine Crocodile** is an entirely different ball game. They grow to well over 7 metres and anything over 3 metres represents a danger to man.

Salties inhabit not only saltwater environments (including the open ocean up to 300 km offshore) but can also be found long distances up freshwater rivers.

In the Dry season crocodiles eat less, but become more active, aggressive and hungrier as the Wet approaches. This is not helped by their nesting season which generally peaks around November/December, and the fact that they are a very territorial animal.

They can be extremely elusive and just because you can't see one doesn't mean that they are not in the immediate vicinity.

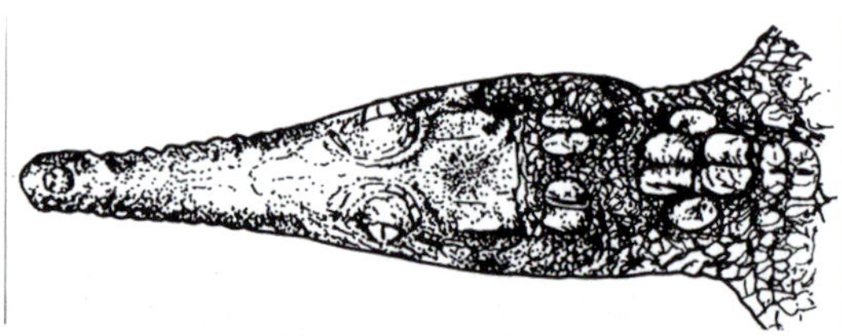

Freshwater Crocodile

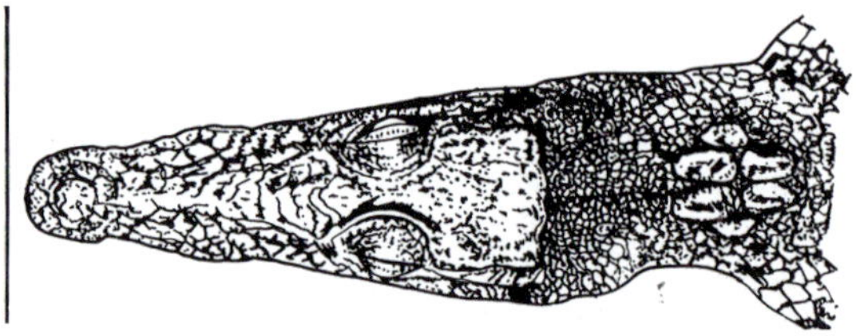

Salt-water Crocodile

How to be 'Crocodile Wise'

- *Observe the warning signs erected at some places where there is a potential danger from crocodiles. Absence of a warning sign does not mean the area is safe.*
- *Seek local or expert advice about crocodiles before swimming, camping, fishing or boating.*
- *There is a potential danger anywhere Salt-Water Crocodiles occur. If there is any doubt, do not swim, canoe or use small boats in estuaries, tidal rivers, deep pools or mangrove shores. Remember that Salt-Water Crocodiles are very capable of surviving in freshwater pools quite some distance upstream.*
- *Be aware. Keep your eyes open for large crocodiles. Children and pets are at particular risk in the water or at the water's edge. Large Salt-Water Crocodiles have no fear of humans.*
- *Do not paddle, clean fish, prepare food or camp at the water's edge. Fill a bucket with water and do your chores at least 50 metres away. Returning daily or regularly to the same spot at the water's edge is dangerous.*
- *Do not lean over the edge of a boat or stand on logs overhanging water, and don't hang articles off the edge of the boat.*
- *Stand at least a few metres back from the water's edge when fishing. Crocodiles have not been known to attack well away from the water.*
- *Dispose of food scraps, fish offal and other wastes properly, and away from your camp site.*

All crocodiles are protected and must not be killed. Obviously if life and limb are being jeopardised that can go by the board, but don't try killing a croc and using that as an excuse!!

CALM produces a very good brochure on being 'Crocodile Wise'. You can download it direct off their web site: **www.calm.wa.gov.au/plants_animals/living_with_wildlife/pdf/crocodiles.pdf**.

MAPS TO THE KIMBERLEY

TOURING MAPS

Hema Maps produces a very good map and guide to the whole region, simply called, *'The Kimberley'*. At a scale of 1:1,250,000 it shows all the major and minor routes through the region as well as Aboriginal land, national parks, etc. Printed on both sides, the back is full of information and details touring throughout the Kimberley. It is available at all good map shops as well as tourist bureaus throughout the region. Check out their web site for details on their maps and retail outlets at **www.hemamaps.com.au**/

The **Department of Land Information (DLI)** produces the ***'StreetSmart Touring Map'*** covering all of the Kimberley on a scale of 1:1 000 000. Detailed maps of the major towns are included, along with informative details on the principal points of interest and brief notes on the history of the areas covered. Contact the Dept of Land Information *(see below for contact details)*. The map can be purchased from good map shops or you can purchase maps directly from DLI's 'Land on Line' web site at: **www.landonline.com.au/**. You can also purchase CALM publications from the web site.

GENERAL MAPS

There are a number of good general maps available that cover the Kimberley.

DLI in Western Australia puts out a general 1:1,000,000 topographic map on the Kimberley and this map is available from them (see above for contact details).

The National Mapping Division (**Natmap** - formerly Auslig) of *Geoscience Australia*, produces topographic maps at scales of 1: 100 000, 1: 250 000 and 1: 1 000 000. It also produces general reference maps of the Kimberley on a 1:1,000,000 scale. You'll need the *'Broome'*, *'Halls Creek'*, *'Brunswick Bay'* and *'Darwin'* maps to fully cover the area.

A series of 1:1,000,000 thematic maps are also produced by Natmap, depicting geographical distribution of natural or cultural occurrences such as climate, nature conservation reserves or population. The maps available for the Kimberley region are *'Broome'* and *'Halls Creek'*. Maps can be purchased online from the Natmap at: **www.ga.gov.au/map/images.jsp**.

Obtaining Maps

Check out your nearest good map shop. The ***Melbourne Map Centre*** (see below), has a wide range of guide books and maps that can be mail ordered.

If you're having trouble getting your favourite map both **DLI** and the **Natmap** have mail order facilities and will supply catalogues of the maps they produce and sell, plus an up-to-date list of their agencies around the country. You can also purchase products online.

Department of Land Information (DLI)
1 Midland Square, Morrison Rd (cnr Great Northern Hwy)
Midland, WA 6056
Ph: (08) 9273 7373, fax: (08) 9273 7666
Email: sales@dli.wa.gov.au
Web: **www.dola.wa.gov.au/** and web: **www.landonline.com.au/**

National Mapping Division, (Geoscience Australia),
Cnr Jerrabomberra Ave and Hindmarsh Drive,
Symonston, ACT 2609
Freecall (within Australia) 1800 800 173, ph: (02) 6249 9966, fax: (02) 6249 9960
Email: mapsales@ga.gov.au
Web: **www.ga.gov.au/nmd/mapping/**

Also check out Hema's web site for a detailed listing of their Australian and overseas retailers :
Hema Maps
Ph: (07) 3340 0000, fax: (07) 3340 0099
Email: manager@hemamaps.com.au
Web site: **www.hemamaps.com.au/**

BIBLIOGRAPHY

These books will give you a better understanding of the Kimberley. Many are available from good bookstores Australia wide. If they are not generally available you'll need to search the antique and second-hand bookstores for them. The State Library in your capital city may have a copy.
(Note: Pub. – means Published) (Hesperian – Hesperian Press, WA)

GENERAL

Broome and Beyond – Plants and People of the Dampier Peninsula. By K. Kenneally and Others. 1996. Pub. by CALM of WA.

Caught Off Guard and Other Poems. By Janet Wells. Pub. by Hesperian.

Drover's Cook . A book of poetry by Tom Quilty. Pub. by Hesperian.

Kimberley Challenge. By Terry Bolland. Pub. by Terry Bolland, Ashfield, WA.

North West Bound. 1994. Pub. by CALM of WA.

North West Panorama. Pub. by West Australian Newspapers Ltd.

Nyibayarri – Kimberley Tracker. By Jack Bohemia. 1995. Pub. by Aboriginal Studies Press.

Our Year In the Wilderness. By Michael & Susan Cusack. Pub. 1989 by Australian Geographic Pty. Ltd., Terrey Hills, NSW.

Penelope – Bungles to Broome. By Tim Bowden. Pub 2001; Allen & Unwin

Raparapa – Stories from the Fitzroy River Drovers. Edited by Paul Marshall. Pub. by Magabala Books, Broome, WA.

The Kimberley – A Journey through NW Australia. By M Leonard. 1995. Pub. by CIS, Cardigan Street Publishers.

The Kimberley – Australia's Unique North-West. By Jocelyn Burt. Pub. by Houghton Mifflin Australia, Vic.

The Kimberley – Horizons of Stone. By A. McGregor and Q Chester. 1992. Pub. by Hodder and Stoughton.

The Land Beyond Time. By John Olsen, with Mary Durack, et al. Pub. by MacMillan Co.

HISTORY

Alexander Forrest – His Life and Times. By G Boulton. Pub 1958; Melbourne Uni Press.

Atlantis: A Flight Into Hell. By Barbara Winter. Pub. by Angus & Robertson.

Australia's North-West Challenge. By W.A. Beattie & M. deLacy Lowe. Pub. by Kimberley Pub. Co. Melbourne.

Big John Forrest. By Frank Crowley. Pub 2000; Uni of WA Press.

Bulls & Boabs – Kimberley People & Places. By Athol Thomas. Pub. by Rigby Publishers.

Chasing the Weight 1886-1912. By F.W.P. Cammilleri. Pub. by Hesperian Press, WA.

Cossack Gold. By W.L. Owen. Pub. by Hesperian.

Curtin's Cowboys – Australia's Secret Bush Commandos. By Richard Walker and Helen Walker. Pub. by Allen & Unwin, Sydney.

Expeditions in Western Australia 1837-1839. By G. Grey. Pub. by Hesperian.

Flight of Diamonds. By Major W. Tyler. Pub. by Hesperian.

Fossil Downs – a Saga of the Kimberleys. By Gordon MacKenzie. 1995. Pub. by the author.

Full Fathom Five. By Mary Albertus Bain. Pub. by Artlook Books, Perth, WA.

Golden Quest: Roaring Days of the West Australian Gold Rushes and Life in the Pearling Industry. By A.C. V. Bligh. Pub. 1958 by Hesperian.

Journals of Australian Explorations 1846-1858 (Gregory). By A.C. & F.T. Gregory. Pub. by Hesperian.

Journey Across the Western Interior Of Australia. By P.E. Warburton. Pub. by Hesperian.

Kimberley Days and Yesterdays. By C.E. Flinders. Pub. by Hesperian..

Kimberley Dreaming to Diamonds. By Hugh Edwards. Pub. by Hugh Edwards, Swanbourne, WA.

Kimberley Gold Rush. By C. Clement and P. Bridge. Pub. by Hesperian.

Kimberley Scenes. Edited by Cathie Clement & Peter Bridge. Pub. by Hesperian.

Kimberley Scrapbook. By Leavy,et al. Pub. by Hesperian.

Kings in Grass Castles. By M Durack. 1959. Pub. by Corgi Australia, 1990.

Lonely Graves of WA and Burials at Sea. By Y. Coates. Pub. by Hesperian.

North of the 26th. Edited by Helen Weller. et al. Pub. by Reeve Books, WA.

Northern Patrol. By Pilmer. Pub. by Hesperian.

Packhorse & Waterhole – With the First Overlanders to the Kimberleys. By G. Buchanan. Pub. by Hesperian.

Patrol to the Kimberleys. By Fred Lane. 1958. Pub. by World Adventure Library.

Port of Pearls. By Hugh Edwards. Pub. by Rigby Pub.lishers.

Spinifex and Sand. By David W. Carnegie. Pub. by Hesperian.

Spinifex and Sand Maps. Pub. by Hesperian.

Tales of the Overland – Queensland to Kimberley in 1885. By G.H. Lamond. Pub. by Hesperian.

The Call of the Kimberley. By Irene Shackcloth. Pub. by Hallcraft 1950.

Do Not Yeild to Despair – The Diaries of Frank Hann. Edited by M. Donaldson. Pub. by Hesperian Press, WA, 1998.

The History of the North West of Australia. Edited By Jas. S. Battye. Pub. by Hesperian.

The Law Provides. By E. Morrow. Pub. by Hesperian.

The Rivers of Home – Frank Lacy – Kimberley Pioneer. By Marion Nixon. 1978. Pub. by Vanguard Press, WA.

The White Divers of Broome. By John Bailey. Pub 2001; MacMillan.

There Were Three Ships – The Story of the Camden Harbour Expedition 1864-65. By C. Richards. Pub. by University of WA Press.

WA's Pearl Harbour – The Japanese Raid on Broome. By Mervyn W. Prime. Pub. by Royal Australian Airforce Assoc. WA.

Where God Never Trod – Australia's Oil Explorers Across Two Centuries. By Rick Wilkinson. 1991. Pub. by David Ell Press P/L.

Outlaws of the Leopolds; The Nor-Westers; One Wet Season; Over the Range; Forty Fathoms Deep. All written by Ion. L. Idriess and published by Angus & Robertson.

ABORIGINAL PREHISTORY, HISTORY & ART

Aboriginal Rock Art of the Kimberley, WA. Edited by KF Kenneally et al. Pub 1997; Kimberley Society

Australia's Greatest Rock Art. By GL Walsh. 1988. Pub. by EJ Brill/Robert Brown & Assoc P/L.

Bradshaw Art of the Kimberley. By Graham Walsh. Pub 2000; Takarakka Nowan Kas Publications.

Kalumburu – The Benedictine Mission and the Aborigines 1908-1975. By Fr. Eugene Perez O.S.B. 1977. Pub. by Kalumburu Benedictine Mission.

King of the Kimberley. By Rocky Marshall. 1988. Pub. by Peacock Publications.

Rock Art of the Dreamtime. By Josephine Flood. Pub 1997; Angus & Robertson.

The Art of the Wandjina. By I.M. Crawford. Pub. by Oxford University Press, Melbourne.

The Bradshaws – Ancient Rock Paintings of NW WA. By Graham Walsh. Pub 1994; Bradshaw Foundation.

The Forrest River Massacre. By N. Green. 1995. Pub. by Fremantle Arts centre Press.

The Riches of Ancient Australia – A Journey into Prehistory. By Josephine Flood. Pub. by University of Queensland Press, St. Lucia, Qld.

The Rock & The Sand. By Mary Durack. Pub. by Constable & Co. Ltd. London.

NATURE

A Field Guide to the Birds of Australia. By G. Pizzey. Pub. by Collins.

Arid Shrubland Plants of WA. By A.A. Mitchell & G.G. Wilcox. Pub. by UWAP, 1994.

Atlas of Australian Birds. By M. Blakers, et al. 1984. Pub. by Melbourne University Press.

Australian Native Plants.. By J. W. Wrigley, et at. Pub. by Reed Books.

Australian Snakes. By Graeme Gow. Pub. by Angus & Robertson.

Broome and Beyond. By KF Kenneally, et al. Pub 1996; CALM

Fishing the Wild West. By Ross Cusack and Mike Roennfeldt. Pub. by St. Georges Books WA.

Flowers and Plants of Western Australia. By Rica Erickson, et al. Pub. by Reed Books, NSW.

Grahame Webb's Crocodiles of Australia. 1989. Pub. by Reed Australia.

Mangroves of Australia. By Richard Lear & Tom Turner. Pub. by University of Qld. Press.

Nature Conservation Reserves in the Kimberley. By Burbidge, et al. Pub. by CALM, WA.

Plants of the Kimberley Region of Western Australia. By R.J. Pethram & B. Kok. 1986. Pub. by University of W.A. Press.

Reptiles & Amphibians of Australia. By Harold G. Cogger. Pub. by Reed Books.

The Birds of Australia. By Simpson & Day. Pub. by Lloyd O'Neil Pty. Ltd.

The Mammals of Australia. Edited by Ronald Strahan. Pub 1995; Reed Books.

The Slater Field Guide to Australian Birds. By P & R Slater. Pub. by Rigby.

Top End Native Plants. By John Brock. 1988. Pub. by John Brock – Winnellie, N.T.

Wildflowers of Western Australia. By C.A. Gardner. Pub. by St. George Books.

Wolfe Creek Crater. By Ken McNamara. Pub. by Western Australian Museum, Perth.

GEMSTONES, GOLD, ETC

Gemstones in Western Australia. By Geological Survey of W.A.

Gold & Ghosts – A Prospectors Guide to Metal Detecting in Australia No. 1 WA. By D.W. de Havelland. Pub. by Hesperian.

Gold Deposits of Western Australia. By A.G. Maitland. Pub. by Hesperian.

Gold – Western Australia. By Geological Survey of WA. Pub. by Dept. of Mines

How & Where to Find Gemstones in Australia and New Zealand. Edited By Bill Myatt. Pub. by Lansdowne Press, Sydney.

While you are in the Kimberley check out the speciality book stores below. They have a great range of books on the area:

BIBLIOGRAPHY

TOUR OPERATORS, LODGES & THE LIKE

4WD VEHICLE & 4WD COACH TOURS

AAT King's Tours Pty. Ltd.
Ph: 1300 556 100
Web: www.aatkings.com

AgTour
Ph: (07) 3236 9889
Web: www.agtour.com.au

All Terrain Safaris
Ph: (08) 9295 6680
Web: www.vianet.net.au/~ats/

Australian Adventure Travel
Ph: (08) 9248 2355
Web: www.safaris.net.au

Aussie Off Road Tours
Ph: (08) 9192 3617
Web: www.aussieoffroadtours.com.au

Australian Pacific Touring
Ph: (03) 9277 8555 or 1800 675 222
Web: www.aptours.com.au

Australian Pinnacle Adventures
Ph: (08) 9417 5555
Web: www.pinnacletours.com.au

Broome Day Tours & Charters
Ph: (08) 9192 1068
Web: www.broomedaytours.com.au

Bungle Bungle Adventures – (Kununurra Backpackers Adventure Centre)
Ph: 1800 641 998.
Web: www.adventure.kimberley.net.au.

Bushtrack Safaris
Ph: (08) 9191 1547
Web: www.bushtracksafaris.com.au

Derby Bus Service
Ph: (08) 9193 1550
Web: www.westkimberleytours.com.au

East Kimberley Tours
Ph: (08) 9168 2213
Web: www.eastkimberleytours.com.au

Easyrider Backpacker Tours
Ph: (08) 9226 0307
Web: www.easyridertours.com.au

Halls Creek & Bungle Bungle Tours
Ph: (08) 9193 7267.
Web: www.bunglebungle.com.au.

Get About 4WD Adventures
Ph: (02) 9831 8385. Web: www.getabout.com.au

Go Bush Safaris
Ph: (02) 9817 4660, web: www.gobush.com.au/
Web: www.bunglebungle.com.au

Gibb River Road Bus Services
Ph: 1800 197 262 or (08) 9169 1880 - drops off freight, tourists or visitors at station access roads along the Gibb River Road, from Kununurra to Derby.
Web : www.gibbriverbus.com.au.

Kimberley Adventure Tours
Ph: (08) 9191 2655
Web: www.kimberleyadventures.com

Kimberley Dreams
Ph: (08) 8942 0971, Web: www.kimberleys.com.au

Kimberley Dreamtime Tours
Ph/fax: (08) 9161 1288
Web: http://aboriginaltouroperators.com.au/blackpages/wa/kimberleydream.htm

Kimberley Getaway Safaris
Ph: (08) 9193 7139
Web: www.kimberleysafaris.com.au/

Kimberley Wild Expeditions
Ph: (08) 9193 7778
Web: www.kimberleywild.com.au

Kimberley Wilderness Adventures
Ph: (08) 9192 5741
Web: www.kimberleywilderness.com.au

Kununurra Backpackers Adventure Centre
Ph: 1800 641 998
Web: www.adventure.kimberley.net.au

Odyssey Safaris
Ph: (08) 8948 0091
Web: www.odysaf.com.au/

Outback Spirit Tours
Ph: (02) 6041 6566 or 1800 805 265
Web: www.outbackspirit.net.au

Outback Track Tours
Ph: (02) 9948 9959
Web: www.outbacktracktours.com

Over The Top Adventure Tours
Ph: (08) 9192 5211
Web: www.4wdtourswa.com/tours/

Oz-Trek 4WD Tours
Ph: (02) 4471 7911
Web: www.southcoast.com.au/oztrek4wdtours

Safari Treks
Ph: (08) 9271 1271, Web: www.safaritreks.com.au

Swagman Outback Safaris
Ph: (03) 5222 2855, Web: swagmantours.com.au

Triangle Tours & Charters
Ph: (08) 9168 1272

Triple J Tours
Ph: (08) 9168 2682, Web: www.triplejtours.net.au

Ultimate Adventures
Ph: (08) 9168 2310
Web: http://members.westnet.com.au/ultimateadvent/welcome.htm

West Kimberley Tours
Ph: (08) 9193 1442
Web: www.westkimberleytours.com.au

Wilderness 4WD Adventures
Ph (08) 8941 2161
Web: www.wildernessadventures.com.au

Wild Adventure Tours
Ph: (08) 9169 1013, Web: www.gowild.com.au

Wilderness Challenge
Ph: (07) 4035 4488
Web: www.wilderness-challenge.com.au

Windjana Tours
Ph: (08) 9193 1550

BUS/COACH TOURS

AAT King's Tours Pty. Ltd.
Ph: 1300 556 100. Web www.aatkings.com

Australian Pacific Tours
Ph: (03) 9277 8555. Web: www.aptours.com.au

Evergreen Tours
Ph: (03) 4929 4333, Web: www.evergreentours.com

ANNIES
BAR

www.guidebooks.com.au

VEHICLE GUIDING SERVICES

Aussie Tracks
Ph: 0408 691 536
Web: **www.outbackadventures.com.au**
Bushtrack Safaris
Ph: (08) 9191 1547
Web: **http://members.westnet.com.au/ricannbt/**
Cape York Connections
Ph: 0418 964 279 or 0147 163 312
Web: **www.capeyorkconnections.com.au/**
Duncans Off Road
Ph: (07) 3264 1877
Web: **www.duncansoffroad.com.au**
Global Gypsies
Ph: (08) 9341 6727
Web: **www.globalgypsies.com.au**
Guides to Adventure
Ph: (07) 4091 1978
Web: **www.guidestoadventure.com.au**
Outback Tag-A-Long Tours
Ph: (02) 6025 6494
Web: **www.outbacktagalong.com.au**
Oz-Trek 4WD Tours
Ph: (02) 4471 7911
Web: **www.southcoast.com.au/oztrek4wdtours**
Red Desert Tours
Ph: (03) 5786 2004, mobile: 0412 179 688
Web: **www.red-desert.com.au**
Tag Along Tours Broome
Ph: (08) 9299 6372
Web: **www.tagalongbroome.com**
Tag–Along 4WD Adventure Tours Australia
Ph: (02) 4471 1235
Web: **www.adventure-tours-australia.com/**

HIRE 4WD/4WD Campervans

There are quite a few car hire companies based in the major town centres of the Kimberley - Kununurra, Derby, Broome and Halls Creek, and these have been listed under the facilities of each town in the appropriate chapter.

Aussie Drive - Self Drive Tours
Ph: (08) 9333 4383
Web: **www.aussiedrive.com.au**
Avis Car Rentals
Broome – ph: (08) 9193 5980
Kununurra Airport – ph: (08) 9169 1258
Web: **www.avis.com.au**
Britz – Broome
Ph: (08) 9192 2647, web: **www.britz.com/**
Broome Broome Car Rentals
Ph: (08) 9192 2210
Web: **www.broomebroome.com.au**
Budget Kimberley Rent A Car
Broome Airport – ph: (08) 9193 5355
Derby Airport - ph: (08) 9191 2044
Kununurra Airport – ph: (08) 9168 2033
Web: **www.budget.com.au**
Europcar
Broome Airport, ph: (08) 9193 7788
Web: **www.deltaeuropcar.com.au**
Four Wheel Drive Hire Service
Broome, ph: (08) 9192 8854
Web: **www.4wdhire.com.au**

HIRE 4WDS CONT'D ...
Handy Rentals – Kununurra
Ph: (08) 9168 1657 or 1800 131 975
4WD and Kimberley camping kit available.
Web: **www.handyrentals.com.au**
Hertz *Wheels over the Kimberley*
Broome, or Broome Airport, ph: (08) 9192 1428
Kununurra – ph: (08) 9169 1424
Web: **www.hertzcampervans.com**
Just Broome Car Hire – Broome
Ph: (08) 9192 6636
KEA Campers – Broome
Ph: (08) 9192 8854, web: **www.keacampers.com/**
Maui Rentals – Broome
Ph: (08) 9192 2647, web: **www.maui-rentals.com/**
Poinciana Roadhouse Handyute and Car Hire
Halls Creek, ph: (08) 9168 6164.
Camping kits available.
South Perth 4WD Rentals
Broome, ph (08) 9193 7946
Web: **www.sp4wd.com.au/**
Thrifty, Broome Airport
Ph: (08) 9193 7712, web: **www.thrifty.com.au**
Topless Rentals – Broome
Ph: (08) 9193 5017
Trailmaster Campervan Rentals – Guildford WA
Ph: (08) 9228 0012 or 1800 651 202
Web: **www.trailmaster.com.au/**
Tru Blu Rentals
Broome, ph: (08) 9192 5177.

HIRE CAMPING EQUIPMENT

Kimberley Caravan & Outback Supplies
65 Frederick St, Broome
Ph: (08) 9193 5909, fax: (08) 9193 6878
Web: **www.kimberleycamping.com.au**
Kimberley Camping Hire
Shop 3/ 65 Frederick St, Broome
Ph: (08) 9193 5354.

SPECIAL INTEREST TOURS

Aboriginal Cultural tours

Bardi Culture Tours
Ph: (08) 9192 4049
www.waitoc.com/kullarri.asp
Barramundi Moon
Ph: (08) 9192 9100 (Dampier Peninsula)
Web: **www.waitoc.com/kullarri.asp**
Bungoolee Tours
Ph: (08) 9191 5633 (Fitzroy Crossing)
Web: **www.diversetravel.com.au/experiencesAboriginal/BungooleeTours.htm**
Goombading Aboriginal Boat Tours
One Arm Point, Ph: 08 9192 4970
Web: **www.kooljaman.com.au**
JBAC Bush Adventures - Bush University
Ph: (08) 9191 7467 (Mt Anderson)
Web: **www.jarlmadangah.com/camtour.htm**
Kimberley Dreamtime Tours
Ph/fax: (08) 9161 1288 (Wyndham)
Web: **http://aboriginaltouroperators.com.au/blackpages/wa/kimberleydream.htm**

Kimberley Wilderness Adventures
Ph: (03) 9277 8444 or 1800 675 222
Web: **www.kimberleywilderness.com.au**

Larwarrdu Aboriginal Cultural Tours
Ph: (08) 9192 5067 (Broome)
Web: **www.waitoc.com/kullarri.asp#lact**

Lombadina Aboriginal Adventures
Ph: (08) 9192 4936 (Dampier Peninsula)
Web: **www.waitoc.com/kularri.asp#laa**

Mamabulanjin Aboriginal Tours
Ph: (08) 9192 2660 (Broome)
Web: **www.waitoc.com/kullarri.asp#mat**

Wedgetails Tours
Ph: (08) 8388 7246
Web: **www.wedgetailstours.com.au**

Woolah Aboriginal Tag-along Tours
Doon Doon Station (see pg 122)

Wundargoodie Aboriginal Safaris
Ph: (08) 9161 1145 (Broome)
Web: **www.aboriginalsafaris.com/**

Photography, Wildlife, Birdwatching, Natural History, Bushwalking, Cycling, Horse Riding, Camel Riding, Etc.

Adventure Tours Australia
Ph: (08) 8309 2277 or 1300 654 604
Web: **www.adventuretours.com.au**

Astro Tours of the Kimberley
Ph: 0417 949 958. Web: **www.astrotours.net**

Broome Camel Safaris, Mob: 0419 916 101
Web: **www.broomecam.com/gold/broomecamel.htm**

Broome Camel Safaris, Mob: 0419 916 101
Web: **www.broomecam.com/gold/broomecamel.htm**

Broome Eco Adventures – Broome Adventure Tours
Ph: (08) 9193 7997

Bushtrack Safaris (See *Vehicle Guiding Service.*)

Coate's Wildlife Tours
Ph: (08) 9330 6066 or 1800 676 016
Web: **www.coateswildlife.tours.com.au**

Didgeri Air Aboriginal Art Tours
Ph: (08)8948 5055
Web: **www.didgeri.com.au**

Diggers Rest Station
Ph/fax: (08) 9161 1029
Web: **www.diggers-rest.com**

El Questro Station
Ph: (08) 9169 1777, Web: **www.elquestro.com.au/**

Environmental Encounters
Ph: (08) 9306 1810
Web: **www.environmentalencounters.com.au/**

Geikie Gorge Boat Tours
Operated by CALM.
Ph: Fitzroy Crossing Tourist Bureau (08) 9191 5355/ Derby Tourist Bureau (08) 9191 1426
Web: **www.naturebase.net/tourism/gg_boat_tours.html**

Go Wild Adventure Tours
Ph: (08) 9169 1013
Web: **www.backpackertours.com.au/members/frames/WA/alltour.php?cid=128**

Kimberley Birdwatching
Ph: (08) 9192 1246
Web: **www.kimberleybirdwatching.com.au**

Kimberley Bushwalks and Camel Safaris
Ph: (08) 9191 7017, web: **www.bushwalks.com**

Kimberley Dreams
Ph: (08) 8942 0971 or 1800 000 521
Web: **www.kimberleys.com.au**

Kimberley Pursuits
Ph: (08) 9161 1029
Web: **www.kimberley-pursuits.com.au/horseTrekking.htm**

Kimberley Wild Outback Tours
Ph: (08) 9193 7778
Web: **www.kimberleywild.com.au**

Landscope Expeditions
Ph: (08) 9380 2433, web: **www.calm.wa.gov.au/tourism/lsexpeditions/index.html**

Red Sun Camel Safaris
Ph: (08) 9193 7423
Web: **www.redsuncamels.com.au**

Remote Outback Cycle (ROC) Tours
Ph: (08) 9279 6969, web: **www.cycletours.com.au**

The Kimberley Specialists
Ph: (08) 9168 2576
Web: **www.kimberleyspecialists.com.au.**

Western Blue Sea Kayak - Broome
Ph: 0419 895 367 or 1300 665 888
Web: **www.westernblue.com.au**

Willis's Walkabouts
Ph: (08) 8985 2134
Web: **www.bushwalkingholidays.com.au**

Canoeing

Big Waters - Kimberley Canoe Safaris
Kununurra, ph: 1800 641 998
Web: **www.adventure.kimberley.net.au**

Go Wild Adventure Tours
Kununurra, ph: 1300 66 33 69
Web: **www.gowild.com.au**

STATION PROPERTIES – ACCOMMODATION & CAMPING

For full details of these stations and all the facilities and activities that they have to offer, see the appropriate chapter in which they are listed.

GIBB RIVER ROAD

Charnley River Station
Ph: (08) 9191 4646, fax: (08) 9191 7878
See page 163 for full details.

El Questro Station
PO Box 909, Kununurra, WA, 6743
Ph: (08) 9169 1777, fax: (08) 9169 1383 (booking office), Station office, ph: (08) 9161 4318, fax: (08) 9161 4355.
Web: **www.elquestro.com.au/**
See page 152-154 for full details.

Ellenbrae Homestead
Ph/fax: (08) 9161 4325
See page 156 for full details.

Emma Gorge
PO Box 909, Kununurra, WA, 6743
Ph: (08) 9169 1777, fax: (08) 9169 1383
Web: **www.elquestro.com.au/emma-gorge-resort/**
See page 152 for full details.

Home Valley Homestead
PMB 15, Kimberley Downs, WA, 6728
Ph: (08) 9161 4322, fax: (08) 9161 4288
Web site: **www.homevalley.com.au**
See page 154-155 for full details.

Imintji Safari Camp – – *Kimberley Wilderness Adventures*
Ph: 1800 655 220, fax: (03) 9521 0721
Web: **www.kimberleywilderness.com.au/**
See page 164 for full details.

Mt Barnett Roadhouse – Manning River Gorge
PMB, Derby, WA, 6728, ph: (08) 9191 7007
See page 160-161 for full details.

Mt Elizabeth Station
Peter & Pat Lacy, via Derby, WA, 6728
Ph/fax: (08) 9191 4644
Web: **www.holiday-wa.net/station.htm**
See page 156-157 for full details.

Mt Hart Wilderness Lodge
PO Box 653, Derby, WA, 6728
Ph: (08) 9191 4645
Web: **www.mthart.com.au/**
See page 168 for full details.

KIMBERLEY REGION

Barn Hill Beachside Station Stay
130 km south of Broome, ph/fax: (08) 9192 4975
See page 206 for full details.

Diggers Rest Station
Ph/fax: (08) 9161 1029
Web: **www.diggers-rest.com**
See page 104 for full details.

Drysdale River Station
Ph/fax: (08) 9161 4326
Web: **www.drysdaleriver.com.au/**
See page 130 for full details.

HOLIDAY LODGE TYPE ACCOMMODATION & CAMPING

Broome Bird Observatory
Ph: (08) 9193 5600,
Web: **www.broomebirdobservatory.com**
See page 213 for full details.

Bush Camp Faraway Bay
Ph: (08) 9169 1214
Web: **www.farawaybay.com.au**/
See page 113 for full details.

Kimberley Coastal Camp
Ph/fax: (08) 9161 4410, or 0417 902 006
Web: **www kimberleycoastalcamp.com.au/**
See page 148 for full details.

Kimberley Wilderness Adventures
Bungie Bungie Wiiderness Cam p – Purnululu NP
See page 113 for full details.
Marunbabidi Wilderness Camp – King Edward River
See page 131 for full details.
Ungolan Wilderness Camp – Mitchell Plateau
See page 141 for full details.
Ph: 1800 655 220, fax: (03) 9521 0721
Web: **www.kimberleywilderness.com.au/**

Mornington Wilderness Camp
Ph: (08) 9191 7406, fax: (08) 9191 7419
Web: **www.australianwildlife.org/**
See page 179 for full details.

DAMPIER PENINSULA

Bells Point
Ph: (08) 9192 4006
Web: **www.waitoc.com/kullarri.asp#nhml**
See page 219 for full details.

Chile Creek
Ph: (08) 9192 4141
Web: **www.waitoc.com/kullarri.asp#bm**
See page 220-221 for full details.

Djoodoon
Ph: (08) 9192 4858
See page 222 for full details.

Gambanan (One Arm Point)
Ph: (08) 9192 4220
See page 223 for full details.

Kooljaman at Cape Leveque
Ph: (08) 9192 4970. Dampier Peninsula.
Web: **www.kooljaman.com.au**
See page 223 for full details.

La Djardarr
Ph: (08) 9192 9100
Web: **www.waitoc.com/kullarri.asp#nhml**
See page 220 for full details.

Lombadina
Ph: (08) 9192 4936
Web: **www.lombadina.com.au**
See page 220-221 for full details.

Maddarr
Ph: (08) 9192 4896
Web: **www.waitoc.com/kullarri.asp#bm**
See page 220 for full details.

Middle Lagoon – Nature's Hideaway
Ph: (08) 9192 4002
Web: **www.waitoc.com/kullarri.asp#nhml**
See page 218-219 for full details.

Mudnunn
Ph: (08) 9192 4930
Web: **www.waitoc.com/kullarri.asp#mtl**
See page 222 for full details.

SPECIALISED TRAVEL AGENTS

The Tourist Bureaus & Visitor Centres in each of the major centres in the Kimberley specialise in local knowledge and can help travellers with all local & Kimberley tour packages & accommodation.

Aboriginal Australia
100% Aboriginal Owned – brings you access to services and information. They offer specialised tours and list Aboriginal tour operators.
Ph: (08) 8952 3408
Web: **www.aboriginalaustralia.com**

Broome & The Kimberley Holidays
Ph: (08) 9193 5790 (Broome)
Specialist travel agent for accommodation and tours in Broome and throughout the Kimberley.
Web: **www.broomekimberley.com/**

Best Of The Kimberley
Ph: 08) 9192 6070 (Broome)
"One Stop Shop" of advice, expertise and booking service. Specialised tour packages around the Kimberley. Web: **www.kimberleytravel.net**

Kimberley Specialists in Tourism
Specialised company dedicated to long term environmental, cultural & tourism sustainability of the Kimberley. Visit remote Kachana Station or take a spiritual, cultural, bushwalking, archaeological guide led package.
Web: **www.kimberleyspecialists.com/index.html**

SPECIALISED WEB SITES

Broome Visitor Centre
www.broomevisitorcentre.com.au/
Shire of Broome: **www.broome.wa.gov.au/**
Derby Visitor Centre: **www.derbytourism.com.au/**
Kununurra Visitor Centre:
www.kimberleytourism.com/kununurra.htm
Shire of Wyndham East Kimberley:
www.eastkimberley.com.au/

TOUR OPERATORS & THE LIKE

Kimberley Development Commission: **www.kimberley.wa.gov.au**
Kimberley Tourism Directory: **www.kimberleytourism.com**
RACWA (Royal Automobile Club of WA): **http://rac.com.au/**
Dept of Mains Roads: **www2.mainroads.wa.gov.au/NR/mrwa/run/startr.asp**
Dept of Indigenous Affairs: **www.dia.wa.gov.au/**
Aboriginal Lands Trust: **www.dia.wa.gov.au/Land/Permits/**
WA Indigenous Tourism Operators Committee: **www.waitoc.com/**
CALM (Dept of Conservation & Land Management): **www.calm.wa.gov.au/**
WA 4WD Association: **www.wa4wda.com.au/**
Dept. of Fisheries: **www.fish.wa.gov.au**
Bureau of Meteorology: **www.bom.gov.au/weather/wa/**
Australian Severe Weather: **http://australiasevereweather.com/index.html**
Coastal Data Centre - Tidal Predictions: **www.dpi.wa.gov.au/imarine/coastaldata/2862.aspl**
FlightAce - List Airstrips: **www.flightace.com/airstrp2.asp**

FLYING AROUND THE KIMBERLEY

SCENIC TOURS & CHARTERS

Airnorth
Ph: (08) 8920 400, reservations: 1800 627 474.
Web: **www.airnorth.com.au/**

Alligator Airways
Ph: (08) 9168 1333 or 1800 632 533
Web: **www.alligatorairways.com.au**

Brindabella Airlines,
Ph: (02) 6248 8711
Web: **www.brindabella-airlines.com.au/**

Broome Aviation
Ph: (08) 9192 1369 or 1300 136 629
Web: **www.northwestregional.com.au**

Broome Airlines *(see Northwest Regional Airlines)*
Ph: (08) 9192 2822

Bush Flights
Derby, ph: (08) 9193 2680, web: **www.bushflight.com.**

Derby Seaplanes
Ph: (08) 9192 6208, web: **www.derbyseaplanes.com.au/**

Broome Helicopters
Ph: (08) 9192 7488
Web: **www.broomehelicopters.com**

Didgeri Air Aboriginal Art Tours
Ph: (08) 8948 5055. Web: **www.didgeri.com.au**

Discover the Kimberley Tours
Ph: (08) 9193 7267. Web: **www.bunglebungle.com.au/**

Fitzroy Helicopters
Ph: (08) 9191 5359

Geikie Air Charter
Ph: (08) 9191 5068

Golden Eagle Airways
Ph: (08) 9168 3103 – Mail Plane run north.
Web: **goldeneagleairlines.com**

Halls Creek & Bungle Bungle Tours
Ph: 9193 7267
Web: **www.bunglebungle.com.au**

Heliwork WA
Ph: (08) 9168 1811 or 1800 095 500 *(see Slingair)*
Web: **www.slingair.com.au**

Kimberley Seaplanes
Ph: (08) 9191 1760
Web: **www.horizontalfalls.com.au/derbyflights.html**

King Leopold Air
Ph: (08) 9193 7155. Web: **www.kingleopoldair.com.au/**

Northern Air Charter
Ph: (08) 8945 5444. Web: **www.flynac.com.au/gallery/**

Northwest Regional Airlines
Ph: (08) 9192 1369 or 1300 136 629
Web: **www.northwestregional.com.au**

Oasis Air
Ph: (08) 9168 6462.

Reef Flight
Ph: (08) 9192 3028, web: **www.reefflight.com**

Seair Broome
Ph: (08) 9192 6208, web: **www.derbyseaplanes.com.au**

Slingair
Ph: (08) 9169 1300 or 1800 095 500
Web site: **www.slingair.com.au**

Wyndham Aviation
Ph: (08) 9161 1335.

INDEX

INDEX

INDEX

INDEX

INDEX

INDEX